Critiquing the Sitcom

The Television Series

Robert J. Thompson, *Series Editor*

Other titles in The Television Series

Critiquing
the Sitcom

A Reader

edited by
Joanne Morreale

Syracuse University Press

Copyright© 2003 by Syracuse University Press
Syracuse, New York 13244–5160

All Rights Reserved

First Edition 2003
03 04 05 06 07 08   6 5 4 3 2 1

The paper used in this publication meets the minimum requirements of American National
Standard for Information Sciences—Permanence of Paper for Printed Library Materials, ANSI
Z39.48–1984.∞™

Library of Congress Cataloging-in-Publication Data

Critiquing the sitcom : a reader / edited by Joanne Morreale.—
1st ed.
        p. cm.—(The Television series)
Includes bibliographical references and index.
ISBN 0-8156-2983-4 (pbk. : alk. paper)
1. Television comedies—United States—History and criticism. I.
Morreale, Joanne, 1956-II. Series. PN1992.8.C66 C75 2002
791.45'617—dc21
2002012757

Manufactured in the United States of America

Contents

Illustrations

Contributors

Paul Attallah is the associate director of the School of Journalism and Communication Studies at Carleton University in Ottawa, Canada. He has written extensively on communication and cultural theory, including two books: *Les théories de la communication: Sens, sujet, savoir* (1991) and *Les théories de la communication: Histoire, context, pouvoir* (1989).

Serafina Bathrick is the author of several essays on film and television criticism. She retired in 1995 from teaching at Hunter College in New York City.

Aniko Bodroghkozy is an assistant professor of media studies in the English department at the University of Virginia. She is the author of *Groove Tube: Sixties Television and the Youth Rebellion* (2001). Her current project is called "Negotiating Civil Rights in Prime Time: TV Audiences and the Civil Rights Era."

Thomas Cripps is a distinguished professor at Morgan State University in Baltimore, Maryland. He has written *Hollywood's High Noon: Moviemaking and Society Before Television* (1997), *Making Movies Black: The Hollywood Message Movie from World War II to the Civil Rights Era* (1993), *Black Film as Genre* (1978), and *Slow Fade to Black: The Negro in American Film, 1900–1942* (1977). He has also published numerous articles on film and television, and has appeared in more than one hundred television and radio programs.

Alexander Doty is an associate professor of English at Lehigh University in Bethlehem, Pennsylvania. He is the author of *Flaming Classics: Queering the Film Canon* (2000), *Making Things Perfectly Queer: Interpreting Mass Culture* (1993), and a coedited book, *Out in Culture: Gay, Lesbian, and Queer Essays on Popular Culture* (1995).

Mary Beth Haralovich is an associate professor of media arts at the University of Arizona in Tucson. She is coeditor of *Television, History, and American*

Culture: Feminist Critical Essays (1999) and several articles on film and television.

Matthew Henry is an instructor of English at Richmond College in Dallas, Texas, where he teaches classes in literature, composition, and cultural studies. He has authored several articles on film, television, advertising, and literature.

Michelle Hilmes is a professor of communication arts and director of undergraduate studies at the University of Wisconsin, Madison. She is the author of *Only Connect: A Cultural History of Broadcasting in the United States* (2002), *Radio Voices: American Broadcasting, 1922–52* (1997), and *Hollywood and Broadcasting: From Radio to Cable* (1990).

Patricia Mellencamp is a distinguished professor of art history at the University of Wisconsin-Milwaukee. She is the author of *A Fine Romance: Five Ages of Film Feminism* (1996), *High Anxiety: Catastrophe, Scandal, Age, and Comedy* (1990), and *Indiscretions: Avante Garde Film, Video, and Feminism* (1990). She is editor of and contributor to *Logics of Television: Essays in Cultural Criticism* and coeditor of *Cinema Histories/Cinema Practices* (1984) and *Cinema and Language* (1983).

Kathleen Rowe Karlyn is an associate professor in the Department of English at the University of Oregon. She is the author of *The Unruly Woman: Gender and the Genres of Laughter* (1995), as well as several articles on film and television. Her current project is *Unruly Girls: Changing Media for the Twenty-First Century*, a book on teen-girl culture, coauthored with Ellen Seiter.

George Lipsitz is a professor of ethnic studies at the University of California, San Diego. He is the author of *American Studies in a Moment of Danger* (2001), *The Possessive Investment in Whiteness: How White People Profit from Identity Politics* (1998), *Dangerous Crossroads: Postmodernism, Politics, and the Poetics of Place* (1994), *Rainbow at Midnight: Labor and Culture in the 1940s* (1991), *Time Passages: Collective Memory and American Popular Culture* (1990), and *A Life in the Struggle: Ivory Perry and the Culture of Opposition* (1988; 1995).

Laura Morowitz is an associate professor in the Performing and Visual Arts Department at Wagner University on Staten Island, New York. She is coeditor of *Artistic Brotherhoods in the Nineteenth Century* (2002), as well as author of several articles on art history and criticism.

Joanne Morreale is an associate professor of communication studies at Northeastern University in Boston, Massachusetts. She is the author of *The Presidential Campaign Film: A Critical History* (1993) and *A New Beginning: A Textual Frame Analysis of the Political Campaign Film* (1991).

Michael Real is the director of the E. W. Scripps School of Journalism at Ohio University. He is the author of *Exploring Media Culture: A Guide* (1996), *Super Media: A Cultural Studies Approach* (1989), and *Mass-Mediated Culture* (1977), as well as numerous articles in anthologies and journals.

Virginia Wright Wexman is a professor of English at the University of Illinois, Chicago. She is the author of *Creating the Couple: Love, Marriage, and Hollywood Performance* (1993). She is editor of *Film and Authorship* (in press) and *Jane Campion: Interviews* (1999). She is also coauthor of *A History of Film,* fifth edition (2002), and coeditor of *Letter from an Unknown Woman: Max Ophuls, Director* (1986).

Introduction

On the Sitcom

Critiquing the Sitcom: A Reader is an anthology of essays that analyze television representations of the family, gender, class, race, ethnicity, and culture in the American situation comedy. While these essays incorporate a variety of methods and perspectives, all share a common concern with articulating the relationship between ideology and culture. Ideology in this sense refers to the way that people think, act, and understand themselves and their relationship to the social order. Television, like all forms of social discourse, helps to shape not only beliefs, values, and attitudes, but also subjectivities, people's sense of themselves and their place in the world. Television portrays "appropriate" and "inappropriate" social relations, defines norms and conventions, provides "common sense" understandings, and articulates the preoccupations and concerns that define particular historical moments. Situation comedies, in particular, center around relationships in the family, workplace, and community; in so doing, they express the ideological tensions that mark particular social and historical moments. Sitcoms address significant ideas and issues within seemingly innocuous narrative frames, and analyzing them can help us account for the complexity and complications involved in the production and reception contexts of popular culture.

The essays in this reader help students and scholars to become more critical television viewers. They demonstrate a wide range of concepts and approaches, such as critical-historical, genre, feminist, psychoanalytic, reception-oriented, and postmodern criticism. Many of these essays were written when television criticism was a fledgling field of study, and the more recent essays in this volume often build upon these earlier works. The essays typically provide textual analysis of one or more episodes of a sitcom so that they can be used as models for analysis for those viewing the same or a similar episode. Most, too, include historical or industry analysis to relate the programs to a wider context. The essays are drawn from scholarly books and journals, and they cover situation comedies that have been widely circulated within popular culture. The majority of these sitcoms are known to viewers because they are currently in syndication or available for rental/purchase; others are familiar primarily to television scholars. Not every article written on sitcoms, even significant ones, could be included in this volume. The essays were selected as much for their methodological variety and merit as for the specific sitcom analyzed. Therefore, I hope that the gaps can be seen as opportunities for further exploration and analysis, and that this work will prompt readers to seek out other deserving articles that do not appear in this book.

Perhaps more so than any other fictional television genre, sitcoms have provided fodder for major cultural controversies and conversations. There was the well-publicized National Association for the Advancement of Colored People (NAACP) threat to organize a boycott of *Amos 'n' Andy*. There were the social and political issues raised by *All in the Family*, the debate incited by the main character's abortion on *Maude*, and the politicization of the fictional Murphy Brown's illegitimate child. More recently, the protests over both the real and the fictional Ellen coming out as a lesbian and the public spectacle that surrounded the closing episode of *Seinfeld* demonstrate the sitcom genre's impact upon the social and cultural terrain. Sitcoms generate emotions because they are so integrally related to who we are as both individual subjects and members of a cultural community. Throughout its history, writes Paul Wells, "the sitcom has become a genre dedicated to offering the popular audience a place to empathize with particular situations, rehearse a variety of responses, and find similar kinds of resolution."[1] At the same time, he adds, sitcoms are often ideologically progressive, "smuggling in" challenging ideas and images under the guise of humor (p. 181). As the various essays in this volume demonstrate, sitcoms both incorporate and contain change; they both address and prevent political action, and they may be read as both conservative and progressive forms, sometimes simultaneously. While their status as commercial products suggests that they will ultimately support the status quo, they may also allow for a multiplicity of discourses. Although their formulaic nature may appear to limit the implications of the debates they engender, many sitcoms allow for contrary readings. They thus provide ideal sites for critical examination of tensions and contradictions involving gender, the family, race, social class, and the dynamics of postmodern culture.

The chronological arrangement of the essays, from the inception of television in the late 1940s to the early twenty-first century, makes apparent how representations of gender, class, race, and the family alter through time, while simultaneously demonstrating the circuitous development of the genre. By viewing sitcoms from a historical perspective, we are better able to witness the terrain upon which subject positions are offered, negotiated, and consented to (or not). The result is a snapshot of the evolution of the genre, which enables us to see shifting ideological positions as meaning is negotiated in the construction of social reality. Overall, *Critiquing the Sitcom* lends insight into the construction of subjectivities, American culture, and the evolution of television itself as a medium of communication. More specifically, it familiarizes us with the critical traditions that inform academic inquiry into television texts, and it also enables students and scholars of television to learn to read television texts by viewing them closely.

The first two chapters provide a historical backdrop for some of the major themes and issues that continue to develop; in particular, they discuss some of the ideological tensions that play out in television discourse. The first essay is George Lipsitz's, "Why Remember Mama? The Changing Face of a Woman's Narrative." Lipsitz relates early television texts to their social and economic milieu, with particular attention to representations of social class and the formation of consumer culture. Sitcoms that aired at television's inception in the late 1940s typically depicted urban, working-class ethnic families, with parents who tried to hold on to the traditional ways of their older culture and children who had begun to assimilate into the new American milieu. Lipsitz observes that these texts were one way of dealing with tensions between the traditional values of the past and the new consumerist values of the post-World War II period. Part of the appeal of *Mama* (1949–56) was that its nostalgic images of the past helped to provide an interpretive framework for contemporary issues, particularly those around work, class mobility, and social status. Shows like *Mama* helped to transform ethnic, working-class identities into consumer identities by valorizing commodities, whether as products inserted into the narrative or as the solution to problems set up by the narrative.

Thomas Cripps's essay, "*Amos 'n' Andy* and the Debate over American Racial Integration," also takes a historical perspective to discuss the controversy that surrounded the television production of *Amos 'n' Andy* (1951–53). Like many of the early television sitcoms (including *Mama*), *Amos 'n' Andy* was originally a successful radio sitcom. Cripps observes that the controversy generated when CBS produced a televised version can only be understood in relation to the post-war social context. By the early 1950s, there was a growing black middle class, empowered both by educational and economic opportunities afforded to black soldiers after the war, and the concomitant burgeoning of the Civil Rights movement. Cripps argues that black activists, led by the NAACP, perceived *Amos 'n' Andy*'s negative portrayals of the black middle class as a regressive parody of their historical struggle for social mobility. Yet, he concludes that because the NAACP's protest against *Amos 'n' Andy* focused entirely upon its representations of the middle class, it failed to gain the support of the entire black community, and thus its protests were ultimately unsuccessful.

Patricia Mellencamp's "Situation Comedy, Feminism, and Freud: Discourses of Gracie and Lucy" discusses the representations of Gracie Burns on *The Burns and Allen Show* (1950–58) and Lucille Ball on *I Love Lucy* (1951–57). Mellencamp argues that television in the postwar period became a tool to encourage women to remain within the domestic sphere. Both Gracie Allen and Lucille Ball were powerful female performers who had made their reputations as vaudeville comedians and then went on to star on radio sitcoms. Mellencamp uses a combination of Freudian, feminist, and narrative analysis to discuss the ways that both women eluded patriarchal control on the narrative level, but succumbed to it on the discursive level on their respective sitcoms. Gracie Allen used language, the dominant discursive code of patriarchy, in her own idiosyncratic manner, and thus refused to be controlled by language or the males who possessed it. Yet, the self-reflexive structure of *The Burns and Allen Show* posed George Burns as authoritative narrator who explained and commented upon Gracie's actions, and thus she was ultimately "contained" by him. Similarly, Lucille Ball played a housewife who was continually trying to escape the bonds of domesticity by breaking into show business. Although she failed on the narrative level in every episode, she succeeded on the discursive level. Viewers witnessed Lucille Ball performing her vaudeville act in various guises before her character Lucy Ricardo ultimately repented and returned to her domestic role. Thus, although the women were empowered on the discursive level of performance, the narrative still kept them contained. Mellencamp accounts for their contradictory positioning by turning to Freudian theory of humor and comedy. She notes that both women used their respective brands of humor as substitutes for anger, replicating the experiences of female spectators faced with similar constraints.

The Honeymooners (1955–56) was another example of a working-class sitcom whose themes and issues reflected the tensions that marked the postwar social milieu. Virginia Wright Wexman's "Returning from the Moon: Jackie Gleason and the Carnivalesque" discusses the way the narrative strategies used in *The Honeymooners* reflected the tensions in gender relations that characterized the postwar period. Although in the mid-1950s the culture was inundated with images of the contented middle-class family, with authoritative patriarch, subordinate wife, and well-adjusted if mischievous children, Wexman observes that there remained an undercurrent of cultural instability regarding male dominance. Whereas most sitcoms repressed images of gender conflict, *The Honeymooners* brought it to the surface and in fact undermined the image of the dominant male. Wexman uses Mikhail Bahktin's notions of classical and grotesque bodies to show how *The Honeymooners* both challenged and supported patriarchal authority. Within the narrative of *The Honeymooners*, Ralph Kramden and Ed Norton were "grotesque" bodies, controlled by the "classical" bodies of their wives Alice and Trixie. However, Wexman also points out how this message was confounded because *The Honeymooners* was originally a segment on *The Jackie Gleason Show.* Host Jackie Gleason was the epitome of the "classical" body, dominant and in control, and it was he who framed the presentation of the fictional Honeymooners. In this way, the larger context of *The Honeymooners* reaffirmed the image of male dominance that permeated the culture.

By the late 1950s and early 1960s, women on television lost even the semblance of narrative resistance to patriarchal authority, while representations of working-class families and any racial or ethnic minorities virtually disappeared. The domestic nuclear family sitcom came to dominate the genre. Mary Beth Haralovich, writing "Sitcoms and Suburbs: Positioning the 1950s Homemaker," discusses the way that television helped to reconstitute the nuclear family after World War II. Suburban, middle-class life and the consumption patterns that it necessitated were "sold" to female consumers in sitcoms such as *Father Knows Best* (1954–62) and *Leave It to Beaver* (1957–63). Haralovich pays particular attention to the way that the spatial layouts in these domestic family sitcoms were ways of promoting middle-class ideology.

Domestic sitcoms remained popular throughout the 1960s, despite a political shift in climate away from the conservatism of the 1950s. Many sitcoms were aimed at the demographic groups identified within the industry as heavy television viewers: teens and rural, socially conservative Americans. Paul Attallah uses genre theory to analyze *The Beverly Hillbillies* (1962–71), a text that appealed largely to these groups. "The Unworthy Discourse: Situation Comedy in Television" considers *The Beverly Hillbillies,* like all television texts, as a specifically televisual form that is subject to institutional constraints and draws upon a range of social meanings and values. It is also, according to Attallah, perceived as "unworthy" of serious academic study because it is both a television sitcom and one that was reviled by critics. Yet, Attallah finds that serious discourses about class and sexuality predominate in the seemingly silly *Beverly Hillbillies,* as they do throughout the sitcom genre. These discourses articulate the cultural anxiety around issues of class and gender that characterized the 1960s social and political context.

Gilligan's Island (1964–67) was another sitcom whose simplistic plots and slapstick humor were aimed at youthful viewers, but was also open to multiple readings. Laura Morowitz's essay "From Gauguin to *Gilligan's Island*" examines *Gilligan's Island* as a text whose form and content reinforce media imperialism.

Its central premise, part of the post-Enlightenment tradition of "escapist" literature, affirmed both the perennial quest for escape from Western civilization and the impossibility of doing so. Not only do the castaways remake the remote island in the image of mainstream middle-class culture, but the program itself was marketed in all corners of the non-Western world. The text thus replicates the dominant ideology of consumerist capitalism that it appears to reject.

Julia (1968–71) was notable as one of the few 1960s sitcoms with any pretensions of social relevance. Aniko Bodroghkozy's " 'Is This What You Mean by Color TV?' Race, Gender, and Contested Meanings in *Julia*" places *Julia* within the context of the social and political unrest of the 1960s. Like earlier domestic sitcoms, *Julia* presented an uncomplicated world with trivial problems that were easily resolved at the end of each episode, and it ignored the racial strife in the world outside of the sitcom. Bodroghkozy uses a reception study to analyze viewer responses to *Julia*. She dissects both criticism in the popular press and letters and scripts from producer Hal Kantor's production file to assess the controversy that surrounded the first sitcom to star a black woman who was a self-sufficient professional rather than a maid. At the time, critics decried *Julia's* assimilationist view of black Americans in white culture, while supporters lauded the "realistic" portrayal of a single black mother. Bodroghkozy found that different audiences constructed vastly different readings of *Julia* depending upon their gender, as well as their social, cultural, and racial backgrounds. Her essay highlights the extent to which meaning is determined by readers rather than solely dictated by narrative strategies within a text; thus viewers from different social positions could read Julia as either a conservative or progressive representation of race and gender.

Julia served as a bridge between the light domestic comedies of the 1960s and what came to be known as the "socially relevant" comedies of the 1970s. Discussions of 1970s sitcoms inevitably revolve around the troika of *The Mary Tyler Moore Show* (1970–77), *All in the Family* (1971–83), and *M*A*S*H* (1972–83). These socially and politically "relevant" sitcoms emerged as the industry's conception of its desirable audience changed.[2] These sitcoms were aimed at an urban audience of 18-to 49-year olds with high consumption patterns, disposable incomes, and sophisticated viewing preferences. Thus, these texts addressed political issues, often had morally ambiguous characters, and aimed at "realism" rather than the superficial escapism of the 1960s sitcoms.

Serafina Bathrick's *"The Mary Tyler Moore Show:* Women at Home and at Work" considers how social change is incorporated into the sitcom form in a manner that still preserves the dominant patriarchal ideology. *The Mary Tyler Moore Show* was the first sitcom to star an unmarried career woman whose sole objective was not marriage (though also an unmarried professional, Julia was constantly involved in romantic relationships, and she was safely defined as a widow). *The Mary Tyler Moore Show* went on the air at the height of the woman's movement, and is often cited as a program that spoke to a new audience of "liberated" women. Bathrick's essay provides an excellent example of close visual analysis, as she considers the manner in which the spatial coding of Mary's home and workplace expresses gender relationships. She finds that while Mary's relationships with other women in the personal sphere are coded as positive, her workplace relations undercut her status as a "liberated" woman. Both the coding of space and her relations with her male colleagues remain rooted in traditional representations of the patriarchal nuclear family, and thus *The Mary Tyler Moore Show,* while appearing to accommodate social change, assures viewers that patriarchal structures remain the basis for institutional, if not personal, relations.

As the nation grew more conservative in the mid-1970s, the industry shifted to less complicated sitcoms such as *Happy Days* (1974–84) and its spinoff *Laverne and Shirley* (1976–83), largely designed for an adolescent audience with high consumption patterns. Alexander Doty's essay, "I Love *Laverne and Shirley*: Lesbian Narratives, Queer Pleasures, and Television Sitcoms" uses queer theory to examine the way that characters on television can be represented and read as simultaneously lesbian and straight. On the surface, texts such as *Laverne and Shirley* use representational codes of straight, heterosexual femininity. But Doty's analysis demonstrates the polysemic nature of television texts as he indicates the ways that texts with two female protagonists simultaneously suggest and deny lesbian meanings.

Despite the shift in the late 1970s, sitcoms based on complex characters reappeared in the 1980s, as networks sought to woo back the young, educated, affluent viewers drawn to cable and new video technologies. *Cheers* (1982–93) is one example of the "quality" 1980s sitcom with plot twists and character development designed to lure upscale viewers. Michelle Hilmes's "Where Everybody Knows Your Name: *Cheers* and the Mediation of Cultures" examines the relationship of media institutions and texts, particularly with regard to representations of social class on *Cheers*. She argues that *Cheers* reproduces the conflict between high art and popular culture that lies at the heart of commercial television. *Cheers,* like television itself, celebrates both high art and popular culture; however, like most television sitcoms, it valorizes the workplace family, itself modeled on the patriarchal nuclear family.

The politically conservative 1980s were also marked by the return of the domestic nuclear family comedy, most notably represented by the highly popular *Cosby Show* (1984–92). The text marked a return to the 1950s model of the comfortably middle-class family, with trivial problems typically resolved at the end of the episode. The Huxtable family, with two well-educated professional parents and five well-adjusted children, happened to be black, a significant departure from the all-white families of 1950s sitcoms, as well as from the negatively charged images of other black families seen on television. (For example, *Sanford and Son* [1972–77], *Good Times* [1974–79], and *The Jeffersons* [1975–85], three popular "black" sitcoms produced by the politically liberal Norman Lear, still reproduced the black male as "buffoon" stereotype.) In the essay "Structuralist Analysis 1: Bill Cosby and Recoding Ethnicity," Michael Real discusses Cosby's ideologically progressive and conservative features. Cosby was a text whose content intended to recode black representations from negative to positive. Yet, it also presented an idealized patriarchal family, celebrated consumerism, and glossed over the real conflicts and contradictions that marked black life in America.

Texts such as *Roseanne* (1988–97) and *The Simpsons* (1990–) presented dysfunctional blue-collar families in a manner that highlighted the social and political issues attributable to class disparities. All of these programs were deliberately created to attract a young audience by standing out from standard network fare. Yet, despite controversies generated by their often deliberately provocative content, they still preserved many traditional stereotypes regarding class and gender. Kathleen Rowe Karlyn's essay *"Roseanne*: Unruly Woman as Domestic Goddess" argues that Roseanne Barr's overweight, sharp-witted, and strongly matriarchal character, which could not be separated from her off-screen persona, subverts traditional female stereotypes. Roseanne was a threatening figure, both within the text and within popular culture. At the same time, despite its respectful depiction of a working-class family, *Roseanne* fails to address issues of social class in any critically meaningful way. Similarly, in "The Triumph of Popular Culture: Situation Comedy, Postmodernism, and *The Simpsons*," Matthew Henry describes *The Simpsons* as a postmodern text that uses irony to spoof the nuclear family, television, and popular culture. Yet, it too still depicts an intact, mutually supportive patriarchal family that is beyond criticism. Ultimately, Henry notes, *The Simpsons* is itself part of the consumer culture that it critiques, just as viewers are themselves part of the cultural milieu that is satirized. These texts reflect a growing awareness of a new type of viewer, steeped in television history and aware of its conventions, who adopts an ironic position but only in the service of the text.

Nineties sitcoms based on a "family" of friends, such as *Ellen* (1994–98), *Friends* (1994–), and *Seinfeld* (1990–98), emphasize the characters' anxiety and neurosis rather than camaraderie; the characters serve as much as signs of cultural dysfunction as points of identification. Joanne Morreale's essay "Sitcoms Say Goodbye: The Cultural Spectacle of *Seinfeld*'s Last Episode" considers the media attention that surrounded the closing episode of *Seinfeld*. She analyzes the last episode as a spectacle that magnified the discursive relationship constructed between text and viewer; in so doing, it illustrated the way that mediated relationships substitute for genuine community in contemporary culture. Both the form and content of *Seinfeld* represented cultural malaise, where the characters' superficiality within the narrative paralleled the discursive relationship set up between text and viewer.

Overall, the essays in this volume allow us to see shifting representations and different modes of addressing ideological tensions within culture. They show us that it is not a simple task to read a particular sitcom, or to determine whether a particular sitcom serves an ideologically conservative or subversive function. If anything, we can see that an individual text is capable of both inflections; often, progressive messages are smuggled into conservative texts, and vice versa. Close analysis of individual texts allows us to see how class, gender, race, the family, and culture are presented in television sitcoms, often in complicated ways. When we watch sitcoms, we are watching ourselves; and when we deconstruct them, we become more aware of how we are constructed. All of the authors in this volume have attempted to do just that, and their analyses provide reflective lenses to help us to see ourselves through television.

Part One | Television in the 1940s and 1950s

It is hard to imagine that television, so deeply embedded in our social fabric, is relatively new. The first television broadcast in the United States occurred in a small station owned by General Electric and RCA in Schenectady, New York, in 1928. But the medium developed slowly, largely as a result of economic constraints during the depression. The onset of World War II further delayed its development, as the government banned the manufacture of new television sets and building of new stations. When the war ended in 1945, the major radio networks, NBC, CBS, and ABC (which was formed when the government ordered NBC to sell one of its two radio networks in 1944), along with the short-lived DuMont network, quickly set to work on developing the medium. Thus, it was no surprise that early television was structured like radio, with similar programs and a similar economic structure. As with radio, commercial sponsors paid for programs with the major objective of securing the largest possible audience. This structure remains intact today.

The sitcom did not immediately dominate television programming. From 1946 to 1948, sports and theatrical drama predominated. Sporting events were relatively inexpensive to air, while theatrical dramas helped to sell television to affluent, well-educated viewers who could most easily afford sets. The first television sitcom, Mary Kay and Johnny, *(1947–50) was adapted from radio. It aired on the DuMont network in 1947 and was picked up by NBC in 1948. But the sitcom, like many other genres, was soon overshadowed by another form adapted from radio—the comedy-variety show. These programs essentially consisted of comedy acts and musical numbers performed live in front of a camera, borrowing from the vaudevillian tradition of early American theater.* The Texaco Star Theatre *(1948–53) hosted by Milton Berle, became the first smash hit on television, leading to a host of imitators.*

In the period from 1948 to 1952, largely due to the success of comedy-variety programs, television overtook radio as the dominant entertainment medium in the United States. Television set ownership grew exponentially, especially on the East Coast, where most broadcast stations were located. Many early television stars, such as

*George Burns and Gracie Allen, Ozzie and Harriet, and Jackie Gleason, were origi-
nally vaudeville comedians who transferred their talents to radio, then to television.
Burns and Allen, for example, were originally a vaudeville comedy team who starred
in* The Burns and Allen Show *on radio, then later on television (1950–58). Early
episodes retain the variety show flavor, with musical numbers inserted into the program and George Burns addressing the television audience with a comedy routine.
Vestiges of the broad physical comedy and verbal repartees of vaudeville acts can still
be seen in more modern programs such as* Seinfeld *(1990–98).*

*While one strain of sitcom emerged out of the comedy-variety show, another was
based upon the model of the family serial. These largely came to television when CBS,
attempting to counter NBC's numerous comedy-variety shows, decided to adapt successful radio sitcoms to television. Many of these concerned urban, ethnic, working-
class families dealing with life in America.* The Goldbergs *(1949–55), a long
running radio serial about a Jewish immigrant family in New York, was the first hit
sitcom on television.* Mama *(1949–56), featuring a Norwegian family at the turn of
the century in San Francisco, followed soon after.* Mama *was even more of a ratings
success than* The Goldbergs, *finishing in the Nielsen Ratings Company's top twenty-
five television programs from 1949 to 1955. It lasted longer than any of the other
ethnic situation comedies that appeared on television in the 1940s and 1950s.*

Both The Goldbergs *and* Mama *ushered in the "domestic" strain of the situation
comedy that would become commonplace on television. Instead of relying upon the
physical antics and one-line repartees of vaudevillian humor, these programs explored the humor that arose out of everyday situations, especially those that expressed
the conflict between traditional and modern values. These shows also demonstrate the
close relationship between early television shows and their sponsors. Lead characters
would sell products in the ads that preceded and followed programs, so it was not unusual to see "Mama" espousing the virtues of Maxwell House coffee just before the
program opened with the family sitting down to breakfast, drinking coffee.*

*Most, but not all, of these early television programs were broadcast live. Because
the East and West Coasts were not yet connected by coaxial cable, many programs
were shot on kinescopes, so that live shows were filmed directly off a television moni-
tor as they played.* The Ruggles *(1949–52), for example, another sitcom about a
working-class family, was performed live in Los Angeles and then shipped to the East
Coast. Kinescopes were often the only way viewers could see some programs, but the
resulting films were of extremely poor quality, and thus most sitcoms shot on kinescopes were short-lived. Cinema provided another alternative, and other early sitcoms, such as* The Hank McCune Show *(1950) or* The Life of Riley *(1949–50),
were filmed on the West Coast rather than being performed live. These "Hollywood"
television sitcoms, featuring assimilated rather than ethnic working-class families,*

borrowed from the screwball comedies of film. The formula revolved around a mis-understood situation that provided a context for characters to react with one-liners. They featured bumbling but well-meaning male leads, which became typical of rep-resentations of working-class males in later television sitcoms. Unlike their middle-class counterparts, working-class males lacked both authority and purchasing power.

Although the networks continued to develop radio sitcoms for television, the genre was not an immediate success. The Burns and Allen Show *went on the air in 1950 but only reached the Nielsen top thirty in 1953, when it reached twentieth in the rat-ings.* Burns and Allen *is often cited as an early example of reflexive television. Both George Burns and Gracie Allen played themselves, although the show took place in their suburban Los Angeles home rather than at work. Further, the show is noted for its reflexive narrative techniques, where George Burns would break out of frame in order to comment upon the action in the story, or he would watch the progress of the plot on his own television.*

In January 1951, there was not one sitcom listed among the top ten shows on tel-evision. That summer, CBS introduced Amos 'n' Andy *(1951–53), adapted from a successful radio sitcom that had been on the air since 1929. The characters in the radio version were played by two white men, Freeman Gosden and Charles Correll (who also created the show), but CBS agreed to produce the television version with an all-black cast.* Amos 'n' Andy *was the first major television sitcom shot on film in Los Angeles with a big budget and high production values. Like other "Hollywood" sit-coms, the show fit into the pattern of the screwball comedy, featuring the adventures of conventional, middle-class Amos, his comic sidekick, the bumbling Andy, and their manipulative friend Kingfish. Like* Beulah *(1950–53), a sitcom portraying the inept antics of a black maid,* Amos 'n' Andy *perpetuated negative stereotypes. Whereas the sitcoms about white ethnic families portrayed them as hard-working and restrained, these sitcoms portrayed black characters as lazy and ignorant.* Amos 'n' Andy *is perhaps most famous because the NAACP threatened to organize a boy-cott of* Amos 'n' Andy*'s sponsor, Blatz Beer, unless the show was taken off the air. Al-though they did not succeed, CBS took* Amos 'n' Andy *off the air when it fell from thirteenth to twenty-fifth in the Nielsen ratings during its second season, claiming that its decision was based on the show's poor ratings. But the controversy generated by* Amos 'n' Andy *made it easier for the networks to concentrate on safe, nondescript, white middle-class suburban families. After the furor over* Amos 'n' Andy*, sitcoms starring black performers virtually disappeared from the airwaves.*

By the fall of 1951, the East and West Coasts were linked by coaxial cable, initi-ating coast-to-coast network television. This meant that viewers across the country could watch the same program simultaneously. The coaxial cable link also con-tributed to the homogenization of television representations; rather than urban, eth-

nic sitcoms aimed at viewers largely clustered in East Coast cities, sitcoms featuring white, middle-class suburban families of indistinct nationality became a fact of television life. For the most part, the experiences of working-class or ethnic families were simply not represented on television.

The newer, blander domestic sitcoms also signaled a shift in social context from the 1940s to the early 1950s. As the postwar economy expanded, many (white) working-class Americans were moving into the middle-class suburbs and losing their ethnic identities. Televised depictions of the suburbs provided idealized images of the white middle classes who had the means to buy the appropriate consumer goods. The Adventures of Ozzie and Harriet *(1952–66), which had begun on radio in the 1940s, exemplified the strain of domestic comedy featuring idealized nuclear families that came to characterize television in the 1950s. The actors played themselves as a happily married suburban show business couple with two sons. The humor came from trivial everyday situations where problems were easily resolved, and their on-screen lives were dominated by leisure rather than work.*

One sitcom that provided a transition between the urban, ethnic, working-class sitcom and the domestic suburban family sitcom was I Love Lucy *(1951–57). Its star, Lucille Ball, had appeared in films and on the CBS radio sitcom* My Favorite Husband. *When CBS encouraged her to produce a television sitcom, she agreed only if her real-life husband Desi Arnaz could star as her husband. CBS balked at portraying what was then considered a "mixed marriage," although they capitulated after Ball and Arnaz agreed to take a pay cut in exchange for complete production control of the series.*

The company formed by Ball and Arnaz, Desilu Productions, both utilized and altered television sitcom formulas. Arnaz, a professional bandleader, basically played himself, but Ball took on a fictional role as his wife, Lucy Ricardo. She played an untalented housewife trying to break into show business and out of her restricted role at home. Not only did the show include both professional and domestic situations, but it merged the broad physical comedy and screwball humor of a show such as Amos 'n' Andy *with some degree of character realism as in* Mama.

I Love Lucy *also used an innovative production style that has since become commonplace. It was shot on film using three cameras, although it retained a live studio audience. Within four months of its 1951 premiere, it became the top-rated show on television, and it remained number one for four years.* I Love Lucy's *success led to an onslaught of new sitcoms, most adapted from radio by CBS. None achieved the same level of popularity, though they did make CBS the number one network. After* I Love Lucy, *even programs that had been broadcast live, such as* Burns and Allen, *began to be shot on film, which meant that reruns could be broadcast during the summer or sold to individual stations. Between 1951 and 1952, the number of filmed television programs doubled, and the rerun became both a possibility and a fact.*

Very few long-running sitcoms departed from the domestic sitcom formula. I Love Lucy *was one notable exception, and* Make Room for Daddy *(1953–64), also a Desilu production, was another successful sitcom that portrayed an urban show business family with relationships that were not always harmonious and happy.* The Honeymooners *(1955–56) also stood apart from the staple television sitcom fare, though it was a ratings failure in its half-hour format.*

Vaudeville comedian Jackie Gleason became host of the DuMont network's comedy-variety show Cavalcade of Stars *(1949–52) in 1950. Gleason introduced* The Honeymooners *as a brief comedy skit in 1951 and continued it when the show moved to CBS in 1952. The skit became a half-hour sitcom in 1955.* The Honeymooners, *like other shows, such as* Burns and Allen *and* I Love Lucy, *can be read in terms of the postwar economic and cultural need to restabilize the family, both by repositioning women within the domestic sphere, and by reaffirming male authority. The show depicted a childless working-class couple, the Kramdens, who were failing to achieve the middle-class ideal of economic prosperity and life in the suburbs. Whereas most television images projected images of blissfully cohesive nuclear families,* The Honeymooners *did otherwise. Repressed in most sitcoms, tensions around class and gender defined* The Honeymooners. *Yet, although the brief comedy sketches had been a hit, the half-hour version of the show failed after a single season. The original episodes from this period, often rebroadcast in syndication, have since achieved cult status with many viewers.*

For the most part, sitcoms such as Ozzie and Harriet, Father Knows Best *(1954–60),* Leave It to Beaver *(1957–63), and* The Donna Reed Show *(1958–66) came to represent the sitcom genre in the late 1950s. These shows presented reassuring images of economically secure families with small problems, all easily resolvable within their thirty-minute time slot.*

Although many of these domestic middle-class sitcoms bridged the 1950s and 1960s, they remained rooted in 1950s conservatism and social values. The essays in this section provide critical analyses of some of the more representative sitcoms of the 1940s and 1950s.

J. M.

1

Why Remember Mama?

The Changing Face of a Woman's Narrative

GEORGE LIPSITZ

Almost every Friday night between 1949 and 1956, millions of Americans watched Rosemary Rice turn the pages of an old photograph album. With music from Edward Grace's "Holverg Suite" playing in the background, and with pictures of turn-of-the-century San Francisco displayed on the album pages, Rice assumed the identity of her television character, Katrin Hansen, on the CBS network program *Mama*. She told the audience about her memories of her girlhood, her family's house on Steiner Street, and her experiences there with her big brother Nels, her little sister Dagmar, her Papa, and her Mama—"most of all," she said, "when I remember that San Francisco of so long ago, I remember Mama."[1] Katrin Hansen's memories of her Norwegian immigrant, working-class family had powerful appeal for viewers in the early years of commercial network broadcasting. *Mama* established itself as one of CBS's most popular programs during its first season on the air, and it retained high ratings for the duration of its prime-time run.[2]

In December 1985, the Museum of Broadcasting in New York City presented a retrospective tribute to *Mama,* featuring a reunion with four members of the cast and crew. In the thirty years since the show had been broadcast, each of the featured guests had gone on to interesting and important careers. Rosemary Rice, who played Katrin, became a featured voice on many popular cartoons and children's records. Dick Van Patten, who played the Hansens' son Nels, went on to establish himself as one of America's best known father figures

A slightly different version of this chapter was originally published in George Lipsitz, *Time Passages: Collective Memory and American Popular Culture* (University of Minnesota Press, 1990), 77–96. It has been reprinted here by permission of the publisher.

7

through his acting role on the popular television show *Eight Is Enough* and through his real-life role as father when his children achieved fame as actors and professional tennis players. Robin Morgan, who played Dagmar, became the author of several highly acclaimed books on feminism that established her as a leading thinker and spokesperson for the radical wing of the feminist movement. Ralph Nelson, the show's director, became one of the leading liberals in Hollywood as well as the creative genius behind magnificent motion pictures, including *Lilies of the Field, Soldier Blue,* and *Charlie.* Despite their busy schedules and varied fields of endeavor, Rice, Van Patten, Morgan, and Nelson came together at the Museum of Broadcasting to pay tribute to their memories of *Mama.*

"Every show had a tear and a laugh, and every show taught you something," Rice remembered, adding that working on that series "Christmas didn't come just once a year, it came every Friday night." Van Patten talked about *Mama's* enormous effect on his life: he named his first son Nels after his character on the show, and he secured his role on *Eight Is Enough* largely because producer Fred Silverman had watched *Mama* as a child and admired Nels. Morgan said that she had learned discipline, professionalism, and team play on *Mama,* and that those skills had been crucial to her success as a political activist. In addition, she discerned a connection between the show's content and her evolution into a feminist. "After all, this was *I Remember Mama* [*sic*], not *Father Knows Best,*" she quipped, explaining that the scripts showed girls to be as important as boys and that Judson Laire's characterization of Papa presented a strong, loving, but gentle male.[3] Ralph Nelson discussed how *Mama* prepared him for Hollywood by giving him the opportunity to direct both the regular cast and skilled guest performers including Paul Newman, Inger Stevens, Jack Lemmon, and Cliff Robertson. "When I did *Lilies of the Field* I followed the same structure as *Mama,* and I was quite conscious of it at the time.[4]

Through sympathetic laughter and applause, the audience at the Museum of Broadcasting symposium registered approval of all the praise for *Mama.* But the discussion took a bizarre turn when the audience began to question the speakers. One woman expressed her appreciation to the cast both for their remarks that evening and for their performances thirty years ago. She explained that while growing up she felt very alienated and unhappy with her own family, so she "adopted" the television Hansen family and pretended that they were her own mother and father, brother and sisters. Rosemary Rice responded, "We really were a family, we grew up together—we became a real family." Rice added that she attended classes at New York University while starring in the show and that she always showed her term papers to Judson Laire, who played Papa, because "I thought I should show my father my homework."[5] Robin Morgan indicated that the show helped to provide a surrogate family for her as well. Her father had deserted her mother shortly after Morgan was born, providing her with a bitter early lesson about the family. But Judson Laire became a parental role model on and off camera for the young Morgan, and Peggy Wood encouraged her in her desire to become a writer, encouragement that, she said, "meant a great deal to me."[6] Ralph Nelson recalled that *Mama* had helped reconcile him to his own family. As a teenager Nelson had argued constantly with his Swedish American father, especially over the latter's racism and anti-Semitism. When his father tried to send him to a reform school, Nelson ran away from home and wandered all across the country. Not until he began directing *Mama* could he muster any affection or nostalgia for his background, but weekly contact with the fictional Norwegian Hansen family reconnected Nelson to his past. Then Nelson made a startling connection between his own negotiations with ethnic memory and those of Kathryn Forbes, the author of the original stories on which *Mama* was based. Nelson said that he had read somewhere that Forbes had fashioned a similar relationship to her own past through the Hansen family. Forbes was ethnically Norwegian, but she had spent much of her childhood in foster homes and felt deserted by her family. In her fiction, she "reinvented" her mother on the basis of the few stories she had heard about her grandmother and presented experiences that she wished had actually happened to her.

In response to this projection of the Hansen family as part of the real family experiences of the woman from the audience, Rice, Morgan, Nelson, and Forbes turned the symposium into an exercise in a different kind of nostalgia from what had been planned. One of the commonplace assumptions about *Mama* among contemporaneous critics and media historians has been that the show succeeded because it reflected the "real" family experiences precious to Americans. But the comments at the Museum of Broadcasting indicate that it played to another frame of reception as well—the past as people wish it had been rather than the past as they actually experienced it. The fact that so many of the speakers at the symposium treasured vicarious memories of a family life that none of them actually had, one that in fact ran directly counter to their own experience, illumines an important function of memory within popular culture in general—memory as managed *misappropriation.*

The popularity of *Mama* among people with unhappy family experiences might be seen as a quintessential example of the media's power to naturalize oppression. No one at the symposium expressed outrage at the program for presenting family life as sweeter and more loving than it actually was for them; instead they treasured a picture of the Hansens as normal and typical. One can well imagine the problems that might follow from this process—unrealistically high expectations about family relations, inability to anticipate problems that cannot be resolved by the final commercial, and the likelihood of blaming individual choices and behaviors for what in fact might be systemic problems between men and women or between children and adults. Indeed, as David Marc points out, much critical anger at the content of television programs revolves around these possibilities: critics understandably enough become alienated from a televised world in which nearly everyone is white and heterosexual, where no one sleeps on a mattress on the floor instead of a bed, where no one drives a used car, and where physical bravery and force always outperform moral courage and intellect.

But memory as misappropriation can have positive as well as negative consequences. It enables us to see beyond our own experience, rendering the oppressions of the past as contingent and unnecessary while modeling an alternate past, one as responsive to human wishes and desires as to the accidents of history. It says that biology is not destiny, that family and ethnicity can be sources of self-affirmation and connection to others, but only if they meet certain conditions of humane behavior. If our own personal pasts cannot be venerated as moral guides for the present, we must choose another from history or art and embrace it as our own. But such leaps cannot be fashioned purely from the imagination; the past has more informative power and more relevance to the present if we believe that it is what actually happened, because what people have done before they can do again, while what they imagine may never be realized. Even when misappropriated, memory has to appear credible, to resonate with lessons of some real past. *Mama* succeeded in that role because even its misappropriations resonated with the lessons of history. Because its core tensions exuded the truths of lived experience and memory, *Mama* enabled audiences to arbitrate the tensions facing them and to negotiate utopian endings.

It was not just the audience, cast, and crew of the television show *Mama* who made creative use of the Hansen family. From its inception in the Kathryn Forbes stories of the early 1940s, the narrative about the Hansen family has provided a particularly fertile field for misappropriation. As stories, a book, a Broadway play, a radio special, a film, and finally as a television program, remembering Mama has engaged the revisionist energies of both artists and audiences. At each stage, alterations in narrative as well as in media responded as much to the larger political and ideological context as to dramatic necessities. Though they appear on the surface to be an uncontrollable obscuring of the historical record, the various versions of *Mama* represent in reality a creative adaptation of memory to arbitrate the indignities and alienations of everyday life. These changes were not always positive; some were obviously steps backward—regressive adaptations that precluded rather than promoted possibilities. But they demonstrate the indispensable dialogue with the past that accompanies any present, and they reflect the enduring potential of the past to help us see beyond the present even while speaking to its psychic and ideological preoccupations. The many incarnations of *I Remember Mama* reflected a continuing dialogue about the family and its proper social roles—a dialogue necessitated by extraordinary social changes between the early 1940s and the mid-1950s. Changes in the succeeding versions of these stories offer a significant index to the transformations in family life and family images during that period, as well as to the ways in which social pressures altered the forms and purposes of families.

This is not to argue that the many individuals involved in shaping the short stories, book, play, film, radio show, and television program about the Hansen family decided consciously to make their efforts relevant to contemporary affairs. Rather, it is to claim that commercial mass culture seeks credibility with its audience, at least in part, by arbitrating the ideological tensions created by disparities between cultural promises and lived experiences. As the core tensions facing families in society changed, intellectuals working in the culture industry participated in bending discursive practices to social realities, shaping their art to speak to current issues. Commercial pressures certainly contributed to their decisions: investors, editors, and advertisers had obvious stakes in supporting the status quo, and no doubt made their preferences known to those on the creative side of the enterprise. But more interesting than the conclusions and plot resolutions of these cultural artifacts are the oppositions that precede the conclusions, oppositions indicative of extraordinary contestation and confusion in society about family identity.

Operative Tensions in a Changing Narrative

As short stories, a book, and a Broadway play, the experiences of the Hansen family revolve around the legacy of the Great Depression. The operative tensions in the stories come from the mother's struggle to protect her family from hard times and from ethnic rivalries and hatreds. In the motion picture, the focus shifts to the differences between Mama and her daughters, to a story of a traditional mother raising independent daughters. The television program rescinds the independence enjoyed by the daughters in the film, presenting instead a narrative about threats to the family posed (or solved) by consumer goods. These three frames of reference responded to changes in American society at large—the remnants of the depression in the early 1940s, the entry of large numbers of women into the workforce during World War II, and the rise of suburbs and increases in consumer spending in the early 1950s.

Kathryn Forbes published her first story about the Hansen family, "Mama's Bank Account," in the *Toronto Star Weekly* early in 1941. The *Reader's Digest* printed two excerpts from the story almost immediately upon publication, and Harcourt published an extended collection as a book titled *Mama's Bank Account*. The book received a warm welcome from reviewers and from the reading public; even the War Department deemed it worthwhile and wholesome reading, purchasing fifty thousand copies for soldiers overseas. The success of *Mama's Bank Account* inspired the play *I Remember Mama* by John Van Druten, which opened in 1944 and ran for 713 performances. Both the book and the play depict Mama as an effective manager of the family's finances, successfully maneuvering around illness, unemployment, and the demands of the children so that she does not have to "go to the bank" and withdraw their savings. When Katrin's success as a writer eventually brings in some surplus cash, Mama can finally admit that there is no bank account, that she talked about one so that the children would be shielded from knowing how desperate their financial circumstances actually were. Now they can go to the bank, but to open an account for Katrin's money, not to use up their "savings."

Forbes's book tells about a battle between family and economy; it delineates the ways in which poverty threatens love. Mama's resolute courage in the face of deprivation connects her to the "Madonnas of the Fields"—the strong and courageous farm women made into icons by 1930s Farm Security Administration photographers. In this ethos, women attain beatific status by keeping families together in the face of the Great Depression. *Mama's Bank Account* also revolves around ethnicity, retracing the steps taken by immigrants to find common cause in a new land filled with not-so-friendly strangers. Mama draws upon her special knowledge and skills rooted in the old country to help her children succeed in America.

The story of the bank account forms the core of the Hansen family narrative, touching effectively on historical memories about the depression—especially its threats to the survival of families and the new roles demanded of women by changing economic circumstances. In the book, Papa turns to carpentry only after failing as a farmer; in the play he responds to Katrin's desire to be a writer by asking how much writers earn. But a subtext of ethnicity in the book and play also addresses the collective memory of the audience. Trade-union organizing drives and new political coalitions ranging from the New Deal to the Communist Party's popular front transformed the meaning of ethnicity in the 1930s, and the unity of the war effort eclipsed some internal ethnic rivalries. In Forbes's book, Katrin enrolls in a school where antiforeign prejudice makes her sensitive about her Scandinavian background. At one point the principal complains about the immigrant children enrolling in his school, fulminating "Italians, Jews, what next? Negroes or even Orientals?" Katrin feels like an outsider—her only friend is an Italian American girl—and she fears total humiliation when Mama is asked to take her turn with the other mothers and cook a meal for the class. Katrin worries that Mama's Norwegian meatballs will draw more antiforeign ridicule, but when her classmates and teachers love Mama's cooking, Katrin sees that she can be accepted in American society by offering her ethnic gifts instead of hiding them.[7]

The ethnic component of *Mama's Bank Account* appealed to actress Mady Christians. Born in Vienna in 1900, Christians first acted in her father's German American theater productions in New York and spent much of the 1930s as both an actress and an activist on behalf of refugees from Nazi persecution. When she heard that Rodgers and Hammerstein were thinking of basing a Broadway play on the book, Christians asked for the part. They eventually decided not to do the play, but they mentioned her interest to John Van Druten, who wrote his adaptation to the stage with her in mind and made sure that she got the part (along with a young Marlon Brando cast as Nels).[8]

But even in its first incarnations, sharp contradictions divided the fictional representations of the Hansen family and the lives of the artists responsible for it. Forbes wrote what most critics and viewers considered "realistic" accounts of Norwegian Americans, even though she had no real firsthand knowledge of them and she fashioned a touching portrayal of family life despite herself having a fragile marriage that ended in divorce in 1946 on the grounds of her husband's "extreme mental cruelty."[9] Similarly, for all Christians's conviction about *I Remember Mama* as testimony to the immigrant presence in America, she was passed over for the film and television roles as Mama because, as the Cold War deepened, her work with the American Committee for the Protection of the Foreign Born drew the ire of xenophobic anticommunists. A parade of "investigators" harassed Christians about her political affiliations, and both the film and television industries blacklisted her even though no evidence of "disloyalty" ever surfaced.[10]

If the story, book, and play versions of the Hansen family's adventures coalesced around New Deal mutuality, director George Stevens's 1948 film *I Remember Mama* focused on the rooted independence of immigrant daughters raised by traditional mothers.[11] Dewitt Bodeen's screenplay retained the emphases on gender, class, and ethnicity pervading previous versions of the Hansen story, but adapted them to the dominant social tensions of the war and postwar periods. As film scholar Andrea Walsh points out, the film reflected the "pressure to grow up" facing young girls in the 1940s, at a time when millions of men served overseas and millions of women embraced new roles as war workers. Within the discourse of the day, *I Remember Mama* steered a middle way between hysterical antifeminist tirades (like Philip Wylie's *Generation of Vipers*) that charged domineering mothers with destroying the independence of American children, and the emerging war and postwar feminist consciousness stimulated by women's success in securing and maintaining war production jobs. The film featured Mama as a source for reconciliation, as a means of proving that threatening changes could be resisted while one accommodated to progress.

Indeed the entire film *I Remember Mama* presents threatening contradictions and then shows that they are not contradictions at all. For example, an opposition between family and money pervades the narrative. Mama has to supervise the budget to see that her family survives, with financial crises popping up at every turn—her daughter Christine needs an operation, a boarder pays his rent with a bad check, her sister Trina has no dowry, her Uncle Chris leaves them nothing in his will. But love proves superior to money. Mama mediates in an argument between her Uncle Chris, who has the money, and a doctor who has the expertise to secure the operation for her daughter. She teaches her children that the works of literature left behind by their deadbeat boarder are worth more than money. Along with Uncle Chris, she neutralizes issues of pride and honor to enable her sister to marry a man who does not insist on a dowry. She finds that Uncle Chris spent all his money on charities for crippled children, and she uses that fact to encourage her son Nels to be a doctor and carry on his uncle's good works. Although Mama works within the home for her family, the narrative suggests that her work has great economic value even though she does not succumb to the self-centered greed of the work world.

Lessons about greed dominate one particularly important exchange between Katrin and Mama. Shortly after Mama makes her only consumer purchase in the film, a bouquet of violets, Katrin promises her, "When I'm rich and famous . . . I'll buy you just lovely clothes: white satin gowns with long trains on them and jewelry. I'll buy you a pearl necklace." [12] Mama replies that she prefers her *solje,* her brooch, to a pearl necklace. Her immigrant loyalties confuse the American daughter who protests that Mama must want to be rich. When Mama replies that being rich is like being ten feet tall, "good for some things—bad for others," Katrin asks why she came to America if not to be rich. Mania tells us, "We came to America because they are all here—all the others. Is good for families to be together." [13] The exchange about the superiority of a *solje* to a pearl necklace and the preeminence of family over wealth prefigures a crucial scene that marks Katrin's maturation into an adult. Katrin admires a dresser set in a store window, even though Mama warns her that what Katrin takes to be ivory is probably just plastic. But Katrin persists, hinting about the dresser set for her high school graduation present. Mama and Papa had intended to give her the *solje,* but pressured by their daughter's consumer desire they pawn the brooch to buy her the dresser set. At this point younger sister Christine intervenes, scolding Katrin for her selfishness and reminding her that with Papa on strike their parents could hardly afford the present she wanted. "Why I don't believe you even know what they're striking for. Do you? All you and your friends can talk about is the presents you're going to get. You make me ashamed of being a girl." [14] Humbled by Christine's priorities, Katrin pawns the dresser set and returns the *solje* to Mama and Papa, who reward her passage to adult responsibility by letting her drink coffee with them.

Yet for all its privileging of love over money, *I Remember Mama* ultimately validates love as one way of securing happiness *and* money. Mama's old-fashioned female identity provides the key breakthrough for Katrin's aspirations to become a professional writer. When Katrin despairs because her stories have been rejected and complains that she needs the critique of an expert, Mama uses her traditional skills to launch her daughter's career. Seeing a picture of "famous author" Florence Dana Moorhead in the paper, Mama decides that Moorhead looks like a woman "who likes to eat." Mama visits the author's hotel and at first appears to be totally out of her element in its magnificent lobby. But she bravely locates Moorhead and explains that her daughter needs criticism from a writer. Initially, Moorhead refuses, but when Mama offers to share her recipe for delicious Norwegian meatballs, Moorhead relents and provides the advice that proves decisive to Katrin's later success. When Katrin sells her first story, she buys Mama a new coat with her earnings. Katrin may reject plastic consumer goods in favor of a family heirloom, but her mother's skills become validated only when they demonstrate their ability to open doors in the outside world.

The ambiguous resolution of the tension between family and money in the film *I Remember Mama* resonates with the value crises about female identity in the 1940s. Confronted with unprecedented opportunities in the job market and fundamentally new definitions of social responsibilities, women of the 1940s could turn to *I Remember Mama* and see that they did not have to disown the past to participate in the present, nor did they have to surrender opportunities in the present out of a misplaced fidelity to the past. Their mothers' traditional skills paved the way for the independence of the present; the moral dilemmas of the present could be kept under control by seeing their continuities with the past. Thus Katrin can have a career, but it is one composed of writing about her family, thereby maintaining her female identity. Katrin works at home, writes for love (of her mother) rather than for money, and measures her success by assisting her mother's work within the family rather than by any narcissistic gratification. At the same time, however, Mama encourages Katrin, Christine, and Dagmar to have careers rather than talking to them about marriage; she provides an example of sisterly solidarity when she defends Uncle Chris's wife from accusations of promiscuity; and she comes to the aid of Aunt Trina, scorned for taking so long to marry. Mama pays lip service to the authority of Papa and Uncle Chris, but she takes action as an independent woman centering her concerns on the welfare of others. She rejects the false lures of consumer goods and gossip, while revering education, creativity, and mutuality. Yet that very identity was a construct of the possibilities of the 1940s, and when women's roles underwent serious alterations in the late 1940s and early 1950s, the next incarnation of the Hansen narrative reflected those drastic changes.

A successful special performance of *I Remember Mama* on the Lux Radio Theater helped to convince CBS and General Foods to make a television version for the 1949–50 season. An instant success, the program often appeared among the ten "most-watched" shows, enjoying an eight-year run before its cancellation in 1957. While retaining the main contours of previous versions, the televised *Mama* shifted focus from ethnicity, class, and gender, using those categories largely as a foil for a more pressing social problem—the family as unit of consumption. Just as economic realities during the war encouraged an emphasis on the gender-centered aspects of Forbes's stories, expansion of the consumer market in the 1950s made commodity purchases the core dramatic and narrative issue of the program.

Structural changes in cast and setting reflected external social changes each time *I Remember Mama* reached a new medium. In the stories and book, the Hansen family lived in a large house with seven boarders. The play and film whittled down the size of the house and featured only one boarder. The television program showed the Hansens as a modern nuclear family, owning their own house, without boarders. Forbes's original stories mentioned four aunts for the family to contend with; the play and the film showed three; and the television program mentioned two but tended to show only one. The Hansen family had four children in the stories, book, play, and film, but only three on television. In the print versions of the family's saga, Papa Hansen had failed as a farmer before becoming a carpenter. In the play and film, his decision to participate in a strike represents an important chapter in the family's history. But the television show made no mention of failed business ventures and trivialized its few references to strikes. Ethnic rivalries provided significant tensions and taught important lessons in the book and the short stories, but they tended to disappear from the stage, screen, and television versions.

Changes in casting and plot no doubt owed something to the demands of different media and their attendant time constraints. Yet most of these changes also represent clear ideological and social changes as well. Over two decades and five forms of media, the Hansens changed from a family deeply enmeshed in family, class, and ethnic associations to a modern nuclear family confronting consumption decisions as the key to group and individual identity. Similarly, the spheres of action reserved for women changed considerably from one version to another. In the stories and book, Mama uses her culinary skills to help her daughter win acceptance from classmates who made fun of her Scandinavian heritage. In the 1940s film, Mama uses those same cooking skills to advance her daughter's aspirations to become a writer. But in the 1950s television show, Mama's skill at cooking only provides hints to Katrin about how to get a husband. As the possibilities of the 1940s became transformed into the gender prison of the 1950s, Mama directed her daughter away from a career and toward a husband. Predictably, the child who was dropped from the family when it shrank for the television version was Christine, an independent, intelligent, and ambitious adolescent whose sisterhood, class loyalties, and integrity had provided important guidance for Katrin.

Not that career ambitions totally disappeared from the television program. But they changed. Katrin voices ambitions to become an actress instead of a writer. She actually becomes a secretary, and in the last episode of the program, becomes a full-time wife. She then receives Mama's *solje* as a gift, a reward for choosing her proper female role, unlike the film, which rewarded her choice of history over consumer goods. Similarly, in the book and film, Katrin's brother Nels seeks to become a doctor because he wants to follow in the footsteps of his Uncle Chris, who helped people by giving away all of his money to lame children in need of operations. In the television program, Nels's ambition to become a physician stems from a desire to own consumer goods and to socialize with "better" people.

The changing role of coffee as an icon in both the film *I Remember Mama* and the television program *Mama* maps the ideological difference between the two versions. In the motion picture, Katrin is allowed to drink coffee when she rejects the dresser set in favor of the *solje,* proving her maturation into adulthood by rejecting consumer goods in favor of tradition. In the television program, tradition serves only to legitimate consumer goods; the entire Hansen family story serves as a lure to bring the audience commercial messages by the program's sponsor, Maxwell House coffee. The narrative sequence that framed every episode of *Mama* demonstrates the centrality of advertising messages and their importance in establishing narrative and ideological closure. As soon as Katrin Hansen introduced the show with the words "I remember Mama," a male narrator announced, "Yes, here's Mama, brought to you by Maxwell House coffee." The camera then panned away from the photograph album to show Mama (played by Peggy Wood) making coffee for the Hansen family in their turn-of-the-century kitchen. The authority of the male narrator's voice established a connection between the continuity of family experiences and the sponsor's product, between warm memories of the past and Mama making coffee in the kitchen. In this progression, the product becomes a member of the Hansen family, while tradition and emotional support become commodities to be secured through the purchase of Maxwell House coffee. The sponsor's introduction announces ownership of the television show *Mama,* but it also lays claim to the moral authority and warmth of motherhood itself.

Coffee drinking also appeared in the dramatic narratives of the show with amazing regularity. In the very first episode, Katrin opens the program with a reminiscence about Mama and Papa drinking coffee in the family kitchen, and subsequent episodes feature the beverage as a means of calming down upset children, as a catalyst for conversations among women, as a requirement for receiving company, as a break from housework, and as an aid to clear thinking and problem solving.[15]

The magical attributes of coffee prepare viewers for equally respectful treatment of other commodities. In keeping with the economic imperatives of commercial television, *Mama* touted not only its sponsors' products, but an entire attitude about consumption as well. In one episode the children make homemade presents for Mama's birthday—a bread box, a pen wiper, and a bookmark. But Katrin tells them "those things don't count," and she argues instead for "a bought present." When Nels needs a new suit for his Sunday school graduation, Mama wants to alter one of Papa's, but her son insists on a "bought" suit. The children demand the purchase of goods that are "necessities" to them but seem foolish to their parents—a telephone, a Victrola, a magic-lantern slide projector, a pedigreed dog. But in these matters, the children are always right: a telephone that the family cannot really afford proves instrumental in securing a job for Papa; a Victrola purchased to mollify the children shows Papa's boss that he is a music lover and worthy of promotion; a picture in the newspaper of Dagmar with her dog motivates yet another employer to offer work to Papa.[16] Unlike the film, in which Katrin's own creativity (nurtured by Mama) enabled her to contribute to the family economy, the television show depicts consumer goods themselves mysteriously adding to rather than subtracting from the family's wealth. The lessons from the film about the false lure of consumer goods become inverted. On television products have no false glitter; instead, they establish the necessary preconditions for continued familial ties.

Commodities not only help the family's financial status on *Mama,* they also minister to emotional needs. When an elderly neighborhood woman dies, Mama's social club delegates her to buy flowers for the deceased. But Mama learns that the woman's grandson is heartbroken because his grandmother had promised to buy him a tricycle before she died. Mama uses the flower money to buy the boy his gift and signs the birthday card from his grandmother. "Tricycles are better than flowers," she tells the club, "they last." [17] Grandmothers with the audacity to die before delivering desired toys to their grandchildren share the problem confronting all parents in *Mama*: the loss of face precipitated by inadequate performance as a consumer. In one episode Nels works as a toy salesman in a department store and confronts a bricklayer who cannot afford the expensive electric train that his son desires. Nels suggests a less expensive model, but the father bristles at the idea that he cannot provide the best for his child. Nels buys a raffle ticket for the train in question, and when he wins he gives it to the young boy because he remembers how he never got over his own disappointment at not receiving a pony when he was younger.[18] When Mama is not asked to join an elite social club, Papa fears it is because of his lowly job as a carpenter, and he wonders if his failures do not also explain Dagmar's exclusion from a prestigious dancing school the year before.[19] Papa's self-doubts receive reinforcement from his children. When Nels cannot afford to make long-distance calls to his girlfriend, he decides to start a business, cautioning his partner that they must be serious about upward mobility. "We can't be like my father. I don't even know what he ever came to this country for." [20]

The blurred distinction between dramatic content and advertising messages in *Mama* did not just depend upon indirect ideological influences; sometimes the connection was intentional. Gordon Webber of the advertising agency that handled the show's accounts wrote several scripts for the show, and a 1954 memo from assistant producer Doris Quinlan to the producer, head writer, and director of the program reveals a sometimes conscious connection to product-plugging. Quinlan reminds her coworkers that

> *Good Housekeeping* magazine is coming out next month with a spread on *Mama*: As you know, we have told them for some time we would make use of the magazine on the program. Could we please try to keep this in mind. It does not have

to be anything elaborate. For example, the next time Katrin or Dagmar is looking at a pattern or a new dress, can they not use *Good Housekeeping* and mention
it by name? We have a period copy of the magazine.[21]

Yet for all its embrace of consumer-commodity society, *Mama* still depended
upon its ability to evoke the moral legitimacy of the past for its success in the
present. Katrin Hansen's retrospective narrative and the pictures from the family
album reassured viewers by depicting events that had already happened in the
emotionally secure confines of the audience's collective childhood memories and
imaginations. This false authenticity encouraged viewers to think of the program as the kind of history that might be created about their own homes. A CBS
press release during the program's first broadcast season proclaimed, "On *Mama*,
we try to give the impression that nobody is acting," and went on to claim success for that effort, quoting an unnamed viewer's contention that the show depicted a real family because "nobody but members of a real family could talk like
that." [22] Free from the real history of ethnic, class, and gender experience, the history presented on *Mama* located its action within the personal spheres of family
and consumer choices. Within these areas, realism could be put to the service of
commodity purchases, as when the narrator followed his opening introduction
with a discussion about how Mama, in her day, "had none of the conveniences of
today's modern products" like Minute Rice, Jello, or Maxwell House instant coffee.[23] Thus, the morally sanctioned traditions of hearth and home could be put
to the service of products that revolutionized those very traditions—all in keeping with Ernest Dichter's advice to his fellow advertising executives: "Do not assert that the new product breaks with traditional values, but on the contrary, that
it fulfills its traditional functions better than any of its predecessors." [24]

Stability and Rupture in a Women's Narrative

In the 1970s, literary and film critics began to stress the conservative functions of narrative. They charged that narrative closure worked to forestall social
change, to inculcate a distrust for contradiction and conflict in readers and viewers. These critics argued that some narratives, especially in popular literature,
film, and television, posed imaginary solutions to real social problems and gave
the appearance of openness but allowed only one possible solution, in fact teaching inevitability. In some ways, the Hansen family narrative, even in its many incarnations, could serve as evidence for that line of argument. Its inscribed
ideological content taught tolerance and self-help as solutions to the ethnic and
class divisions of the Great Depression, favored a rooted independence as an ar-

bitration of changes in women's roles in the 1940s, and presented consumer purchases as the key to family happiness in the 1950s. But narrative closure is not so easy to achieve. It is difficult to soothe anxieties without first aggravating them, and impossible to predict in any given case whether the emotional appeal of closure will silence the questions and criticisms provoked by narrative's evocation of the real hurts of history.

One significant failure to ensure narrative closure in the television program *Mama* may illumine more general principles. The single strongest ideological element in the transfer of the Hansen story to television came from the focus on the home. Television shifted the site of popular culture reception away from the public theater to the home, and both commercial and creative personnel thought of it as a medium where "families watched families." Yet as feminist literary critics have observed, the notion of the home as a safe haven from society encompasses some dramatic contradictions, for the glorification of domesticity traditionally draws legitimacy from the idea of the home as the moral center of society, as a social institution whose influence extends outward.[25] On *Mama* the narrative need to reaffirm the Hansen home as such a center of morality opens up rather than contains social contradictions. In one Halloween episode, delinquent street toughs harass the Hansens, throwing stones at their house. When Papa captures two of the youths, Mama serves them cider as they wait for the police to arrive. One asks her, "How do you think we feel when we look in windows and see kids eating ice cream and ducking for apples and stuff like that?" Mama says, "Like throwing stones . . . I would too." [26] Mama tells Katrin to invite her friends over, and instead of turning the youths over to the police she invites them to join the party. Even Mama can feel the pain of economic deprivation, her class loyalties connecting her to the youths despite their decidedly unfamilial behavior.

Even the pursuit of consumer goods takes on some odd wrinkles because of the role of the home as the moral center of society. When the Hansens purchase a telephone that they cannot afford, Papa's boss fires him, claiming that a man who could afford such luxuries does not need work as badly as the other men. But Mama does not believe him. She says (in her accented television Swedish English), "No, Lars, he do it because he do not like you to have same things that he has. That is not nice thing to say about Mr. O'Hara or any man, but is true. That is why we keep telephone, because I do not ever want anyone in this house to be afraid of men like Mr. O'Hara." [27] In this context, acquisition of consumer goods is no longer posed as a universal private need, but, rather, it becomes part of a class-conscious sense of entitlement to the good things in life. Awareness of a larger world outside the home also produces criticism of the home itself. In one episode Katrin bristles at the constant surveillance of her close-knit extended family and expresses a desire to move to Los Angeles to enjoy some freedom. Even though the plot reaches narrative closure by showing Katrin that her gossipy family protects her from malevolent strangers, the suffocating confinement of family identity leaves a bitter residue to the episode.

Similarly, Mama could glorify domesticity only by "containing" the allure of work outside the home. A parade of glamorous opera singers, cultured heiresses, and famous female actresses and writers tempt Karin and her sister in ways that make Mama appear uninteresting, at least temporarily. Mama herself discloses the negative side of her life. She is jealous of women with public roles and fearful that they will attract Papa's interest. "I am someone who cooks and sews and makes the beds and takes care of the children, but when Lars sits and smokes his pipe and thinks thoughts they are not always of me."[28] Another time she complains after a frustrating day of housework, "Sometimes I wish I was an old maid. What does a family mean? Work. And who appreciates it?" Again, the resolution of these shows reassures us that Mama is loved and valued for her work, but for any given viewer the ruptures opened by the show might carry as much impact as the narrative resolution.

Frankfurt school marxist T. W. Adorno claims that the culture industry opens such ruptures only to close them, that it disciplines all potential opposition by showing the possibility and then the futility of criticism. But as long as ruptures and closures accompany each other within media texts, at least the possibility of oppositional readings remains alive. One reason for that possibility comes from the contradictions of those fashioning the narratives. The tension between the ideological imperatives of commercialized leisure and the need for making the narratives credible creates a space for the airing of historical memories and contradictions. The sources of "authenticity" for these artists often belie the narrative closures and preferred readings demanded from their work. Earlier we saw how Rice, Morgan, Forbes, and Christians created parts of the Hansen narrative both with and against the grain of their own experiences; some of the contradictions about social reality and family roles evident within *Mama* resonate with the tension between life and art for its two main creators, writer Frank Gabrielson and director Ralph Nelson.

As the chief writer for *Mama,* Frank Gabrielson created some of the warmest and most touching images of family harmony in the history of television. But his own behavior often conflicted with the values that he projected onto the screen. His wife sacrificed her own career in radio to allow him to move to Hollywood and work as a writer for Twentieth Century Fox, and she supported him with her earnings when he could not find paying work. But Gabrielson abandoned his wife and young daughter in 1947, shortly before securing his position on *Mama*. As head writer he often took the entire cast out to dinner at expensive restaurants while neglecting to send alimony checks to his own family. His writings beautifully portrayed a kind of family loyalty and responsibility that had nothing to do with his own life. "He created the ideal family out of what we were not," observes his daughter, Hale Lamont Havers.[29] But however reprehensible his behavior, Gabrielson obviously drew upon his unhappy family experiences in his scripts. "Audiences are willing to accept the idea that good things are not the only things that happen in families," he told one interviewer, citing in particular an episode where Mama fears she will lose Papa's interest if she wears the eyeglasses that have been prescribed for her.[30]

Gabrielson's writing not only disclosed the contradictions of domesticity, with Ralph Nelson's encouragement it also used the moral concerns of the Hansen household to critique society. An episode about Halley's comet provided a pretext for airing concerns about nuclear war metaphorically; the presence of a Chinese laundryman provoked a lesson about the evils of racial prejudice, and an episode set during World War I gave Mama an opportunity to question the "glories" of war and the enthusiasms of uncritical nationalism. Nelson viewed his own liberal politics and his commitment to acting as part and parcel of a rebellion against his father's values, and he welcomed opportunities to combine the two. Censorship pressures within the industry only redoubled his resolve. Executives from a company that bought large amounts of commercial time on television once warned Nelson that he was to hire "no communists, no socialists, and we're even thinking of eliminating Democrats."[31] But he did not give in to that pressure, joining Martin Ritt in refusing to sign a loyalty oath. Nelson told the network, "There's nothing in my background that's subversive, and the loyalty oath is unconstitutional."[32] Like the creators of earlier incarnations of the Hansen family narrative, Nelson and Gabrielson developed the contradictions within *Mama* because those contradictions formed an important part of their lives. Their work both resisted and reinforced dominant ideology by highlighting operative ideological tensions in the social context in which their art appeared.

The serial nature of television situation comedies and the recombinant nature of popular culture texts inhibit premature closures. Narrative devices that fix meanings in other media leave them unstable and subject to revision on television. When combined with the continual changes in social life characteristic of our era, they contain the possibility for opening up previously closed discussions. It is certainly possible that the Hansen family narrative served the interests of patriarchy, capitalism, and the state, but it is also possible that it exposed contradictions conducive to resistance to those institutions. As long as people's needs and desires remain unsatisfied, the prospects for narrative and ideological closure are always incomplete. As the old people used to say in the days of slavery, "You can hide the fire, but what you gonna do with the smoke?"

2

Amos 'n' Andy and the Debate over American Racial Integration

THOMAS CRIPPS

By 1948, the American popular press, the ruling Democratic Party, and even the most conservative of entertainment media, the movies, had signaled to their constituencies that the touchy issue of racial integration would move to the center of American attention. At the same time, African Americans, especially the growing middle class, swelled the ranks of activist organizations dedicated not merely to older, ambiguous goals of "fair play" and "equality of opportunity," but to full participation in the main social and economic activities of American life.

The Columbia Broadcasting System, like most American broadcasters, had often behaved as though blacks did not exist. But as post-World War II racial activism grew into a genuine social movement, CBS departed from its usual indifference by announcing its plans to produce a television version of its twenty-year-old radio program *Amos 'n' Andy*. A comic anachronism that depended for its humor on stereotypical racial traits, the new television program provided the occasion for blacks to debate, both with CBS and among themselves, the precise nature of racial prejudice.

At stake was the right to a nationwide monopoly of broadcasting facilities through which the image of African Americans was to be presented to an enormous American audience. On one side was a complex, increasingly political black bourgeoisie; on the other a highly visible weekly comedy that depicted

A slightly different version of this chapter was originally published in *American History, American Television: Interpreting the Video Past*, ed. John E. O'Connor, 33–54 (Ungar, 1983). It has been reprinted here by permission of the author and the publisher.

blacks as feckless, verbally crippled, ineptly conniving parvenus with hearts of gold.

More than any other point of contention, the misrepresentation of the black middle class set black activists on edge. For decades, black intellectuals ranging from racial nationalists to assimilationists had looked to this class for leadership. Whether rooted in the antebellum free Negro community, in the sturdy southerners who had graduated from Booker T. Washington's Tuskegee Institute, or in the urban northerners who formed "the talented tenth" symbolized by the black philosopher W. E. B. DuBois, this class had distinguished itself from the mass of blacks. The middle class—churched, stably employed, and affiliated with an intricate network of clubs and fraternal orders—found in *Amos 'n' Andy* a polar opposite that demeaned aspiration, burlesqued the complex distinctions that marked black social classes, and presented to a national white audience an image of maddening oversimplicity.[1]

As early as 1931, black educator Nannie Burroughs spoke for the middle class when she complained of broadcasters who characterized blacks as a uniformly "ignorant, shouting, fighting, rowdy element," a contention summed up by John H. Law, a part-time actor: "The Negro intelligentsia dislikes the lump into one social group." By 1951, the year *Amos 'n' Andy* reached the television screen, these sentiments had been solidified into a movement led by the NAACP, which had already attained considerable success in changing the black image in Hollywood movies. Among the dissenters were Hollywood blacks who viewed the NAACP as a threat. As one of them, Ernestine Wade, put it, "Agitation from officials of Negro organizations in the past jeopardized the progress of Negro shows."[2]

Amos 'n' Andy, till then a blessedly invisible and therefore relatively innocuous comedy, came to television in 1951 after more than twenty years on radio. On radio it had never aroused the single-minded wrath that seemed to mark the black response to the television version. For every critic who had complained, another could be found who saw merit in the show. As early as 1932, a survey of black students and "adult leaders" revealed a spectrum of opinion ranging from enjoyment to "marked resentment and emphatic disapproval," a finding later confirmed by a Chicago Urban League study reported in the black *Los Angeles Sentinel*. When another early critic, Bishop W. J. Walls, attacked the show, he emphasized not its substance but the uses to which it was put—"a commercialization of primitive weakness." Later, at the height of the NAACP campaign against the show, some of the nation's prestigious black newspapers expressed similar ambivalence toward the TV series.[3] To this day, despite persistent hostility toward the show, black collectors, scholars, and fans divide on the question of the racism in *Amos 'n' Andy*.[4]

Why did black activists devote so much time, energy, and expense to snuffing out *Amos 'n' Andy* if they knew as well as its makers and sponsors did that the black community split in its opinion of the show and its impact? The answer is to be found in the rise of the black bourgeoisie to postwar political awareness and its success in influencing the racial content of motion pictures. Wartime propaganda had hinted at an enhancement of postwar black status; NAACP memberships had risen tenfold during the 1940s; CBS's announcement of the proposed series came in 1948, less than a year before the release of Harry S. Truman's Civil Rights Commission report, which had called for a "year of rededication" to American ideals of social justice; and, beginning in 1949, Hollywood dramatized these social changes in a cycle of "message movies."[5] In this social mood, CBS's decision to broadcast a television version of *Amos 'n' Andy* seemed a regressive flaunting of lily-white power in the faces of a formerly vulnerable minority. Moreover, CBS stood alone in its programming preferences, if we may credit a report written by the agent of Hugh Wiley, a writer of black southern local-color stories. Wiley's agent explained a dry spell that began in 1947 as follows: "Stories dealing with the Negro character are, unfortunately impossible to sell," not merely because *Amos 'n' Andy* preempted the field but because of "extreme pressure" from blacks.[6]

Wiley's man had hit on the central difference between postwar and prewar black America—the national "pressure" that black middle-class Americans were capable of mounting against the networks. It was their taste, sensibility, and identity that CBS violated in its narrow depiction of blacks as urban riffraff, tricksters, Falstaffs, and snarling matriarchs marked by naïve cunning, languid manners, and drawling malapropisms.

Before the war the NAACP had been a mere shadow of its postwar bulk, and black protest had been limited to empty protests over racial epithets and a few bids for ownership of low-wattage stations. Broadcasters, therefore, had done little to cultivate black listeners, and blacks had appeared on the air only in local broadcasts of religious music, prime-time guest shots by musicians, and a few servile roles in situation comedies and soap operas. As a social scientist put it, the black performer "introduces the humor, the clowning, and also enables the middle-class housewife to smile in a sort of superior, patronizing way."[7] At their best, radio programs occasionally included, "on a 'sustaining' or unsponsored basis," the Hampton Institute Choir, Paul Robeson, Ethel Waters, and bits of jazz and vaudeville. Years passed between dramas such as CBS's *John Henry* (1932) and

WMCA's made-for-New York show *A Harlem Family* (1935).[8] The narrowest, most stereotyped black roles were reserved for the huge prime-time audiences, who saw blacks only as obstreperous maids and valets in popular situation comedies. One of the best, *The Jack Benny Show,* played limitless variations on the relationship between a parsimonious employer and his irreverent, bumptious valet, Rochester (Eddie Anderson).[9]

Before World War II, blacks had felt powerless to act against this white monopoly of access to broadcasting, but the war helped to shake the foundations of the social order, at the least in the form of necessitarian gestures toward enlisting blacks in a national effort, and at the most in the form of hints and promises of a better life after the war. Black journalists exploited the situation by demanding a "Double V"—a simultaneous victory over foreign fascism and domestic racism, thereby linking American war aims to black social goals.[10]

The broadcasters responded to the heat of the moment with dozens of shows, among them Roi Ottley's *New World a'Comin'*; Wendell Willkie's *Open Letter on Race Hatred,* following the Detroit riot of 1943; Kate Smith's guest shot on *We the People* (1945), in which she urged an end to racism, not "at a conference table in Geneva" but in "your own home," a plea that drew twenty thousand requests for transcripts; a black doctor and a black soldier in the soap operas *Our Gal Sunday* and *The Romance of Helen Trent*; CBS's black situation comedy *Blueberry Hill*; and scattered dramas written by leftists such as Norman Corwin. Together they eroded the monopoly held by the comic servants in *Fibber McGee and Molly, The Great Gildersleeve,* and their epigones.[11]

After the war, the liberal mood became, said Walter White of the NAACP, a "rising wind" of social change. New shows that reflected the times included ABC's *Jackie Robinson Show,* which ranged from sports to social issues; WDAS's (Philadelphia) prize winning *Bon Bon Show*; and CBS's production of Katherine Dunham's *The Story of a Drum.*[12] Typical of these programs was Richard Durham's self-proclaimed "rebellious, biting, scornful, angry, cocky" *Destination Freedom* (1948–50), a series of 105 historical sketches produced at WMAQ (Chicago). Durham, a writer for *Ebony* and the *Chicago Defender,* introduced listeners to black history through such characters as abolitionist Harriet Tubman, rebels Denmark Vesey and Toussaint L'Ouverture, and a number of modern activists.[13]

Coincident with the trend of programming, black organizations took up fresh strategies: giving awards, prodding sponsors, enlisting the support of foundations, and joining in cooperative ventures. Sometimes they actually sponsored programs such as the Urban League's production of Erik Barnouw's *The Story*

They'll Never Print, a drama about an unemployed black veteran that was chosen for Joseph Liss's book, *Radio's Best Plays.*[14]

Within the industry itself, researchers began to identify a heretofore untargeted audience of prosperous black listeners. WLIB, Harlem's station, for example, reported a "vast Negro market potential" of billions of dollars, a population then bursting into Greater New York, a college enrollment that had risen by one thousand percent, and an unemployment rate of only four percent. The trade magazine *Sponsor* confirmed the boom in black wealth in a story on "the forgotten 15,000,000" black consumers. *Ebony,* a glossy magazine that catered to this new class, ventured a linkage between black wealth, political power, and the coming medium of television. Pointing to evidence that blacks outpurchased whites in the pursuit of consumer goods, *Ebony* characterized sponsor-dominated television as "an amazing new weapon which can be all-powerful in blasting America's bigots."[15] With each new exposure of the prospective black audience, the broadcasters increased their repertoire of gestures from mere slanted programming to appointing Jackie Robinson a vice-president of WNBC. Among the performers, no less than nine groups campaigned for improved black opportunity in broadcasting.[16]

Coincident with this rising black presence, commercial television emerged as a visual medium that had only just become profitable after nearly two decades of technical development. As early as 1939, Julius Adams of the *Amsterdam News* had anticipated black attitudes toward the new medium and even toward *Amos 'n' Andy.* Because television seemed unconstrained by a racist tradition and not yet dominated by entrenched whites, Adams touted it as "Our New Hope." As to *Amos 'n' Andy,* Adams argued that although blacks had tolerated it during its invisible radio period, "it would be suicide to put a show like this on television."[17] By 1950, *Variety* agreed with Adams on the basis of a wave of black performers who had broken into TV: "Negro Talent Coming into Own on TV Without Using Stereotypes: A Sure Sign That Television Is Free of Racial Barriers."[18]

Indeed, in the three years from 1951 to 1953, the lifespan of the *Amos 'n' Andy* show, network executives embarked on "a new policy of cultivating the Negro audience"—at least according to the trade papers. When NBC hired a public relations firm to direct a series of seminars intended to lead toward "a more realistic treatment of the Negro on the air and the hiring of more Negro personnel," *Variety* characterized it as part of a "movement." In fact there was something to the story; all manner of memoranda passed among the topmost broadcasting executives urging cooperation with the Urban League, "integration without identification" in casting radio shows, more black material, and "the creation of new program ideas designed to realize these new goals." [19] But at lower levels, executives complained of wooden, unresponsive black auditions, or claimed that "there are certain positions where you feel it might not be advisable to use Negroes." [20]

For a brief moment during the same period, a black production company broke the white monopoly on filmmaking for television. The All America company—a creature of William D. Alexander, a sometime functionary in a black college and in the Office of War Information; Claude A. Barnett, president of the Associated Negro Press; and Emmanuel Glucksman, a white producer of B movies—made a deal with Chesterfield Cigarettes to combine stock shots from their own inventory and other sources with topical news film of black celebrities.[21] Unfortunately, ambition outstripped execution, and this idea, which had been pressed by black entrepreneurs for more than thirty years, ended up in syndication in small markets and profitless dates in southern grind houses. Glucksman, who hated the rough-and-tumble of location shooting, settled for "talking heads" in claustrophobic office settings, stills, fabricated events, canned ceremonies such as sorority inductions, honorary degrees, Ralph Bunche laying a wreath on Gandhi's tomb, and a black family in Queens enmeshed in its symbols of, as the voice-over said, "gracious living," all of them punctuated by shots of Barnett plugging "our cigarette." *Variety* sniffed at the pioneering effort as "little more than a lot of name-dropping with pictures" fit only for the "southern markets" that eventually bought them at bargain prices.[22]

Into this world of newly felt, newly flexed, black middle-class consciousness, activism, and wealth descended *Amos 'n' Andy,* complete with baggy pants, plug hats, foul cigars, pushy wives, misfired schemes, and mangled grammar. Organized blacks were shocked, not so much at what they saw, but at the timing of its release in the year of liberal "rededication," at a cresting of black political consciousness. Indeed, at first it was not even altogether clear that Freeman Gosden and Charles Correll, the two white originators of the radio series, would decide to abandon blackface in favor of using black actors. In any case, organized blacks reckoned that no good could result from a genre of visual humor that made fun of the black bourgeoisie.[23]

From the moment the story broke in 1948, when the *Los Angeles Sentinel* reported that the *Amos 'n' Andy* radio show had begun integrating blacks into its cast, a confrontation between the NAACP and CBS seemed inevitable. And yet, it should be seen that ambiguity clouded the issue. On one hand, organized middle-class blacks winced at the thought of their collective image resting in the charge of two white men whose adult life had been devoted to week after week of creating a nationwide running gag about blacks. On the other hand, blacks in show business pointed to increased opportunities for actors to be generated by the show. On the side of the NAACP, James Hicks of the *Amsterdam News* refused CBS advertising and complained that the show "stinks"; speaking for the actors, Billy Rowe of the *Pittsburgh Courier* labeled the NAACP group "pinks." [24]

With blacks unable to marshal a united front, CBS assembled a production team composed of two executives; Gosden and Correll; director Charles Barton; the veteran vaudevillian Flournoy Miller as consultant on racial matters; and a corps of black actors composed of new recruits, as well as Johnny Lee and Ernestine Wade from the radio show. They began shooting at the Hal Roach Studio. The decision to record the show in film was a pioneering strategy founded upon hoped-for profits in syndication. [25] Their creature enjoyed a national premiere on June 28, 1951, impervious to the ineffectual black pressure against the show.

At this point CBS seemed to have won the day. Blatz Beer proved to be an eager sponsor. The Roach studio, working with an uncommonly high budget of forty thousand dollars, gave *Amos 'n' Andy* a showman-like gloss: In Charles Barton, a veteran director of Abbott and Costello farces at Universal, they possessed an early master of television style with its cadenced sequences of medium close-ups and two-shots that quickly became conventions of situation comedies. Fortunately for CBS, Barton proved not a good journeyman director but an amiable, sentimental buffer between the originators of the show and the black staff, one of whom remembered Gosden as "an old Southern hardcore general" who tried to "make us mouth their words . . . to imitate them." For Barton the company was "the greatest family you ever saw," while one of the black actors agreed that "there was not a lot of tension . . . because our director, Charlie Barton, was so human and considerate." CBS shrewdly played this angle in its press releases, which minimized the racial basis of the shows while emphasizing the "warm feelings" shared by the members of the company. [26]

The product of their labors played on similar sentiments. Putting aside the racial material that grated upon the sensibilities of organized blacks, from the premiere onward the shows presented happy people with small problems that were solved each evening by restoring equilibrium to some momentarily ruffled situation. The winsome characters were models for the next generation of television heroes—neutral, bland, goodhearted Amos (Alvin Childress) was an island of sanity in a sea of manic connivance; Andy (Spencer Williams), a mixture of innocence and eye-winking worldliness; and Kingfish (Tim Moore), the potentate of a gimcrack lodge and a fabricator of rickety schemes. The women displayed a similar range of sense and eccentricity: even-tempered Amos had a wife to match; flirtatious Andy, a string of shallow disappointments; and Kingfish, a shrew who was the equal of his own comic pushiness. The supporting characters, all played by veterans such as Johnny Lee, Nick Stewart, Jester Hairston, and the Randolph sisters, represented various extremes of virtue and vice that provided a frame for the principals. As the show matured, the malleable characters grew away from some of the premises of the radio show in ways that allowed Kingfish to serve as a pejorative model beside which the others seemed saner, wiser, less avaricious, and therefore more humane, decent folk. In this way, the dignity of African Americans seemed less at risk, and the race of the characters seemed to matter less than it had in radio.

Predictably, the first round of criticism of the show focused on the fringe characters and on Kingfish, whose malapropisms, feckless scheming, and anachronistic costumes and manners seemed a caricature of black middle-class aspiration. Even *Variety,* usually a defender of show business, complained of "the molasses-tempered janitor who is a throwback to the Stepin Fetchit era" and called for a toning down of exaggerated manners and stereotypes and a shifting of focus from burlesque to sympathy for the plight of the race. Led by the NAACP, the black middle class challenged what they took to be a parody of their historical struggle for social mobility in a hostile society.[27]

At first the NAACP protest, which *Variety* played on page one, began with letters of complaint to the sponsor—Schenley Distilleries, the parent company of Blatz Beer—only hours after the premiere. In a few days, the protest spread to various white liberal groups such as the American Jewish Committee, which proposed a team of consultants that included black psychologist Kenneth Clark of City College of New York and political scientist Robert MacIver of Columbia. The team was to draft an "unobjectionable" substitute program similar to the "loveable [and] admirable" *Goldbergs* and other ethnic shows that had avoided alienating ethnic activists.

With many shows already "in the can," the network pointed out that the slightest changes would take weeks to reach television screens. Nevertheless, through the summer of 1951, the activists pressed on by means of outraged press releases, a rousing resolution at the NAACP convention in Atlanta, and nominal support from a small cluster of allies such as the United Auto Workers—and yet with scant results save for isolated gestures such as the decision of WTMJ-TV (Milwaukee) to drop the show.[28]

The snag in the NAACP campaign was not in its tactics but in the fact that the issue rested upon the ability of the organized black middle class to translate its own resentments into a collective black will to act. Instead of this intended outcome, however, the campaign exposed an undercurrent of dissension in black circles. Newspaper columnists, actors with deeply felt loyalties to show business, and television viewers compromised the NAACP's claims to solidarity, thereby softening the drive for dignified portrayals of the black bourgeoisie. As Bill Rowe of the *Pittsburgh Courier* pointed out, if black audiences wished "to look at people of their own color," this desire was in itself an aspect of racial integration that doomed the NAACP to "fighting a losing battle."[29]

Indeed, Rowe had hit upon the vulnerable center of NAACP demands. Walter White of the NAACP, in attacking the white monopoly on American broadcasting, depicted this nettlesome fact only in terms of its slandering the middle class. By focusing on *Amos 'n' Andy*'s caricature of the middle class as indecorous, prone to using "street slang," and no more than a nest of "quacks and thieves [and] slippery cowards, ignorant of their profession," White appeared to concede that the CBS show had been accurate in its depiction of the black lower classes.[30]

With few exceptions, the black newspapers took a position in the middle between the NAACP and CBS, either because they reflected their readers' attitudes or because they hesitated to offend the broadcasters and advertisers from whom they derived revenue. Occasionally, a paper played both angles, blasting the show as "disgusting" while also running CBS press releases. On the extremes were the *Amsterdam News,* which refused advertising for *Amos 'n' Andy,* and Billy Rowe of the *Courier,* who touted the show as "the greatest television show on earth."[31]

Actors heatedly denied the NAACP's charge that *Amos 'n' Andy* smeared the middle class. Clarence Muse, for example, spoke for black Hollywood when he praised the show as an "artistic triumph" that played upon "real Negroes you and I know." In a swipe at the NAACP he announced, "I have switched to Blatz Beer." One of the most senior members of the cast and a former director of feature films, Spencer Williams, also asserted the case for verisimilitude in opposition to the NAACP. Of one scene he asked rhetorically: "Now there's a situation that could happen in any home with any race of people, isn't that right?" Yet the actors' main concern was not so much art or social messages, but with their own version of striving for integration—job opportunities in Hollywood. One of their guilds, the Coordinating Council of Negro Performers, threatened to picket the New York NAACP to make their point. Individual dissenters kept their counsel. "I knew it was wrong," said Nick Stewart years later, but "I went along with it."[32]

As the split in black opinion became evident, broadcasters, advertisers, and white journalists joined in a collective expression of astonishment at the inflexibility of the NAACP position. Indeed, one ad executive felt "nonplussed" because Blatz's advertising agency drew such vigorous fire while "making a frank bid for Negro trade . . . [through] a policy of integration in hiring . . . [and] taking pains to assure the show's complete acceptance." The advertising trade papers agreed; *Printers' Ink* predicted that the show would "be with us for a long, long time," while *Advertising Age* reported that "most Negroes in this area do not go along with the NAACP." In general, the white press probably believed, with Harriet Van Horn of the *New York World Telegram and Sun*, that the NAACP was "a trifle touchy." [33]

The central issue in the debate never came into focus. Both sides assumed that they were in essential agreement on the future of blacks in American life—a benignly liberal drift toward an eventually painless, fully integrated place in the American social order. Indeed, in its primitive stages, the genre of television situation comedy tended to promote, ratify, and reinforce this bland, center-left vision of the future by depicting American society as a self-correcting system that was responsive to demands for "fair play."

Television producers had quickly invented a formula that expressed their sentiments as they applied to various ethnic groups—the Jews in *The Goldbergs;* Nordics in *I Remember Mama* (a novel, a drama, and a movie before its TV debut); and the Italians in *Luigi* (a "thoroughly moral character . . . [and] not a one-sided stereotype," according to *Variety*), *Papa Cellini,* and *Bonino,* the latter starring Ezio Pinza of the Metropolitan Opera. All of them shared a pool of interchangeable parts: an extended family, crotchety but warmly sentimental old folks, happy problems happily resolved in twenty-eight minutes of air time, and a division of characters into an older generation encrusted with cultural survivals from the old country and a younger group of super-Americans who had assimilated the virtues of the new land. [34]

Unfortunately, *Amos 'n' Andy* was asked to perform similar service for an ethnic group whose history included slavery, discrimination, and exclusion from the opportunity for easy assimilation implied in the gently comic plots of the European ethnic shows. Thus their traits of eccentric manners, dialect, and other cultural baggage were perceived not as vestiges of a national culture but as the mocking of racial subculture that was an aberration of white American culture. Moreover, the black middle class that spoke against *Amos 'n' Andy* perceived itself as having successfully struggled to overcome the cultural bondage that the characters in the show seemed locked into. In fact, within the shows this point was given emphasis in that the central figures, Andy and Kingfish, spoke in rural dialects, wore slightly off-center-clothing such as derbies and flashy suits, and behaved with exaggerated, hat-in-hand diffidence and cunning obsequiousness, while only the minor figures—the clerks and functionaries—were allowed the crisp Yankee accents and officious surroundings that marked them as middle-class successes. Thus, the NAACP activists were correct in their resentments, especially in view of the fact that the American broadcasting system allowed them no adversarial voice on the air.

At the same time, the writers engaged to write the television version—Bob Ross, Bob Mosher, Joe Connelly, Jay Sommers, Paul West, Dave Schwartz, and others—took pains to depict most of the supporting characters with a neat, pristine middle-class politesse. The actors—Jeni LeGon, Napoleon Simpson, and others—reinforced the writers' intentions with self-confident, solid bits of business; well-spoken, modulated voices; and a firm sense of place as though they had been born in paneled offices. The set decorators followed the same line of thought. Exteriors—even an alley through which a white thief had escaped—were clean and devoid of trash. In the kitchens were full refrigerators, four-burner stoves, matching china; on the walls were the stock symbols of middle-brow culture—Barbizon landscapes, Van Gogh's *Bridge at Arles,* and Kingfish's favorite painting, Hals's *Laughing Cavalier*; scattered about their parlors were the candy dishes and books of a typical middle-class room.

In the scripts, the writers left the blocking, shot selection, movement and business, and other fragments of characterization entirely to the director and the actors on the set. Thus the development of specific details of character were placed in the hands of the actors—an important factor to black viewers who might get derivative pleasure from seeing Sam McDaniel, or some other actor forced by Hollywood circumstance into a lifetime of demeaning roles, play a straight role, uncluttered by heavy-handed dialect. Finally, in the few shows in which a heavy criminal appeared, he was sure to be played by Anthony Warde or some other white denizen of B movies.[35]

The ambience of the sets was matched by the equally bourgeois motivations of the characters. While it is true that neither of the two principals succeeded at their erratic careers, their failure never resulted from want of striving. The premise of the episode entitled "Jewel Store Robbery," for example, is that Kingfish and Andy ruefully reminisce about wasted opportunity. "Sapphire was right, Andy," says Kingfish. "I done wasted my entire life. Me who had such a brilliant record in school." Often at moments like these, the supporting characters appear as contrasts against which to measure the principals. In this show, Roy Glenn appears as a sleek, imposingly dressed, basso-voiced success. The comic plot turns on the humiliating fact that Kingfish's circumstances have forced his wife, Sapphire, to hire out as Glenn's maid. At the denouement Amos hammers home the point in a brief exchange with Andy: I feel kinda sorry for the Kingfish. But you know, you can't much blame the Kingfish for wantin' the folks down in Marietta to think he's a bigshot up here. It's just human nature for everybody to want somebody to think they is important. I guess that's what keeps a lot of us going in life.

Moreover, the attention of the viewer is never allowed to stray from the plot and the characters into current events along the racial front. White characters, for instance, are never allowed to refer to race or even to notice that the principals are black. In one show in which a gang of white counterfeiters appear, they have a private opportunity to discuss the blacks but identify them only as "those two birds upstairs."[36]

The plots reinforced the message put forth by the set decorations and characterizations. In "Happy Stevens," for example, Kingfish and Sapphire, cranky and backbiting from a marriage gone stale, seek help from "the happy Harringtons," two white talk show hosts. But in the end, they not only learn that they can live with themselves, unpropped by the "cultured, charming chitchat" advocated by their radio counselors, but also that the station prefers them to the white Harringtons. In "Kingfish's Secretary" the situation is used not so much to depict some small victory but rather to show how Kingfish has matured beyond his origins in Marietta. The dramatic contrast is provided by a Southern woman who has come north in answer to a matrimonial advertisement. The country woman suffers from comparison with the chic secretaries, primly dressed neighbors, well-stocked Harlem stores, and flippant dialogue of Harlem. Kingfish and Andy, with their slurred diction, outdated clothes, and perpetual suspension in midcareer between golden opportunities, suggest that although they are no longer bumpkins like the woman from the south, they are also still marching toward some form of bourgeois success. "That must be the scrubwoman!" says Kingfish as he casually compares her with his own evolving parvenu style of life.[37]

Of all the shows, the most well known and affecting was a Christmas story that *Variety* described as "an almost classic bit." A simple story of a child's dream fulfilled at Christmastime, it provided a showcase for Andy to display his most deeply felt sentiments while seeking work that would allow him to buy a brown-skinned, talking doll for Arabella, Amos's precocious daughter. Andy's laying of the gift under the Christmas tree inspires Amos to compose a bedtime story in the form of a sentimental exegesis of the Lord's Prayer as it plays on the radio in the background, set to the music of Albert Hay Malotte.

As though challenging the NAACP, every incident, character, and set contributed to a touching domestic drama that was anything but an exploitation of black life. Indeed, the most persistently nettling quality of the program in the minds of black activists was not in the substance of plot or character but mainly in the survival of a stylized Negro dialect. Nevertheless, it often seemed balanced or disarmed by the middle-class accents that marked many of the shows. Thus, when Arabella asks crisply, "Wouldn't it be wonderful to have a white Christmas?" Andy replies with a favorite uncle's devotion, "Them's the best kind." Whatever Andy's small crimes against the language, he is treated with deferential respect by the janitor, who calls him "Mistuh Andy." And if Andy professes that poverty is "rebarrassin'," or uses some other comic neologism, the preponderance of supporting characters speak in Yankee accents appropriate to the setting. A coolly professional nurse; a department store executive played by Napoleon Simpson, a veteran of Hollywood jungle movies; a floorwalker played by Milton Woods, a star in "race movies"; and a string of winsome kids who sit on Andy's lap as he plays the store's Santa Claus all speak in radio-announcer American.

In the end, Andy has played out a perfect bourgeois scenario: he has focused on a goal, worked for wages to accomplish it, deferred his own gratification, and ceremonially presented the fruits of his labors in a socially correct call on Arabella's parents. And he has accomplished all this at considerable psychic cost to himself in that he chose not to present Kingfish with a gift and had been insulted for it.

Every setting, prop, and gesture reaffirmed the form and substance of middle-class life. When Andy calls, Amos and his wife are enjoying a Christmas Eve pause in front of their tree. At the sound of the doorbell, Amos puts on a dark jacket, straightens his tie, and receives his old friend with a formal handshake. The rooms are jammed with the same icons of conventionality that have dressed the sets of all the programs in the series.

As though to confirm the theological sources of Andy's selfless behavior, the last scene is devoted entirely to Amos's interpretation of the Lord's Prayer. Up to this moment, every two-shot close-up of the characters has been in conventional television style—a succession of fixed, eye-level shots of "talking heads," intercut with reaction shots edited for easy continuity. Here, however Barton lowers the camera angle, tilting up on Arabella's bed, a setup broken by cutaways that tilt down on the recumbent and reverent girl. The sequence asserts Amos's fatherly authority and gives him an imposing presence through which to give a line-by-line exegesis of the prayer—which plays, sotto voce, on the radio. Amos's resonant expression of humanity's need for a deity, and his evoking of a natural order in which mankind may live with a hope for community, harmony, and brotherhood ends with a shot of falling snow, seen through the window from Arabella's point of view.[38]

Over the seventy-odd weeks of production, these softly decent characters and homilies balanced the shambling presence of Kingfish, thereby blunting the case of the NAACP. *Variety,* which frequently spoke for show business and for liberalism, used the Christmas show as a swipe at what it considered off-target militance. "Despite the hassle over civil rights currently engulfing the nation in this Presidential election year, *Amos 'n' Andy* isn't going to influence any viewer one way or the other," declared the trade paper. "If anything, the series shrewdly brings out some of the best characteristics of the Negro." Indeed, even though the cast was solidly black in almost every show, *Variety* inferred a subtle integrationist message that logically followed from "the great value of showing a Negro family living normal lives in normal surroundings sharing the emotional and religious experience of all people."[39]

Gradually the NAACP saw its image as defender of the oppressed take on an unaccustomed ambiguity as a pressure group whose "touchiness" in attacking the "most liberal" of the networks ruined the careers of black actors and polarized black opinion. Apart from the younger generation of black Hollywood, which shared the dismay of the NAACP at "the harm" done by *Amos 'n' Andy*, countless black actors and loyal listeners felt put upon by "outsiders" and, according to actress Lillian Randolph, "various white groups" who used the NAACP as a weapon to "eliminate the Negro actors [and] put [me] out of business."[40] Musician Lionel Hampton, the most conservative of black performers, set forth this economic line in its broadest social terms: "I look upon the new *Amos 'n' Andy* television show as an opening wedge toward greater opportunities and bigger things for scores of our capable artists who haven't been able to get a break in video until this new Blatz-CBS show started." Blatz released the results of a poll that supported the performers against the NAACP, claiming that seventy-seven percent of black New Yorkers liked the show. In 1952, Estelle Edmerson, a young graduate student, surveyed the actors and confirmed a deep vein of resentment at the NAACP pressure on their livelihoods, a strong sense of accomplishment, and gratitude toward the sponsor and network. They felt grateful for "a toe in the door" (Willie Best) and to be able "to eat three times a day" (Roy Glenn); they refused to "see anything objectionable" on the air (Eddie Anderson); they complained of organized blacks that "we, as a race, are too sensitive" (Johnny Lee); and they praised "the baby entertainment medium, television, [that] has accepted the Negro entertainer" (Cab Calloway). Ruby Dandridge extended Calloway's opinion by pointing to CBS's hiring of Flournoy Miller, whom "they ask for opinions when in doubt as to the insults to the Negro people." Whites such as Ed Sullivan also testified "that TV as a medium was made to order for Negro performers." Dissenters—most of them trained actors such as James Edwards, Juano Hernandez, and Frank Silvera—insisted on "the harm" done to liberalism by the show.[41]

In the end, the ambiguities both in the content of *Amos 'n' Andy* and in the splintered black response to it undercut the NAACP campaign to remove the show from the air. This is not to cast the organization as a lone figure in a hopeless cause. By August 1951 the National Urban League had opened its own letter-writing campaign, which also attracted several white liberal groups. But intellectuals such as George Norford, drama critic of the *Amsterdam News,* and G. James Fleming, a political scientist from the Virgin Islands and an *Amsterdam News* reporter, began to hope to divert the attention of blacks toward a demand for "an open communications system" rather than the divisive question of whether or not *Amos 'n' Andy* excluded or burlesqued black bourgeois behavior. Indeed, the NAACP itself by 1954 turned its attention to studying the black broadcasting marketplace, ways to develop a "National Negro Broadcasting Council," and eventually a means of producing "network-calibre, quality programming" for independent Negro-appeal stations. One enthusiastic advocate told Walter White of the NAACP that radio—if not television—was "potentially the greatest instrument of progress that has ever been available to a minority race," a source of "cultural self-expression on a mass scale," and a source of jobs and income.[42]

Nevertheless, in the short run the NAACP had failed to cast *Amos 'n' Andy* as an enemy of the entire black world. Instead, the show had been characterized as a slander against only the black middle class. Thus, instead of fulfilling a Chicago Defender prediction that the "disgusting" revival of "stereotyping" would "be crushed . . . by the frontal assault of an enlightened and protesting people," the campaign merely sputtered out. Blatz's decision to withdraw from sponsorship at the end of the 1953 season was depicted in the trades not as a defeat at the hands of the NAACP, but as a quest for a higher-class image accomplished by picking up the prestigious *Four Star Playhouse*.[43] The show survived in syndication, often earning solid ratings and audience shares. Far into the 1960s, *Amos 'n' Andy* played as a "strip," or daily program, usually in fringe time but occasionally in prime.[44] In the large markets such as New York, heavyweight sponsors like Trans-World Airways bought the time slots. And when it finally expired in major markets it played on in small-time southern metropolitan areas, remembered not as a vanquished enemy, but almost as a martyr—"one of the all-time major casualties of the radio-to-video transition," according to *Variety*.[45]

Why had the NAACP engaged in what seemed like a fruitless enterprise that split blacks and alienated white liberals? What had been gained by the playing out of the episode? The answers are not entirely clear, but they lie in the shifting goals and rising hopes of the postwar black leadership. World War II had enlarged black goals to include the possibility of eventual full integration into American life at the precise moment of a boom in memberships in black activist organizations. Simultaneously, *Amos 'n' Andy* arrived in full view of the television audience, complete with symbolic baggage from an older time in black history and broadcasting history. Solidly rooted in a segregated world, by its existence, even on television, it seemed to cast doubt over black social goals and to mock the newly powerful, organized black middle class. The virtues of black aspiration and success were simply too deeply imbedded in the fabric of the programs to invite appreciation by organized black activists—even though evidence suggests a faithful audience of black viewers.

3

Situation Comedy, Feminism, and Freud

Discourses of Gracie and Lucy

PATRICIA MELLENCAMP

> Since we said "I do," there are so many things we don't.
> —Lucy Ricardo

> This is a battle between two different ways of life, men and women. The battle of the sexes? Sex has nothing to do with it.
> —Gracie Allen and Blanche Morton

During the late 1940s and the 1950s, linked to or owned by the major radio networks, television recycled radio's stars, formats, and times through little proscenium screens, filling up the day. Vaudeville and movies fed both of these voracious, domestic media, each reliant on sound, and each influential in the rapidly developing suburbs. With a commercial collage of quiz, news, music, variety, wrestling/boxing, fashion/cooking, and comedy shows, both media were relatively irreverent toward well-fashioned narrative and worshipful of audiences and sponsors. Television was then (and continues to be) both an ecology—a repetition and recycling through the years—and a family affair, in the 1950s conducted collectively in the living room, with the dial dominated by Dad. A TV set

A slightly different version of this chapter was originally published in *Studies in Entertainment: Critical Approaches to Mass Culture,* edited by Tania Modleski, 80–95 (Bloomington: Indiana Univ. Press, 1986). It has been reprinted here by permission of the publisher.

was a status symbol, a rooftop economic declaration, and an invitation to other couples to watch.

Like suburban owners of TV "sets," the four television networks were also concerned with status; thus "the news" was made a separate category of the real and legitimate, presumably distinct from "entertainment." At the beginning of the 1950s, the United Nations debates were prestigiously broadcast. The proceedings of the Kefauver congressional committee, which was investigating organized crime, were televised by WPIX in New York; the networks carried these "real life" dramas with good ratings. In April 1951 General Douglas MacArthur's speech to Congress was broadcast; his words attacked the "containment" and limited warfare policies of the Truman administration, revving up the paranoiac or conspiracy interpretation of not only world but also social events. In July 1952 the GOP convention was televised, and Stevenson and Eisenhower fought part of the subsequent election on television. The Army-McCarthy hearings began on April 22, 1954, and received high ratings for the many hours during which Senator Joseph McCarthy accused the military of "communist infiltration" and then was undone on live television.[1]

Coincident with these prestigious broadcasts of the "real"—events of power, politics, and "truth"—and the massive licensing of broadcast air and time, women were being urged to leave the city, work force, and salaries; to move to the suburbs, leisure, and tranquillity; to raise children; and to placate commuting, overworked husbands for free. In reality, of course, not all women did so. Most women over thirty-five remained in the paid work force; when allowed, instead of building battleships, they took other jobs. That TV and particularly situation comedies would, like radio, both serve and support the new, imaginary, blissful domesticity of a ranch-style house, backyard barbecue, and a bath-and-a-half seems logical—it is, of course, historical. "Containment" was not only a defensive, military strategy developed as U.S. foreign policy in the 1950s; it was practiced on the domestic front as well, and it was aimed at excluding women from the work force and keeping them in the home.

To argue that television was a powerful machinery for familial containment of women is hardly original. Yet the specifics of program strategies are intriguing and complex—rather than monolithic or perfectly generic, as most discourses presume. For me, two issues are central: the importance in early 1950s comedy of idiosyncratically powerful female stars, usually in their late thirties or forties; and the gradual erosion of that power that occurred in the representation of women within comedy formats. In situation comedy, pacification of women occurred between 1950 and 1960 without a single critical mention that the genre's terrain had altered: the housewife, although still ruling the familial roost, changed from being a humorous rebel or well dressed, wise-cracking, naïve dis-senter who wanted or had a paid job—from being out of control via language (Gracie) or body (Lucy)—to being a contented, if not blissfully happy, under-standing homebody (Laura Petrie). With this in mind, we need to review specific programs, particularly in TV's early stages. This essay is based on a general analy-sis of forty episodes of *The Burns and Allen Show*, which was on the air Wednes-day nights from October 1950 until June 1958, when Gracie left the show; and of 170 of the 179 episodes of *I Love Lucy*, which was broadcast Monday evenings from October 1951 until May 1957. It also begins to rethink Freud's construc-tion of the radical underpinnings and "liberating" function of jokes, the comic, and humor—perhaps yet another "foreign" policy of potential containment for U.S. women.

In fifteen-minute segments, broadcast live three times a week in 1949, Gertrude Berg—writer, producer, and star—disguised herself as Molly Gold-berg, the quintessential Jewish mother, a melange of chicken soup malaprops and advice. Leaning out of her window, she would intimately confess to us: "If Mr. Goldberg did not drink Sanka decaffeinated coffee, I don't know what I would do—I don't even know if we'd still have a marriage . . . just try it once, and that's what I'm telling you." The program and its popularity were emblem-atic of the subsequent televised avalanche of situation comedies, a direct descen-dant of radio, vaudeville's "husband and wife" sketches, music hall, and *comedia del arte's* stereotypical scenes and characters. The elision of program and star with sponsor was another version of television's corporate coupling/ownership.

In the 1950–51 season, *The Burns and Allen Show* debuted, continuing in this tradition. Burns and Allen funneled their 1926 marriage, their vaudeville, radio and film routines, and their characters/stars into an upper-middle class sit-uation comedy—a historical agglutination suggesting that what is monolithi-cally termed "mass culture" is a process: a collection of discourses, scenes, or turns recycled from various media and contextualized within historical mo-ments. Despite its similarity to the Molly Goldberg type of program, this show represented a new version of the happily married couple, featuring the zany, fashionable Gracie of bewildering non sequiturs and the relaxed, dapper George of one-liners and wisecracks living in suburban, affluent Beverly Hills. Gracie was certainly unlike TV's nurturing-yet-domineering mothers who dwelled in city apartments. Yet she was familiarly different as "Gracie." Derailing the laws and syntax of language and logic, her technique was a referral back to either the nearest or the most unexpected referent as a comic turn on the arbitrary and con-ventional authority of speech (and she would continually break her own rules just when her friends and we caught on). She baffled all the male and most of the female characters, concocting improbable stories and schemes that were invariably true in amazing circumlocutions that became that week's "plot."

The casual narratives of each week's program were used merely as continuity for vaudeville routines and existed primarily to be mocked by George. The scenario is often as follows: an ordinary event—shopping, going to the movies—would be "misinterpreted" and then complicated by Gracie, who would then connect a second, random event to the first. For example, their college son, Ronnie, needs a story for his campus newspaper; Blanche Morton, her next-door neighbor and confidante, wants new dishes. Linking these two unrelated problems, Gracie contrives a fake theft of Ronnie's wealthy friend's car. When the car is initially found in the Mortons' garage, Blanche's husband is so relieved not to have to pay for this "new" car, which he believes Blanche has bought, that he gladly buys the plates; and Ronnie scoops the story of the theft.

Adding to the shaggy dog quality of the plots were the many bewildered characters (including the postman) who would drop by the house and would then be involved by Gracie. The more unrelated the character or innocent bystander to the plot, the better; a large measure of Gracie's comedy depended on the other characters' astonishment. Her naïve, friendly non sequiturs rendered them speechless, reluctantly agreeing, finally reduced to staring in reaction shots. (This is diametrically the opposite of what occurs in *I Love Lucy,* where Lucy is invariably given the last word or look, the editing indicating that different mechanisms of identification and spectator positioning are operative in each show.) Then, winking, George would either join in the linguistic mayhem or sort things out. His intervention was not, however, for our understanding, but for that of the confused, speechless characters; his Aristotelian analyses of Gracie's behavior and illogic left bystanders doubly amazed. Finally, at the end of each show, George would issue the imperative, "Say goodnight, Gracie."

Garbed in dressy 1950s fashion, set in an upper-middle class milieu of dens, patios, and two-car garages, constantly arranging flowers or making and serving coffee but not sense, Gracie equivocally escaped order. Despite being burdened by all the clichés applied to women—illogical; crazy; nonsensical; possessing their own, peculiar bio-logic and patronized accordingly—in certain ways, she seemed to be out of (or beyond) men's control. Unlike the ever loyal and bewildered Harry VonZell, the show's and the story's announcer, and other characters in the narrative sketches, neither she nor her neighbor Blanche (who both loved and understood Gracie) revered George or were intimidated by his cleverness; in fact, Gracie rarely paid attention to him or to any authority figure. She unmade decorum, she unraveled patriarchal laws, illustrating Jean Baudrillard's assertion through Freud: "The witticism, which is a transgressive reversal of discourse, does not act on the basis of another code as such; it works through the instantaneous deconstruction of the dominant discursive code. It volatilizes the category of the code, and that of the message."[2] The "dominant discursive code" of patriarchy tried, through benevolent George, to contain Gracie's volatilization, her literal deconstruction of speech, and her tall tales of family. Whether or not the system won can be answered either way, depending on where the analyst is sitting—politically with George in his den, or in the kitchen with the women.

Gracie's forte was the shaggy dog story—either as verbal riff or as the very substance of the narrative: the first use led to illogical nonsense, a way of thinking definitive of Gracie's comedy; the second led to instigation and resolution of the week's episode. Furthermore, the shaggy dog event, preposterous as it was, would always prove to be "true." Take for example the following episode. The scene is Gracie's sunny, ruffle-curtained kitchen with table in the center, an auto-replenishing coffee pot, and numerous exits. The initial situation is explicated in the dialogue:

> GRACIE. Thanks for driving me home, Dave.
>
> DAVE. As long as I towed your car in, I didn't mind at all, Mrs. Burns.
>
> GRACIE. There's some coffee on the stove. Would you like some?
>
> DAVE. I've been wondering, Mrs. Burns. How are you going to explain this little repair job to your husband?
>
> GRACIE. I'll just tell him what happened. I went shopping and bought a blouse and on my way home I stopped to watch them put up the tents and this elephant came along and sat on my fender and smashed it.
>
> DAVE. He'll never believe it.
>
> GRACIE. Of course he will. He knows a fender isn't strong enough to hold up an elephant. George is smarter than you think he is.[3]

To prove her story to George, Gracie will show him the blouse. Her idiosyncratic cause-effect connections have nothing (or everything) to do with physics, the arbitrary conventions of language, or common sense. In many ways, her style of speech is uncommonly funny because it is ahistorical, ignoring the speaker and the situation while obeying language's rules. Like Chico Marx, she takes language literally; unlike Chico, she is unaware of her effect on other characters.[4] Gracie delivers her deadpan lines without reaction or expectation, obliviously using the same expressive tone no matter what the terms of the discursive contract—which she ultimately reconstructs anyway.

The rest of this episode consists of retelling the story—first to Blanche, who then tells her husband, Harry; then to the insurance salesman, Prescott; and simultaneously to Harry VonZell and Stebbins, the circus man. George, basically a solo, narrative entrepreneur, keeps breaking and entering Gracie's dilemma of credulity with comments ("All I wanted was a little proof"), observations on life, and ironic maxims about marriage: "Married people don't have to lie to each other. We've got lawyers and friends to do that for us." George bribes Gracie with a promise of a mink coat for the "true" story, which, of course, she has already told him. The show culminates in a final courtroom scene with all of the participants sitting in the Burns's living room validating the truth of Gracie's initial story, which is confirmed by Dave, the "seeing is believing" mechanic. The truth of male vision verifying Gracie's words is endlessly repeated, both in the series and in this program. Dave says, "If I hadn't come down to the circus grounds to tow away your car, I wouldn't have believed it myself."

During the last scene, he reiterates: "If I hadn't seen it with my own eyes, I wouldn't have believed it myself." During this conclusive trial, presided over by George, a new character—Duffy Edwards, the furrier—enters with Gracie's newly won fur coat and says to George: "I always watch your show. I knew you were going to lose." Unlike Lucy, Gracie always wins in the narrative, which thereby validates her story.

Other codes are also operative, however: George is center-framed in the mise-en-scène and by the moving camera; he is taller than all the other characters; and he has access to the audience via his direct looks at the camera. He nods knowingly, with sidelong collusive glances at us (or perhaps at eternal husbands everywhere). In the end Gracie is frame left. She wins the narrative and the mink coat, but loses central screen space; perhaps most importantly, she never was in possession of "the look." Roland Barthes, placing power firmly in language, asks: "Where is speech? In locution? In listening? In the returns of the one and the other? The problem is not to abolish the distinctions in functions . . . but to protect the instability . . . the giddying whirls of the positions of speech."[5] The whirls are giddying; yet George Burns, the dapper entertainer as Hollywood gossip, critic, and golf partner of CBS president William Paley, presides over the show with benign resignation, a wry smile, and narrative "logic" firmly grounded in bemused knowledge of the frothy status of the situation, comedy, and television. Throughout each program, Gracie is blatantly dominated not only by George's looks at the camera and direct monologues to the audience, but also by his view of the program from the TV set in his den, and by his figure matted or superimposed over the background action as his voice-over comments on marriage, Gracie, her relatives, movie stars, show business, and the "story."

In his analysis of Freud's *Jokes and Their Relation to the Unconscious,* Samuel

Weber suggests an intriguing reading of the Aufsitzer, or shaggy dog jokes—nonsense jokes that create the expectation of a joke, causing one to search for concealed meaning. "But one finds none, they really are nonsense," writes Freud. Weber argues that the expectation rests in the desire "to make sense of the enigmatic assertion with which the joke begins . . . such jokes 'play' games with the desire of the listener. . . . By rousing this 'expectation' and then leaving it unsatisfied . . . such jokes function in a manner very reminiscent of the discourse of the analyst, who refuses to engage in a meaningful dialogue with the analysand."[6] It is, however, difficult to apply Weber's insight to Gracie, to compare *her* rather than George to the analyst. After all, it is George with whom the listener is in collusion; it is George who hears Gracie from his tolerant, central, bemused vantage point. It is as if he occupies the central tower in the panopticon, or the analyst's chair behind the couch, unseen, with all scenes visible to his gaze.

As Weber writes, these jokes are "come-ons," taking us for a ride. "For at the end of the road all we find is nonsense: 'They really are nonsense,' Freud states, thus seeking to reassure us, and himself as well."[7] Perhaps *Burns and Allen* could be interpreted as a massive, male reassurance that women's lives are indeed nonsense. The Aufsitzer is a joke played on the expectation of a joke, and is clearly a complicated matter—in the case of Gracie Allen, it is a refusal of conventional meaning gleefully accepted and encouraged as rebellion by Blanche Morton and contained for the audience by the omniscience of George, who narcissistically strives as super/ego to "unify, bind . . . and situate [himself] as a self-contained subject."[8]

Nor should we be misled by the fact that George is the "straight man" and thus seems to occupy a slightly inferior position, which he himself describes as follows:

For the benefit of those who have never seen me, I am what is known in the business as a straight man. If you don't know what a straight man does, I'll tell you. The comedian gets a laugh. Then I look at the comedian. Then I look at the audience—like this . . . That is known as a pause . . . Another duty of a straight man is to repeat what the comedian says. If Gracie should say, "A funny thing happened on the streetcar today," then I say, "A funny thing happened on the streetcar today?" And naturally her answer gets a scream. Then, I throw in one of my famous pauses . . .

But George was never *just* a straight man; the monologue continues:

I've been a straight man for so many years that from force of habit I repeat every-thing. I went out fishing with a fellow the other day and he fell overboard. He yelled "Help! Help!" So I said, "Help? Help?" And while I was waiting for him to get his laugh, he drowned.

This gag defines quite precisely George's actions, as well as indicating their vaudeville origins. Inevitably, like the male leads in most situation comedies, he got the final and controlling look or laugh. Containment operated through laughter—a release that might have held women to their place, rather than "lib-erating" them in the way Freud says jokes liberate their tellers and auditors. As radical as the nonsense joke might be (when it comes from the mouth of the male), it's different, as is the rest of life, for the female speaker. The audience, too, is measured and contained by George, whom both the camera and editing fol-low: the husband as television critic, solo stand-up comic, female psychologist, and tolerant parent/performer. Yet, unlike in most situation comedies, it was clear that George depended on Gracie, who worked both in the series' imaginary act and the program's narratives. Thus, the contradiction of the program and the double bind of the female spectator and comedian—women as both subject and object of the comedy, rather than the mere objects that they are in the Freudian paradigm of jokes—are dilemmas which, for me, no modern critical model can resolve.

In its original version, *I Love Lucy* debuted on Monday, October 15, 1951, at 8:00 P.M. Held to the conventional domesticity of situation comedy, Lucy Ricardo was barely in control, constantly attempting to escape domestic-ity—her "situation," her job, in the home—always trying to get into show busi-ness by getting into Ricky's "act," narratively fouling it up, but brilliantly and comically performing in it. Lucy endured marriage and housewifery by trans-forming them into vaudeville: costumed performances and rehearsals that made staying home frustrating, yet tolerable. Her dissatisfaction, expressed as her de-sire for a job, show business, and stardom, was concealed by the happy endings of hug/kiss (sometimes tagged with the line, "now we're even")/applause/titles/theme song. Her discontent and ambition, weekly stated, were the show's working premises, its contradictions massively covered up by the audience's pleasure in her performances, her "real" stardom. The series typified the paradox of women in comedy—the female performer caught somewhere between narra-tive and spectacle, historically held as a simulation between the real and the model.

As was the case with *The Burns and Allen Show*, the entire *I Love Lucy* series was biographically linked to the marriage of the two stars. Lucille Ball, movie star, and her husband Desi Arnaz, Cuban band leader, became Lucy and Ricky Ricardo; their "friends" appeared on programs as bit players or as "themselves." At the end of one episode, for instance, the voice-over announcer said: "Harpo Marx played himself." Image/person/star are totally merged as "himself," the "real" is a replayed image, a scene, a simulation—what Jean Baudrillard calls "the hyperreal." The most extraordinary or bizarre example of the elision of "fact" and fiction, or the "real" with the simulation, marshaled by the "formal coherency" of narrative, was Lucy's hyperreal pregnancy. In 1952, with scripts supervised by a minister, a priest, and a rabbi, seven episodes were devoted to Lucy's TV and real pregnancy (without ever mentioning the word). The first of these episodes was aired on December 8, timed with Lucy's scheduled caesarean delivery date of Monday, January 19, 1953. Lucy's real, nine-month baby, Desi, Jr., was simulated in a seven-week TV gestation and electronically delivered on January 19 at 8:00 P.M. as Little Ricky, while forty-four million Americans watched. (Only twenty-nine million tuned in to Eisenhower's swearing-in ceremony. We liked Ike. We loved Lucy.) As were all the episodes in the series, this one was given a children's book title, "Lucy Goes to the Hospital." [9]

But if the "real" domestic and familial details of the star's life were so oddly mixed up with the fiction, perhaps the supreme fiction of the program was that Lucy was not star material, and hence needed to be confined to domesticity. Thus the weekly plot concerned Lucy's thwarted attempts to break out of the home and into show business. Unlike Gracie's implausible connections and overt machinations, though, all of Lucy's schemes failed, even if failure necessitated an instant and gratuitous reversal in the end. Lucy was the rebellious child whom the husband/father Ricky endured, understood, loved, and even punished, as, for example, when he spanked her for her continual disobedience. However, if Lucy's plots for ambition and fame *narratively* failed, with the result that she was held, often gratefully, to domesticity, *performatively* they succeeded. In the elemental, repetitive narrative, Lucy never got what she wanted: a job and recognition. Weekly, for six years, she accepted domesticity, only to try to escape again the next week. During each program, however, she not only succeeded, but demolished Ricky's act, upstaged every other performer (including John Wayne, Richard Widmark, William Holden, and even Orson Welles), and got exactly what she and the television audience wanted: Lucy the star, performing off-key, crazy, perfectly executed vaudeville turns—physical comedy as few women (particularly beautiful ones, former Goldwyn girls) have ever done.

The typical movement of this series involves Lucy performing for us, at home, the role that the narrative forbids her. She can never be a "real" public performer, except for us: she must narratively remain a housewife. In the episode entitled "The Ballet," for example, Ricky needs a ballerina and a burlesque clown for his nightclub act; Lucy pleads with him to use her. Of course he refuses. Lucy trains as a ballet dancer in one of her characteristic performances: dressed in a frothy tutu, she eagerly and maniacally imitates a dancer performing ballet movements which she then transforms through automatic, exaggerated repetition into a charleston. Whenever Lucy is confident that she has learned something new, no matter how difficult, she gets carried away. These are the great comic scenes, occurring after the narrative setup: pure performances during which the other characters show absolutely no reactions. This is the first "story" line, before the mid-program "heart break": "curtains" as halves of a heart lovingly open/close, or frame and divide each episode. Then, the second: Lucy will now train to be a burlesque comic. Her baggy pants clown/teacher arrives at their apartment, she pretends she's a man, and he tells his melodramatic tale of woe about Martha and betrayal; Lucy becomes involved in the story, says the Pavlovian name, Martha, and is hit with a pig bladder, sprayed with seltzer water, and finally, gets a pie in the face. The scene ends with Lucy saying, "Next time, you're going to be the one with the kind face"—in other words, the victim of the sketch. Then, as in all the episodes, and in this one more literally than in most, the two stories are condensed in a final, onstage performance. At his nightclub, Ricky is romantically singing "Martha" in Spanish. Ethel calls Lucy to inform her that Ricky needs someone in his act. She dresses up as the burlesque clown (not the needed dancer), and steps onstage with her clown's props. When Ricky sings the refrain, the word "Martha" is now her Pavlovian cue: she beats the male ballet dancers with the bladder; squirts the female ballerina with seltzer water; and, in a conclusion that uses all the previous setups, slams a pie in the singing face of tuxedoed, romantic crooner Ricky. (The Saudi Arabian government detected an element of subversion in this series and banned it because Lucy dominated her husband.) This episode, like so many others, is a rehearsal for a performance, involving in the end a comical, public upstaging of Ricky. We are simultaneously backstage and out front in the audience, waiting for Lucy's performance and Ricky's stoic, albeit frustrated, endurance; thus, expectation is not connected to narrative, but to anticipation of the comic—a performative or proairetic expectation.

An exemplary instance of Lucy's upstaging, or humiliation, of Ricky may be seen in the episode entitled "The Benefit," in which Ricky's attempts to be the comedian rather than the straight man are utterly foiled. In this episode Lucy, along with the audience, discovers that Ricky has re-edited their benefit duo, taking all the punchlines for himself. Fade. Onstage, in identical costumes of men's suits, straw hats and canes, Ricky and Lucy perform a soft-shoe sketch. Ricky stops, taps his cane, and waits for Lucy to be the "straight man." Of course, she won't. While singing "Under the Bamboo Tree" about marriage and happiness, Lucy, with the camera closeup as her loyal accomplice in the reaction shots, outrageously steals all of Ricky's lines, smirking and using every upstaging method in the show biz book. Applause, exit; the heart, this time as a literal curtain, closes. Lucy gets the last word and the last laugh during this ironic "turn" on the lyrics of the romantic song. It is interesting to compare Ricky, the would-be comedian forced by his partner/wife to be the straight man, to George Burns, the "straight man" who always gets the final, controlling laugh. That Ricky can be so constantly upstaged and so readily disobeyed is not insignificant, for with his Cuban accent (constantly mimicked by Lucy), he does not fully possess language, and is not properly symbolic as is George, the joker or wielder of authoritatively funny speech. The program's reliance on physical rather than verbal comedy, with Lucy and Ethel as the lead performers, constitutes another exclusion of Ricky. Unlike George, Ricky is not given equal, let alone superior, time. He constantly leaves the story, and his departure becomes the cue for comic mayhem and audience pleasure. Although he is "tall, dark, and handsome," not the usual slapstick type, his representation as the Latin lover/bandleader/crooner and slapstick foil for Lucy's pies in the face suggests that Lucy's resistance to patriarchy might be more palatable because it is mediated by a racism that views Ricky as inferior.

In "Vacation from Marriage," the underside of situation comedy's reiteration of the same is briefly revealed. Lucy, with Ethel in the kitchen, is talking about the boredom and routine of marriage. "It isn't funny, Ethel, it's tragic." The rest of this show and the series make marriage funny and adventurous. Week after week, the show keeps Lucy happily in her confined, domestic, sitcom place after a twenty-three-minute tour-de-force struggle to escape. That neither audiences nor critics noticed Lucy's feminist strain is curious, suggesting that comedy is a powerful and unexamined weapon of subjugation. In most of the episodes' endings, the narrative policy was one of twofold containment: every week for seven years, she was wrong and duly apologetic; and while repeating discontent, her masquerades and escapades made Monday nights and marriage pleasurable. Allen, on the same network, untied legal language and the power polarities implicit in its command; Ball took over the male domain of physical comedy. Both unmade "meaning" and overturned patriarchal assumptions, stealing the show in the process; yet neither escaped confinement and the tolerance of kindly fathers. "That's entertainment!"—for women a massive yet benevolent containment.

As theorists of historiography have argued, discourses of "truth" and the "real" move through a cause-effect, narrative chronology to a resolute closure without gaps or discontinuities. There is something at stake in this strategy, and it is related to power and authority. Narrative embodies a political determinism in which women find a subordinate place. But narrative in situation comedy is only the merest overlay, perhaps an excuse. As George Burns said, "more plot than a variety show and not as much as a wrestling match." This implausible, sparse "situation" exemplifies—in its obsessive repetition of the domestic regime, of marital bliss as crazy "scenes" and competitive squabbles—a social plaint if not a politics.

Situation comedy, with "gaps" of performance and discontinuities, *uses* narrative offhandedly. The hermeneutic code is not replete with expectation, not in need of decipherment, not ensnaring us or lying to us. Expectation of pleasurable performance—the workings of the comic and humor—rather than narrative suspense are currencies of audience exchange. Perhaps this system might challenge "narrative's relation to a legal system";[10] certainly narrative is not viewed as sacred or authoritative any more than husbands are. It is necessary but not equal to performance. In trying to determine how comedy works to contain women and how successfully it does so, theories of narrative will thus be of little help to us. It is necessary to turn to theories of the comic and humor.

I will hesitantly begin an inquiry into the consequences of Freud's assessment of the comic and humor in situations where both subject and object are women. In his study of jokes, particularly tendentious or obscene jokes, Freud assigns woman to the place of object between two male subjects. However, there must be a difference, perhaps an impossibility, when "woman" becomes the joke-teller. Also, given that the process between spectator/auditor and joker is, according to Freud, a mutually timed, momentary slippage into the unconscious, one wonders what occurs when that "unconscious" is labeled "female"—without essentialist or biological simplifications, but with historical and cultural difference in mind. Yet, while the "joke" comprises the majority of Freud's study, and while the joke is for Freud a more complicated process than is the comic, its structure is not applicable to the structure of either of these television series (with the crucial exception of the role of George Burns, for whom Freudian joke analysis works perfectly), possibly because the joke *is* such a strong male preserve.

Unlike the three-way dealings of jokes, the comic, for Freud, is a two-way process; it is not gender-defined, and it derives from the relations of human beings "to the often over-powerful external world."[11] We experience a pleasurable empathy with the person who is pitted against this harsh world, whereas if we were actually in the situation, "we should be conscious only of distressing feelings" (p. 197). We laugh at Lucy's comic moments, yet I wonder whether women might not also have experienced a certain amount of distress, particularly given the constraints of the 1950s and the constant subtle and not-so-subtle attempts to confine women to the home. Freud notes that "persons become comic as a result of human dependence on external events, particularly on social factors" (p. 199). Lucy is caught in her economic subservience to Ricky, as well as in the social mores of the 1950s, a decade that covertly tried to reduce women to the status of dependent children. Lucy and Gracie are continually referred to as children; the women are "helpless" or economically dependent on males—particularly Lucy and Ethel, who do not have jobs as Gracie does. Thus it is interesting to note that what Freud calls the "comic of situation is mostly based on embarrassments in which we rediscover the child's helplessness" (p. 226) (one thinks perhaps of Lucy's exaggerated crying when she is frustrated or thwarted in her desires). Moreover, just as one rediscovers the helplessness of children in the comic of situation, so too the pleasure that it affords is compared by Freud to a child's pleasure in repetition of the same story. Situation comedy endlessly repeats mise-en-scène, character, and story; this pleasure, like the pleasure derived from *most* television, must depend to a degree on weekly forgetting as well as on repetition of the intimately familiar. Freud concludes his meandering thoughts on the comic and its infantile sources: "I am unable to decide whether degradation to being a child is only a special case of comic degradation, or whether everything comic is based fundamentally on degradation to being a child" (p. 227). "Degradation" is the crucial word here. Featuring the perennially disobedient and rebelliously inventive child, *I Love Lucy* hovers somewhere between the comic of situation and what Freud calls the "comic of movement"; or better, the "situation" (the external world) is the problem that necessitates the comic of movement, of which Lucy is the master" (p. 228).

An appendage ten pages before the end of *Jokes and Their Relation to the Unconscious,* and a later, brief essay by Freud entitled "Humour," are especially interesting for our purposes. Freud's analysis of "humor"—epitomized by "gallows jokes," the clever, exalted diversions of the condemned victim just before the hanging—as a category distinct from either the joke or the comic better explains the female victim (both subject and object, both performer and spectator) and her place in the internal and external conditions of *Lucy's* production. Endlessly repeating that she wanted to work, to perform, Lucy saw humor as "a means of obtaining pleasure in spite of the distressing affects that interfere[d] with it. It acted precisely 'as a substitute' for these affects." Humor was "a substitute" produced "at the cost of anger instead of getting angry."[12] As Freud observes, "the person who is the victim of the injury, pain . . . might obtain *humourous* pleasure, while the unconcerned person laughs from *comic* pleasure" (p. 228). Perhaps, in relation to husband and wife sketches, and audiences, the sexes split right down the middle, alternating comic with humorous pleasure depending on one's view of who the victim is; this invocation of different pleasures suggests a complexity of shifting identifications amidst gendered, historical audiences.

Trying to revive Lucy for feminism, I have suggested that throughout the overall series, and in the narrative structure of each episode, she is the victim—confined to domesticity and outward compliance with patriarchy. Yet this series is complex; Ricky is often the immediate victim of Lucy, a role more easily accepted due to his Cuban rather than Anglo-Saxon heritage. Given this perhaps crucial qualification, Lucy is, finally, rebelliously incarcerated within situation comedy's domestic regime and mise-en-scène, acutely frustrated, trying to escape via the "comic of movement," while cheerfully cracking jokes along the way to her own unmasking or capture.

It is important that humorous pleasure for Freud comes from "an economy in expenditure upon feeling" rather than from the lifting of inhibitions that is the source of pleasure in jokes—not a slight distinction. Unlike the supposedly "liberating" function of jokes, humorous pleasure "saves" feeling because the reality of the situation is too painful. As Lucy poignantly declared to Ethel, "It's not funny, Ethel. It's tragic." Or as Freud states, "the situation is dominated by the emotion that is to be avoided, which is of an unpleasurable character." In *I Love Lucy*, the avoided emotion "submitted to the control of humour"[13] is anger at the weekly frustration of Lucy's desire to escape the confinement of domesticity. This desire is caricatured by her unrealistic dreams of instant stardom in the face of her narrative lack of talent: her wretched, off-key singing, her mugging facial exaggerations, and her out-of-step dancing. Her lack of talent is paradoxically both the source of the audience's pleasure and the narrative necessity for housewifery. Using strategies of humorous displacement (the "highest of defensive processes," says Freud—a phrase that takes on interesting connotations in light of 1950s containment policies) and of the comic, both of which are "impossible under the glare of conscious attention," (p. 233) situation comedy avoids the unpleasant effects of its own situations. The situation of Lucy was replicated by the female spectator—whether working as a wife or in another "job"—moving between comic and humorous pleasure, between spectator and victim, in tandem with Lucy.

In this later essay, Freud elevates humor to a noble, heroic status:

[Humour] is fine . . . elevating . . . the triumph of narcissism, the ego's victorious assertion of its own invulnerability. It refuses to be hurt . . . or to be com-
pelled to suffer. It insists that it is impervious to wounds dealt by the outside
world, in fact that these are merely occasions for affording it pleasure. Humour
is not resigned, it is rebellious. It signifies the triumph of not only the ego but the
pleasure principle . . . it [repudiates] the possibility of suffering . . . all without
quitting the ground of mental sanity . . . it is a rare and precious gift.[14]

For Lucy, Gracie, and their audiences, humor was "a rare and precious gift."
Given the repressive conditions of the 1950s, humor might have been women's
weapon and tactic of survival, ensuring sanity, the triumph of the ego, and pleasure; after all, Gracie and Lucy were narcissistically rebellious, refusing "to be
hurt." Comedy replaced anger, if not rage, with pleasure. The double bind of the
female spectator, and of the female performer, is replicated in the structure of the
programs—the shifts between narrative and comic spectacle, the latter being
contained within the resolute closure of the former—and the response of the
spectator is split between comic and humorous pleasure, between denial of emotion by humor and the sheer pleasure of laughter provided by the comic of
movement and situation of Lucy's performances. Whether heroic or not, this
pleasure/provoking cover-up/acknowledgment is not a laughing but a complex
matter, posing the difficult problems of women's simulated liberation through
comic containment.

4

Returning from the Moon

Jackie Gleason and the Carnivalesque

VIRGINIA WRIGHT WEXMAN

The study of television as a textual system has thus far devoted scant attention to the issue of character, even though, as Sarah Kozloff and others have pointed out, "it is characters and their relationships that dominate television stories."[1] The few critics who have dealt with this topic have focused on the audience's tendency to view television personages as real people embodying their own projected fantasies. Ien Ang's discussion of the evening soap opera *Dallas,* for example, explores the inclination of viewers to respond to the show's characters as though they were actual people. In the chapter devoted to character in *Television Culture,* John Fiske similarly focuses on the issue of realism when he claims that "character portrayal on television works to deny the difference between the real and the representation in both the production and the reception processes."[2] The studies that contrast television stars with film stars, such as those by Molly Haskell, Dave Kehr, John Langer, and David Thorburn, also focus on television's aura of verisimilitude. These critics point out how television performers seem ordinary in relation to the larger-than-life images cultivated by movie actors; they also stress the continuum that exists between actor and role in the realm of TV entertainment. In short, it is generally agreed that television promotes an aesthetic of realism: TV characters strike us as being just like the actors who play them, who, in turn, seem like the audiences who watch them and fantasize about them.

To be sure, most of these critics deal with realism as a criterion that is cultur-

A slightly different version of this chapter was originally published in the *Journal of Film and Video* (winter 1990): 20–32. It has been reprinted here by permission of the author and the publisher.

ally constructed and historically variable. Thus, their discussions are often aimed at dismantling the pervasive popular discourses surrounding acting in general in which the sine qua non of performance is taken to be its true-to-life quality. While this project has led to valuable insights, it also tends to perpetuate the conflation of performers with nonperformers. For example, in an excellent article on the television star Mr. T, Jimmie Reeves emphasizes the continuum that exists between the actor's role and his off-screen identity, concluding that Mr. T's construction of an image represents an exaggerated version of what occurs in the lives of all of us; thus, Mr. T emerges as somehow "ordinary." In analyses such as this, Reeves and other commentators have constructed a sophisticated framework that explains the ways in which television audiences approach performers as models that can help them to formulate their own subjectivity.

My purpose here, by contrast, is to explore qualities that set performers apart rather than those they share with others, to understand the ways in which actors like Mr. T are not ordinary. Television comedy in particular has achieved some of its most memorable effects not through performers that the audience approaches simply as surrogates, but rather through actors who embody skills and talents that are understood as uncommon.

Surely one of the most masterful comic actors in the history of television was Jackie Gleason, whose creation of the hapless bus driver Ralph Kramden on *The Honeymooners* series (which was first aired during TV's "Golden Age" of the 1950s) stands as his most celebrated achievement. Gleason's elaborately histrionic style stood in contrast to the performance conventions that characterized most of the other situation comedies of the period, which remained well within television's familiar realist aesthetic. In programs like *The Adventures of Ozzie and Harriet* and *The Burns and Allen Show,* the identification of the stars with the characters they played was taken to the extreme of featuring eponymous titles that foregrounded the use of the same name for both actor and role. By contrast, the comic caricatures created by Gleason and Art Carney, who played Ralph Kramden's friend and neighbor Ed Norton, enabled *The Honeymooners* to rely heavily on virtuoso performance turns, such as Ralph doing the mambo or Norton walking in his sleep. Among the other TV comedians of the era, only Lucille Ball, whose exaggerated makeup played on similarities between feminine glamour and clownish hyperbole, created a character as stylized as those created by Gleason and Carney. Significantly, *I Love Lucy* and *The Honeymooners* are the two programs from the period that have remained most popular with viewers and critics. This popularity is largely founded on the performance techniques practiced by the stars of both shows.

The Honeymooners was initially developed as one of a number of irregularly aired skits that made up an hour-long variety show that Gleason hosted every Saturday night beginning in 1951. In these skits, Gleason assumed a variety of personas, among them The Poor Soul, Joe the Bartender, and Reggie Van Glea-son III. Later, the popularity of *The Honeymooners* became so great that it was given a regular half-hour slot during the show. It is generally agreed that the half-hour episodes of *The Honeymooners* aired during the 1955–56 season (the so-called "classic thirty-nine") represent the show's most successful period. It is these episodes that reappear time and again as reruns and form the basis of my discussion of Gleason's achievement.[3]

Perhaps the most satisfactory framework for analyzing Gleason's artistry can be derived from Mikhail Bakhtin's study of Rabelais, which understands the human body as the site of a variety of discursive formations that represent op-posing strategies for conceptualizing relations of power within the culture at large. Bakhtin's interest in representations of the body is related to the concerns of more recent theorists like Mary Douglas, Michel Foucault, Elaine Scarry, and Klaus Theweleit. In contrast to these authors, however, Bakhtin associates such uses of the body not with the activities of everyday life but with performative events such as carnivals and artistic representations. Further, Bakhtin is specifi-cally concerned with the role played by the exaggerated forms associated with comedy in the articulation of these meanings. Bakhtin is not the only theorist to focus on this issue: character and performance also figure in other theories of comedy including those of Bergson, Sartre, and Freud. In a well-known formu-lation, Bergson relates the effects of comedy to the representation of mechanical behavior. Sartre also speaks to the issue of performance when he characterizes comic actors as people disassociated from any authentic sense of self. Freud's de-scription of comedy as "an expenditure that is too large" emphasizes perform-ance as well, citing clowns as the major example of physical expenditure of this type.[4]

Far more precisely than any of these other theorists, Bakhtin specifies partic-ular bodily attributes that may be exploited for comic effect, and he develops a suggestive conceptual scheme of contrasting body types. Gleason's artistry read-ily lends itself to an analysis based on such a scheme, for his achievement lies in his ability to use the exaggerated modes of comic performance to draw out a number of contradictory meanings inherent in his body image. Some of these meanings participate in discourses associated with realism, while others do not.

The Gleason Persona and the Issue of Male Dominance

To understand the Bakhtinian implications inherent in Gleason's complex star persona, it is first necessary to isolate its various facets. David Marc has usefully divided the Gleason star image into three parts.

> The television personality develops in one or more of three general modes: the representational, in which he dons the mask of a frankly fictional character; the presentational, in which, as "himself," he addresses the audience within the context of theatrical space; and the documentary, in which his "real life"—his exploits, his opinions on matters of public concern, his lifestyle—becomes the subject of other television programs or presentations in other media. Gleason, like many of the early TV clowns, went the grand route of developing all three.[5]

In Marc's view, Gleason, in all three of his manifestations, spoke to American class aspirations. "In both life and art he projected the persona of the Depression-bred blue-collar ethnic who demanded the right to live like a king" (p. 102).[6] Marc's analysis is in keeping with the program's strong emphasis on class distinctions in an era when sitcoms were situated in comfortable middle-class settings. If *The Honeymooners* aggressively raised the issue of class, however, it was also notably overt in its representation of gender conflict, for the ideal of class privilege inherent in Gleason's idea of living like a king was largely dependent on his ability to dominate women.

The show's depiction of such gender conflict was connected to uncertainties regarding gender roles in the culture as a whole during the 1950s. On the surface the relations between men and women appeared untroubled, and images of harmonious interactions within the nuclear family were frequently promoted. As Barbara Ehrenreich and Benita Eisler have shown, however, this surface masked deeper currents of unrest.[7] Women's educational level and recent experiences in the workplace during World War II made them ill-suited to their 1950s roles as homemakers. Joseph Pleck has observed that a similar situation existed for men, whose newly domesticated positions as the heads of households or as anonymous corporate functionaries contrasted sharply with the more heroic and male-identified activities they engaged in during the war.[8] Further, as John D'Emilio and Estelle Freedman have pointed out, the emergence of gay and bohemian subcultures during this period began to mount serious challenges to the hegemony of the nuclear family, and the conception of sexual fulfillment as a mainstay of personal identity increasingly supplanted the more traditional view of reproduction as the purpose of sex.[9] These conflicting conceptions of gender relations were signaled by an unprecedented outpouring of popular books on the male role during the decade. Taken together these developments reflected growing instabilities within the established system of patriarchal power, which was largely founded on a principle of male dominance in the realms of sexuality and family life.

For the most part, the underlying strains in gender roles during the 1950s were repressed in television sitcoms. Programs like *December Bride, Father Knows Best,* and *Leave It to Beaver* focused on an idealized portrait of family life. By contrast, *The Honeymooners,* which derived much of its energy from the multifaceted image of its famous star, addressed the dissonances inherent in contemporary gender roles. This dimension of the program was most obviously apparent in its portrayal of domestic strife, but it also lay at the heart of the conception of Gleason's tripartite persona.

Though not a romantic idol in terms of physical appearance, Gleason's money and fame allowed him to cultivate a lifestyle based on popular fantasies about successful and desirable males. Such fantasies were acted out through well-publicized anecdotes about the star's personal life and in his widely distributed record album "For Lovers Only." These themes were further developed in the presentational mode of his appearances as master of ceremonies on *The Jackie Gleason Show,* where beautiful women called "Glea Girls" announced his entrance and served him liquor in a coffee cup as he confided to the audience, "How sweet it is!"[10] Gleason was later to marry a showgirl, thereby providing such images with a further dimension of documentary verisimilitude.

The larger-than-life romantic persona Gleason established by these means is strikingly at odds with the down-to-earth images of most television personalities of the 1950s, especially situation comedy stars like Eve Arden, Ozzie and Harriet Nelson, and Robert Young. Nonetheless, Gleason's ability to surround his pursuit of male power with an aura of glamour and romance both on and off the air was extremely effective. The season premiere of his show on CBS in 1954 was marked by the highly publicized switch of its sponsor Buick from *The Milton Berle Show* to Gleason. In an era in which outsized and elaborate cars were displayed as symbols of power and prestige, Buick could claim to be one of the most desirable modes of transportation available. To enhance this image of grandeur, the company severed its connection with Berle, whose comic persona was based in large part on transvestitism, in favor of Gleason, whose image was more unambiguously associated with masculine dominance, and who had by then become known as "The Great One."

Ralph Kramden has little in common with the glamorous presentational image Gleason otherwise cultivated. Though Gleason the star makes an ostentatious display of dominating women, Ralph, his alter ego, is unable to dominate even the woman to whom he is married. Ralph is motivated by an obsessive desire to be "king of his castle" and to cast his wife Alice in the role of peasant. His will to male dominance is further exemplified by his pathological jealousy, for he fears that the strong-minded Alice could easily slip away. Where Gleason is supremely confident, Ralph is eternally anxious. This anxiety, however, is firmly positioned within the context of Gleason's own more authoritative confidence. For Ralph's status as an artificially created character is stressed by the role Gleason assumes as host in introducing *The Honeymooners* and in his presentational reappearance dressed in a bathrobe and towel after his performance as Ralph.[11]

The Honeymooners and Bakhtinian Performance Modes

The model proposed by Bakhtin speaks to the disparity between Gleason and his alter ego Ralph by distinguishing between two types of bodies: the grotesque and the classical.[12] The grotesque body is, according to Bakhtin, "a body in the act of becoming. It is never finished, never completed; it is continually built, created, and builds and creates another body. . . . It is looking for that which protrudes from the body's confines. Special attention is given to the shoots and branches, to all that prolongs the body and links it to other bodies or to the world outside" (p. 317).

Comic in its grandiosity, the grotesque body is most explicitly personified in the figure of the clown. Bakhtin argues that such a body is created in response to two related and universal fears: the fear of the cosmos and the fear of death. In folk celebrations, such fears are dispelled by laughter, which arises from the clown's symbolic refiguration of these threatening forces as aspects of his own grotesque physicality. The clown conquers fear by incorporating it, so to speak. This act of incorporation is achieved by his celebration of what Bakhtin terms "the lower bodily stratum," the site of sexuality and defecation. Through his grotesque antics, which invert the bodily hierarchy of spiritual upper functions and vulgar lower ones, the clown negates accepted epistemological hierarchies that place cosmic issues "above" the mundane concerns of humankind. "The entire logic of the grotesque movements of the body . . . is of a topographical nature. The system of these movements is oriented in relation to the upper and lower stratum; it is a system of flights and descents into the lower depths" (p. 353). The fear of death is similarly dispelled by re-presenting it as an aspect of the grotesque body, for this body deals with death not as an end but as a part of the ongoing life process. "Eating, drinking, defecation, and other eliminations (sweating, blowing of the nose, sneezing) as well as copulation, pregnancy, dismemberment, swallowing up by another body—all these acts are performed on the confines of the body and the outer world, or the confines of the old and new body. In all these events, the beginning and end of life are closely linked and interwoven" (p. 317). Bakhtin identifies the grotesque body with the medieval carnival, which celebrated a joyous bodily spirit of vitality and renewal in opposition to the abstract order of the "official" culture. In the Renaissance, he argues, a new figuration of the body emerged, in which all signs of duality and proliferation were erased. This he terms the classical body.

> The new bodily canon, in all its historic variations and different genres, presents an entirely finished, completed, strictly limited body, which is shown from the outside as something individual. That which protrudes, bulges, sprouts, or branches off (when a body transgresses its limits and a new one begins) is eliminated, hidden, or moderated. All orifices of the body are closed. The basis of the image is the individual, strictly limited mass, the impenetrable facade. The opaque surface and the body's valleys acquire an essential meaning as the border of a closed individuality that does not merge with other bodies and with the world. (p. 320–21)

Bakhtin relates the emergence of this well-ordered classical body to the emerging consciousness of historical time. By contrast, the grotesque body is understood in terms of a concept of biological time that sees generations following each other in the absence of historical progress. Here as elsewhere Bakhtin sees the modern era as one marked by increasing confusion among competing conceptions of time in relation to the image of the body: thus, the grotesque clown continues to exist alongside the individualized "classical" body, which defines itself as part of history.

The contrast between the Gleason of *The Jackie Gleason Show* and the Gleason of *The Honeymooners* can thus be understood as a Bakhtinian opposition. As the star moves from the role of gracious host to that of harried bus driver, his body image changes from classical to grotesque. In particular, the smooth, finished appearance of Gleason the host is transformed in his portrayal of Ralph Kramden into ungainly clownishness. Though in his role as host Gleason's sizable stomach is concealed by well-cut clothing, his corpulence is exaggerated by Ralph's bus driver's uniform, and it repeatedly makes Ralph the butt of the other characters' "fat" jokes. As host, Gleason's utterances are mellow and measured, but as Ralph his laugh often ends in loud, uncontrolled coughing. Ralph's eyes habitually bug out. He is frequently characterized as having "a big mouth," a description that contains literal as well as figurative truth, in view of the fact that his mouth is often agape as he roars in rage or pain. All of these elements position Ralph's body in Bakhtinian terms as one "in the act of becoming."

Ralph's grotesquery is also opposed to the sleek image of Gleason as host in terms of the way each relates to his surrounding space. The host of *The Jackie Gleason Show* moves gracefully around an ample, precisely organized stage. This orderly arrangement closely conforms to Bakhtin's description of the classical body. "The exact position and movements of this finished body in the finished outside world are brought out, so that the limits between them are not weakened" (pp. 32–33). On the stage of *The Jackie Gleason Show,* order is articulated as a visual display of male supremacy, for this order is represented primarily by means of the choreographed activities of the showgirls who populate the space. The June Taylor dancers, all dressed in similar costumes, typically open the program by creating the kind of intricate visual patterns familiar from Busby Berkeley musicals. Then another series of attractive women appear in sequence to announce the arrival of the star, whose entrance is marked by the parting of two rows of women to create an aisle through which he walks.

This lavish and meticulous frame for the male body is set against the constricted and tumultuous spatial configurations that characterize *The Honeymooners.* To mark the transition between the two segments of the show, Gleason customarily engages in a few dance steps, an action that begins to suggest the massiveness of his body under the flattering clothing he wears. In *The Honeymooners* itself, this massiveness is continually emphasized. Ralph's very name suggests a person who must be "crammed in" to his surroundings. The Kramden apartment, in which the show is largely set, is conspicuously cramped, and Ralph, especially when angry (which is much of the time) can hardly be contained by it. As he stalks around the kitchen, his gestures constantly threaten the space of others in the room as he throws his arms wide, jabs his finger in the air, or thrusts his head aggressively forward. On one occasion, when Ralph belligerently tells his wife that "There isn't enough room in here for both of us," she pointedly replies, "There isn't enough room in here for you and anybody." Ralph's job, which is often referred to on the program, consists of driving a bus down Madison Avenue, one of the most congested thoroughfares in the nation; thus, when at work he presumably participates in a human maelstrom even greater than the one he creates in his own home. Ralph's oversized body also acts as a visual analogue to his inflated ego, which is equally ill-suited to the dimensions of the socially constricted world in which he finds himself.

If in one sense Ralph's world is constricted, in another sense it is breathtakingly vast, for he aspires to incorporate the cosmos into himself. Gleason manages the transition between his two environments by asking for "a little traveling music" for his dance. Then he announces, "And away we go!" These allusions to traveling are picked up in *The Honeymooners'* credit sequence, which literally transports the viewer into outer space. There, against a backdrop of a starry sky, the show's title appears inscribed in a floating white ball intended to represent an unspecified heavenly body. Similar floating balls carry the names of the cast, and the head of Gleason himself is pictured as the man in the moon. Such a depiction speaks most obviously of Gleason's grandiose conception of his stardom, accompanied as it is by a triumphal fireworks display and the ascending chords of "Melancholy Serenade." The portrayal of Gleason as the man in the moon identifies the star's prodigious body with the vast space of the cosmos.

In the show itself, this grandiosity takes on a quality of comic overreaching. Ralph's most famous threat to Alice, that he will "send her to the moon," suggests a capacity to transcend fear by representing the entire universe as part of his own personal space. It is not simply that Ralph's body is too massive to fit comfortably into the space in which it finds itself; rather, it overflows all spatial confines and yearns to be embodied in the endless reaches of the universe itself. The spectator's laughter at such a representation is generated by the spectacle of an ego so outsized that it is unable to function in terms of any plausible limits. Yet it is also laughter that celebrates the magnitude of the human aspiration that such grandiosity represents.

Because of their association with reproduction, grotesque bodies often come in pairs, and in *The Honeymooners* Gleason's clowning is complemented by the antics of Art Carney. Carney's Ed Norton personifies another kind of grotesque. He is given to conspicuous nose-blowing and his mouth is usually half-open. The symbiotic pairing of Carney with Gleason emphasizes the dual unfinished nature of both of their bodies—one fat, the other thin. Norton's customary mode of dress, a T-shirt and baggy vest, calls attention to his thinness, and his airy, loose-limbed movements complement the weighty vigor of Ralph's. The dialogue that is thus fostered between Ralph and Ed is further elaborated by their relation to food: though Ralph is the one who is fat, Ed is the one with the enormous appetite. The convention of such complementary depictions of fat and thin clowns has a long and notable history, including such famous pairs as Laurel and Hardy and Don Quixote and Sancho Panza.[13]

In the spirit of this tradition, *The Honeymooners* pairs a fat clown whose overweening ego manifests itself in the expansiveness of his physical presence with a thin one whose more subtle grandiosity is revealed in his excessive concern with time. Ed's watch is often a conspicuous element in his attire, and he frequently consults it. Many of the interactions between the two men center on

Ralph's irascibility in the face of Norton's fussiness about time, when, for example, Norton uses Ralph's telephone to find out what time it is or when he explains to Ralph how he can tell the precise hour and minute by means of the odors wafting up from the Chinese restaurant across the street. Most significantly, Ed repeatedly uses his body to take up inordinate amounts of time in a manner analogous to the way Ralph takes up too much space. He can never begin a task such as writing or playing the piano without an elaborate and lengthy preliminary flourish. These rituals invariably infuriate Ralph, who is as impatient as his friend is laggardly.

As with Ralph's excessive girth, Ed's job in the sewer is made into the object of much of the show's humor. Viewed in Bakhtinian terms, the sewer represents a projection of the lower bodily stratum, the body seen as organic waste, as part of the natural world. This image of the body is, in turn, identified with the image of a grotesque underworld. Thus, when Ed emerges each day from this world, he undergoes a kind of rebirth. For Bakhtin such grotesque representations of the triumph over death are associated most notably with conflicts over the burial of the past. "The image of the netherworld in folk tradition becomes the symbol of the defeat of fear by laughter," Bakhtin writes. "The fear is dual: the mystic fear inspired by hell and death and the terror of the authority and the truth of the past, still prevailing but dying, which has been hurled into the underworld." [14] Thus Ed's daily journeys into the sewer-underworld can be seen as indications of his unwillingness to allow the past to be definitively buried.

Ed's trips down into the sewer are also related to his dawdling in that both behaviors seek to slow the passage of time and thereby avoid the changes the future promises to bring. Ed recognizes the inevitable passing of an anachronistic order but is determined to hold on to each remaining moment of it. In short, he wishes to resist history. Though his anxiety about time is never tied to any specific issue, its elaboration within the context of the domestic sphere (the home environment in which the show is set) suggests that gender relations constitute its source. In contrast to the Kramdens' marriage, the Nortons' relationship is a harmonious one because Ed, unlike Ralph, does not aspire to be "king of his castle." But Ed's ambivalence about the reduced status he is allotted in his household and in society at large is nonetheless still displayed, acted out through comic behavioral symptoms.

Performance and Narrative

The role played by the two clowns in *The Honeymooners* is intimately associated with the show's conflicting narrative principles. Commentators such as

David Grote, Mick Eaton, and Roger Rollin argue that TV sitcoms are conservative in nature because they end where they begin.[15] This formulation has been challenged by Jane Feuer, who points out that some sitcoms begin from what she describes as a "progressive" situation (for instance, with Mary Tyler Moore in the role of an independent career woman).[16] Both of these formulations, however, are too sweeping to account for the varied narrative patterns followed by different sitcom series. An analysis that attends to the effect of contrasting performance styles within individual programs is in a position to construct a more complex narrative model in which the issue is not simply beginnings and endings but tensions surrounding the development of the story as a whole, which are generated by the styles of its various characters.

As has been observed by many theorists of television narrative, including Robert C. Allen and John Ellis, the classic narrative progression of cause and effect is, in this medium, ordinarily less important than character-centered vignettes, or to use Ellis's term, "segments."[17] In *The Honeymooners* such segments are typically motivated by the activities of Ralph and Ed. Though these segments create much of the pleasure of the show, they do not in themselves constitute a story, insofar as stories create an impression of causal progression. The principle of narrative flow is represented in the show by yet another character, Alice Kramden.

In some ways the image of Alice, as portrayed most famously by Audrey Meadows,[18] echoes the classical model associated with Gleason the star. Neatly dressed, with her hands on her hips or thrust into her pockets, she presents a more modestly scaled image of a classical body. Like Gleason, she dominates her surrounding space, though in a less grandiose and more functional manner. Scenes are most often set in the Kramden's kitchen, a room over which Alice exercises complete mastery (in contrast to Ralph, who is conspicuously ill at ease with all of its culinary appurtenances).[19] Alice invariably stands her ground in the face of the inflated male egos with which she must cope. As the still presence around which her husband revolves, she is capable of calling a halt to his extravagant gestures simply by saying, "Now you listen to me, Ralph."

Alice's image differs most importantly from that of Gleason the star in that she participates in a narrative, and therefore in a principle of orderly temporal progression. She is the one who customarily brings *The Honeymooners* to a harmonious conclusion by straightening out the errors of the men, thereby ordering the chaos they wreak and creating a story in time. Her goals are pragmatically conceived, and she usually manages to achieve them. By contrast, as we have seen, the two clowns are out of step with the progress of time: Norton is a laggard and Ralph is overly hasty. In this sense Alice's role suggests a version of the notion of historical progress that Bakhtin associates with his concept of the classical body.

A typical *Honeymooners* episode is most accurately described as a play of oscillations between the various segments (in which the clowns enact bits of comic business) and the story proper (in which Alice soberly straightens out the plot's complications). Such a play of oscillations has been described by Rick Altman, who borrows the Bakhtinian term "dialogic" to refer to the dual focus effect of narrative structures that shift between the cause-effect strategies associated with classical "realistic" storytelling and the more local, sensational effects associated with popular melodrama.[20] Altman suggests psychoanalytic dream interpretation as an appropriate model for the reading of this multidimensional system. A model of this sort has been elaborated by Peter Brooks, who draws on Freud's late work *Beyond the Pleasure Principle* to explain the conflicting forces at work in all narrative structures. Brooks opposes a story's metonymic dimension (its narrative cause-effect chain) to its metaphoric dimension (its play of significant repetitions). According to Brooks, the metaphoric dimension is justified by its capacity to create an energy that makes the story not only pleasurable but also significant.

> The energy generated by deviance, extravagance, excess—an energy which belongs to the textual hero's career and to the reader's expectation, his desire of and for the text—maintains the plot in its movement through the vacillating play of the middle, where repetition as binding works toward the generation of significance, toward recognition and the retrospective illumination which will allow us to grasp the text as total metaphor but not therefore to discard the metonymies that have led to it.[21]

By "binding" Brooks refers to the capacity of repetitions to allow the psyche to master trauma and thereby free itself to experience pleasure. "Repetition in all its literary manifestations may in fact work as a 'binding,' a binding of textual energies that allows them to be mastered by putting them into serviceable form within the energetic economy of the 'narrative.'"[22]

The Honeymooners achieves this quality of significant repetition through the "deviance, extravagance, [and] excess" generated by Ralph and Ed, the show's grotesque clowns. The appeal of the obsessive grandiosity of these two figures is based on their repeated "shticks," which the audience responds to as familiar pleasures. By contrast, the more realistically drawn figure of Alice is identified with the metonymic chain that brings the story to its conclusion.

The oscillation between these two poles speaks to the repressed cultural contradiction centered on gender roles in the 1950s. The exaggerated performance styles of Ralph and Ed serve as significant metaphors of an excessive masculine reaction to the trauma signified by the loss of dominance that was then threatening men—and that the presentational and documentary persona of Gleason the star went to extravagant lengths to deny. By contrast, the measured and deliberate style embodied by Alice offers an image of feminine empowerment that is seen as a realistic alternative to the absurd postures of the men. *The Honeymooners* is not in a position to resolve this tension, but through its contrasting performance styles it is able to represent alternative frameworks through which various aspects of the dilemma can be expressed. Perhaps most significantly, a Utopian ideal of an egalitarian union between men and women is announced at the end of almost every *Honeymooners* skit when Gleason, the Great One, as Ralph Kramden, announces to his wife Alice, "Baby, *you're* the greatest!"

5

Sitcoms and Suburbs

Positioning the 1950s Homemaker

MARY BETH HARALOVICH

The suburban middle-class family sitcom of the 1950s and 1960s centered on the family ensemble and its home life: breadwinner father, homemaker mother, and growing children placed within the domestic space of the suburban home. Structured within definitions of gender and the value of home life for family cohesion, these sitcoms drew upon particular historical conditions for their realist representation of family relations and domestic space. In the 1950s, a historically specific social subjectivity of the middle-class homemaker was engaged by suburban housing, the consumer product industry, market research, and the lifestyle represented in popular "growing family" sitcoms such as *Father Knows Best* (1954–62) and *Leave It to Beaver* (1957–63). With the reluctant and forced exit of women from positions in skilled labor after World War II and during a period of rapid growth and concentration of business, the middle-class homemaker provided these institutions with a rationale for establishing the value of domestic architecture and consumer products for quality of life and the stability of the family.

The middle-class homemaker was an important basis of this social econ-

An earlier version of this chapter, entitled "Suburban Family Sitcoms and Consumer Product Design: Addressing the Social Subjectivity of Homemakers in the 1950s," was presented as a paper to the 1986 International Television Studies Conference and appears in Phillip Drummond and Richard Paterson, eds., *Television and Its Audience: International Research Perspectives* (London: British Film Institute, 1988), 38–60. This chapter is also an abbreviated version of an article that was published in the *Quarterly Review of Film and Video* 11 (1989): 61–83. It has been reprinted here by permission of the publisher. The author thanks Beverly O'Neil for suggesting and participating in the survey of design journals, and Robert Deming, Darryl Fox, and Lee Poague, who made helpful comments.

omy—so much so that it was necessary to define her in contradictions that held her in a limited social place. In her value to the economy, the homemaker was at once central and marginal.[1] She was marginal in that she was positioned within the home, constituting the value of her labor outside of the means of production. Yet she was also central to the economy in that her function as homemaker was the subject of consumer product design and marketing, the basis of an industry. She was promised psychic and social satisfaction for being contained within the private space of the home; and in exchange for being targeted, measured, and analyzed for the marketing and design of consumer products, she was promised leisure and freedom from housework.

These social and economic appeals to the American homemaker were addressed to the white middle class whom Stuart and Elizabeth Ewen have described as "landed consumers," for whom "suburban homes were standardized parodies of independence, of leisure, and most important of all, of the property that made the first two possible."[2] The working class is marginalized in and minorities are absent from these discourses and from the social economy of consumption. An ideal white and middle-class home life was a primary means of reconstituting and resocializing the American family after World War II. Because access to property and home ownership were defined within the values of the conventionalized suburban family, women and minorities were guaranteed economic and social inequality. Just as suburban housing provided gender-specific domestic space and restrictive neighborhoods, consumer product design and market research directly addressed the class and gender of the targeted family member, the homemaker.

The relationship of television programming to the social formation is crucial to an understanding of television as a social practice. Graham Murdock and Peter Golding argue that media reproduce social relations under capital through "this persistent imagery of consumerism conceal[ing] and compensat[ing] for the persistence of radical inequalities in the distribution of wealth, work conditions and life chances." Stuart Hall has argued that the ideological effects of media fragment classes into individuals, masking economic determinacy and replacing class and economic social relations with imaginary social relations.[3] The suburban family sitcom is dependent upon this displacement of economic determinations onto imaginary social relations that naturalize middle-class life.

Despite its adoption of historical conditions from the 1950s, the suburban family sitcom did not greatly proliferate until the late 1950s and early 1960s. While *Father Knows Best,* in 1954, marks the beginning of popular discussion of the realism of this program format, it was not until 1957 that *Leave It to Beaver* joined it on the schedule. In the late 1950s and early 1960s, the format multiplied, while the women's movement was seeking to release homemakers from this social and economic gender definition.[4] This "nostalgic" lag between the historical specificity of the social formation and the popularity of the suburban family sitcom on the prime-time schedule underscores the sitcom's ability to mask social contradictions and to naturalize woman's place in the home.

The following is an analysis of a historical conjuncture in which institutions important to social and economic policies defined women as homemakers: suburban housing, the consumer product industry, and market research. *Father Knows Best* and *Leave It to Beaver* mediated this address to the homemaker through their representations of middle-class family life. They appropriated historically specific gender traits and a realist mise en scène of the home to create a comfortable, warm, and stable family environment. *Father Knows Best,* in fact, was applauded for realigning family gender roles, for making "polite, carefully middle-class, family-type entertainment, possibly the most non-controversial show on the air waves."[5]

"Looking Through a Rose-tinted Picture Window into Your Own Living Room"

After four years on radio, *Father Knows Best* began the first of its six seasons on network television in 1954. This program about the family life of Jim and Margaret Anderson and their children, Betty (age fifteen), Bud (age thirteen), and Kathy (age eight), won the 1954 Sylvania Award for outstanding family entertainment. After one season the program was dropped by its sponsor for low ratings in audience polls. But more than twenty thousand letters from viewers protesting the program's cancellation attracted a new sponsor (the Scott Paper Company), and *Father Knows Best* was promptly reinstated in the prime-time schedule. It remained popular even after first-run production ended in 1960 when its star, Robert Young, decided to move on to other roles. Reruns of *Father Knows Best* were on prime time for three more years.[6]

Contemporary writing on *Father Knows Best* cited as its appeal the way it rearranged the dynamics of family interaction in situation comedies. Instead of the slapstick and gag-oriented family sitcom with a "henpecked simpleton" as family patriarch (this presumably refers to programs such as *The Life of Riley*), *Father Knows Best* concentrated on drawing humor from parents raising children to adulthood in suburban America. This prompted the *Saturday Evening Post* to praise the Andersons for being "a family that has surprising similarities to real people": "The parents . . . manage to ride through almost any family situation without violent injury to their dignity, and the three Anderson children are presented as decently behaved children who will probably turn into useful citizens." [7]

These "real people" are the white American suburban middle-class family, a social and economic arrangement valued as the cornerstone of the American social economy of the 1950s. The verisimilitude associated with *Father Knows Best* is derived not only from the traits and interactions of the middle-class family, but also from the placement of that family within the promises that suburban living and material goods held out for it. Even while the role of Jim Anderson was touted as probably "the first intelligent father permitted on radio or TV since they invented the thing," [8] the role of Margaret Anderson in relation to the father and the family—as homemaker—was equally important to post-World War II attainment of quality family life, social stability, and economic growth.

Leave It to Beaver was not discussed as much or in the same terms as *Father Knows Best*. Its first run in prime-time television was from 1957 to 1963, overlapping the last years of *Father Knows Best*. Ward and June Cleaver raise two sons (Wally, age twelve; Theodore, the Beaver, age eight) in a single-family suburban home that, in later seasons, adopted a nearly identical floor plan to that of the Andersons. Striving for verisimilitude, the stories were based on the "real life" experiences of the scriptwriters in raising their own children. "In recalling the mystifications that every adult experienced when he [*sic*] was a child, '*Leave It to Beaver*' evokes a humorous and pleasurably nostalgic glow." [9]

Like *Father Knows Best*, *Leave It to Beaver* was constructed around an appeal to the entire family. The Andersons and the Cleavers are already assimilated into the comfortable environment and middle-class lifestyle that housing and consumer products sought to guarantee for certain American families. While the Andersons and the Cleavers are rarely (if ever) seen in the process of purchasing consumer products, family interactions are closely tied to the suburban home. The Andersons' Springfield and the Cleavers' Mayfield are ambiguous in their metropolitan identity as suburbs in that the presence of a major city nearby is unclear, yet the communities exhibit the characteristic homogeneity, domestic architecture, and separation of gender associated with suburban design.

Margaret Anderson and June Cleaver, in markedly different ways, are two representations of the contradictory definition of the homemaker in that they are simultaneously contained and liberated by domestic space. In their placement as homemakers, they represent the promises of the economic and social processes that established a limited social subjectivity for homemakers in the 1950s. Yet there are substantial differences in the character traits of the two women, and these revolve around the degree to which each woman is contained within the domestic space of the home. As we shall see, June is more suppressed in the role of homemaker than Margaret is, with the result that June remains largely peripheral to the decision-making activities of family life.

Yet these middle-class homemakers lead a comfortable existence in comparison with television's working-class homemakers. In *Father Knows Best* and *Leave It to Beaver,* middle-class assimilation is displayed through deep-focus photography exhibiting tasteful furnishings, tidy rooms, appliances, and gender-specific functional spaces: dens and workrooms for men, the "family space" of the kitchen for women. Margaret Anderson and June Cleaver have a lifestyle and domestic environment radically different from that of their working-class sister, Alice Kramden in *The Honeymooners.* The suburban home and accompanying consumer products have presumably liberated Margaret and June from the domestic drudgery that marks Alice's daily existence.

The middle-class suburban environment is comfortable, unlike the cramped and unpleasant space of the Kramdens' New York City apartment. A major portion of the comedy of *The Honeymooners'* (1955–56) working-class urban family is derived from Ralph and Alice Kramden's continual struggle with outmoded appliances, their lower-class taste, and the economic blocks to achieving an easy assimilation into the middle class through home ownership and the acquisition of consumer goods. Ralph screams out of the apartment window to a neighbor to be quiet; the water pipe in the wall breaks, spraying plaster and water everywhere. The Kramdens' refrigerator and stove predate the postwar era.

One reason for this comedy of mise en scène is that urban sitcoms such as *I Love Lucy* (1951–57) and *The Honeymooners* tended to focus on physical comedy and gags generated by their central comic figures (Lucille Ball and Jackie Gleason) filmed or shot live on limited sets before studio audiences.[10] *Father Knows Best* and *Leave It to Beaver,* in contrast, shifted the source of comedy to the ensemble of the nuclear family as it realigned the roles within the family. *Father Knows Best* was praised by the *Saturday Evening Post* for its "outright defiance" of "one of the more persistent clichés of television scriptwriting about the typical American family . . . the mother as the iron-fisted ruler of the nest, the father as a blustering chowderhead and the children as being one sassy crack removed from juvenile delinquency." Similarly, *Cosmopolitan* cited the program for overturning television programming's "message . . . that the American father is a weak-willed, predicament-inclined clown [who is] saved from his doltishness by a beautiful and intelligent wife and his beautiful and intelligent children."[11]

Instead of building family comedy around slapstick, gags, and clowning, the Andersons are the modern and model American suburban family, one in which—judging from contemporaneous articles about *Father Knows Best*—viewers saw themselves. The *Saturday Evening Post* quoted letters from viewers who praised the program for being one the entire family could enjoy; they could "even learn something from it." In *Cosmopolitan,* Eugene Rodney, the producer of *Father Knows Best,* identified the program's audience as the middle-class and middle-income family. "It's people in that bracket who watch us. They don't have juvenile delinquent problems. They are interested in family relations, allowances, boy and girl problems."[12] In 1959 *Good Housekeeping* reported that a viewer had written to the program to thank *Father Knows Best* for solving a family problem: "Last Monday my daughter and I had been squabbling all day. By evening we were both so mad that I went upstairs to our portable TV set, leaving her to watch alone in the living room. When you got through with us, we both felt like fools. We didn't even need to kiss and make up. You had done it for us. Thank you all very much." *Good Housekeeping* commented fondly on the program's "lifelike mixture of humor, harassment, and sentiment that literally hits home with some 15 million mothers, fathers, sons, and daughters. Watching it is like looking through a rose-tinted picture window into your own living room." In its last season, *Father Knows Best* ranked as the sixth most popular show on television.[13]

The verisimilitude of *Father Knows Best* and *Leave It to Beaver* was substantially reinforced by being based at major movie studios (Columbia and Universal, respectively), with sets that were standing replications of suburban homes. *The Saturday Evening Post* described the living environment of *Father Knows Best*:

> The set for the Anderson home is a $40,000 combination of illusion and reality. Its two floors, patio, driveway and garage sprawl over Columbia Pictures Stage 10. One room with interchangeable, wallpapered walls, can be made to look like any of the four different bedrooms. The kitchen is real, however. . . . If the script calls for a meal or a snack, Rodney insists that actual food be used. . . . "Don't give me too much food," [Young said] "Jim leaves quickly in this scene and we can't have fathers dashing off without cleaning their plates."

The home is a space not for comedy riffs and physical gags but for family cohesion, a guarantee that children can be raised in the image of their parents. In *Redesigning the American Dream,* Dolores Hayden describes suburban housing "as an architecture of gender, since houses provide settings for women and girls to be effective social status achievers, desirable sex objects, and skillful domestic servants, and for men and boys to be executive breadwinners, successful home handy men, and adept car mechanics."[14]

"The Home Is an Image . . . of the Household and of the Household's Relation to Society"

As social historians Gwendolyn Wright and Dolores Hayden have shown, housing development and design are fundamental cornerstones of social order. Hayden argues that "the house is an image . . . of the household, and of the household's relation to society."[15] The single family detached suburban home was architecture for the family whose healthy life would be guaranteed by a nonurban environment, neighborhood stability, and separation of family functions by gender. The suburban middle-income family was the primary locus of this homogeneous social formation.

When President Harry Truman said at the 1948 White House Conference on Family Life that "children and dogs are as necessary to the welfare of this country as is Wall Street and the railroads," he spoke to the role of home ownership in transforming the postwar American economy. Government policies supported suburban development in a variety of ways. The forty-one thousand miles of limited-access highways authorized by the Federal Aid Highway Act of 1956 contributed to the development of gender-specific space for the suburban family: commuter husbands and homemaker mothers. Housing starts became, and still continue to be, an important indicator of the well-being of the nation's economy. And equity in home ownership is considered to be a significant guarantee of economic security in the later years of life.[16]

But while the Housing Act of 1949 stated as its goal "a decent home and a suitable living environment for every American family," the Federal Housing Administration (FHA) was empowered with defining "neighborhood character." Hayden argues that the two national priorities of the postwar period—removing women from the paid labor force and building more housing—were conflated and tied to: "an architecture of home and neighborhood that celebrates a mid-nineteenth century ideal of separate spheres for women and men . . . characterized by segregation by age, race, and class that could not be so easily advertised."[17]

In order to establish neighborhood stability, homogeneity, harmony, and attractiveness, the FHA adopted several strategies. Zoning practices prevented multifamily dwellings and commercial uses of property. The FHA also chose not to support housing for minorities by adopting a policy called "red-lining," in which red lines were drawn on maps to identify the boundaries of changing or mixed neighborhoods. Since the value of housing in these neighborhoods was designated as low, loans to build or buy houses were considered bad risks. In addition, the FHA published a technical bulletin titled "Planning Profitable Neighborhoods," which gave advice to developers on how to concentrate on homogeneous markets for housing. The effect was to "green-line" suburban areas, promoting them by endorsing loans and development at the cost of creating urban ghettos for minorities.[18]

Wright discusses how the FHA went so far as to enter into restrictive or protective covenants to prevent racial mixing and "declining property values." She quotes the 1947 manual:

> If a mixture of user groups is found to exist, it must be determined whether the mixture will render the neighborhood less desirable to present and prospective occupants. Protective covenants are essential to sound development of proposed residential areas, since they regulate the use of the land and provide a basis for the development of harmonious, attractive neighborhoods. Despite the fact that the Supreme Court ruled in favor of the NAACP's case against restrictive covenants, the FHA accepted written and unwritten agreements in housing developments until 1968.[19]

The effect of these government policies was to create homogeneous and socially stable communities with racial, ethnic, and class barriers to entry. Wright describes "a definite sociological pattern to the household that moved out to the suburbs in the late 1940s and 1950s": the average age of adult suburbanites was thirty-one in 1950; there were few single, widowed, divorced, and elderly; there was a higher fertility rate than in the cities; and nine percent of suburban women worked, as compared to twenty-seven percent in the population as a whole. According to Hayden, five groups were excluded from single-family housing through the social policies of the late 1940s: single white women; the white elderly working and lower classes; minority men of all classes; minority women of all classes; and minority elderly.[20]

The suburban dream house underscored this homogeneous definition of the suburban family. Domestic architecture was designed to display class attributes and reinforce gender-specific functions of domestic space. Hayden describes Robert Woods Kennedy, an influential housing designer of the period, arguing that the task of the housing architect was "to provide houses that helped his clients to indulge in status-conscious consumption . . . to display the housewife 'as a sexual being' . . . and to display the family's possessions 'as proper symbols of socio-economic class,' claiming that [this] form of expression [was] essential to modern family life." In addition to the value of the home for class and sexual identity, suburban housing was also therapeutic for the family. As Hayden observes, "whoever speaks of housing must also speak of home; the word means both the physical space and the nurturing that takes place there."[21]

A popular design for the first floor of the home was the "open floor plan," which provided a whole living environment for the entire family. With few walls separating living, dining, and kitchen areas, space was open for family togetherness. This "activity area" would also allow children to be within sight and hearing of the mother. Father could have his own space in a den or workroom and a detached garage for his car, while mother might be attracted to a modern model kitchen with separate laundry room. Bedrooms were located in the "quiet zone," perhaps on the second floor at the head of a stairway, away from the main activities of the household. While children might have the private space of individual bedrooms, parents shared the "master bedroom," which was larger and sometimes equipped with walk-in closets and dressing areas.[22]

This housing design, built on a part of an acre of private property with a yard for children, allowed the postwar middle-class family to give their children a lifestyle that was not so commonly available during the depression and World War II. This domestic haven provided the setting for the socialization of girls into women and boys into men, and was paid for by the labor of the breadwinner father and maintained by the labor of the homemaker mother. The homemaker, placed in the home by suburban development and housing design, was promised release from household drudgery and an aesthetically pleasing interior environment as the basis of the consumer product industry economy.

Televisual Life in Springfield and Mayfield

One way that television distributed knowledge about a social economy that positioned women as homemakers was through the suburban family sitcom. The signifying systems of these sitcoms invested in the social subjectivity of homemakers put forth by suburban development and the consumer product industry. In their representation of middle-class family life, series such as *Father Knows Best* and *Leave It to Beaver* mobilized the discourses of other social institutions. Realistic mise en scène and the character traits of family members naturalized middle-class home life, masking the social and economic barriers to entry into that privileged domain.

The heterogeneity of class and gender that market research analyzed is not manifested in either *Father Knows Best* or *Leave It to Beaver.* The Andersons and the Cleavers would probably rank quite well in the Index of Social Position. Their neighborhoods have large, arid, well-maintained homes; both families belong to country clubs. Jim Anderson is a well-respected insurance agent with his own agency (an occupation chosen because it would not tie him to an office). Ward Cleaver's work is ambiguous, but both men carry a briefcase and wear a suit and tie to work. They have the income that easily provides their families with roomy, comfortable, and pleasing surroundings and attractive clothing; their wives have no need to work outside the home. Both men are college-educated; the programs often discuss the children's future college education.

Father Knows Best and *Leave It to Beaver* rarely make direct reference to the social and economic means by which the families attained and maintain their middle-class status. Their difference from other classes is not a subject of these sitcoms. By effacing the separations of race, class, age, and gender that produced suburban neighborhoods, *Father Knows Best* and *Leave It to Beaver* naturalize the privilege of the middle class. Yet there is one episode of *Leave It to Beaver* from the early 1960s that lays bare its assumptions about what constitutes a good neighborhood. In doing so, the episode suggests how narrowly the heterogeneity of social life came to be defined. Wally and Beaver visit Wally's smart-aleck friend, Eddie Haskell, who has moved out of his family's home into a rooming house in what Beaver describes as a "crummy neighborhood." Unlike the design of suburban developments, this neighborhood has older, rambling two-story (or more) houses set close together. The door to one house is left ajar, paper debris is blown about by the wind and left on yards and front porches. Two men are working on an obviously older model car in the street, hood and trunk open, tire resting against the car; two garbage cans are on the sidewalks; an older man in sweater and hat walks along carrying a bag of groceries. On a front lawn, a rake leans against a bushel basket with leaves plied up; a large canvas-covered lawn swing sits on a front lawn; one house has a sign in the yard: "For sale by owner-to be moved."

Wally and Beaver are uneasy in this neighborhood, one which is obviously in transition and in which work activities are available for public view. But everyone visible is white. This is a rare example of a suburban sitcom's demarcation of good and bad neighborhoods. What is more typical is the assumption that the homes of the Andersons and the Cleavers are representative of the middle class.

In different ways, the credit sequences that begin these programs suggest recurring aspects of suburban living. The opening of *Father Knows Best* begins with a long shot of the Anderson's two-story home, a fence separating the front lawn from the sidewalk, its landscape including trellises with vines and flowers. A cut to the interior entryway shows the family gathering together. In earlier seasons, Jim, wearing a suit and with hat in hand, prepares to leave for work. He looks at his watch; the grandfather clock to the left of the door shows the time as nearly 8:30 A.M. Margaret, wearing a blouse, sweater, and skirt, brings Jim his briefcase and kisses him goodbye. The three Anderson children giggle all in a row on the stairway leading up to the second floor bedrooms. In later seasons, after the long shot of the house, the Anderson family gathers in the entryway to greet Jim as he returns from work. Margaret, wearing a dress too fancy for house-work, kisses him at the doorway as the children cluster about them, uniting the family in the home.

The opening credits of *Leave It to Beaver* gradually evolved from an emphasis on the younger child to his placement within the neighborhood and then the family. The earliest episodes open with childlike etchings drawn in a wet con-crete sidewalk. Middle seasons feature Beaver walking home along a street with single-family homes set back behind manicured, unfenced lawns. In later sea-sons, the Cleaver family is shown leaving their two-story home for a picnic trip: Ward carries the thermal cooler, June (in a dress, even for a picnic) carries the basket, and Wally and Beaver climb into the Cleavers' late model car. Whereas *Father Knows Best* coheres around the family ensemble, *Leave It to Beaver* decen-ters the family around the younger child, whose rearing provides problems that the older child has either already surmounted or has never had.

The narrative space of these programs is dominated by the domestic space of the home. *Father Knows Best* leaves the home environment much less often than does *Leave It to Beaver,* which often focuses on Beaver at school. This placing of the family within the home contributes in large measure to the ability of these programs to "seem real." During the first season of *Leave It to Beaver,* the Cleavers' home was an older design rather than a suburban dream house. The kitchen was large and homey, with glass and wood cabinets. The rooms were sep-arated by walls and closed doors. By the 1960s, the Cleavers, like the Andersons, were living in the "open floor plan," a popular housing design of the 1950s. As you enter the home, to your far left is the den, the private space of the father. To the right of the den is the stairway leading to the "quiet zone" of the bedrooms. To your right is the living room, visible through a wide and open entryway the size of two doors. Another wide doorway integrates the living room with the for-mal dining room. A swinging door separates the dining room from the kitchen. The deep-focus photography typical of these sitcoms displays the expanse of liv-ing space in this "activity area."

Although the Cleaver children share a bedroom, it is equipped with a private bathroom and a portable television set. Ward and June's bedroom is small, with twin beds. Since it is not a site of narrative activity, which typically takes place in the boys' room or on the main floor of the home, the parents' bedroom is rarely seen. These two small bedrooms belie the scale of the house when it is seen in long shot.

The Andersons' home makes more use of the potential of the bedrooms for narrative space. With four bedrooms, the Anderson home allows each of the children the luxury of his or her own room. Jim and Margaret's "master" bedroom, larger than those of their children, has twin beds separated by a nightstand and lamp, a walk-in closet, a dressing table, armchairs, and a small alcove. In this design, the "master" bedroom is conceived as a private space for parents, but the Anderson children have easy access to their parents' bedroom. The Andersons, however, have only one bathroom. Betty has commented that when she gets married she will have three bathrooms because "there won't always be two of us."

The Andersons and the Cleavers also share aspects of the decor of their homes, displaying possessions in a comfortably unostentatious way. Immediately to the left of the Andersons' front door is a large, freestanding grandfather clock; to the right and directly across the room are built-in bookcases filled with hardcover books. In earlier seasons of *Leave It to Beaver,* the books (also hardbound) were on shelves in the living room. Later, these books were relocated to Ward's study, to line the many built-in bookshelves behind his desk.

The two families have similar tastes in wall decorations and furnishings. Among the landscapes in heavy wood frames on the Cleavers' walls are pictures of sailing vessels and reproductions of "great art," such as "Pinkie" by Sir Thomas Lawrence. Although the Andersons do not completely share the Cleavers' penchant for candelabra on the walls and tables, their walls are tastefully decorated with smaller landscapes. Curiously, neither house engages in the prominent display of family photographs.

The large living room in each home has a fireplace. There is plenty of room to walk around the furniture, which is overstuffed and comfortable or of hardwood. The formal dining room in both homes includes a large wooden table and chairs that can seat six comfortably. It is here that the families have their evening meals. A sideboard or hutch displays dishes, soup tureens, and the like. The kitchen contains a smaller, more utilitarian set of table and chairs, where breakfast is eaten. Small appliances such as a toaster, mixer, and electric coffeepot sit out on counters. A wall-mounted roll of paper towels is close to the sink. The Andersons' outdoor patio has a built-in brick oven, singed from use.

Although both homes establish gender-specific areas for women and men, *Father Knows Best* is less repressive in its association of this space with familial roles. Both Jim Anderson and Ward Cleaver have dens; Ward is often shown doing ambiguous paperwork in his, the rows of hardcover books behind his desk suggesting his association with knowledge and mental work. June's forays into Ward's space tend to be brief, usually in search of his advice on how to handle the boys. As Ward works on papers, June sits in a corner chair sewing a button on Beaver's shirt. Ward's den is often the site of father-to-son talks. Its doorway is wide and open, revealing the cabinet-model television that Beaver occasionally watches. While Jim also has a den, it is much less often the site of narrative action, and its door is usually closed.

Workrooms and garages are also arenas for male activity, providing storage space for paint or lawn care equipment or a place to work on the car. The suburban homemaker does not have an equivalent private space. Instead, the woman shares her kitchen with other family members, while the living and dining rooms are designated as family spheres. In typical episodes of *Leave It to Beaver,* June's encounters with family members generally take place in the kitchen, while Ward's tend to occur throughout the house. As her sons pass through her space, June is putting up paper towels, tossing a salad, unpacking groceries, or making meals. Margaret, having an older daughter, is often able to turn this family/woman space over to her. She is also more often placed within other domestic locations: the patio, the attic, the living room. Both Margaret and June exemplify Robert Woods Kennedy's theory that housing design should display the housewife as a sexual being, but this is accomplished not so much through their positioning within domestic space as through costume. June's ubiquitous pearls, stockings and heels, and cinch-waisted dresses are amusing in their distinct contradiction of the realities of housework. Although Margaret also wears dresses or skirts, she tends to be costumed more casually, and sometimes wears a smock when doing housework. Margaret is also occasionally seen in relatively sloppy clothes suitable for dirty work but marked as inappropriate to her status as a sexual being.

In one episode of *Father Knows Best,* Margaret is dressed in dungarees, sweatshirt, and loafers, her hair covered by a scarf as she scrubs paint from her youngest daughter, Kathy. When Betty sees her, she laughs, "If you aren't a glamorous picture!" As Jim arrives home early, Betty counsels Margaret, "You can't let father see you like this!" Betty takes over scrubbing and dressing Kathy while Margaret hurries off to change before Jim sees her. But Margaret is caught, embarrassed at not being dressed as a suburban object of desire. Jim good-naturedly echoes Betty's comment: "If you aren't a glamorous picture!" He calms Margaret's minor distress at being seen by her husband in this departure from her usual toilette: "You know you always look great to me."

As this example shows, the agreement among Jim, Margaret, and Betty on the proper attire for the suburban homemaker indicates the success with which Betty has been socialized within the family. Yet even though both programs were created around "realistic" story lines of family life, the nurturing function of the home and the gender-specific roles of father and mother are handled very differently in *Father Knows Best* and *Leave It to Beaver*.

By 1960, Betty, whom Jim calls "Princess," had been counseled through adolescent dating and was shown to have "good sense" and maturity in her relations with boys. Well-groomed and well-dressed like her mother, Betty could easily substitute for Margaret in household tasks. In one episode, Jim and Margaret decide that their lives revolve too much around their children ("trapped," "like servants") and they try to spend a weekend away, leaving Betty in charge. While Betty handles the situation smoothly, Jim and Margaret are finally happier continuing their weekend at Cedar Lodge with all of the children along.

Bud, the son, participates in the excitement of discovery and self-definition outside of personal appearance. A normal boy in the process of becoming a man, he gets dirty at sports and tinkering with engines, replaces blown fuses, and cuts the grass. Unlike Betty, Bud has to be convinced that he can handle dating; Jim counsels him that this awkward stage is normal and one that Jim himself has gone through. Kathy (whose pet name is "Kitten"), in contrast to her older sister, is a tomboy and is interested in sports. By 1959, *Good Housekeeping* purred that "Kathy seems to have got the idea it might be more fun to appeal to a boy than to be one. At the rate she's going, it won't be long before [Jim and Margaret] are playing grandparents."[23]

Film and television writer Danny Peary was also pleased with Kathy's development, but for a very different reason: in the 1977 *Father Knows Best* "reunion" show, Kathy was an unmarried gym teacher. Peary also felt that *Father Knows Best* was different from other suburban family sitcoms in its representation of women. "The three Anderson females . . . were intelligent, proud, and resourceful. Margaret was Jim's equal, loved and respected for her wisdom."[24] The traits that characterize Margaret in her equality are her patience, good humor, and easy confidence. Unlike Ward Cleaver, Jim is not immune to wifely banter.

In one episode, Jim overhears Betty and her friend Armand rehearsing a play, and assumes they are going to elope. Margaret has more faith in their daughter and good-naturedly tries to dissuade Jim from his anxiety: "Jim, when are you going to stop acting like a comic strip father?" In the same episode, Jim and Margaret play Scrabble, an activity that the episode suggests they do together often. "Dad's getting beat at Scrabble again," observes Bud. Kathy notices, "He's stuck with the 'Z' again." Margaret looks up Jim's Z-word in the dictionary, doubting its existence. Margaret is able to continually best Jim at this word game and Jim is willing to play despite certain defeat.

In contrast to this easy-going family with character traits allowing for many types of familial interaction, *Leave It to Beaver* tells another story about gender relations in the home. June does not share Margaret's status in intelligence. In a discussion of their sons' academic performances, June remarks, "We can't all be 'A' students; maybe the boys are like me." Ward responds, "No, they are *not* like you" and then catches himself. Nor does June share Margaret's witty and confident relationship with her husband. She typically defers to Ward's greater sense for raising their two sons. Wondering how to approach instances of boyish behavior, June positions herself firmly at a loss. She frequently asks, mystified, "Ward, did boys do this when you were their age?" Ward always reassures June that whatever their sons are doing (brothers fighting, for example) is a normal stage of development for boys, imparting to her his superior social and familial knowledge. Like her sons, June acknowledges the need for Ward's guidance. Unlike Margaret, June is structured on the periphery of the socialization of her children, in the passive space of the home.

Ward, often a misogynist, encourages the boys to adopt his own cynical attitude toward their mother and women in general. In an early episode, Ward is replacing the plug on the toaster. He explains to Beaver that "your mother" always pulls it out by the cord instead of properly grabbing it by the plug. Beaver is impressed by Ward's knowledge of " 'lectricity," to which Ward responds by positioning his knowledge as a condition of June's ineptness. "I know enough to stay about one jump ahead of your mother." Unlike *Father Knows Best, Leave It to Beaver* works to contain June's potential threat to patriarchal authority. When June asks why Beaver would appear to be unusually shy about meeting a girl, Ward wonders as well: "He doesn't know enough about life to be afraid of women."

In the episode in which Eddie Haskell moves out of the home, Ward sides with the Haskells by forbidding both his sons to visit Eddie's bachelor digs. As Ward telephones another father to ask him to do the same, June timidly asks (covering a bowl to be put in the refrigerator), "Ward, aren't you getting terribly involved?" Ward answers that if this were their son he would appreciate the support of other parents. June murmurs assent as Ward and June continue the process of defining June's function within the family in terms of passivity and deference.

While *Father Knows Best* and *Leave It to Beaver* position the homemaker in family life quite differently, both women effortlessly maintain the domestic space of the family environment. In their representation of women's work in the home, these programs show the great ease and lack of drudgery with which Margaret and June keep their homes tidy and spotlessly clean. In any episode, these homemakers can be seen engaged in their daily housework. June prepares meals, waters plants, and dusts on a Saturday morning. She brings in groceries, wipes around the kitchen sink, and asks Wally to help her put away the vacuum cleaner (which she has not been shown using). Margaret prepares meals, does dishes, irons, and also waters plants. While June is often stationary in the kitchen or sewing in the living room, Margaret is usually moving from one room to another, in the process of ongoing domestic activity.

While one could argue that this lack of acknowledgment of the labor of homemaking troubles the verisimilitude of these sitcoms, the realist mise en scène that includes consumer products suggests the means by which the comfortable environment of quality family life can be maintained. Margaret and June easily mediate the benefits promised by the consumer product industry. They are definitely not women of leisure, but they are women for whom housework is neither especially confining nor completely time-consuming.

The visible result of their partially visible labor is the constantly immaculate appearance of their homes and variously well-groomed family members. (The older children are more orderly because they are further along in the process of socialization than are the younger ones.) The "real time" to do piles of laundry or the daily preparation of balanced meals is a structured absence of the programs. The free time that appliances provide for Margaret and June is attested to by their continual good humor and the quality of their interactions with the family. Unrushed and unpressured, Margaret and June are not so free from housework that they become idle and self-indulgent. They are well-positioned within the constraints of domestic activity and the promises of the consumer product industry.

We have seen how the homemaker was positioned in the postwar consumer economy by institutions that were dependent on defining her social subjectivity within the domestic sphere. In the interests of family stability, suburban development and domestic architecture were designed with a particular definition of family economy in mind: a working father who could, alone, provide for the social and economic security of his family; a homemaker wife and mother who maintains the family's environment; children who grow up in neighborhoods undisturbed by heterogeneity of class, race, ethnicity, and age.

The limited address to the homemaker by the consumer product industry and market research is easily understood when seen within this context of homogeneity in the social organization of the suburban family. Defined in terms of her homemaking function for the family and for the economy, her life could only be made easier by appliances. The display of her family's social status was ensured by experts who assuaged any uncertainties she may have had about interior decor by designing with these problems in mind. By linking her identity as a shopper and homemaker to class attributes, the base of the consumer economy was broadened, and her deepest emotions and insecurities were tapped and transferred to consumer product design.

The representation of suburban family life in *Father Knows Best* and *Leave It to Beaver* also circulated social knowledge that linked the class and gender identities of homemakers. Realist mise en scène drew upon housing architecture and consumer products in order to ground family narratives within the domestic space of the middle-class home. The contribution of the television homemaker to harmonious family life was underscored by the ease with which she negotiated her place in the domestic arena.

This brief social history has placed one television format—the suburban family sitcom—within the historical context from which it drew its conventions, its codes of realism, and definitions of family life. Yet we must also ask about resistances to this social subjectivity by recognizing the heterogeneity of the social formation. For example, in the late 1950s and 1960s, when the suburban family sitcom proliferated on prime-time television, the women's movement was resisting these institutional imperatives, exposing the social and economic inequalities on which they were based.[25]

Oppositional positions point to the inability of institutions to conceal completely the social and economic determinations of subjectivity. But the durability of the suburban family sitcom indicates the degree of institutional as well as popular support for ideologies that naturalize class and gender identities. Continuing exploration of the relationship between the historical specificity of the social formation and the programming practices of television contributes to our understanding of the ways in which popular cultural forms participate in the discourses of social life and diverge from the patterns of everyday experience.

Part Two | **Television in the 1960s**

Although the television networks and the major Hollywood film studios saw themselves as competitors at the beginning of the 1950s, this relationship shifted throughout the decade. By the 1960s, almost all television programming, apart from news and sports, was produced either by Hollywood studios or independent companies. There were several advantages to this for the networks, though it resulted in standardized television fare. First of all, it was cheaper for the networks to buy programs than to make their own, and it also enabled them to select from the best of what was offered. The Hollywood studios, however, produced predictable, formulaic programs based upon their B-films rather than innovative forms and formats. The competition for ratings also led the networks to eschew risky, high quality programming in favor of formulas that would draw the largest number of viewers, thus reinforcing the Hollywood B-film approach. By the mid-1950s, it was also apparent that huge amounts of money could be made from syndication, so many shows, particularly sitcoms, were deliberately structured so that they could be repeated endlessly without appearing dated; this also meant that they did not address controversial subjects. Further, the quiz show scandals of 1959 contributed to the need for television programming to be inoffensive and reassuring in order to win back the public trust.

It was not surprising, then, that conventional domestic sitcoms remained television staples throughout the 1960s. Social and political issues were addressed only obliquely. As in the 1950s, CBS continued to take the lead in airing sitcoms. Dennis the Menace *(1959–63),* My Three Sons *(1960–72), and* The Andy Griffith Show *(1960–68) were some examples of hit CBS sitcoms that emerged in the 1959–60 season. The latter two slightly modified the domestic sitcom formula by focusing upon a widowed father raising children with the help of a live-in relative.* The Andy Griffith Show *also made the rural sitcom a successful formula, where the idiosyncratic characters who populated the small town of Mayberry were as much a part of the program as the not-so-nuclear family. Yet, Mayberry was a southern town devoid of black residents. Although civil rights demonstrations were increasingly part of the cultural landscape throughout the 1960s, most sitcoms ignored race altogether. It was in this context of bland, all-white programming that Newton Minow, Chair of the Federal Communications Commission (FCC), made his famous speech to the National Association of Broadcasters in 1961, condemning television as a "vast wasteland."*

Despite Minow's criticism, there were two innovative television sitcoms that made it on the air. Early on, this shift was represented by The Many Loves of Dobie Gillis *(1959–63), one of the first sitcoms aimed at the burgeoning teen audience. Its main claim to unconventionality was its satirical, cynical edge and the beatnik character Maynard G. Krebs.* The Dick Van Dyke Show *(1961–66) clearly represented the liberal political climate that came to characterize the Kennedy era. Not only was this one of the first sitcoms to give equal space to home and work, city and suburb, but it modernized the television image of the sitcom family. It attempted to represent the everyday life of the middle-class suburban family in a more realistic manner than typical domestic sitcoms. Unlike sitcoms that portrayed a simple, homogeneous small town America,* The Dick Van Dyke Show *portrayed a more complex world where race and ethnicity existed and the genders had a semblance of equality.*

Whereas The Dick Van Dyke Show *was slow to build an audience,* The Beverly Hillbillies *(1962–71) quickly became one of television's most popular programs. Within six weeks of its introduction, it became the number one show in the nation and was the highest rated television show of the 1960s. Its success could be accounted for by a new focus on demographics. The networks began to try to reach heavy viewers rather than families gathered together around the set. These types of viewers were more likely to be working class, rural, and socially conservative.* The Beverly Hillbillies*' popularity, along with that of* The Andy Griffith Show, *suggested that light, rural-based situation comedies were successful formulas.*

Sitcom spinoffs of these shows attempted to capitalize on their success, so that a specific character or gimmick from a well-known sitcom was reintroduced in a new setting. Petticoat Junction *(1963–70), for example, starred Bea Benaderet who played son Jethro's mother in* The Beverly Hillbillies, *and featured the exploits of a backwoods family much like the Beverly Hillbillies. When* Petticoat Junction *became a hit, it spawned* Green Acres *in 1965.*

*The nation's mood became somber following the assassination of President Kennedy in 1963. Further, television increasingly conveyed images of unrest over U.S. involvement in Vietnam, racial tensions, and the women's rights movement. At the same time, television sitcoms became increasingly escapist. The airwaves were filled with martians (*My Favorite Martian *[1963–66]), monsters (*The Addams Family *[1964–66] and* The Munsters *[1964–66]), talking animals (*Mr. Ed *[1961–66]), women with magical powers (*Bewitched *[1964–72],* I Dream of Jeannie *[1965–70], and* The Flying Nun *[1967–70]), and castaways (*Gilligan's

Island *[1964–67])*. *Military escapades* (F Troop *[1965–67]*, Hogan's Heroes *[1965–71]*, *and* McHale's Navy *[1962–66])*, *far removed from the realities of war, were also popular. Although critics complained that these sitcoms were childish and unimaginative, most did quite well in the ratings. As the chapters in this section indicate, many of these sitcoms indeed included social criticisms of gender, race, class, and even the Vietnam War, yet these criticisms were oblique rather than overt.*

Color television sets had been available since the mid-1950s, but it wasn't until the mid-1960s that the networks began broadcasting in color and large numbers of viewers began buying color sets. By fall of 1964, half of NBC's programs were in color, and CBS followed suit in 1965. ABC, lagging behind, suffered in the ratings, and as a result began the now established practice of initiating a new, "second" season in January. But CBS continued to dominate in the ratings, largely because of its reliance upon sitcoms. Some noteworthy sitcoms were NBC's The Monkees *(1966–68), aimed at the increasingly large teen market and another example of innovative television in the sixties. ABC's* Love on a Rooftop *(1966–67), about a newly married couple, and* That Girl *(1966–71), about an aspiring actress living alone in New York, were designed for young adults. That* Girl *was the most successful of these new comedies, although its potentially feminist slant was undercut by its slapstick humor, ludicrous situations, and the fact that she was constantly bailed out of difficult situations by her dad or boyfriend. The success of the latter two shows suggested that there was an audience for more adult comedies, although the networks didn't take this idea seriously until the 1970s.*

After the assassinations of Martin Luther King and Robert Kennedy in 1968, and a resurgence of protests about television violence, the networks responded accordingly. Action-adventure shows, typically relying on violent interactions, took a new approach. ABC's Mod Squad *(1968–73), for example, initiated a move to relevant, youth-oriented programming. This sensibility filtered through to sitcoms, too. It was in this context that NBC presented* Julia *(1968–71), the first modern sitcom to star a black woman. Julia was often criticized for the main character's seemingly effortless assimilation in her predominately white, middle-class world at a time when the nation was torn by racial strife. Yet, the show did provide a link between the trivial sitcoms of the 1960s and the socially relevant sitcoms of the 1970s.*

The essays in this section illuminate some of the issues that characterized television in the 1960s.

J. M.

6

The Unworthy Discourse

Situation Comedy in Television

PAUL ATTALLAH

Ever since television was made commercially available in the late 1940s, a great deal has been written in North America about it. Oddly enough, however, most of that writing has been heavily marked by a high degree of sameness. Not only are the contents and the conclusions of most television writing remarkably similar but, more important, so are their fundamental presuppositions about the very nature of television. The most widely shared and tenacious presupposition insists on seeing television almost exclusively as a technology producing both social and psychological effects. Indeed, most television research has been devoted to exploring precisely that proposition. Whatever its merits, this fundamental presupposition springs from the following factors: (1) the introduction of television as a privately consumed commodity within the family rather than along the lines of other popular attractions such as movies, vaudeville, or the circus; (2) the consequent concerns about child rearing and psychology, social propriety, and education; (3) widely shared attitudes towards science and technology and their place in society; and (4) the predominance of behaviorist and positivist modes of thought in the institutions most likely to study television.

These factors are important to bear in mind because what is said about situation comedy, as about any type of television, will be dependent on what is believed about television and society as a whole. Clearly, if you believe society and individuals to operate in a certain way, your television will in all likelihood dis-

A slightly different version of this chapter was originally published in *Interpreting Television: Current Research Papers,* ed. Willard D. Rowland Jr. and Bruce Watkins, 222–49 (Newbury Park, Calif.: Sage Annual Reviews of Communication Research 12, 1984). It has been reprinted here by permission of the publisher.

play contents and formats consonant with your presuppositions; and so will your television research. Indeed, the reader need only refer to the vast body of literature known as effects studies in order to see how certain conceptions of human psychology, of the relationship between mind and machine, and of the place of technology in society lead directly to highly specific and particular types of research and to no less specific conclusions and policy recommendations.

These presuppositions are also operative in the case of situation comedy, but they naturally assume a form appropriate to that type of television show. What I wish to argue is that situation comedy can be understood as a *genre*. To understand a genre, however, one must also understand the institution that produces it. No genre exists or has meaning independently of its context. The context of situation comedy includes basically not only the institution of television and all that it produces, but also the social meaning and values upon which it draws and which it reformulates.

Situation Comedy

As a rule, one does not talk about situation comedy. To quote Mick Eaton: "There has been virtually nothing written about television situation comedy as a specifically televisual form."[1] This is due to the way television is talked about in general, to the unworthiness that accrues to it and its products, to its institutional functioning, and to the various modes of availability of its products. In a sense, the absence of sitcoms in television writing can be seen as an effect of the institutionalization of television, which prefers to draw attention to its other achievements. Nonetheless, one may adopt a number of points of view in order to talk *around* the subject of situation comedy.

One may take, for example, an industrial perspective and discuss the situation comedy as an economic proposition: is it successful and does it earn money? In this case, only its status as a commodity is of interest and one might just as easily be talking about any other commodity; the situation comedy has no specificity.

One may adopt a social scientific and critical point of view and choose simply to ignore situation comedy either because it has no discernible effect or because it appears to be generally irrelevant and to make no contribution whatsoever to society. This goes a long way towards explaining the dearth of material on situation comedy.

One may also, on the other hand, occasionally take the inverse stance and talk profusely about certain "quality" or "relevant" situation comedies such as *M*A*S*H, All in the Family,* or *The Dick Van Dyke Show.* These shows are seen as

important precisely to the extent to which they do not resemble situation comedies, because they make significant social statements, or because of strong characterization and good scripting. In this case, it is the content of the situation
comedy that is singled out for praise and attention, and especially that content's
resemblance to "serious drama." One may also talk about *I Love Lucy*, for example, as an incomprehensible social phenomenon: why do people watch *Lucy*? She
just must be a very talented/zany/gifted lady. Again, it is the content (star) of the
show that is singled out and, again, questions of textual specificity or of audience
reception are neglected.

Finally, one may adopt a historicist point of view and attempt either to clas-
sify types of humor or to retrace the origins of the situation comedy through
films, radio, vaudeville, and the theater, as Raymond Williams has begun to do.[2]
Both of these approaches can be interesting, but they do tend to deny the situation comedy's *televisual* specificity and to see it as a variation on a preexisting
form, which it may not be, and on a previous content, which it may not share.

Occasionally, sitcoms are approached genealogically with all the attendant
pitfalls of unproblematized genre theory.[3] But on the whole, one does not talk
about situation comedy as a mode of address or as a televisual form. This is due,
primarily, to the unworthiness of the object.

Unworthiness

There is a strong sense in which television and everything connected to it is
seen as unworthy: unworthy certainly as a serious intellectual pursuit, unworthy
as a source of ideas or of stimulation, unworthy of critical evaluation, unworthy
even as a pastime. The entertainment it provides has long been considered inferior to the entertainment provided by books or films or plays; its information
more ephemeral and less substantial than that provided by newspapers, books,
magazines, or journals. In short, in the classic dichotomy between high art and
low art, television definitely occupies the region of low art. And, as innumerable
books proclaim, television is a "mass" medium, a business and not an art, which
consequently obeys the law of the lowest common denominator. As an activity,
television is generally held to induce both passivity and violence, and ranks far
behind sports, play, or socializing, and especially reading. Furthermore, there are
few television theorists or scholars in the sense that there are film theorists and
literary scholars, that is to say people inspired by a genuine passion for their object of study above and beyond its content, supposed effects, and presumed uses.
There is no television equivalent of an auteur or of an auteur theory, nothing
that might correspond to film or literary theory. There are very few journals de-

voted to television, there is exceptionally little inquiry into the forms and language of television, no network of references, debate, and response. If, like film and literature, television does spark love in some people, the love that fuels inquiry, debates, and theory, then it is a love that dares not speak its name, for it is almost nowhere present.[4]

Instead, television is studied as a technology: effects studies, uses and gratifications studies, sociological and psychological studies, impressionistic studies, and these are clearly overdetermined by its unworthiness. Does anyone attach electrodes to opera lovers in order to determine the behavioral effects of an aria? Does anyone claim that the meaning of poetry can be exhausted by knowing the economic state of the publisher, or that sculpture corresponds to certain uses and gratifications? The whole approach to television is akin to saying that if you write with a typewriter, that is to say with a machine, your writing is more objective or more likely to have an effect. Such positions are clearly only possible because of the maintenance of certain untenable theories of high art and television's relegation to the status of low art.

Television is, in fact, so undeserving of our interest that only two types of people may legitimately attend to it. The first type consists of people who may be defined as suffering some lack: children, housewives, old people, the poor, off-duty laborers. They lack the knowledge to know better, or they lack interest in other activities, or they lack resources. For them, television is obvious and self-explanatory, if still undesirable. Their very social status exhausts their relationship to television and television's relationship to them. As a matter of course, we expect children to like television precisely because they are easily amused and do not know any better, but we also expect them to grow out of it. Television is definitely a phase in life. The other type of people that may legitimately attend to television are those who may be defined as having a surfeit: social scientists, commentators, reformers. They have a surfeit of knowledge and typically apply it to explaining what the first type is doing. Their social status gives them a privileged and authoritative view on television. They approach the object through a forest of precautions and justifications: "We wished to find out why . . ."; "We were commissioned by X to discover . . ."; "It is our aim to explain that . . ."; and so on. One of the major purposes of these studies is to sanitize the object as much as possible, to objectify it, and to demonstrate manifestly that they themselves, the researchers, take no pleasure in it. The first type's relationship to television, then, is entirely personal and insignificant, whereas the second type's is entirely social and authoritative. The second type provides a metadiscourse on the first.

This is the dominant attitude toward television. The immediate temptation is, of course, to say exactly the opposite, to say that television is good and wonderful and enlightening and valuable. Such a reaction would, however, merely confirm the terms of the original debate and set us off on a search for the quality of television, hoping to prove that representations of peace on television cause peace in society. In fact, it is the terms of the debate themselves that need to be understood and modified.

My original object of study for this paper was *The Beverly Hillbillies,* and one can imagine how the unworthiness of the object was greatly amplified by that fact, for, though it was probably one of the most watched programs in the history of television, it was also one of the most vilified and despised. Its unworthiness stems from two causes: the type of program that it is (situation comedy), and the specific program that it is. It appears that in an undeserving medium, situation comedy constitutes a particularly undeserving form equaled only perhaps by the game show and the locally produced commercial.

As a sitcom, *The Beverly Hillbillies* is particularly interesting on a number of levels. Some sitcoms are much discussed (*All in the Family*); some are loved and fondly remembered (*I Love Lucy, The Mary Tyler Moore Show*); some are honored and praised (*The Dick Van Dyke Show, M*A*S*H*). In every case it is because of some element extrinsic to the show's status as sitcom: the issues raised, good acting, or good casting. *The Beverly Hillbillies* apparently had none of that. On the contrary, it remained doggedly at the level of sitcom, refusing to rise above its status or to transcend itself. Consequently, very little was written about it, and almost all of that was uncomplimentary. Within the institutional blind spot that designates situation comedy, *The Beverly Hillbillies* seems to stand out as one of the greatest absences of all.

This silence is surprising, and one should try to make it speak. In its inclusions and exclusions, in what is spoken and in what is not, one detects a pattern or a system, an order of regularity, a recurrent way of approaching, ordering, and constituting objects, in short, a discourse.

Genre

One of the most useful ways to discuss situation comedy in general and *The Beverly Hillbillies* in particular, which I shall use as a somewhat privileged example, is from within genre theory. An excellent discussion of genre in the cinema is to be found in Stephen Neale's monograph.[5]

There is no doubt that situation comedy exists for us as a category quite distinct from westerns, newscasts, police dramas, documentaries, or even variety. The *TV Guide* listings even go so far as to identify shows according to their generic type: *Three's Company*—situation comedy; *Dragnet*—police drama;

Carol Burnett—variety. Television writing, as a whole, easily categorizes shows into generic groups. Nonetheless, most of us can easily imagine which shows would properly belong under the rubric "situation comedy" and which would not. There would undoubtedly be some problematic entries, a few test cases, but by and large, the sorting process occurs quite smoothly. It seems, in fact, that the entire television industry is organized around the production of specific genres. Everything that appears on television effectively fits into one genre or another. Television could be said not to exist outside of its genres. There is nothing that is just "television." It is always a specific "type" of television: police show, soap opera, and sportscast. Genres would appear, then, to be a fundamental institutional category. Certain production companies, actors, directors, writers, or producers specialize in making only one type of show and come to be known and appreciated for precisely that reason. Quinn/Martin Productions, for example, specializes in police drama (*The FBI, Barnaby Jones, The Streets of San Francisco, Quincy*); Norman Lear Productions specializes in "relevant" situation comedy (*All in the Family, Maude, The Jeffersons*); and Hannah-Barbera specializes in cartoons. It might even be possible to sketch a history of television through the rise and fall of different production companies and their corresponding generic cycles, from MCA-Revue Studios in the 1950s, to Filmways and Screen Gems in the 1960s, to Norman Lear and MTM in the 1970s. This is, of course, highly reminiscent of the history of Hollywood wherein certain small studios and certain units within large studios made nothing but certain types—genres—of films. And much like current television production, the films of these studios or units all had the same "look"—similar production values, characters, and situations.

So, it is probably fair to say that the concept of genre has a certain sociological resonance. It is something with which we feel comfortable and that helps us organize the output of television. It also has a certain institutional and industrial resonance. Shows self-consciously offer themselves as belonging to specific genres, and production is organized around them. Beyond that, however, genres seem also to have a life of their own; they exercise a determinate and clearly visible pressure. For example, if I were to make a western tomorrow, its final shape would not be determined solely by institutional organization, by the industrial mode of production, distribution, and exhibition, or by economic, ideological, and other interests, but also, and perhaps more importantly, by the history of the genre itself. I would want to argue, therefore, that genres have something that might be called "relative autonomy" and that the variations in and between generic cycles can be explained by it.

We would probably all agree that *The Beverly Hillbillies* belongs to the genre known as situation comedy. Very few books have been written about situation comedy and none about *The Beverly Hillbillies*. This is the zero degree of unworthiness. The one book devoted entirely and solely to sitcom is Rick Mitz's *Great TV Sitcom Book*.⁶ It is essentially a large coffee-table book abundantly illustrated with photographs. Overall, the book is sociologically interesting in that it represents what gets written about television and certainly about situation comedy. Nonetheless, the interest of the book resides in its explicit though inadequate use of the concept of genre. This is not so surprising, as other books on popular phenomena also seem spontaneously to adopt the genre approach. For example, Will Wright's *Sixguns and Society* (westerns) and Gary Gerani's *Fantastic Television* (science fiction) also root their observations in a generic understanding of the object of study.⁷ Why they should turn to this methodology is a moot point. Perhaps it is the popular appropriation of what is seen as "scientific" structuralism. Perhaps it is only the mirror image of television's own institutional organization around the necessity of genre. Whatever the reasons, and whatever the value of the generic approach, it remains fraught with serious theoretical difficulties that must be negotiated before this approach can be said to be of any use. Most writers do not successfully negotiate these difficulties.

The Problem of Content

The greatest danger of all lies in the conflation of genre with content. It is often thought that genres can be defined on the basis of their content: a western is a western because it contains horses, guns, cowboys. As Mitz states: "A sitcom has its own special set of characteristics. . . . There's [*sic*] the credits, then a commercial, then the show, then a commercial, then more of the show, then more commercials, then a short 'tag,' then the closing credits. . . . There's the sit—the things that happen—and the com—the laughs that, hopefully, come out of the sit."⁸ Here, Mitz's emphasis is placed on the content of the show. He refers to the sit and the com, the commercials, the show, the tag, the credit sequence, all elements that refer us to content. The problem with content is that it can cut across genres. A cowboy can be in a documentary, a horse in a sitcom (*Mr. Ed*), a gun in a cop show, and so on. This is the single, most monumental error of those who would adopt genre theory. It rests on a fundamental misunderstanding of the institution of which genre is a component. How then can we define genre?

Whenever we look at a western, for example, the most studied genre, we realize that it is not exactly like everything else we can see on television or at the movies. We define it by difference. We begin, then, by positing a background against which are played out a number of differences, and which gives these differences their meaning. The answer to what constitutes difference is what gives us the notion of genre.

Usually, the difference of the western is answered as follows: the western is different from the nonwestern because of its subject matter (the settlement of the western United States between 1860 and 1880, order versus disorder, civilization versus barbarity), because of its treatment of the subject matter (use of space and natural elements, actors whose demeanor suggests ruggedness), and because of its supposed effects (reaffirmation of the triumph of good over evil, pride, patriotism). It is clear, however, that the important element is the second: the treatment of the subject matter. If the settlement of the western United States were not treated with a particular use of space and nature, with the establishment of specific types of hierarchies between all the show's elements, then it would not be a western but possibly a documentary.

It is usually argued that the manner in which subject matter is treated constitutes a convention and that certain conventions signify certain genres. And yet, as with content, the same conventions can cut across generic boundaries. The good guy can get the girl in any genre, black and white can symbolize good and evil in any context, and so on. The definition of genre as a bundle of conventions remains unsatisfactory because it does not get away from the conflation of genre and content, and ends up either imposing an a priori category or turning genre into an ahistorical and transcultural essence. Let me explain.

Conventions are the element upon which most genre theory fastens as definitive of the very concept of genre. If we say that the western is characterized by X and Y conventions, we have, besides returning to the level of content, selected out a number of arbitrary characteristics and said that all objects exhibiting these characteristics will be westerns. What is the justification for selecting those characteristics and not others? There is none. A given choice of characteristics can only be justified on the basis of preexisting conceptions of what the western is. That is to say, in order to select those characteristics and in order to know that they are the definitive ones, we must already have a definition of the genre before the selection occurs. There is no necessary link between the category (western) and its characteristics (whichever conventions we may choose) other than that we have chosen to see a link. To proceed in this manner says more about the selecting agency than it does about the object of study. This then constitutes an a priori category.

In order to deny the charge of imposing an a priori category on the genre, it is sometimes argued that such categories are not arbitrary but are in fact derived from actual observation. The "actual observation" sends us even deeper into content analysis and totally fails to answer the question of why the observer actually observed some characteristics and not others. Nonetheless, it is argued that any category naturally groups dissimilar objects and that, when the same dissimilar objects are found together time and again, they form a category and thereby become similar objects. One of the problems with this argument is that categories are never natural and are always constructed, so to say that a category naturally groups anything is simply naïve. Furthermore, such a category, if it could be said to exist, could only be applied to a closed system for, if a category were observed to contain all the usual dissimilar objects save one, or one too many, then it would cease to be the category in question. To say, therefore, that all westerns share certain characteristics is to imply that all westerns have been produced and that no new ones will ever be produced. This statement is essential lest a new western introduce a new characteristic and thereby destroy the existing category. However, claiming that all westerns share certain characteristics also implies that should any new western ever be produced, it will somehow partake of the essential nature of all previous westerns. If one begins to define the category "western" as soon as the first western is produced, then either the category contains only that one western or it is constantly being destroyed and modified as a category in order to accommodate all the new westerns that bring new elements into play. Or else, all those other "things" are not really westerns. Since, obviously, all westerns may not yet have been produced, we are not dealing with a closed system and such a category (the western) cannot yet exist.

To avoid such a logical obstacle, it is usually argued that a category such as the western exists above and beyond all the specific instances that have been or are yet to be produced; that is to say, there exists an *essence* of the western. Bazin argued along precisely those lines when he posited the existence of a "superwestern" from which all other westerns derived and of whose essence they all partook.[9] How did Bazin know a film was a western? Because it partook of the essence of westerns. What was the essence of westerns? It was composed of the mass of all western films. The essence justified the corpus and the corpus justified the essence. Bazin began by assuming the existence of that which he set out to prove and then, upon having discovered that which he had constructed in the first place, congratulated his logic for having been so effective. We are then arguing that all westerns share some common third element, across all their similarities and dissimilarities, that marks them unmistakably as westerns. This third element has to be some ideal-perfect state of the genre that all specific instances of the genre only approximate to a greater or lesser degree. This establishes genres as a tautological essence and mystifies them more than it explains them. In fact, by essentializing them, it places them beyond the realm of explanation.

The Problem of the Sitcom

If we were to take all this and apply it to the sitcom, what would we call its subject matter, which distinguishes it from the nonsitcom, what would be its treatment of that subject matter, and what would be its presumed effects? The difficulty with using the sitcom as an example can be seen immediately. It would be fairly easy to state the supposed effect of the sitcom: laughter, and the feeling that all is well with the world, that our problems are not that important, and that they are not insurmountable. It might even be fairly easy to say what the treatment of the subject matter is: the resolution of conflict in the mode of humor. We would be rather hard-pressed, however to say what the subject matter or pretext of the sitcom is. Is it zany, exaggerated, or eccentric characters? Not necessarily. *Leave It to Beaver, Father Knows Best, Family Ties, My Three Sons,* and *The Brady Bunch* are hardly notable for the eccentricity or outrageousness of their characters. On the contrary, they, like most sitcoms, insist on the utter normality of their characters. Is it a certain type of situation? Not necessarily. Sitcoms have been set in prisoner of war camps (*Hogan's Heroes*), in police stations (*Barney Miller, Car 54, Where Are You?*), and in other historical eras (*Happy Days, Laverne and Shirley, It's About Time*). Is it the presence of certain types of conflict? Possibly, but one would be hard pressed to argue that the conflicts of *Gilligan's Island, Mork and Mindy,* and *Maude* were of the same order or intensity, or concerned with the same themes or issues, or even, at times, worth calling conflicts. And at any rate, are any of these elements—zany characters, situations, conflict—specific to situation comedy? Hardly. In fact, the subject matter of sitcoms is very difficult to define, and when we come to it, it will retroactively redefine many of the other categories we shall have been using.

All this might seem to add up to a convincing argument for the dismissal of the concept of genre: it is tautological, essentialist, a priorist, content-laden, and unspecific. These are genuine dangers, but they spring from a misunderstanding of the institution of television and not from some inherent flaw in the concept of genre. What I want to draw attention to is the question of treatment, the way in which the elements of a genre are handled. *Genres are ways of organizing, regulating, and hierarchizing themes, signifiers, and discourses.* To reject genre on the basis of the objections raised above is to misunderstand the institution of which genre is a regulator. For though these are serious dangers, they stem from a misuse of the notion of genre. They stem from a belief that genre is a reified category. They fail to see genre in relationship to the large institution of television. Instead of seeing genre as a feature of the institution, they try to make genre exist absolutely, independently of the institution. How does the institution of television work, what is characteristic of it? Why should its manifestations be genres?

Institution

Television as an institution is a highly complex phenomenon. It is perhaps first and foremost an industry, with all the problems of specialization, capital, technology, production, and distribution that implies. As an industry, however, it is crucially dependent upon audience appreciation for its very survival. Indeed, if audiences do not watch the shows offered, the shows become unprofitable, and the institution must ultimately cease production altogether.

The problem for the institution of television is to link its output to audience approval, to get the audiences somehow to want to watch its shows. This is not necessarily an easy task to accomplish, as the enormous number of flops attests. And obviously the production of desirable shows does not happen in a pure or unmediated manner. It is subject to the constraints of competition, of habit, of the socially acceptable, and so on.

Television, furthermore, like any institution, produces a discourse. That is to say, in an ordered and regular manner it constructs representations. The content of its representations can vary enormously but the manner of their construction is consistent. It is this regularity or redundancy that is a discourse. For example, television sitcom can include everything from *I Love Lucy* to *All in the Family*, and within that range any number of contradictory and even antagonistic positions can be assumed. Yet, across these various specific instances, there are certain invariants:

(1) The same tropes reappear. This can be something as banal as the physical appearance of the characters, the necessity of a funny look or gesture.

(2) The same ways of setting up arguments or points to be resolved recur.

(3) The same mode of address (wit) recurs.

(4) The same way of imagining a situation that will be both funny and significant recurs; hence the necessity of establishing a homeostatic situation with well-defined, nonevolving main characters who nonetheless encounter an endless stream of minor, outside characters.

(5) The same relationship between the product (sitcom) and the institution (television) recurs; the various products must all achieve the same goal; hence, the same mode of address.

(6) The same relationship between the product and the empirical reality it is said to represent recurs. The same theory of representation is at work in all sit-

coms; the way reality is thought to look and operate is heavily coded into every aspect of the representation, from the construction of narrative space to the definition of character types.

(7) Ultimately the same conception of the audience recurs. The discourse of the institution of television, which, like all discourses, is intended for someone, systematically arranges, orchestrates, and constitutes its audience through its construction of representations.

In a social context, however, in which no constraints compel television viewing, it is necessary that television as an industry produce products that will provide some form of satisfaction to large numbers of people. Therefore, though on the one hand the television industry seeks to produce shows for profit, it must also simultaneously produce a certain pleasure in the viewer. The viewer must want to watch television, and the television program must, to a certain extent, meet the viewer's wish.

Furthermore the viewer's past experience of television will inform his future choice of programming and future viewing patterns. If the industry failed to produce pleasure, the viewer would be unwilling to watch, and without the viewer's attention, the television industry would be unable to sell commercial time and hence unable to maintain itself. It must present itself, institutionally, as something desirable. Television must present itself as a body to be loved. All its products must attempt to produce pleasure such that the pleasure of the past will be inducement for the pleasure of the future. Clearly, then, for television to be successful, to establish itself as an industry with a public wanting its product, it must get the audience to like it. And the best way to do that is to have the audience internalize and expect the repeated experience of pleasure. This process occurs over time and is therefore a historical internalization of the institution by the audience.

The institutionalization of television occurred quite rapidly because the audience had already internalized the experience of pleasure from movies, radio, novels, and so on. The institutional, economic, and psychological structures upon which television depends were already largely in place by the time it was introduced. Naturally, television inflected those structures in its own way and as a function of the constraints that surrounded it. Television brought certain tropes and devices together into configurations that began to acquire, or had already acquired from earlier institutional settings, standardized meanings that came to be expected and recognized. The persona of Walter Cronkite is a good example of how a specific configuration of personal style, institutional setting, and the constraints of journalistic professionalism come to be stabilized, generalized, recognized, and expected. These configurations, which provided forms of stabilization and coherence, also produced enough pleasure and found sufficient resonance within viewers, for whatever reasons, for them to want to watch these configurations again and again, thereby making it profitable for the institution to repeat them again and again.

One of the most successful inflections of the institution was the production of genres. Different segments of the audience responded more or less favorably to certain configurations. It was possible to refine these configurations and, in the process, attract viewers willing to attend to them because they offered a special type of satisfaction. Genres appear out of this process of specialization. A genre is a highly specialized configuration requiring an equally specialized viewer who knows how to expect pleasure from it. And though the genre may fragment the market, it also strengthens it. Those viewers not likely to watch a soap opera might watch a detective story instead.

The institution, then, in the sense given it by Christian Metz in *The Imaginary Signifier,*[10] is not just a technology or an industry but also a set of mental or psychological practices that are, to a certain extent, an internalized mirror reflection of the outside institution. The history of American prime-time network television, which arguably represents one of the most successful attempts at historical internalization, is, in fact—with its adoption of the ideology of realism, its insistence on continuous flow, the dominance of narrative as a form for virtually everything, a television star system, the fragmentation into genres, and the development of highly specialized production processes—a collection of strategies designed to increase the viewer's pleasure. "Like cinema, television is not only a set of economic practices or meaningful products (but) also a constantly fluctuating series of signifying processes, a 'machine' for the production of meanings and positions, or rather positions for meaning; a machine for the regulation of the orders of subjectivity." [11]

In other words, it is an institution constituted at the site of the intersection among several discourses, strategies, positions, and interests, but also inflecting these and producing its own. What every institution does by virtue of the historical internalization of its discourses is to provide meanings and subjects for those meanings, literally positions for meaning. And those meanings and subject positions are imbedded in and constituted through and through by *narrative.*

Television produces endlessly, across the totality of its output, countless stories—tales that may be funny or tragic or exemplary or slices-of-life. In this respect it is hardly different from the other cultural institutions of the current social formation. Everything on television is given narrative form, that is, the successive posing and resolution of enigmas. Even this chapter is structured as a narrative, with an original enigma (what's wrong with sitcom studies?), followed by its eventual resolution. Sports events are the confrontation of opposing camps, and the resolution of their conflict is offered as narrative closure. Newscasts are structured as the telling and retelling of the day's events. Educational programming is usually presented as the posing and subsequent resolution of an enigma. Even commercials are routinely constructed as microscenarios. Narrative is the massively dominant form of television, and one can say of television exactly what Stephen Neale says of cinema:

> The focus of the cinematic institution, of its industrial, commercial and ideological practices, of the discourses it circulates, is narrative. What mainstream cinema produces as its commodity is narrative cinema, cinema as narrative. Hence, at a general social level, the system of narration adopted by mainstream cinema serves as the very currency of cinema itself, defining the horizon of its aesthetic and cinematic possibilities, providing the measure of cinematic "literacy" and intelligibility. Hence, too, narrative is the primary instance and instrument of the regulatory processes that mark and define the ideological function of the cinematic institution as a whole.[12]

It is my contention that television, for a variety of reasons having to do with its greater availability, its insertion within the family, and its greater turnover of images, has in North America taken over the position here assigned by Neale to the cinema. As for narrative, it may be defined as

> a process of transformation of the balance of elements that constitute its pretext: the interruption of an initial equilibrium and the tracing of the dispersal and refiguration of its elements. The system of narration characteristic of the cinema is one which orders that dispersal and refiguration in a particular way, so that dispersal, disequilibrium is both maintained and contained in figures of symmetry, of balance, its elements finally re-placed in a new equilibrium whose achievement is the condition of narrative closure.[13]

The difference between genres, that which characterizes them, will then reside at least partially in how they conceive the initial equilibrium—what discourses make it up, in what order or sphere they situate it—in what disrupts the equilibrium—and in how a new equilibrium is achieved. *Genres, then, are specific ways in which equilibrium is conceived, disrupted, and replaced.* They are, quite literally, regulators of televisual narrative.

We may turn now to any sitcom to see where this concept of genre gets us. What is the nature of the original equilibrium in, for example, *The Beverly Hillbillies*? Here, the equilibrium is situated in the social order. The discourses that make it up have manifestly to do with class, wealth, and modes of social interaction; in short, those discourses that go to make up the social order of most television shows, the look of normality. The disruption is then provided by the arrival of outsiders clearly marked as belonging to another social class into a world of which they are entirely ignorant. Here, then, we have the confrontation of two discursive hierarchies and the question becomes, How will these people insert themselves into their new class?

If in *The Beverly Hillbillies* the disruption is figured by the intrusion of a new discursive hierarchy, this is not necessarily so in other genres. In the western, for example, the equilibrium is usually figured by some state of society disrupted specifically by violence: Indians disrupted by white men, settlers by Indians or bad guys, farmers by ranchers, and so on. In the musical and the melodrama, the disruption is figured by the irruption of desire. Stephen Neale states:

> For example, in the western, the gangster film and the detective film, disruption is always figured literally—as physical violence. Disequilibrium is inaugurated by violence which marks the process of the elements disrupted and which constitutes the means by which order is finally (re)established. In each case, equilibrium and disequilibrium are signified specifically in terms of Law, in terms of the presence/absence, effectiveness/ineffectiveness of legal institutions and their agents. In each too, therefore, the discourses mobilised in these genres are discourses about crime, legality, justice, social order, civilisation, private property, civic responsibility and so on. Where they differ from one another is in the precise weight given to the discourses they share in common, in the inscription of these discourses across more specific generic elements, and in their imbrication across the codes specific to cinema.[14]

In *The Beverly Hillbillies,* and indeed in situation comedy as a genre, equilibrium and disequilibrium are signified specifically in terms of social class. The situation comedy as a genre may then be said to rest upon the encounter of dissonant or incompatible discursive hierarchies. Each hierarchy mobilizes different values, different codes, different modes of social interaction, different semantic fields, different ideas about sex, art, religion, and politics. These latter can be said to be the discourses that make up the discursive hierarchies. The disruption, then, occurs and operates in terms of the discursive hierarchies themselves. Whereas in the western disruption happens in terms of violence, and in the musical and melodrama it happens in terms of desire, neither violence nor desire is a discourse. They are events or forces that cause an activation or a reorganization of the discourses involved. In the situation comedy, disruption and discourse are conflated; it is the discourse itself that is the disruption. And that is the specificity of the situation comedy, to organize disruption in terms of discourse. This further specifies the difficulty in establishing the subject matter of situation comedy. That subject matter is discourse itself. This in turn can cause us to view the "subject matter" of other genres in terms of discourses that are mobilized and that come into conflict with each other.

Disruption as discourse or discourse as disruption can take two forms. It can set into play forms of behavior or of linguistic usage that become nonsense and gibberish (Lucille Ball, Jerry Lewis, the Marx Brothers), or it can set into play forms of behavior and action that are simply incommensurate with the situation (*The Beverly Hillbillies,* Charlie Chaplin). These two forms of humor are simply what have been called the screwball or crazy comedy and the social comedy. They have also been called American and British humor, respectively. As Stephen Neale again states: "Crazy comedy tends to articulate order and disorder across the very mechanisms of discourse, producing incongruities, contradictions and illogicalities at the level of language and code, while social (situation) comedy, on the other hand, tends to specify its disorder as the disturbance of socially institutionalised discursive hierarchies. It is important to stress that these two forms are indeed only tendencies." [15]

The Beverly Hillbillies, with its love of puns and sight gags, draws on both types of comedy. Most sitcoms fit somewhere between the two extremes of discursive disruption. *I Love Lucy,* for example, tends towards the screwball comedy. When Lucy gets her head caught in a vase, for example, the disruption is figured in terms of incongruous or illogical behavior. In fact, it is possible to see screwball comedy in "linguistic" terms. Elements are brought into contiguity and turned away from their intended or expected use, much as in the word plays of screwball comedy. The elements (Lucy, the vase) are discrete units inscribed into new semantic fields much as the dialogue between the Clampetts and any outsiders. *Barney Miller* tends more towards the social comedy. Discourses of law, justice, and morality, which are very close to those held or believed in by the viewers, are brought into continuity with individuals or institutions who order those discourses differently. In *Barney Miller,* furthermore, the prisoners are usually "crazies." This allows the discursive hierarchies to remain closed to each other and dispenses with the need for any of the characters to gain experience by integrating elements of another discursive hierarchy into their own, and thereby allowing the basic situation to continue. *Leave It to Beaver* is clearly the encounter of dissonant discursive hierarchies: that of the children and that of the adults. The children gain experience but always inflect it through their own discourses such that it remains childish. Only Beaver's biological aging determined the end of that situation. *Mork and Mindy* is likewise clearly about the encounter of radically other discursive hierarchies, though the emphasis is again heavily on the screwball elements. Like Beaver, Mork gains experience, but only through the filter of his own discourse, again allowing the situation to remain essentially unchanged.

So, whereas other approaches to situation comedy attempt to define it in terms of its antecedents (vaudeville, radio, film, theater), or in terms of its types of humor (as in Freud, Bergson, and the like), it is my contention that situation comedy can be dealt with and defined from within genre theory in terms of the discourses it sets into play. I would further contend that specific instances of situation comedy can be specified by the precise weight given each of the discourses in play and that generic cycles are largely explicable in terms of the weight given specific discourses in specific socioeconomic and institutional circumstances.

It is a narrative necessity of situation comedy that the "situation" remain unchanged. If the program is to be repeated week after week, the characters and their mode of interaction must not be allowed to evolve. Were they to acquire experience, then evolution would occur and the show could not continue. The ideal situation, therefore, is one that is both open and closed at the same time: open to outsiders or to other discursive hierarchies but closed to experience or to the modification of discursive hierarchies. This is usually handled by establishing a character or group of characters (the stars) whose discursive hierarchy is the one that will be repeated again and again. The privileged site for the establishment of a discursive hierarchy is the family, both literally and metaphorically. There are the "real" families of *Happy Days, Father Knows Best,* and *Donna Reed,* and the "metaphorical" families of *M*A*S*H, Hogan's Heroes,* and *Taxi.* But then, the family is probably the dominant metaphor for all North American television. In this, the sitcom shares an important element with other genres. Nonetheless, once the discursive hierarchy that is to be repeated weekly has been established, the ideal situation requires that it come into contact with other discursive hierarchies. Narratively, this is handled through a device such as the family or the place of work, wherein a number of repeatable characters can come into contact with nonmembers. Usually, on a narrative level, the situation manages never to be resolved through some "natural" or diegetically motivated obstacle: Hawkeye will never leave Korea because of the army, Gilligan will never get off the island because of a number of accidents, and Uncle Martin will never fix his spaceship because the parts are not available on earth. Narratively, then, a small closure is provided to each week's episode while never providing a larger narrative closure to the fundamental situation.

Sitcoms use a number of strategies to preclude the possibility of the characters acquiring experience and thereby altering the fundamental situation. *The Beverly Hillbillies,* for example, frequently fails to provide even a microclosure to each weekly episode such that any number of questions (what happened to Elly May's boyfriend? what happened to the horse Jed bought? what happened to the man who fell into the swimming pool?) remain unresolved. The narrative has no real ending, so the question of experience cannot even be posed. Also, because of their discursive hierarchy, the Clampetts systematically and tenaciously invest a private semantic field; they literally do not understand what is said to them and therefore cannot acquire experience. Likewise, other characters do not understand what the Clampetts say to them, and the "situation" can therefore remain stable.

The narrative nonclosure of *The Beverly Hillbillies* also dispenses with the need for *vraisemblance* (real-seemingness). *The Beverly Hillbillies* makes little or no attempt to claim that it is a faithful representation of reality. In this respect, it is significantly different from many other so-called "relevant" sitcoms that not only make that claim but use it in order to establish some type of value. *M*A*S*H* and *All in the Family,* for example, are clearly intended to have a beneficial effect on the viewer such that the viewer will be a better person after having watched those shows.

The "Relevant" Sitcom

This raises briefly the issue of the so-called "relevant" sitcom. Many writers have noted that sitcoms in the 1970s seemed to become more socially aware, seemed to deal with much more delicate issues, and to deal with them more sensitively. There can be no doubt that the sitcoms of the 1970s were experienced differently by their audiences than were the sitcoms of the 1960s. Indeed, it is the opposite that would be surprising. The real problem with the so-called "relevant" sitcom lies in whether it represents some sort of qualitative shift, as some writers have suggested.

A very good sense of the newness and importance of the "relevant" sitcom is provided by Horace Newcomb when, comparing the old comedy of the 1960s to the new comedy of the 1970s, he says:

> When the problems encountered by the families become socially or politically
> significant (the sitcom) form can be expanded. The frame of the ordered world is
> shattered. Families find themselves living in the world of the present without
> magical solutions and, to some extent, without the aid of peaceful and laughing

love. Comedy, in the form of *All in the Family* or *Maude* or *M*A*S*H*, *is* changed into the perfect vehicle for biting social commentary. Clearly this has long been the case with traditional comic forms . . . For television, however, the sense of satire and commentary was long in coming. When it did begin to present answers that were not totally acceptable at the mass cultural level, a new stage had been reached.[16]

The idea that the new sitcoms were biting social commentary beyond that which was generally acceptable gives a good sense of the excitement and interest that they generated. It might, furthermore, seem that the relevant sitcom, by virtue of its very relevance, somehow breaks with the type of generic considerations discussed so far, as though relevance really did break with discursive hierarchies by having some sort of direct hold on reality. There is, however, a slight problem with the concept of relevance.

When people talk about the relevance of sitcom, they are invariably talking about its content and not about its form or any specifically televisual trait it might possess. The very issue of relevance returns us, therefore, once again to the problem of content. Relevance is hardly a defining characteristic of sitcom. News shows, police dramas, documentaries, made-for-television movies all lay claim to relevance. Relevance cuts across genre, it does not constitute it.

Nonetheless, it is maintained that the "relevant" situation comedy marks a new stage in television comedy because it is socially and politically aware. And yet, does not a generic study of sitcom suggest that every sitcom, precisely because it is concerned vitally with class, is already socially and politically aware? Obviously, the distinction being argued between *M*A*S*H* and *Father Knows Best* is that the former is conscious of its class implications whereas the latter merely acts them out. But it seems to me that the question of awareness in sitcoms is largely a question of fashion, and that if some sitcoms are indeed more conscious of their liberalism, it is as part of an attempt to capture an audience. The extent to which all sitcoms deal with social and political issues can be measured by the frequent condemnations of sitcoms. There have also always been those who have objected to the inanity of *I Love Lucy* or of *Gilligan's Island* precisely because of its sociopolitical implications. But this again returns us to content analysis and effects studies. Does *Gilligan's Island* lull viewers into a false sense of happiness and deaden them to the really important issues of the day; and does *All in the Family* encourage bigotry or not; and does *M*A*S*H* glorify war or denounce it? The most sophisticated response possible is that for some viewers under some circumstances, they do, and for others they do not. Indeed, the extent to which social relevance is merely another discursive hierarchy, subject to infinite permutations as are all discourses, can be deduced from the emergence of shows such as *Family Ties* and others that attempted to make traditional conservative values seem cool and fashionable. *Family Ties* is about hippies of the 1960s whose children in the 1980s turn out to be right-wing Republicans. The liberalism of the 1970s is the conservatism of the 1980s, and both types of social awareness are equally "relevant." The only difference is that the relevance of the 1970s came to liberal conclusions on social issues whereas the relevance of the 1980s came to conservative conclusions. The discursive hierarchy of relevance remains quite unperturbed by its specific content; it continues to construct its arguments in the same manner.

It is ultimately more fruitful to see the emergence of the so-called "relevant" sitcom as an industrial strategy. People with somewhat different concerns from those of the 1960s came to positions of prominence within the television institution and discovered that it was still possible to ensure the institution's survival by a reordering of its discourses. Of course, television has always worked that way. Whether this makes the sitcom more relevant is debatable. The presumed relevance of modern sitcom is but another effect of the institution of television, part of the way in which it maintains its currency as the most important and relevant medium of our time and its purchase on our attention. Advertising uses exactly the same content and concerns as socially relevant sitcom. Is it therefore more relevant? The more important question to ask is whether the sitcoms of the 1970s structure their humor differently, whether they use a different mode of address, whether they conceive of disruption and equilibrium in new terms. Clearly, they do not. *All in the Family, M*A*S*H,* and *Maude,* to name but three, all conceive of disruption in class terms. This is the whole point about Archie Bunker: that he is a blue-collar worker. And also the point behind Maude: that she is an overbearing liberal. And one would be hard put to ignore or deny the importance of the class origins of the various characters on *M*A*S*H,* each of whom is stereotypically middle class and good, or upper class and boorish, or socially mobile and untrustworthy.

Relevance is merely another discursive hierarchy that has come to prominence because of a certain historically contingent articulation of the personal, the social, and the institutional. It will no doubt change as that articulation changes. At most, one might wish to detect a generic cycle built around the prominence of the discursive hierarchy of relevance, but it would be an error to claim any qualitative shift in sitcom on the basis of that discursive hierarchy.

So far, we have said that situation comedies mobilize a discourse on class. The other extremely important discourse they mobilize has to do with sexuality.

All situation comedy, inasmuch as it is concerned with discursive hierarchies, is also concerned with sexuality, the latter being one of the dominant modes of manifestation of class difference. Sexuality is usually presented in its most highly domesticated form: the leading characters are married, have been married, or envisage marriage as a likely outcome in their lives. The discourse of sexuality in situation comedy constitutes it as necessarily heterosexual and necessarily unconsumable outside of matrimony. This is a discourse of sexuality as it is spoken in many of the dominant institutions of the present social formation. As Stephen Neale says, "Social comedy proper proceeds by mapping the field of a socio-discursive order, a field whose nodal points tend constantly to be those of class and sexuality.[17]

Sexuality as a discourse comes into contact with the discourse of class, and each provides a means of manifestation to the other. The social class of the Cleavers in *Leave It to Beaver* is clearly indicated by the very proper relations between Mr. and Mrs. Cleaver, but also by the coming to sexual awareness of both Wally and Beaver in the most hackneyed boy-meets-girl terms. Indeed, in one episode in which Eddie Haskell gets Wally to talk to a girl who works at a movie theater, Wally's mother complains that she does not want Wally picking up girls at movie theaters because "this girl works" and is therefore of a lower social order. The same can be said of *Happy Days* or of *The Bob Newhart Show* or of *All in the Family*. In fact, the only way in which sexuality can be explicitly mentioned in situation comedy is in the tone of amused embarrassment. To mention it is already to be funny. Shows in which there is no married couple have characters who wish they were (*Laverne and Shirley, Rhoda, Cheers*), who have been married (*The Doris Day Show, Petticoat Junction, Andy Griffith*), or for whom marriage is a natural possibility (*The Courtship of Eddie's Father, The Many Loves of Dobie Gillis*). Always, sexuality bespeaks class origin. One of the most striking of recent examples is to be found in the character of the Fonz on *Happy Days*. The Fonz's sexual prowess is explicitly valorized not only by the fact that various women are perpetually at his beck and call but also by his manliness and knowledge of things technical (his motorcycle, his ability to make jukeboxes and telephones work on command). His overt sexuality is also a clear indication of his class origin. The Fonz is then slowly integrated into the camp of the "normal" kids on the show, into middle-class mores. Indeed, in the famous Christmas Day episode in which the Cunninghams invite the Fonz to spend Christmas Day with them so that he will not be alone, the show ends with the family gathered around the piano singing Christmas carols and the Fonz saying: "I love middle-class families." As he is integrated into middle-class values, his sexual potency undergoes a corresponding decline: he is seen to be not always successful, to be insecure, and to be rejected by women who are as cool as he (Pinky Tuscadero); and finally, he too was married in the 1982–83 season.

The "relevant" sitcoms also are organized in terms of the discourse of sexuality. Many of the characters of *M*A*S*H* have a relationship to sexuality that bespeaks their class origin. Radar's perennial virginity refers explicitly to his rural origin and innocence about the ways of the world. B.J.'s faithfulness to his wife is indissociable from his dream of one day owning property and consequently from his very proper middle-class background. The mutual lusting of Frank Burns and Major Hoolihan, as well as the major's subsequent unhappy marriage, are manifestations of their somehow unseemly desire for class mobility. And of course Klinger's constant transvestism, besides being a ploy to evade the army, is also an expression of his inability, because of his ethnic and class background, to abide by the rules of an authoritarian institution. An enormous number of *Maude* episodes were constructed around questions of sexual appropriateness, and of course the whole plot of *The Mary Tyler Moore Show* was dependent on the idea of a young woman setting out in the world in order to break sexual stereotypes. *Barney Miller* is forever parading cops in drag who are sent out to catch various muggers and rapists in the park, and the only women who appear on that show are either sexually repressed or sexually unsatisfied. It is one of *Barney Miller*'s standby jokes to have a female cop be hurt because a rapist found the male cop in drag more appealing. And of course much of the story line of *All in the Family* was bound up with Archie's disapproval of his daughter's marriage to a man who was of a different ethnic and class origin. The humor was to be generated by the clash of their dissonant discursive hierarchies with their attendant highly divergent attitudes toward politics, sex, religion, and so on.

In *The Beverly Hillbillies,* the discourse of sexuality is manifested literally as a crisis of gender identity, perhaps as a metaphor of the characters' class identity crisis. Before proceeding, however, it is perhaps interesting to note that *The Beverly Hillbillies* in particular, and sitcoms in general, seem to contain all those elements—authority and sexuality—to which the television writing discussed earlier was trying to give shape. It is as if there were a continuity from television programs to television writing to this particular article, with each attempting to give shape to class and sexuality in a particular manner.

Let us now consider the discourse of sexuality. To begin with, the very bodies of the hillbillies are visibly marked as different. Not only do they dress differently, but they are almost freaks of nature. Elly May, for example, is designated as being excessively nubile: not only does she pop the buttons on her shirt, but she is also consistently marked out as the most desirable woman on the show. Like Jethro, she is also remarkably strong. Jethro is not only unusually strong, but he is also indicated as being unusually big for his age, and a prodigious eater. What he has in strength, however, he more than lacks in intelligence. As for Granny, she is not only tremendously old, having lived through the Civil War, but also incredibly spry and feisty. Jed is, in fact, the only one of the hillbillies to be unmarked by physical abnormality. And he is also the only one who comes to any understanding or appreciation of urban life and who tries to come to terms with it without compromising his values.

The crisis of gender seems to superimpose itself upon the physical difference of the hillbillies. Elly May, though she is nubile and a girl, also dresses and acts like a boy. In herself, she combines excessive nubility and affirmed boyishness. As for Jethro, he knows nothing about sex. Jed is constantly saying about him: "Someday I'm gonna have to have a long talk with that boy." Though he wants a girlfriend, he does not know how to get one (his attempts are invariably disastrous), and whenever a girl expresses a liking for him, he is mortified with embarrassment. In himself, he combines great potency with utter impotence. He even crosses gender boundaries as he has a sister, Jethrine, who is in every respect similar to him and who is played, for obvious laughs, by the same actor.

Granny and Jed operate as inverse functions of each other. Though she has never remarried, Granny effectively occupies the position of surrogate mother, and though he is now widowed, Jed occupies the symbolic position of father, even to Jethro, who is his nephew. Both combine parenthood with celibacy. What appears to be spoken here is a discourse on the proper public conduct of sexuality, which is a combination of chastity and the denial of sexuality, something safe enough for even the most impressionable child viewer to watch.

The only other person whose body is visibly marked by signifiers of difference is Miss Jane Hathaway. She is, for all intents and purposes—by her association with the bank, her efficiency, insight, and intelligence—a man who just happens to be a woman. She combines within herself a pronounced feminine desire with all the traits of masculinity, right down to her manner of dress and comportment. Interestingly, she is the only one of the nonhillbillies who is specifically accepted by the others as a member of the family and who comes to understand and even love them. She is forever defending them and decrying her boss's schemes to dupe them. Significantly, she is the only nonhillbilly whose body undergoes physical change similar to that of the hillbillies. Whenever someone must wear a ridiculous costume, or submit to one of Granny's haircuts, or whatnot, it is she. Difference is written right on to her body and she thereby crosses over into the camp of the hillbillies. *The Beverly Hillbillies* is perhaps one of the most striking examples of the discourses of class and sexuality at work in sitcoms. But to a very large extent, the way in which these two discourses serve as manifestations of each other is to be found in all sitcoms. Sexuality is usually inscribed onto the very bodies of the characters as class difference, and class difference finds its expression in sexuality. It is never an accident, for example, that so many sitcom characters are spouseless despite their explicit desire not to be so. This allows for all the possible modalizations of sexual relationships within the confines of what the institution of television will allow. Hawkeye's spouselessness is no more surprising than Doris Day's in her show or Diane Carroll's in hers. It allows the expression of an attitude toward sexuality that is itself exemplary of class origin.

So, from the mass of television writing to the content of situation comedy, the same themes recur: class, sexuality, authority, and modes of social interaction, but with markedly different emphases. In *The Beverly Hillbillies,* the discourse of sexuality is explicitly signaled as "the inscription of a disruption in the spatio-temporal scales governing the order of the 'human' and of 'nature,' producing figures such as giants—be they animals or humans—or, alternatively, homunculi, dwarfs, and so on." [18]

In other words, were *The Beverly Hillbillies* not a situation comedy, that is to say a genre in which discursive hierarchies themselves constituted the disruption, we could well be dealing with another genre altogether in which variations of the scales of the human and of nature also occur: the fantastic or the horror genre. It is, therefore, the presence of the discourses of class and sexuality, and the status of discourses as the agent of disruption, that specifies the situation comedy as a genre. In the fantastic or the horror genre, the discourse of class would be absent and would be replaced by a discourse of metaphysics.

Indeed, a metaphysical discourse is not entirely absent from *The Beverly Hillbillies.* Many objects, animals, and people are mistaken by the hillbillies for that which they are not. A pink flamingo is mistaken for a giant chicken, a croquet ball for an egg, and a camel for a horse. Spatiotemporal variations abound. Furthermore, Granny dabbles in black magic and on more than one occasion believes that she has transformed someone into an animal.

Besides the dominant discourses on class and sexuality, there are in *The Beverly Hillbillies* minor discourses on nature and on the metaphysical. It is perhaps the specificity of *The Beverly Hillbillies* that the discourses of class and sexuality figure not only the very disruption of the initial equilibrium but also that they are articulated across other minor discourses on nature and the metaphysical, and thence across spatiotemporal distortions. Other situation comedies could perhaps likewise be specified through the specific weight given to the discourses of class and sexuality and through their articulation across other minor discourses, which would have to be specified in each case. Generic cycles are then the relative recurrence of these minor discourses. Perhaps a generic cycle can be detected in 1960s sitcoms such as *I Dream of Jeannie, My Favorite Martian,* and *Bewitched,* all of which deal with the order of the metaphysical and with magic. In these, the metaphysical is more pronounced than in *The Beverly Hillbillies,* but it is also allied with questions of sexuality, class, and correct behavior. Perhaps there is a general discourse of 1960s sitcom that links the metaphysical to questions of class and sexuality. It might also be worthwhile to explore further the links between these themes and other television genres. It should not be overlooked that sitcoms such as *I Dream of Jeannie* explicitly link the metaphysical with technology, featuring both spaceflight and the genie's powers as two types of magic. What then could be the relationship between this and other genres more explicitly interested in technology (science fiction) and in the metaphysical (the fantastic)? And what then of other genres, such as news programming, which explicitly foreground their own technology and consistently display its limitless possibilities?

Perhaps we can also find another generic cycle more appropriate to the 1970s that links a didactic and moralizing attitude to questions of class and sexuality. Perhaps, on the basis of this one study, we can begin to identify other discourses at work in other genres and begin to see the surprising relationships between genres.

7

From Gauguin to *Gilligan's Island*

LAURA MOROWITZ

Videoculture, it has been argued, can recreate on a national, or even a global scale, the mystical unity possessed by primitive tribes.

—Frank Coppa, 1979 (xi)

"Unga bunga!"
—Gilligan,
1964

In episode no. 34 of *Gilligan's Island,* "Goodbye Old Paint,"[1] a Russian artist named Gregor Duvol is discovered living on the "deserted" island. After ten years of isolation from "Western civilization," he refuses to return. Greed (fostered by the actions of the castaways) convinces Duvol that he should try to resume life back in Russia. The episode ends, however, with Duvol still "stuck" on the island, with no immediate mode of rescue in sight. Curiously enough, the names of da Vinci, Picasso, Chagall, and Toulouse-Lautrec are uttered throughout the episode, but the one figure most clearly evoked by Duvol is never once mentioned: that of the nineteenth-century artist-gone-primitive Paul Gauguin. Even though Duvol paints Ginger's portrait as a Balinese dancer, the name of Gauguin is never referenced. Nor need it be. For in the themes, plots, and char-

A slightly different version of this chapter was originally published in the *Journal of Popular Film and Television* 26, no. 1 (spring 1998): 2–11. It has been reprinted here by permission of the publisher. The author thanks friends and colleagues who offered their insights, encouragement, and suggestions on this project: Maura M. Reilly, Jessica Falvo, Eric Schechter, Lori Weintrob, and Ariella Budick. Special thanks go to Maura for her thorough grammatical editing.

acters of *Gilligan's Island*, Gauguin is as powerfully present as if he had landed, paintbrush in hand, on the shore of that island.

Despite its facile plot lines and goofball humor, *Gilligan's Island*, the most syndicated television show in history, resonates with powerful post-Enlightenment artistic themes and obsessions. At its core (and central to its long-running appeal) are the quest for escape from Western civilization and the ultimate impossibility of achieving that goal. Indeed, the underlying structure of *Gilligan's Island* can be traced to Daniel Defoe's *Robinson Crusoe* (1719), to the imaginative novels of Jules Verne, and to the life and art of Paul Gauguin. Central to the novels are the themes of primitivism, the inability to leave behind the West, and the impulse to remake the world in the image of bourgeois society.

Just as central to the works and others in their genre lies the ubiquitous and undeniable theme of colonization. Entangled in the figures of primitivism and nostalgia is the potent urge to conquer and to bring "advanced" Western civilization to the farthest corners of the globe. In *Gilligan's Island* this theme is realized and figured in the medium of television itself. In contrast to earlier manifestations of the genre, *Gilligan's Island* parallels its content on a formal level, for during the years of its production (1964–66), television became a tool of "global conquest," of media imperialism. In its endless return of the same, its penetration of the world, and its creation of a "global village," television provided the medium for escapism and the yearning for distance that haunted the voyager of mysterious islands, tropical Edens, and false paradises.

The Lure of the Primitive

The lure of the primitive is part of culture, but the "call of the wild" reached a new height in the Western world of the late eighteenth century.[2] The Enlightenment project of spreading knowledge and reason unleashed a simultaneous longing for preindustrial life. To leave behind Western civilization, it was necessary to travel a great distance, in time or in space. The site of the escapist text—the dream, the work—must be distant, characterized by its Otherness.

In the works of Jules Verne, difference is figured through remote islands and the outermost reaches of space. In *The Mysterious Island* (1875), Verne pays direct homage to Defoe's story. But Verne's island is marked by the nineteenth-century longing for "purity." In contrast to Crusoe's stores of bullets and food supplies, the castaways on Lincoln Island can salvage no provisions and must learn to rebuild the world from scratch: "The imaginary heroes of Daniel Defoe, of Wyss, as well as Selkirk and Raynal,[3] were never in such absolute destitution.

But here, not any instrument whatever, not a utensil. From nothing they must supply themselves with everything." [4]

If Verne's novels rework Enlightenment texts such as *Robinson Crusoe,* they also point forward to *Gilligan's Island.* Pierre Macherey observed in an essay on Jules Verne that the underlying themes of Verne's novels are voyage, scientific invention, and colonization. [5] Such themes come to be embodied, respectively, in the characters of *Gilligan's Island:* the Skipper (voyage), the Professor (invention), and the Howells (colonization). Moreover, the trajectory of Verne's oeuvre from remote island to outer space is followed through in an animated series created by the show's producers in 1982. Titled *Gilligan's Planet,* the series premised that a NASA spacecraft had landed on the island, was reconstructed by the Professor, and accidentally landed the castaways on a distant planet. So, too, the shift in setting from Europe to the United States is foreshadowed and prepared by Verne's *Mysterious Island,* in which the castaways are escaped prisoners of war from Grant's army. Their ultimate goal is to turn the island into the property of the United States. [6]

Although it takes the form of a romantic quest for the self, the story of Gauguin is also a tale of escape, primitivism, the ideology of colonization, and the retreat from bourgeois civilization. [7] Tahiti was the terminus of Gauguin's endless journey (from Brittany, to Indochina, to Madagascar, to the Marquesas Islands) to the ever more "backward," the ever more distant. [8] Nor was Gauguin's choice of Tahiti purely fortuitous, as Abigail Solomon Godeau and others have shown. [9] Acquired as a colony by the French in 1881, Tahiti had been repeatedly portrayed as a sexual paradise, and one in which labor (and wages) were entirely unnecessary. Gauguin's letters abound with this vision of Tahiti:

> I am going soon to Tahiti, a small island in Oceania, where the material necessities of life can be had without money. . . . The Tahitian has only to lift his hands to gather his food, and in addition he never works. When in Europe men and women survive only after increasing labor, during which they struggle with convulsions of cold and hunger, a prey to misery, the Tahitians, on the contrary, happy inhabitants of the unknown paradise of Oceania, know only the sweetness of life. [10]

Thus Gauguin reverses the industriousness of Crusoe, whose endless labor is embodied formally in Defoe's novel through the densely worded descriptions and endless details of survival. The eighteenth-century faith in endless progress, in an almost systematic diligence, is replaced by the late-nineteenth-century longing for leisure. But along with the "sweetness of life," Gauguin's letters and journals tell of the bitterness of disappointment. No matter how far he goes, he is unable to escape. "The dream which enticed me to Tahiti was cruelly contradicted by the present. It is the Tahiti of another time that I love. . . . I quickly took my resolve: to leave Papeete, to distance myself further from the European center."[11] For all its abundance and fruitfulness, Gauguin's Tahiti is a place of loss. The remote island is always already inhabited by the greed and consumption of the West, by those who have come before to appropriate and spoil. The precious virgin island has always already been deflowered.

Gilligan's Island

A close analysis of *Gilligan's Island*—its conception, characters, plot, and production—reveals an intense reworking of the themes of progress and primitivism, imperialism and escape. With *Gilligan's Island* the themes leave the world of high art, literature, and the avant-garde to settle firmly within popular culture. The shift in medium (from the exhaustive prose of the novel, to the immediately grasped painting, to the effortless projection of the television screen) parallels the shift in value from eighteenth-century industriousness to the vacation ethic of the 1960s. The way home points not to Europe now, but to the very heart of mid-twentieth-century America.

In the 1950s and 1960s, television conquered the world.[12] Television sets increased from two hundred thousand to three million from 1940 to the 1970s. By the mid-1960s, Western Europe could count eighty thousand sets, while ninety-two percent of U.S. homes were equipped with at least one television. Powerfully symbolized by Armstrong's 1969 walk on the moon (which reached 723 million viewers in fifty countries), the literal colonizing of space took place simultaneously with the colonizing of the earth via videoculture.[13] Terms such as *cultural colonialism* and *electronic imperialism* were used to describe the ubiquity and speed with which television spread around the globe.

With the mounting conflicts and controversies of the 1960s, television became ever more escapist. Moreover, a backlash or rejection of the "bourgeois perfection" dominant in the 1950s sitcom, and symbolized by the patriarchal nuclear family, can be detected in the shows originating in the mid-1960s. Tellingly, *Leave It to Beaver* was canceled in 1963. Indeed, the shows of that period are characterized by a conspicuous lack of "normal" suburban families, who had become a rare (if not yet extinct) breed. Two distinct alternative patterns or strategies emerged.

On the one hand, a large number of shows were marked by the physical abandonment of (or flight from) bourgeois culture. A variety of rural oddities came to dominate prime time: the most popular show of the 1960s, *The Beverly Hillbillies,* as well as its country cousins, *Green Acres, Petticoat Junction, Andy Griffith,* and *Gomer Pyle.* The shows' rural retreats, demonstrating a rejection of urban life for a return to a more "deep-rooted" and "natural" existence, correspond to Gauguin's initial "escape" to the peasant countryside of Brittany.[14]

In the second pattern of shows, the bourgeois and suburban environment is maintained, but a decided break from "normality" has occurred. Under the surface, the families and characters of the shows are freaks, quite literally alien or nonhuman, although living in the sterile environment of the 1960s suburb. Shows that fall into this category include *The Munsters* and *The Addams Family* (both of which were canceled in 1966, the same year as *Gilligan's Island*), *Bewitched, I Dream of Jeannie,* and *My Favorite Martian.* The plots of these series often revolve around the nonhumans' failed attempts to conform to mainstream society; for the characters are ultimately exotic, challenging bourgeois normality from within.[15]

If the shows in both of those categories abandon and critique American middle-class culture, *Gilligan's Island* takes the notion further, leaving behind not only the suburbs, but in a far more radical turn, civilization itself.

First airing on CBS in 1964 and canceled three years later, *Gilligan's Island* would come to be the most repeated series in television history.[16] By 1971, the show was being syndicated to more than three dozen countries; by the 1980s, viewers in places as remote as Solomon's Island were familiar with the antics of the castaways. Dawn Wells, the actress who played Mary Anne, relates an anecdote about visiting Solomon's Island—a place without running water or electricity—and being astonished that she was recognized by the inhabitants for her role on the show.[17]

The brainchild of Sherwood Schwartz, the show was never a favorite of network executives, despite its consistently high ratings. Championed by the public, *Gilligan's Island* was routinely derided by critics, and its time slot moved three times in three years.

The show was sponsored by the corporate giants Proctor and Gamble and Phillip Morris (companies well known for expanding their global reach in the years following the series' demise).[18] In its first year, the show did so well that a "shipwreck party" was thrown in celebration at the CBS studio's center stage. Encouraged to dress in island wear, guests dined on Polynesian food and danced to exotic melodies. The highlight of the evening was a treasure hunt, with the winner receiving an all-expense-paid trip to Tahiti.[19]

Schwartz (whose favorite childhood book was *Robinson Crusoe*) intended the show to be an "allegory," a "social microcosm" from the very beginning. The show was first pitched to network executives in January 1963.[20] Whereas network executives pictured the island as a fantasy resort, with different guests arriving each week, this notion clashed with Schwartz's original conception. Schwartz related his idea: "Just as these seven people were on this little island, the nations of the world are all on Earth, which is a little island in space. And just as those Castaways learn to get along with each other, that's how the countries of the world eventually are going to have to get along with each other."[21]

From its inception, the show was meant to function as a global metaphor. Emerging from the discourse surrounding the space explorations of the 1960s, Earth could now be described as a "little island in space." Like its post-Enlightenment predecessors, *Gilligan's Island* shares the theme of contact between different peoples, the "shrinking" of the world, and a nationalist vision. Moreover, the title of the show implies appropriation; the island, linguistically, "belongs" to Gilligan.

Where exactly is Gilligan's island? Described in the original script as "a little south of no place and a little west of nowhere,"[22] the original title song with its swaying calypso beat implied a Caribbean setting.[23] Before filming began, however, Schwartz insisted that the show be shot in an area that looked like the South Seas.[24] In an episode titled "X Marks the Spot," the exact location of the island is "accidentally" given away. A warhead launched by the Pentagon lands on the island and is determined to have set down in the South Seas between Mexico City and Hilo, Hawaii (140 degrees latitude, 10 degrees longitude).[25] Thus the setting for the show is the same as that of Verne's island, "presumed to be some land in the Pacific,"[26] (as well as the islandscape that inspired the fertile dreams of Gauguin).

Aside from the castaways, is Gilligan's island occupied? From episode to episode, the answer is inconsistent. We are assured that the island is free of other inhabitants, only to learn that someone has been living there, unbeknownst to the castaways, for many years. Such inconsistency may be explained as a thematic device: the island (like all sites of colonization) is always already occupied. As Macherey writes of Verne, "The journey, in all its progressive stages, is disclosed as having ineluctably happened before."[27] The theme is played out on the level of intertextuality as well: *Gilligan's Island* repeats Gauguin's tale, which repeats the nineteenth-century travel literature, which in turn echoes the tales of Captain Cook, whose eighteenth-century voyages to Polynesia were documented and published by the nineteenth century.

This leitmotif appears in the first episode aired, "Two on a Raft." Gilligan and the Skipper find a bottle washed upon the shore, with a note asking for rescue. But the note turns out to have been launched by Gilligan himself. In the same episode, Gilligan, determined to scout the island from the top of the tallest tree (thus repeating exactly the surveying act of Verne's *Mysterious Island* character, Herbert[28]) is excited to spot a party on the other side of the island. When he runs to tell the castaways of his discovery, they turn out to be the ones he had spotted. The ambiguity, the puzzle of whether the island is or is not inhabited, is constantly shifting, and a sense of déjà vu is repeatedly evoked. Though seemingly vacant, the island is perpetually haunted by those who have disappeared; the ghosts of the colonized are forever present.

The hope of rescue raises another essential metatheme of the series: the castaways' constant desire to return to Western civilization. We might well wonder why the castaways would want to leave the island; material abundance, companionship, and an absence of the stresses and dangers of "civilized" life render Gilligan's island a tropical paradise. Yet the castaways are forever in search of a way "home." The reality of elsewhere can never match the dream, as Gauguin knew all too well. Just as important, the castaways can only "exist" in some relation to the West. As postindustrial Westerners, they cannot remain in the realm of the timeless and ahistorical (a realm reserved only for "natives").[29] Movement is a prerequisite of their condition: bourgeois ideology and colonialism require constant change and expansion to new markets, new regions, new uncharted territories. Capitalism always seeks an elsewhere.

If the castaways are cut off from civilization, their remaining link to the outside world is embodied in one precious object: the inexpensive transistor radio that fails to give out despite three years of almost constant use and tinkering. It is their lifeline to the world beyond; the castaways are often depicted huddled around the radio listening to news reports. The radio serves as a symbol of the outside world and as a powerful metaphor for the "technological colonization" of the communications industry.[30] Just as the castaways receive broadcasts even in their remote locale, so, too, in the years of the series it became possible for viewers in the most scattered regions of the world to receive television broadcasts. In May 1965 (the second year of the series), the Early Bird Communications Satellite made possible the simultaneous transmission of broadcasts to countries in North America, Europe, and the Dominican Republic.[31] The importance of such events is reflected in individual episodes of the show, such as "Smile, You're on Mars Camera."[32] In this episode a television camera probe, headed for Mars, lands on the island. It is only a missing lens (broken, of course, by Gilligan) that prevents Cape Kennedy from learning of the castaways' plight and rescuing them. The camera and the radio (in many more episodes) serve as instruments of salvation and as images of technological promise.

If the colonialism dominant during earlier manifestations of the island genre

(Crusoe, Verne, Gauguin) was primarily military,[33] in the 1960s we can speak of "economic" and "technological" colonialism. The phenomenon of vast industrial expansion is present on Gilligan's island, figured by a recurring reference to the hotel industry. The tourist and leisure trade saw immense increases in mid-century (including the rise of hotel consortia and a shift from domestic to global travel), with the United States leading in tourism spending. In the years from 1950 to 1990, there was a huge increase of tourists from 25 million to 159 million.[34] By 1980, twelve percent of the world GNP would derive from tourism, and smaller, less developed countries and islands would be especially targeted.[35]

In the first episode, "Two on a Raft," the leisure and hotel industry is invoked, as in this dialogue between the Skipper and Howell just moments after they are stranded on the island:

> HOWELL. Drop us at the nearest hotel.
> SKIPPER. I don't even know where we are!
> HOWELL. Oh, nonsense, Mr. Hilton has hotels everywhere.

In Howell's logic, no place can truly be "off the map" if it exists as a potential resort or market. One episode was dedicated to this theme: Erika Tiffany Smith, a wealthy socialite, lands on the island determined to turn it into a luxury resort.[36] Years later, in a made-for-television "reunion" film, this wish—also that of the CBS executives to whom the show was originally pitched—was fulfilled. In *The Castaways on Gilligan's Island* (airing March 3, 1979) the group returns to the island after being rescued and transforms it into an elegant private resort, chicly devoid of television sets and telephones. The island also functions as a resort attracting an international clientele in the final reunion show, *The Globetrotters on Gilligan's Island* (1981). The castaways no longer need to return to bourgeois civilization—they have remade the island in its image.

Like the larger-than-life characters in myth (or a celebrity who has reached mythic status), the characters in *Gilligan's Island* are mostly known to us by a single name or title. As in the novels of Verne, the characters exist as types rather than individuals. We are introduced to each one in the opening sequence: Gilligan, the Skipper, the Millionaire and his wife, the Movie Star, the Professor, and Mary Anne.[37] It comes as something of a shock to realize that all of the castaways have "real," full names, which are revealed in various episodes.

In their carefully delineated representations of class, profession, and gender, the castaways in *Gilligan's Island* make up a microcosm of bourgeois society. At the top of the island's hierarchy reign the Millionaire, Thurston Howell III, and his wife Lovey. Howell (played by Jim Backus) is a caricature of the entrepreneur/aristocrat/exploiter, a tycoon and self-made millionaire who is nevertheless character-ized by his refusal to perform any kind of labor, no matter how dire the circum-stances. Howell is baffled when a sweat drop appears on his forehead; he's never seen one before.[38] Even on the island Howell somehow continues to grow richer. Lovey's role (Natalie Shafer) is chiefly that of supportive wife. As a married woman (and more important, one who did not meet the 1960s requirement of youthful beauty) she serves as a comic companion rather than as an object of desire.

The Professor (Russell Johnson), a former high school teacher named Roy Hinkley, in his bland khakis and starched white shirt, is not only a representa-tion of science, but also of the intelligentsia. Indeed, the generic term *professor* serves him well, for he seems to have mastered every kind of intellectual task and discipline from chemistry, biology, physics, and engineering to psychology and anthropology. The Professor remains remarkably aloof—asexual, the odd man out, an embodiment of objectivity and rationality. He is above sensual and ma-terial concerns; a rare glimpse inside his hut reveals it to be entirely undecorated.

In charge of his own private charter, the Skipper (Alan Hale Jr.) has the hard-working ethic and self-dependence of the petit bourgeois. He is well aware of his rank above Gilligan. Gilligan (Bob Denver), at the constant beck and call not only of the Skipper, but of all the castaways, is the exploited worker, Howell's caddy, and the Professor's gofer. He is marked by a taste for simple pleasures and an incurable laziness, those qualities that the "higher" classes have always attrib-uted to the lower ones.

Ginger (Tina Louise), the Movie Star, and Mary Anne (Dawn Wells), as fe-males, exist "outside" of history and the class structure; in their perfect dualities, they represent the eternal (and ahistorical) Woman. If Ginger is the whore, the city, the knowing, and the sexual, then Mary Anne is the virgin, the country (born and bred in the wheatfields of Kansas), the innocent, and the childlike. Together they embody the angel in the kitchen and the devilish seductress in the bedroom.

The character of Ginger, however, has an extraordinarily important func-tion; her role marks Gilligan's Island as a particularly modern entity. She is the only character who could not possibly appear in earlier manifestations of the is-land genre. Ginger, the Movie Star, is a paradigm of late capitalism and a repre-sentation of the small screen itself. In the character of Ginger, the colossal fields of leisure and entertainment come together beautifully. Importantly, the sex goddess role that Ginger embodies was one that would already, in the 1960s, have registered as nostalgic. The gown-draped, high-voiced sexuality of Marilyn Monroe had already given way to the swinging casualness of Bridget Bardot.[39] Ginger's "take" on Monroe coincides with Andy Warhol's images of Monroe as a sex icon and reveals an intense self-consciousness about the culture industry and media representations.

The limits of *Gilligan's Island* as a "radical" experiment are revealed in the characters; escape from bourgeois civilization is not possible. There is no reason why the class system should continue to be followed on the island; there is no money economy, but a limited market with a production system based on need rather than commodity logic. And yet the castaways continue to occupy their prior class positions: Howell refuses to work; Gilligan refuses to rebel; Ginger and Mary Anne continue to do all the domestic chores. The island society is not a rejection but a replication of bourgeois society. Despite the island's "primitive" trappings, the society there is not Rousseau's tabula rasa but a place already deeply marked. The American audience of the 1960s could easily recognize the values necessary to the continued existence of their own culture operating on Gilligan's island. Moreover they could see those values as universal because they are displaced onto a "primitive" world.

It is not only the setting, themes, and characters of *Gilligan's Island* that invoke and repeat earlier works such as *Robinson Crusoe,* but also the show's individual (if slightly ludicrous) plots. Indeed, the vast majority of its story lines revolve around a disturbance, an invasion, of the hermetic world of the island. The plots can be divided into those that focus on "savage" or non-Western visitors and those that reveal how "civilization" (and all of its attendant dangers) penetrates the peaceful microcosm of the island, undermining the notion of total escape.

Many episodes of *Gilligan's Island* play out the familiar tropes and discourses of nineteenth-century primitivism epitomized by Gauguin and present in the work of artists from Delacroix to Picasso.[40] The literary and artistic encounter of the West with the *primitif* or the "noble savage" is evoked in countless images and references in the show. In "High Man on the Totem Pole,"[41] a carved head at the top of a totem pole resembles Gilligan and recalls the terrifying row of heads, staked on fences, in Joseph Conrad's classic *Heart of Darkness* (1902). The constant references to head-hunting summon up a myriad of nineteenth-century precedents, from Karl May's novels on the "savage Indians" of the New World to the "professional" anthropological literature of the late nineteenth century. From "Two on a Raft":

> GILLIGAN. Those savage Marubis what do they do?
> PROFESSOR. They're collectors.
> GILLIGAN. That doesn't sound too bad—what do they collect?
> PROFESSOR. Heads.

Several plots revolve around the simultaneous absence and presence of "savages" on the island. In "Two on a Raft," the castaways mistake a fire set by Gilligan and the Skipper on the other side of the island as evidence of native presence. The entire show consists of a play of identity, as the castaways erroneously assume each other to be members of the Marubi tribe. The plot of "Waiting for Watubi" [42] involves the unearthing of an idol of evil Kona that, due to the machinations of the castaways, keeps reappearing and spooking the Skipper. The resurfacing idol functions, like Poe's tell-tale heart, as a symbol of bad conscience, this time that of the West. The island is haunted by the ghosts of the banished; memories of the colonized lurk around every bush.

Relations between the castaways and the "natives" are almost always hostile and threatening. [43] Evidence of the natives' "primitive" presence is equated with imminent attack, as in "Topsy Turvy." [44] To correct the results of a head injury, Gilligan must drink a brew made from kiphbora berries that causes him to see in multiples. The few natives that come to attack appear to Gilligan as a large army. Such plots play out the repressed but ever-present fear of revenge against the colonizer. Gilligan's hallucinations turn the "real" power relations topsy-turvy, as the dominated now appear as the more powerful and victorious. Other episodes that deal with attacks by the "savages" on the island include "How to Be a Hero," "Music Hath Charms," "The Chain of Command," and "Voodoo."

Within the "primitivist" mentality, the natives are always seen as Other. Their difference must be maintained at all costs: at the colonial and universal expositions of nineteenth-century France and Britain, indigenous peoples were taken from their lands and forced to perform their traditional dances and "rites" within the safe precinct of the fairs. [45]

The unbridgeable cultural differences between the castaways and the natives are underlined by "Gilligan's Mother-in-Law," [46] an episode in which Gilligan is chosen to marry a young native woman whose outer appearance and cultural habits are made to seem repulsive and comic. Likewise, the "irresistible" Ginger repels the male head of the tribe. Despite the differences, however, the proximity of the West is also revealed. Just as the natives invade the peace of the castaways, the world of the natives is "tainted" by encounters with the West. In "Gilligan the Goddess," [47] King Kaliwani lands on the island in search of a "white goddess." His desires have been shaped by those of the West. For example, he is extraordinarily proud of a Zippo lighter he has obtained. Like the missionary-supplied muumuus that covered the beautiful Tahitian Vahine who greeted Gauguin (he had envisioned the women naked), the Zippo lighter disturbs the dream. Someone has been there before; the mythic vacuum in which the natives exist has been exploded.

If natives such as King Kaliwani could not escape the reach of Western civilization, the castaways surely have no way of eluding it. Their distance and remote locale cannot protect them from the dangers and threats of the modern Western world. Despite the tropical climate, even the chill of the cold war is felt on *Gilligan's Island*. In fact, all of the major American wars of the twentieth century are alluded to in the plots of the show. In one episode, the castaways discover Wrongway Feldman, a downed World War I ace pilot, who had been living on the island for many decades.[48] The cultural trauma of World War II is embodied in the person of the Skipper, whose "past" life included battles between American and Japanese forces on the island of Guadalcanal in 1942.[49] (Ironically, Alan Hale, who played the Skipper, had served in the coast guard during World War II.) In contrast to the historical "ruin" of World War I, World War II is treated in a far more vivid (and still threatening) manner. Memories of that war would have been closer to viewers of the 1960s, and the "Asian" soldier was still regarded as a danger (even if he was now Korean or Vietnamese). The Japanese soldier who appears on the island in "So Sorry My Island Now"[50] is not even aware that the war has ended; he immediately makes the castaways his prisoners. The Skipper suffers a form of post-traumatic disorder in "Forget Me Not."[51] When some stray missiles hit the island, he is convinced that the war is still on and suffers hallucinations that his fellow castaways are really Japanese soldiers.

Nor are the islanders safe from the forces of communism and the fallout from the cold war. In separate episodes both a Cuban dictator and a Russian spy find their way to the island,[52] with imperialist fantasies of taking it over. In the last year and a half of the series, an even more terrifying threat shakes the peaceful, enclosed world of the island: that of global nuclear disaster. In "Meet the Meteor,"[53] the Professor must build a special screen to protect the island from powerful radiation. Even the tropical flora and fauna of the island are not immune to the effects of nuclear buildup. "Please Pass the Vegetables"[54] focuses on radioactive seeds that sprout strange and poisonous food in the soil. Like the stray missiles that repeatedly land on the island from episode to episode, the realities of life in post-cold war America penetrate *Gilligan's Island*.

The themes of global expansion, racism, exploitation, primitivism, and technology reach a grand apotheosis in the plot of *Gilligan's Island's* final made-for-television film based on the series, which aired on May 15, 1981. In *The Globetrotters on Gilligan's Island,* the original hopes of the CBS executives are realized—the island now functions as a luxury resort.[55] A billionaire discovers the island to be rich in the precious substance of "suprematism" (a word that simultaneously evokes gasoline and Russian avant-garde ideology). His plot to steal the substance and take over the island results in a call for a showdown basketball match between the Harlem Globetrotters and a group of Russian-made robots called the Invincibles. The Globetrotters (who fight for the castaways) combine the racial "Other" (Harlem) and the world traveler and jetsetting globetrotter. The old cold war is over; the war is now fought in the field of technology and economics that is combined in the sports broadcasting industry, and the winner takes all.

No matter how far out at sea Gilligan's island may be, it cannot leave the world behind. Like cheap reproductions of Western masterpieces on the wall of Gauguin's Tahitian hut, the bourgeois world is always present. Nor can the lingering legacy of colonialism, exploitation (of both land and populations), "progress," and a retreat that has its roots in the Europe of the Enlightenment be erased. In *Gilligan's Island,* the escapism of travel (the true underlying theme of our island genre) is transferred to television; the great escape does not exist in a far-off tropical locale, but everywhere at once in the form of a medium that conquered the world.

8

"Is This What You Mean by Color TV?"

Race, Gender, and Contested Meanings in Julia

A N I K O   B O D R O G H K O Z Y

America in 1968: Police clash with the militant Black Panthers while one of the group's leaders, Huey Newton, is sentenced for murder; civil rights leader Martin Luther King is assassinated in Tennessee, sparking violent uprisings and riots in the nation's black ghettos; the massive Poor People's Campaign, a mobilization of indigent blacks and whites, sets up a tent city on the mall in Washington, D.C.; at Cornell University, armed black students sporting bandoliers take over the administration building and demand a black studies program.[1] In the midst of all these events—events that many Americans saw as a revolutionary or at least an insurrectionary situation among the black population—NBC introduced the first situation comedy to feature an African American in the starring role since *Amos 'n' Andy* and *Beulah* went off the air in the early 1950s.[2] *Julia,* created by writer-producer Hal Kanter, a Hollywood liberal Democrat who campaigned actively for Eugene McCarthy, starred Diahann Carroll as a middle-class, widowed nurse trying to bring up her six-year-old son, Corey. After the death of her husband in a helicopter crash in Vietnam, Julia and Corey move to an integrated apartment complex, and she finds work in an aerospace industry clinic.

A slightly different version of this chapter was originally published in *Private Screenings: Television and the Female Consumer,* ed. Lynn Spigel and Denise Mann (Minneapolis: Univ. of Minnesota Press, 1992), 143–68. It has been reprinted here by permission of the publisher. The author extends thanks to Lynn Spigel, John Fiske, Charlotte Brunsdon, David Morley, Julie D'Acci, the graduate students of the Telecommunications section of the Communications Arts Department, University of Wisconsin-Madison, and David Aaron for their suggestions and comments on various drafts of this paper.

NBC executives did not expect the show to succeed.[3] They scheduled it opposite the hugely successful *Red Skelton Show*, where it was expected to die a noble, dignified death, having demonstrated the network's desire to break the prime-time color bar. Unexpectedly, the show garnered high ratings and lasted a respectable three years.

Despite its success, or perhaps because of it, *Julia* was a very controversial program. Beginning in popular magazine articles written before the first episode even aired and continuing more recently in historical surveys of the portrayals of blacks on American television, critics have castigated *Julia* for being extraordinarily out of touch with and silent on the realities of African American life in the late 1960s. While large numbers of blacks lived in exploding ghettos, Julia and Corey Baker lived a luxury lifestyle impossible on a nurse's salary. While hostility and racial tensions brewed, and the Kerner Commission Report on Civil Disorders described an America fast becoming two nations separate and unequal, tolerance and colorblindness prevailed on *Julia*.

The show came in for heavy criticism most recently in J. Fred MacDonald's (1983) *Blacks and White TV: Afro-Americans in Television Since 1948*. MacDonald describes *Julia* as a "comfortable image of black success . . . in stark juxtaposition to the images seen on local and national newscasts."[4] The show, according to MacDonald, refused to be topical; when dealing with racial issues at all, it did so only in one-liners. He also describes black and white discomfort with the show, claiming that the series was a sell-out intended to assuage white consciences and a "saccharine projection of the 'good life' to be achieved by those blacks who did not riot, who acted properly, and worked within the system."[5]

MacDonald's text-based criticism of *Julia* would appear to be quite justified. However, there was a whole range of politically charged meanings attributed to the program during its network run that critics like MacDonald haven't discussed. What critics of the program have ignored are the diverse and often conflicted ways in which both the producers and viewers of *Julia* struggled to make sense of the show in the context of the racial unrest and rebellions erupting throughout American society. Historically situated in a period of civil dislocations when massive numbers of black Americans were attempting, both peacefully and not so peacefully, to redefine their place within the sociopolitical landscape, *Julia* functioned as a symptomatic text—symptomatic of the racial tensions and reconfigurations of its time.

The extent to which *Julia* functioned as a site of social tension is particularly evident in the viewer response mail and script revisions in the files of producer Hal Kanter, and it is also apparent in critical articles written for the popular press at the time.[6] These documents allow us to begin to reconstruct the contentious dialogue that took place among audiences, magazine critics, and the show's producer and writers. They also provide clues to how such conflicts materialized in the program narrative itself. A key feature of this dialogue was a discursive struggle over what it meant to be black and what it meant to be white at the close of the 1960s. Black viewers, white viewers, and critics all made sense of the program in notably different ways. Although a struggle over racial representation was the overt issue, their responses to the program also occasionally exhibited a nascent, if conflicted, attempt to speak about gender and the representation of women.

Producing Difference

The script files in the Hal Kanter papers provide a particularly rich case study of how *Julia's* audiences attempted to make sense of the program and how they grappled with racial difference and social change in the context of the civil rights movement. Particularly revealing is the file for a 1968 episode entitled "Take My Hand, I'm a Stranger in the Third Grade," which contains the initial six-page outline (the first working out of the episode's storyline) and a thirty-six page first draft script (the first fleshing out of the story in dialogue form) written by Ben Gershman and Gene Boland, the latter one of the series' four black writers.[7]

The story revolved around Corey's friend Bedelia Sanford, a black schoolmate who tries to win his affection by stealing toys for him. In the original storyline, Julia confronts Bedelia's mother, who lives in a slum with numerous children. She flares up at Julia's expressions of sympathy for her situation, calling Julia "one of the uppitty [*sic*] high-class Colored ladies who thinks she's somebody because she went to college and has a profession. Well, says Mrs. S., she's got a profession too—she's on welfare." Hal Kanter underlined that final line and wrote in the margin next to it, "NO, SIRS!"

In the first draft script, Mrs. Sanford has suddenly metamorphosed into an upper-class black woman whose preoccupation with money-making has pulled her away from attending to her daughter. When Julia accuses her of trying to buy Bedelia's love, Mrs. Sanford accuses Julia of "always trying to tear down our own." She calls Julia a mediocre Negro who has attained all the status she will ever have. Julia retorts, "[B]ut that Gauguin print and that Botticelli and your *white maid* all rolled together isn't going to change the fact that you are a failure as a mother."

The adjustment of the Sanford's economic status upward indicates that Kanter and his writers were uncertain and anxious about their depiction of black Americans. The characters were either demeaning ghetto stereotypes or they were upper-class "white Negroes," a term used by critics to describe Julia. The stereotypical images of African American life that most whites had previously taken for granted had, by the late sixties, become, at least to *Julia*'s creators, problematic constructs. As predominantly white creators of black characters, Kanter and his writing team wanted to avoid racist representations but appeared stumped in their attempt to come up with something that wasn't merely a binary opposition. The repertoire of black images was inadequate and there was no new repertoire on which to draw.

While racial depiction and definition functioned as a highly politicized dilemma for the producers of *Julia,* the question of gender representation was another matter. On might expect that a program dealing with a working woman's attempts to raise her child alone would open a space for questioning sexual inequality. If scenes from the series' first episode and pilot are any indication, this appears not to have been the case. While racist depictions of blacks were being questioned, sexist portrayals of women were not. The show and its creators seemed as blithely unconscious in their portrayal of women as they were self-conscious in their portrayal of blacks.

The first episode of the series, "The Interview," written by Hal Kanter and aired September 24, 1968, includes the following scene between Julia and her future boss, Dr. Chegley.[8] Julia has just entered Chegley's office to be interviewed for a nurse's position. Chegley has his back to Julia as she enters. He looks at an X ray and, without looking at her, asks her to identify it. She replies that it is a chest X ray. He then turns to face her and the following dialogue ensues:

> CHEGLEY. You have a healthy looking chest . . . I believe you're here to beg me for a job.
> JULIA. I'm here at your invitation, Doctor, to be interviewed for a position as a nurse. I don't beg for anything.
> CHEGLEY. I'll keep that in mind. Walk around.
> JULIA. Beg your pardon?
> CHEGLEY. You just said you don't beg for anything.
> JULIA. That's just a figure of speech.
> CHEGLEY. I'm interested in your figure without the speech. Move. Let me see if you can walk.
> JULIA. I can. [*Walking*] I come from a long line of pedestrians.
> CHEGLEY. Turn around. [*As she does*] You have a very well-formed fantail. [*As she reacts*] That's Navy terminology. I spent thirty years in uniform. [*Then*] Do you wear a girdle?
> JULIA. No, sir.
> CHEGLEY. I do. I have a bad back. Now you can sit down.

The pilot, "Mama's Man," also written by Kanter, contains a similar scene.[9] Julia is being interviewed by a manager at Aerospace Industries, Mr. Colton, who becomes very flustered when he sees Julia. He tells her that all her qualifications are in order, but that she is not what he expected. Julia asks whether she should have been younger or older, or, "Should I have written at the top of the application—in big, bold, letters, 'I'm a Negro?!'" Colton tells her that had nothing to do with it. The problem is that she is too pretty. "When we employ nurses far less attractive than you, we find that we lose many man-hours. Malingerers, would-be Romeos, that sort of thing. In your case, you might provoke a complete work stoppage."

In contemporary terms these two scenes display examples of the most egregious sexism and sexual harassment. However, when the episodes aired, the women's liberation movement, which dates its public birth to the Miss America pageant protest on September 7, 1968, was not yet a part of public consciousness. *Julia's* creators thus did not yet have to contend with the oppositional voices of the women's movement. In contrast, the producers were quite concerned with the highly visible civil rights and black power movements, and were well aware of the fact that representations of racial discrimination and harassment were now socially and politically unacceptable. The scenes from these two episodes of *Julia* reveal a self-conscious understanding of that unacceptablity; however, anxiety about that situation resulted in a displacement. Discrimination and harassment were shifted from racism onto sexism. Both job interview scenes needed to relieve the anxiety created over Julia's difference. The writers could not allow her racial difference to function as an appropriate reason for the denial of a job or for demeaning banter, but there were no such political taboos in relation to her sexual difference.

Conflicted Reception

The conflicted production process can indicate some of the ways in which *Julia* worked through social and political anxieties in American culture in the late 1960s. However, the interpretive strategies brought to bear upon the text both by critics and viewers are even more significant because they can show us how these tensions and conflicts were dealt with by different social groups within American society at the time.

Recent work in cultural studies has demonstrated that meanings are not entirely determined by the text or its producers. As Stuart Hall's "encoding-decoding" model has shown, readers of a text are active agents and need not accept the meanings constructed by a text's producers. Readers can oppose or negotiate with the meanings that the text promotes as the correct or preferred interpretation.[10] By examining how audiences interpreted *Julia,* we can see how the crisis in race relations grew as people attempted to come to grips with the meanings of racial difference in the face of militant challenges by a black opposition movement.

By juxtaposing the interpretive strategies and discourses mobilized by critics writing in the popular press and by viewers writing to Kanter or to the network, we can examine how privileged cultural elites interpreted the show as well as how television viewers constructed meanings often at odds with those of the critics. The viewer mail (some 151 letters and postcards) filed in the Hal Kanter papers provides a particularly rich case study of how *Julia's* audiences attempted to make sense of the program and how they grappled with racial difference and social change through their engagement with the show. At times, the statements in the letters echo those in the popular press; more frequently, both the reading strategies and the debates are different. Many of the letters have carbon copy responses from Kanter attached, setting up a fascinating, often contentious dialogue. But what is most compelling about the letters is the way they reveal the remarkably conflicted, diverse, and contradictory responses among audience members.

These letters, the majority of which came from married women, should not be seen as representative of the larger audience's responses to the program.[11] Letter writers tend to be a particularly motivated group of television viewers. There is no way to determine whether the sentiments that crop up over and over again in the letters were widespread among viewers who did not write to the producers. Thus my analysis of these letters is not an attempt to quantify the *Julia* audience or to use the documents as a representative sample. While neither the letter writers nor the critics in the popular press were representative of the audience as a whole, their readings were symptomatic of struggles over racial definition. Perhaps, then, the best way to work with these documents is to see them as traces, clues, or parts of a larger whole to which we have no access. Indeed, like all histories of audience reception, this one presents partial knowledge, pieces of the past that we must interpret in a qualified manner.[12]

One trend that became evident almost immediately among the favorable letters written by white viewers was a marked self-consciousness about racial self-identification: "I am white, but I enjoy watching '*Julia.*' "[13] "Our whole family from great grandmother down to my five year old, loved it. We just happen to be caucasian." "As a 'white middle class Jewish' teacher, may I say that it is finally a pleasure to turn on the T.V. and see contemporary issues treated with honesty, humor, and sensitivity." [14]

One way in which to account for the self-consciousness of many letter writers identifying themselves as whites was that the novelty of a black-centered program raised questions about traditional and previously unexamined definitions of racial identity and difference. One mother of two boys in Ohio struggled with this very issue in her letter: "Being a white person I hope this program helps all of us to understand each other. Maybe if my children watch this program they will also see the good side of Negro people [rather] than all the bad side they see on the news programs such as riots, sit-ins, etc. I know this program will help my two sons so when they grow up they won't be so prejudice [*sic*]." Although the woman made some problematic distinctions between good black people and bad black people, there was an attempt to grapple with racial difference. Definitions of what it meant to be white had suddenly become an uncertain terrain. The crisis in race relations signified by "riots, sit-ins, etc." made the black population visible, and the depiction of African Americans had ceased to be a stable field. As representations of black people had become an arena of contested meanings, so too had self-representations of whites become uncertain. One manifestation of that uncertainty was self-consciousness. In the aftermath of the Civil Rights movement and in the midst of black power sentiment, the question of what it now meant to be white in America was an issue that needed working through.

Another way to think about race was, perhaps, paradoxically, to deny difference. A letter from a rather idealistic fifteen-year-old girl in Annandale, Virginia, affirmed, "Your new series has told me that at least SOME people have an idea of a peaceful and loving existence. So what if their skin pigmentation is different and their philosophies are a bit different than ours *they are still people*." Another woman, from Manhattan Beach, California, who described her race as Caucasian and her ancestry as Mexican, wrote, "I love the show. Keep up the good work. This way the world will realize that the Negro is just like everyone else, with feelings and habits as the Whites have." A mother of twins in Highland Park, New Jersey, observed, "And it's immensely valuable to the many non-Negroes who just don't know any Negroes, or don't know that all people mostly behave like people."

Perhaps these viewers engaged in a denial of the "Otherness" of black people in an attempt to reduce white anxiety about racial difference. By affirming that blacks were "just people" and just like everyone else, these viewers defined "everyone else" as white. White was the norm from which the Other deviated. In

their sincere attempts to negotiate changing representations of race, these viewers denied that blacks historically had not fit the constructed norm of the white
middle-class social formation. In this move, the viewers were, of course, assisted
by the program itself. The show's theme music was a generic sitcom jingle lacking any nod to the rich traditions of African American musical forms. Julia's
apartment, while nicely appointed, and with a framed photo of her dead hero
husband prominently displayed, was also completely generic. Unlike a compara-
ble but more recent black family sitcom, *The Cosby Show,* with its lavish town-
house decorated with African American artworks, Julia's home contained no
culturally specific touches. Diahann Carroll's speech was also completely unin-
flected, on the one hand differentiating her from her prime-time predecessors
such as *Amos 'n' Andy* and *Beulah,* but on the other hand evacuating as much ethnic and cultural difference as possible. For viewers picking up on the interpretive
clues provided by the show, black people were "just people" to the extent that
they conformed to an unexamined white norm of representation.

While this denial of difference may have been typical, it was by no means the
dominant interpretive strategy employed by viewers who wrote letters. In fact,
many viewers were clearly struggling with the problem of representation, both of
blacks and of whites. The criticism leveled by many viewers—that the show was
unrealistic and was not "telling it like it is"—reveals a struggle over how reality
should be defined.

The refrain "tell it like it is" became a recurring theme in debates about *Julia,*
both in the popular press and among the viewer letters. In a rather scathing review, *Time* magazine criticized the show for not portraying how black people really lived: "She [*Julia*] would not recognize a ghetto if she stumbled into it, and
she is, in every respect save color, a figure in a white milieu." [15] Robert Lewis
Shayon, the TV-radio critic for *Saturday Review,* was also particularly concerned
with *Julia's* deficiencies in representing this notion of a black reality. In the first
of three articles on the series, he, like the *Time* reviewer, castigated the program
for turning a blind eye to the realities of black life in the ghettos. For Shayon, the
reality of the black experience was what was documented in the Kerner Commission report: "Negro youth, 'hustling in the jungle' of their 'crime-ridden, vi-
olence-prone, and poverty-stricken world'—that's the real problem, according
to the commission report." [16] The world of *Julia,* on the other hand, was a fantasy because it did not focus on the problems of black youth (which for Shayon
meant young black males) and because it did not take place in a ghetto environment. The unconsciously racist notion that the black experience was essentially
a ghetto experience remained unexamined in these popular press accounts.

This attempt to define a singular, totalized "Negro reality" became a point of dispute in Shayon's follow-up columns on May 25 and July 20, 1968. Shayon received a letter in response to his first column from M. S. Rukeyser Jr., NBC's vice-president for press and publicity. He also received a letter from Dan Jenkins, an executive at the public relations firm handling television programming for General Foods, one of *Julia*'s main sponsors. Shayon juxtaposed the responses of these men to an interview given by Hal Kanter, which affirmed that the show would tell the truth, show it like it is. Shayon noted that Jenkins appeared to hold a contradictory view: "Jenkins, the publicity agent, wrote: 'It is not, and never has been the function of a commercial series to "show it as it is, baby." On those rare occasions when the medium has taken a stab at limning the unhappy reality of what goes in much of the world (e.g., *East Side, West Side*), the public has quickly tuned out.' " [17] Shayon went on to quote from Rukeyser's letter: "We have no real quarrel with your [Shayon's] subjective judgment on the degree of lavishness of Julia's apartment, wardrobe, and way of life. There has been no controversy within our own group about this." [18] Shayon also quoted from another interview with Kanter, who seemed to step back from his earlier stance. By " 'showing it like it is,' [Kanter] was talking not of ghetto life, but of 'humourous aspects of discrimination . . . properly handled . . . without rancor, without inflammation, and withal telling their attempts to enjoy the American Dream.' " [19] In his article of July 20, 1968, Shayon added Diahann Carroll's response, quoting from an Associated Press story about the controversy generated by Shayon's initial article: "We're dealing with an entertainment medium . . . *Julia* is drama-comedy; it isn't politically oriented. Because I am black that doesn't mean I have to deal with problems of all black people." [20]

By bringing together the sentiments of the show's creator and its network, sponsor, and star, the Shayon pieces revealed just how conflicted the production process for *Julia* was. There was no consensus on what "telling it like it is" meant. Rukeyser's letter openly admitted to controversy over how Julia and her world should be depicted. Shayon's series of articles opened up for examination the problem of representation. If black identity had become a shifting field in the wake of the crisis in race relations, then "telling it like it is" would be impossible. Shayon thought he knew how *Julia* should tell it, but his articles indicated that in 1968 the program's creators were far less certain.

Unlike the critics, viewers generally did not want to relocate Julia and Corey to a ghetto. Instead, viewers who criticized the show for not "telling it like it is" were more concerned with the presentation of black characters than they were with the upscale setting. A male viewer in Chicago wrote:

On another point which bears remarks is the unwillingness to allow the program to be "black." I do not object to white people being in the cast. What I do object to is selecting the black cast from people (black people) who are so white oriented that everyone has a white mentality, that is, their expressions are all that of white people. Choose some people whose expressions and manners are unquestionably black. The baby-sitter was, for example, so white cultured that you would have thought she was caucasian except for the color of her skin.

Hal Kanter's reply to this letter indicates how contested this issue was: "We all make mistakes, don't we, Mr. Banks? Please try to forgive me for mine in the spirit of universality and brotherhood we are attempting to foster."

Mr. Banks's letter revealed an uncertainty over how to portray black people. Kanter's reply indicated that, despite his rhetoric of brotherhood (and sameness), this was a problem that plagued the show's creators—a problem already evident in the script development for "Take My Hand." How would one represent "unquestionably black" expressions and manner? The representation of "black" was defined by Mr. Banks negatively by what it was not: it was not white. The dilemma over what "black" signified outside a cultural system in which "white" was the norm was still left open to question.[21]

Other viewers, also uncomfortable with the unrealistic quality of the program, pointed out more problems in the representation of blacks. A woman in Berkeley, California, observed:

Your show is in a position to dispell [*sic*] so *many* misconceptions about Black people & their relationships to whites. I am just one of many who are so *very* disappointed in the outcome of such a promising show.

Please, help to destroy the misconceptions—not reinforce them! Stop making Miss Carroll super-Negro and stop having blacks call themselves "colored" and make your characters less self-conscious and tell that "babysitter" to quit overacting.

This concern with representing blacks as "super-Negro" was also voiced in the popular press. In a *TV Guide* article in December 1968, Diahann Carroll was quoted as saying: "With black people right now, we are all terribly bigger than life and more wonderful than life and smarter and better—because we're still proving. . . . For a hundred years we have been prevented from seeing accurate images of ourselves and we're all overconcerned and overreacting. The needs of the white writer go to the superhuman being. At the moment, we're presenting the white Negro. And he has very little Negro-ness."[22] These references to the "super-Negro" or the "white Negro" indicated an unmasking of an ideologically bankrupt representational system unable to come to terms with a representation of blacks that was independent of white as the defining term. The self-consciousness to which Diahann Carroll and the letter writer alluded was similar to the self-consciousness of other viewers who felt a need to identify themselves by race. Racial identity and its representation may have become an uncertain and contested field as "black" and "white" became unhinged from their previous definitions, but they were still imbricated within a white representational system.

This problem of racial definition was raised by other viewers who objected to blacks being differentiated and defined at the expense of white characters. Many viewers, particularly white housewives, took exception to the juxtaposing of Julia to her white neighbor, Mrs. Waggedorn. One mother of a four-year-old in Philadelphia said she would not watch the program anymore "as I believe you are protraying [sic] the white mother to be some kind of stupid idiot. —The colored boy & mother are sharp as tacks which is fine but why must the other family be portrayed as being dumb, dumb, dumb." Another "white suburban mother of four" in Fort Worthington, Pennsylvania, complained that Mrs. Waggedorn was a "dumb bunny" while Julia was a "candidate for 'Mother of the Year.' " A third letter, from a "quite typical New England housewife and mother of three" in Hyde Park, Massachusetts, stated:

> If Diahann Carroll were to play the roll [sic] of the neighborly housewife, and vice verser [sic], the black people of this country would be screaming "Prejudice." Why must Julia be pictured so glamorously dressed, living in such a luxurious apartment, dining off of the finest china while her white neighbor is made to appear sloppy, has rollers in her hair . . .
>
> If your show is to improve the image of the negro woman, great! But—please don't accomplish this at the expense of the white housewife.

The reading strategy these viewers brought to the text was one of polarization. They saw a form of reverse discrimination. Explicit in their letters was an anxiety over the representation of race, black versus white. Implicit, however, was a nascent critique of the representation of gender. All three of these letter writers self-consciously defined themselves by occupation: white housewives and mothers. In the depiction of Mrs. Waggedorn, they saw a stereotypical representation of themselves and were quite aware that they were being demeaned as women.

The positions articulated by these women to a certain extent mirror concerns raised in a number of women's magazines. Articles written about the series, or more specifically the series' star, Diahann Carroll, focused not on questions of race but rather on questions of motherhood. An article in *Ladies Home Journal* written by the widow of slain civil rights activist Medgar Evers, while not ignoring the question of race representation, emphasized a theme of female bonding between Mrs. Evers and Diahann Carroll, two black women forced to raise children on their own.[23] A *Good Housekeeping* article completely evacuated the issue of race, dealing only with dilemmas Diahann Carroll faced attempting to raise her daughter while pursuing a career.[24]

Thus, while questions of race representation were highly politicized both in the popular press and among viewers, questions about the representation of gender and motherhood were rendered entirely apolitical in both articles in the women's magazines. Instead, the issues were personalized; they were Diahann Carroll's problems or Mrs. Medgar Evers's problems, but they were not discussed as social problems. Similarly, the white housewives who objected to the portrayal of Mrs. Waggedorn had no political discourse through which to articulate their anger at an offensive female stereotype. Both the women's magazine writers and the housewives seemed aware that there was something problematic about the gender-based positions of mothers and housewives within the social order. However, they lacked the means to shift their analysis of the problem from the personal to the social. One could argue that the women's movement, still in its infancy in the late 1960s, provided such an analysis, at least for middle-class white women who formed the main constituency for the emergent women's liberation movement. Just as the black oppositional movement revealed that the position of African Americans within the social landscape was politically, economically, and socially circumscribed and required political solutions, so the emergence of the women's movement revealed a similar set of concerns about the position of women. However, such an analysis, widely available in relation to race, was not yet accessible to a female audience.[25]

The viewer response letters examined so far attempted, either by denying difference or by trying to grapple with it, to engage with the program in order to think through ways in which to rework race relations. Although many of the letters exhibited unexamined racist discourses, the racism seemed unintended and unconscious, a manifestation of the shifting ground. *Julia,* as a text that worked hard to evacuate politically charged representations and potentially disturbing discourses of racial oppression, would appear to be an unlikely candidate for overtly racist attacks. However, a surprisingly large number of the letters in the Hal Kanter papers reveal an enormous amount of unmediated anxiety felt by some viewers about changes being wrought in the wake of the Civil Rights and black oppositional movements.

Concerns that reappeared in these letters tended to focus on a discomfort with seeing increasing numbers of African Americans on television, fears that traditional racial hierarchies were being eradicated, and anxieties about interracial sexuality. While *Julia* never dealt with issues of miscegenation or intermarriage, many of these viewers read them into the program anyway. Some of these viewers may have done so because, unlike the black mammy figures traditionally predominant in the mass media, *Julia* conformed to white ideals of beauty. That her white male bosses were shown recognizing her sexuality may have provided the cues some viewers needed to construct scenarios such as the one provided by an anonymous viewer from Los Angeles: "What are you trying to do by making '*Julia.*' No racial problems—she is playing opposite a white, she is suppose [*sic*] to live in an all white apt house. It's racial because you will have it so Nolan [Dr. Chegley, Julia's boss] will fall in love with her and have to make her over-repulsive—You had better write a part for a big black boy so he can mess with a white girl or they will get mad." Anxiety over social change and transformations in race relations erupted here in a full-blown fear of interracial sexuality. For this viewer, integration created a moral panic whereby the sudden visibility of blacks in "white society" could only mean that "big black boys" wanted to mess with white girls.

Other viewers, less obsessed with questions of miscegenation, exhibited fears about integration by expressing anger at television as an institution. They blamed television for creating social strife and causing blacks to forget their proper place. One anonymous viewer from Houston, Texas, who signed her or his comments "the silent majority," wrote: "Living in Texas all my life I have always lived around the negroes and they used to be really fine people until the T.V. set came out & ruined the whole world! Not only have you poor white trash taken advantage of them & ruined their chances now you have ruined the college set. You are good at getting people when they are most vulnerable and changing their entire thinking!" These letters indicate how besieged some people were feeling in the midst of the turmoil of the late 1960s. In Julia, some viewers may have seen the "new Negro" as one who threatened their racially hierarchized universe. All the anxiety-reducing mechanisms employed by the program's creators to defuse notions of difference merely exacerbated anxiety for these viewers. They did not need to see explicit interracial sexuality dealt with on the television screen to see miscegenation as the logical (and inevitable) outcome of the erasure of racial difference. Such letters show the ideological extremes viewers could go to in their meaning-making endeavors. *Julia* as a text certainly did not encourage these interpretations. But since meanings are neither entirely determined nor controlled by the text, and since viewers are active agents in the process of constructing their own meanings, we can see how disturbing the process can be. Cultural studies theorists analyzing oppositional reading strategies have generally focused on how such viewers position themselves against dominant ideology. By implication such reading positions are often seen as positive evidence of cultural struggle against the constraining policies, perspectives, and practices of the ruling social order or "power bloc." [26] However, as these letters show, an oppositional reading strategy need not be a liberatory or progressive strategy.

Another issue that seemed to bother the hostile viewers was the mere presence of blacks on television. Blacks were slowly becoming more visible as supporting players in such popular programs as *I Spy, The Mod Squad, Hogan's Heroes,* and *Daktari.* Blacks were also occasionally being featured in commercial advertisements by 1967. But in the summer of 1968, the networks, at the urging of the Kerner Commission, outdid themselves by offering an unprecedented number of news documentaries on the state of black America, including CBS's acclaimed *Of Black America,* a seven-part series hosted by Bill Cosby. [27] For some viewers this was clearly too much: "We have had so much color shoved down our throats on special programs this summer its [*sic*] enough to make a person sick," wrote one viewer from Toronto. An anonymous viewer from Eufaula, Oklahoma, wrote, "After the riots and [the] network filled 'Black American' shows all summer, white people aren't feeling to [*sic*] kindly toward colored people shows. You are ahead of the time on this one." Yet another anonymous viewer, from Red Bluff, California, asserted, "I will not buy the product sponsoring this show or any show with a nigger in it. I believe I can speak for millions of real americans [*sic*]. I will write the sponsors of these shows. I am tired of niggers in my living room." A third anonymous viewer, from Bethpage, Long Island, asked, "Is this what you mean by color T.V. ugh. *Click!!*" Moreover, many of these people made no distinction between documentary representations of civil strife and the fictional world of *Julia.* Because both in some way concerned black people, *Julia* was really no different from the news specials about ghetto riots.

In the end, the reason it is useful to consider these disturbing and offensive letters is because of what they can tell us about the polysemic nature of reception. *Julia* was heavily criticized for constructing a "white Negro," for playing it safe in order not to scare off white viewers, for sugar-coating its racial messages. While all of that may be true, the show's "whiteness," middle-classness, and inoffensiveness did not defuse its threat to entrenched racist positions. This threat was also made evident by the fact that many of the hostile letters carried no return address. Unlike other viewers who wrote letters, both favorable and unfavorable, these letter writers were not interested in opening up a dialogue with the show's producers. The anonymity both shielded their besieged positions and revealed that such positions were no longer easily defensible.

Although the majority of letters in the Hal Kanter papers appear to be from white viewers, there are a significant number of letters from viewers who identified themselves as black.[28] Some of these letters share minor similarities with some of the responses from white viewers. For the most part, however, the reading strategies differ markedly. Jacqueline Bobo, drawing on the work of David Morley and Stuart Hall, has discussed the importance of "cultural competencies," or cultural codes, in order to make sense of how black women made their own meanings of *The Color Purple*.[29] As David Morley has stated: "What is needed here is an approach which links differential interpretations back into the socio-economic structures of society, showing how members of different groups and classes sharing different 'cultural codes' will interpret a given message differently, not just at the personal idiosyncratic level, but in a way 'systematically related' to their socio-economic position."[30] Bobo shifts the emphasis from social and economic structures to those of race in order to determine what codes black women employed when interpreting the film. This model can also help us understand the unique ways in which black viewers of *Julia* made sense of the program.

One crucial distinction between black and white viewers was that many of the black viewers displayed a participatory quality in their engagement with the program. They tended to erase boundaries between themselves and the text. Many letter writers asked if they could write episodes or play parts on the show. An eleven-year-old boy from the Bronx wrote: "I am a Negro and I am almost in the same position as Corey . . . Your show really tells how an average black or Negro person lives. I like your show so much that if you ever have a part to fill I would be glad to fill it for you."[31] A teenage girl from Buffalo wanted to create a new character for the show: *Julia*'s teenage sister. She proceeded to describe what the sister's characteristics would be and how she would like to play the part. A female teacher from Los Angeles wrote: "The thought occurred to me that Julia may be in need of a close friend on your television show—and/or Corey Baker may need a *good* first grade teacher (me). . . . I am not a militant but a *very proud Negro*."[32] The viewers who wanted to write episodes generally made their offer at the end of the letter after having detailed what they considered wrong with the show. Other viewers wanted to get together with Kanter personally to discuss the matter. One young woman from Detroit, studying mass media at college, suggested a meeting with Kanter: "Perhaps I can give you a better idea of what the Black people really want to see and what the white person really *needs* to see."[33]

While white viewers offered criticisms of the program, only the black viewers took it upon themselves to offer their assistance in improving the show. Their participatory relationship to the text indicated a far more active attempt at making the show meaningful. For the black viewers, the struggle over representation was between the actual program as created by the white producers and a potential, but more authentic, program to be created by the black viewers. By acting in and writing for the show, they became producers of meaning rather than mere recipients of meaning constructed by whites. Asserting the values of their cultural codes, they attempted to bring their own knowledge to the text. The positive engagement evidenced by these viewers arose from an articulation of self-affirming representation.

Ebony, a mass-circulation magazine targeted at a primarily middle-class black readership, also tried to find racially affirming representations in the program. Unlike other popular press accounts, Ebony took pains to emphasize the show's positive aspects while acknowledging its shortcomings. Pointing to *Julia's* four black scriptwriters, the article indicated that the show would provide new opportunities for African Americans in the television industry.[34] *Ebony* appeared to support the program specifically because the magazine saw that blacks were assisting (even if in a limited way) in its production.

One of the main areas of concern for many black viewers was whether the representation of blacks was realistic or whether the program portrayed a white world for white viewers. The denial of difference that numerous white viewers applauded was challenged by many, although not all, black viewers. A black woman from Los Angeles wrote: "Your show is geared to the white audience with no knowledge of the realness of normal Negro people. Your work is good for an all white program—but something is much missing from your character—Julia is unreal. To repeat again—Julia is no Negro woman. I know & I'm Negro with many friends in situations such as hers." Kanter replied somewhat sarcastically: "I'm glad you think our work is 'good for an all white program.' I'll pass your praise along to our black writer and black actors."

Whereas some of the white viewers, who had self-consciously identified themselves by race, appeared to think *Julia* was addressed primarily to a black audience, this black viewer had the opposite impression. The black audience was evacuated by a text that denied the "realness" of black identity. The mass-media student quoted above made a similar observation: "The show does not portray the life of the typical probing Black woman, it is rather a story of a white widow with a Black face. Even though she does possess the physical appearance of a Black woman (minus expensive clothing, plush apartment, etc.) she lacks that certain touch of reality." The problem of realism was again a manifestation of a crisis in representation, a crisis in how to define black identity and who would be authorized to do so. In his reply to the student, Kanter acknowledged the problem, stating, "I have considered its [your letter's] content and have come to the conclusion that you may be right."

Those white viewers who agreed that the show was unrealistic and that Julia was a "white Negro" were more likely to do reality checks with other white characters with whom they could identify, like Mrs. Waggedorn. Black viewers who found the show unrealistic and who found Julia to be a "white Negro" had difficulty identifying with any of the characters. The woman with many friends in Julia's situation searched the text in vain looking for confirmation of her identity as a black woman. Unlike the black women Jacqueline Bobo studied who found positive, progressive, and affirming meanings about black womanhood in *The Color Purple,* this particular woman found nothing in *Julia.* The text did not speak to her experiences. It did not construct a reading position from which she could use her cultural codes and find useful meanings. On the contrary, her experience as a black woman, along with those of her friends, blocked any possibility of finding a place for herself within the text. The strategy of breaking down textual boundaries and inserting oneself into the program by offering to write episodes or play a role may have functioned to avert this problem. It may have given some black viewers a mechanism by which to place themselves within the program and assert their own identities as African Americans.

The other major arena of concern for black viewers, as well as for some white critics, was the depiction of the black family. This issue is a difficult one for feminist theory. The reading strategies employed by black viewers of *Julia* present a problematic situation since, from a (white) feminist perspective, it would be difficult to see their readings as empowering for women. Only one of the viewers who commented on the portrayal of the black family took an antipatriarchal position. The other black viewers (all of whom were women) criticized the show for not having a strong male head of the family.

The one woman who did not take the creators of *Julia* to task for omitting a strong patriarch was herself reacting to *Saturday Review* critic Shayon's remarks that *Julia* was perpetuating the "castration theme in the history of the American Negro male."[35] Offering her services as a writer of short stories and plays, the viewer went on to provide the following observations: "No one ever let the Negro woman have her say even the middle class one. No one really knows how hard it is for the Negro woman when her man walks out on her leaving her with four or five babies." Another woman from Chicago offered an analysis more representative of black viewers:

> I don't think any more of you for excluding the black man from this series than I think of the "original" slave owners who first broke up the black family!

You white men have never given the black man anything but a hard time.

If you really want to do some good you'll marry "Julia" to a strong black man before the coming TV season is over and take her from that white doctor's office and put her in the home as a housewife where she belongs!

Otherwise a lot of black women—like me, who love, respect, and honor their black husbands will exclude "Julia" from our TV viewing just as you have excluded our black male from your show!

A married woman from Brooklyn who signed herself "An Ex-Black Viewer" wrote: "After viewing the season premiere of 'Julia,' I, as a black woman find myself outraged. Is this program what you call a portrayal of a typical Negro family (which is, incidentally, fatherless?) If so, you are only using another means to brainwash the black people who, unfortunately, may view your program weekly."

The problems associated with the show's portrayal of black family life were also discussed in black academic circles. In an article on blacks in American television that appeared in *The Black Scholar* in 1974, Marilyn Diane Fife strongly attacked *Julia* for ignoring black men. By making the central character a widowed black woman, the program neatly sidestepped the critical issue of black men and their position within African American culture, as well as their position within American society. Fife observed: "Traditionally the black female has accommodated more to the white power structure. The real social problems of blacks have always turned around the black man's inability to have dignity, and the power and respect of his family. 'Julia' disregards all this by turning the only black male roles into potential suitors, not actual male figures involved in the overall series." [36] Fife thus suggested that the focus on a female black lead rendered the series safer, less likely to grapple with issues that might upset white viewers.

White feminists may be particularly uneasy with such analyses since they seem to affirm the very conditions of patriarchal family structures that they have challenged. However, for black women, this critique of patriarchy has ignored questions of racism that are seen as crucial to an understanding of the situation of black women. The historically different positions occupied by black and (middle-class) white women within the social order should alert us to the problems of grafting feminist perspectives developed within a white middle-class milieu onto the experiences of black women. However, this necessity of acknowledging difference seems to render problematic the mobilization of much feminist theory to apply to anything but the experiences of white women. Given this dilemma, I (along with other feminists) would suggest that feminist theory needs to respond to the specific historical situations of different women living in patriarchal systems.[37]

Indeed, a more historically grounded examination of the unique experiences of black women within family structures can help explain the responses of these women to *Julia*. As Angela Davis and Jacqueline Jones have pointed out in their histories of black women, the life of a housewife within a patriarchal familial structure was quite uncommon for black women. For these women, work generally meant exploitative labor for whites that took black women away from their own families and communities.[38] Unlike middle-class white women, who may have seen work outside the home as potentially liberating, the history of work for black women had no such emancipatory connotations. The viewer who wanted Julia taken out of the white doctor's office was thus making sense of Julia's labor from within this larger history of black women's work. That Julia resorted to leaving Corey locked up in their apartment while she went off to her job interview may have had deeper meanings for black women who historically had been forced to leave their children to fend for themselves while they cared for the children of either white owners or white employers.

Another way to examine the perspectives of these black women is to situate them in relation to dominant ideas about the black family that were in circulation at the time. It is likely that these discourses would have been familiar to educated, professional, middle-class members of the African American community. Many of the black letter writers identified themselves by profession—teachers, nurses, students—and tended to write grammatically and stylistically sophisticated letters. This leads me to assume that they were most likely middle-class viewers. The dominant perspective on the black family, with which these viewers were likely to be familiar, was an intensely misogynistic view of a destructive "black matriarchy."

This thesis was first put forth by the influential African American sociologist E. Franklin Frazier, who began writing about the black family in the 1930s. He attributed a matriarchal character to black familial structure and found its source in the dislocation and stresses of slavery and discrimination. While this familial structure remained strong within the black community after emancipation, Frazier contended that matriarchal formations predominated in mostly lower-class, impoverished urban and rural families. Rather than give much credit to the strength and resiliency of black women, Frazier saw their power within the family as a sign of dysfunction. Those families who managed to achieve middle-class or upper-middle-class status assumed patriarchal characteristics mirroring white families, thus assimilating more successfully into the American norm. Frazier felt that blacks had been unable to retain their African cultural heritage when ripped away from their homeland by slave traders. He therefore felt blacks needed to adopt the familial arrangements dominant in their new homeland in order to survive as a people. Thus the two-parent nuclear family with a strong male head, a structure Frazier saw in upwardly mobile black families, was desirable.[39]

Frazier, like many of the white viewers of *Julia* who attempted to deny difference, did not see any problems with this white norm. Patriarchy seemed to work in constructing successful families if we view the white middle-class model as normative. But Frazier, like most theorists of the black family, was concerned primarily with the black male and was thus rather blind to the position of the female in familial structures, whether black or white.

Frazier's perspective can help us understand why the familial structure in *Julia* was considered so problematic for many black viewers as well as for numerous critics who may also have been familiar with this thesis. On the one hand, the Baker family seemed the epitome of an upwardly mobile black family. Julia, as a nurse, was a professional who had joined the middle class. She and Corey, living in an integrated apartment building with white neighbors, appeared to be completely assimilated into white society. On the other hand, this assimilated, middle-class black family had no male head. As was the case in lower-class and ghettoized black families, a woman took sole responsibility for running the family. The black family depicted in *Julia* thus threatened the dichotomized model Frazier had described. The Bakers collapsed the distinctions between the upwardly mobile middle-class family predicated on patriarchy and the impoverished and dysfunctional lower-class family predicated on matriarchy.

The Moynihan Report was even more influential in distributing ideas about the black family in the 1960s.[40] Produced by the Department of Labor in 1965 (around the time of the Watts uprising), the report described black families caught within a "tangle of pathology." One characteristic of this so-called pathology was the supposed preponderance of female-headed black households in comparison to white households. Echoing the misogynist stance of Frazier, Moynihan felt this situation had grave consequences for African Americans as a people: "In essence, the Negro community has been forced into a matriarchal structure which, because it is so out of line with the rest of the American society, seriously retards the progress of the group as a whole, and imposes a crushing burden on the Negro male and, in consequence, on a great many Negro women as well."[41] The report was denounced by many in the black community who felt that it put as much, if not more, of the blame on the black family structure as it did on white racism and discrimination in order to explain the dire situation of many blacks in American society.[42] While some scholars attempted to trace matriarchal or matrilineal familial structures back to black cultural ancestry in West

Africa, few in the 1960s were championing female-dominated families within scholarly or popular discourses.

Within this cultural climate, where so much attention was being focused on the apparently pathological and destructive quality of female-headed black households, *Julia* was a likely target for criticism from black viewers. As an unattached, independent woman, Julia could be seen as a threatening figure, yet another strong matriarch perpetuating in the realm of popular culture a familial model menacing African American social life. It is unfortunate that the emergent women's movement, which would most likely embrace a figure such as Julia precisely because she was independent and career-oriented, would find it impossible to speak to the unique oppressions of black women. The perniciousness of the black matriarchy myth remained unexposed.[43]

The readings provided by viewer letters and popular press critics should indicate that there was no one preferred, dominant, or definitive set of meanings attached to *Julia.* Different viewers brought their socially, culturally, racially, and historically determined interpretive strategies to bear upon the program. And because of the historically specific moment of *Julia*'s appearance, a moment of racial strife when previously unquestioned categories of racial identity and definition no longer held firm, the program itself was as conflicted as the interpretations of it. Even Kanter at times acquiesced to the dissenting views of his audience.

By looking at *Julia* as a symptomatic text—symptomatic of the crisis in race relations and its concomitant representations—we can see how a document of popular culture can serve as a piece of historical evidence, embodying within itself tensions working their way through American society at a particular moment. The social and political turmoil of the 1960s manifested itself within a multitude of institutions and sectors of American civil society. Even television, saddled with the moniker "the vast wasteland" for its vapid and blithely apolitical programming in the 1960s, could not escape the turmoil. *Julia* straddled the vacuous "wasteland" and the more socially relevant programming inaugurated at CBS with *All in the Family* in 1970.[44] Despite flirting with relevance, *Julia* tended to slide toward innocuous cuteness. When we shift our attention away from the program and onto its audiences, however, we find contentious and sometimes highly politicized responses. By concentrating on reception, we can thus begin to chart the dynamics of historical and social change. In the process, American television in the 1960s starts to look less and less like a vast wasteland.

Part Three | Television in the 1970s

By the 1970s, the networks began to rely more heavily on audience demographics as the key to a program's success. Total numbers of viewers mattered less than who was watching when. Young adults in their late teens and early twenties were more desirable than the rural, older viewers who watched more television. In order to reach more youthful viewers, CBS, known for "rural" sitcoms such as The Beverly Hillbillies *or* The Andy Griffith Show, *initiated the shift to "socially relevant" programming that addressed contemporary issues and concerns.* The Mary Tyler Moore Show, *which premiered in September 1970 and ran until 1977, was one of the first of these sitcoms to incorporate contemporary social trends into a familiar sitcom structure. It featured a single, professional working woman in "slice of life" situations that arose both at home and work. The main character, Mary Richards, worked in a television newsroom, which also enabled television to poke fun at itself. The show captured the ambiance of the 1970s as it dealt with problems and issues typical of the era.*

Norman Lear's All in the Family *followed in January 1971 and lasted until 1983. The show was based on an English sitcom called* 'Til Death Do Us Part, *and it depicted a working-class family headed by Archie Bunker, a bigoted conservative who tried to dominate his wife and daughter while constantly arguing with his liberal son-in-law. Although CBS was initially hesitant to air the controversial program, favorable audience reaction to the pilot prompted them to give it a try. For the first time since* The Honeymooners, *a sitcom about a working-class family returned to television. But* All in the Family *was unlike any other sitcom that had been on American television, both in Archie Bunker's free use of racial and ethnic epithets and the show's focus on controversial social and political issues. Although it began with poor ratings, it gradually built an audience, especially after reruns aired from late March through May. By late May* All in the Family *became number one in the ratings.*

With the success of All in the Family, *the networks began to cultivate the new "urban" sitcom, with complex characters that faced complicated situations. These new sitcoms added elements of drama to the sitcom form. The humor was character-based rather than a consequence of characters facing absurd situations. Moreover, sitcoms became a forum for examining social problems and issues, which were perhaps easier to confront in the context of humor. Death, alcoholism, and divorce, previously taboo as sitcom topics, were present in both* Mary Tyler Moore *and* All in the Family. *Storylines often continued from show to show, and the characters developed over time. The sitcom began to tackle difficult topics and to adopt the serial form previously the domain of the soap opera.[1]*

By the fall of 1972, CBS continued to expand this new form of sitcom by introducing M*A*S*H *(1972–83) and* Maude *(1972–78), the latter a spinoff of* All in the Family. Maude *was remarkable for being one of the first sitcoms to star a middle-aged woman who had been divorced three times (preceding the divorced mother of two on* One Day at a Time, *which ran from 1975 to 1984). Not only did* Maude *challenge previous stereotypes of middle-aged women, but it also acknowledged that divorce and single parents had become commonplace.* Maude *also incited controversy when her character became pregnant and decided to have an abortion. Many CBS affiliates refused to air the two-part episode, thus providing a clear example of a sitcom serving as a site of social controversy.*

CBS also presented M*A*S*H *the same year. Although it was a typical war comedy in its first year, its themes gradually became more complex. Demographics showed that it was popular with young viewers, and thus the network allowed it time to build an audience. As it improved in the ratings, it began to shift its content to more dramatic, innovative material. It became one of the first successful dramedies on television, where it seamlessly merged comedic and dramatic material. It featured an ensemble cast and introduced the idea of multiple storylines, one which of was often serious. Scenes shot within the operating room did not have a laugh track. It commented on the futility of war while also developing deep characters who evolved over time.* M*A*S*H *was also one of the first sitcoms to have a major character "die"—when actor McLean Stevenson decided to quit the show, the writers had him killed off when his plane was shot down as he headed home. Not typical sitcom fare, but appropriate for a dramedy such as* M*A*S*H. *In fact, there have been very few successful dramedies after* M*A*S*H. *Its dark humor and political cant may have especially appealed to audiences demoralized by Watergate and the inconclusive end of the Vietnam War.*

The 1970s was also the era of the spinoff. There were Norman Lear spinoffs of All in the Family *such as* Maude, Good Times *(1974–79), and* The Jeffersons *(1975–85), as well as a plethora of spinoffs of* The Mary Tyler Moore Show: Rhoda *(1974–78),* Phyllis *(1975–77), and* The Betty White Show *(1977–78).* Lou

Grant *(1977–82) was also a spinoff of* Mary Tyler Moore, *but it became a drama rather than a sitcom, the only such case of generic shifting in television history. Other shows produced by MTM Productions such as* The Bob Newhart Show *(1972–78)* WKRP in Cincinnati *(1978–82), and* Taxi *(1978–83) became successful sitcom staples. Ethnic sitcoms reappeared on television, with* Sanford and Son *(1972–77),* Chico and the Man *(1974–78), and* Diff'rent Strokes *(1978–86) also achieving solid ratings. Although these shows still perpetuated negative racial stereotypes, others such as* Barney Miller *(1975–82) or* Taxi *began to portray a more integrated world full of a range of characters from different ethnic and racial backgrounds.*

As television began to move to more "realistic" programming geared to a younger, sophisticated, urban (and affluent) audience, public groups organized to protest the excessive amounts of sex and violence on television. In response to FCC pressure, the networks decided at the end of 1974 to dedicate a "family" hour from eight to nine o'clock each evening. Few popular programs resulted, and the idea was abandoned in May 1976. But ABC did achieve ratings success with family-hour shows such as Happy Days *(1974–84) and* Laverne and Shirley *(1976–83), both of which portrayed a nostalgic, essentially white view of 1950s America. Yet,* Happy Days *became a hit only after it altered its format and showcased "The Fonz," a prototypical bad boy in the mold of Eddie Haskell from* Leave It to Beaver. Laverne and Shirley *marked a return to the slapstick humor characteristics of sitcoms like* I Love Lucy, *but it also featured two strong single women in leading roles on television. Both of these shows, while avoiding "relevance," became solid television fare from the mid-1970s into the 1980s.*

After the failure of the family viewing hour, the networks began to substitute sex for violence as a means to quell public protest. Norman Lear achieved a hit when his Mary Hartman, Mary Hartman *(1976–77)—part sitcom and part soap opera spoof—was the first syndicated show to become a national hit. When the networks passed on the controversial show, Lear went directly to independent television stations to sell the idea. After* Mary Hartman *became a success, ABC decided to launch* Soap *(1977–81), its own sitcom/soap opera spoof. Even before the pilot aired, advance publicity led to public protests over the sexual content. Yet, ABC persevered, and* Soap *became a hit. This was followed by* Three's Company *(1977–84), another successful sitcom based on sophomoric sexual humor. This show featured three single young adults sharing an apartment (with the male pretending to be gay to fool the landlord). The plots and dialogue were laced with sexual innuendo, which has remained a strong component of much sitcom humor to the present day.*

The essays in this section discuss two representative sitcoms from the 1970s: The Mary Tyler Moore Show *and* Laverne and Shirley.

J. M.

9

The Mary Tyler Moore Show
Women at Home and at Work

SERAFINA BATHRICK

Situation comedy situates us. More than any other television genre, it provides us, as viewers whose everyday experience may be shaped by TV's presence and programming, with a powerful model for private life in the age of broadcast culture. Sitcom humors us with its comic portrayals of the collisions that characterize our conflicting attitudes toward technology. By personalizing the tensions that exist between our real needs as human beings and the dictates of a highly rationalized society, these comedies encourage us to "fit in" and even to enjoy our efforts at doing so. But we may also continue to feel a sense of regret as we organize our lives around the televised image of the everyday. And although the representation of life at home has changed since the early years of television, we are confronted with our own loss of experience as we watch situation comedy. For while the video image seeks to be ever-relevant so as to integrate and ingratiate itself into our present lives through its visual style and narrative conventions, it also confronts us with what we have lost historically since the arrival of industrially produced culture.

By the mid-nineteenth century, a systematically cultivated ideology of the nuclear family compensated for the dissolution of community. A belief in individualism replaced the needs for collectivity, and rigidly imposed sex-gender differences helped explain the schism between private and public life. At this time the birth of a culture industry that printed and circulated the facts and fictions of this new era became essential to the shaping of a modern consciousness. In the

A slightly different version of this chapter was originally published in *MTM: Quality Television,* ed. Jane Feuer (British Film Institute, 1984), 99–131. It has been reprinted here by permission of the author and the publisher.

155

mid-twentieth century, with the advent of a mass medium that brought a constant flow of images and information into the very center of private life, the focus on the bourgeois family ideal gave way to an ideology of the familial. The old opposition between family and society had begun to collapse. Contemporary sociologists Michèle Barrett and Mary McIntosh describe this phenomenon: "Just as the family has been socially constructed, so society has been familialized. Indeed it can be argued that in contemporary capitalist society one dominant set of social meanings is precisely an ideology of familialism. The meaning of family life extends far beyond the walls of concrete households in which proverbial 'co-residing close kin' go about their business of marrying and raising children."[1] Social and economic factors thus widened the gap between the promise and the reality of family life. In this way the ideology of the familial may be viewed as a new effort to salvage what is most positive about family-as-community, while at the same time it is used to reinforce some of the conservatism associated with gender and family hierarchy. Pivotal to this ideological shift is the changed position of the middle-class woman: from domestic True Woman in the nineteenth-century family idyll to the career True Woman in the twentieth-century familial workplace.

It is woman who provides situation comedy with its capacity to mediate historical change through its representation of both the family and the familial. This tendency began with the ideology of the nineteenth-century True Woman, who was worshipped as she was assigned the role of family maintenance-expert. Ever devoted to her home and family, she was estheticized by the mass media as fragile and feminine while she was in fact asked to function as the powerful preserver of individualism in a newly competitive industrial society. Monumentalized as one who could "uphold the pillars of the temple with her frail white hand," the True Woman functioned as an essential ally-and-invention of the culture industry.[2] Above all, she was to preserve her home as a refuge from the marketplace, while at the same time she would grow increasingly dependent on that marketplace for its goods and services. Thus, many of the values that she maintained as alternatives to the rationalized work sphere were eroded by the invasion of consumer culture into the home. By the 1950s the arrival of television insured an almost complete "occupation" of the private by the public. For the True Woman, there was surely the experience of seeing her own family replaced by the TV family. But there was also the new economic reality that confronted Americans in the post–World War II era: middle-class women, wives, and mothers were entering the labor force as never before. Between 1950 and 1970, the number of married women who worked doubled, and the percentage of women who made up the workforce grew from thirty-four to forty-three percent.[3]

When TV sought legitimacy as a made-for-the-family product during its first decade, situation comedy and nostalgic drama combined in popularity to recall a previous time in history when the nuclear family was in mother's keeping. The reality of the working housewife was denied completely as old-fashioned mothers on TV spoke family wisdom to America's new postwar mothers. There were real married couples who played comic married couple routines for newlyweds who were learning to stay home with their TVS. Because family "togetherness" was synonymous with Americanism in the 1950s, the middle class who could afford the first televisions cooperated in front of their screens, their couches and chairs lined up as if to mirror the living-room sets in domestic dramas and sit-coms like *I Love Lucy* and *Ozzie and Harriet.* They rearranged their dinnertimes to allow for watching the dining-room-table-as-family-forum in *Mama.* That San Francisco-based Norwegian mother and her New York Jewish immigrant counterpart Mrs. Goldberg wanted nothing more than to stay at home. Lucy always complained that she wanted to be in show business, and we knew Lucille Ball was a powerful entrepreneur, but as Ricky's dizzy wife, she too stayed at home and had babies. (More people tuned in to the birth of little Ricky on *I Love Lucy* than to Eisenhower's inauguration spectacle; Americans were increasingly familiar with the television family.) Ozzie and Harriet, another married couple who performed as a TV family, provided broadcast fans with a continuous and seamless family album as they moved from radio to television, bringing their sons into the picture when they were old enough to take on public person-alities. All of these series preserved the mythic nuclear family ideal for postwar audiences.

Mary Richards and her working women friends appear in 1970 as television's first serious concession to a changed world where middle-class daughters leave home, earn their living, and remain single. This new image emerged at first quite tentatively. *TV Guide* presented Mary Tyler Moore the actress and Mary Richards the central character on *The Mary Tyler Moore Show* to a first-season audience as if they had both been helped substantially in their efforts to perform as modern women by the television industry itself. The rhetoric of a September 1970 article in *TV Guide* describes the star's capacity as a television actress, and maintains its own self-promotional interests by presenting Mary Tyler Moore as an "instinctual" performer who has "never had a lesson in her life," and who is thus a natural "fit" for the medium that seeks to validate daily life as sitcom. Not a professional who had made it on stage or in the movies, this star is quoted in an article entitled "You've Come a Long Way, Baby": "I'm not an actress who can create character. I play *me.* I was scared if I tampered with it I might ruin it." As if to suggest that the television medium is best for the untrained but trusting neophyte, Mary Tyler Moore is also credited with having grown up to success as "middle-class America's zingiest housewife" on *The Dick Van Dyke Show* from 1961 to 1966.[4] As is characteristic of *TV Guide* and of television culture, this actress's inability to succeed in any other of the performing arts of mass media is attributed to her own gender-determined priorities: she has a private life and works to protect a happy marriage to her business partner. All of these points are made as preface to the season's new show—about a single career woman of thirty. Surely such a mixture of self-congratulatory praise for television and for the inherently home-loving nature of this star must remind us that *The Mary Tyler Moore Show* stepped cautiously into the American living-room.

Soon after *The Mary Tyler Moore Show* had become a successful Saturday night prime-time program, *TV Guide* published a second kind of commentary dealing with women who sought jobs in TV production, and women's roles in current TV series. Much like the self-aggrandizing prose that had previously hyped the responsibility of the industry as it "looked after" its female star, these articles promote an image of a responsive medium that is granting women opportunities to work behind the scenes. In both instances, the sexism is blatant: the female star who appears on screen is a virtuous homebody, while the working woman who produces is revealed as a pin-up on the job in articles entitled "The Writer Wore Hotpants" and "Cameraperson in Hotpants."[5] It is in this context that *TV Guide* readers encountered a number of serious attacks by feminist journalists who were finally voicing and publishing their outrage about TV roles for women. Early in 1971 Caroline Bird, author of *Born Female,* reviewed the roles played by women in the so-called "relevant" shows of the recent seasons. In an essay entitled "What's Television Doing for Fifty Percent of Americans?" Bird asserts that working women portrayed on TV are never granted private lives and that mothers are denied any relationship to the workplace. The few "shadowy" female characters who exist as independent women in responsible jobs take no initiative within the narratives, and frequently disappear for weeks at a time. Caroline Bird sees and names covert hostility on the part of network television toward working women, claiming that "none of these shows is challenging the family system, demanding a new kind of sexual relationship or a new division of labour in the home."[6]

Diane Rosen contributed an attack on "TV and the Single Girl," in another 1971 *TV Guide* article, where she remarks that fifteen years have passed since *Father Knows Best,* and yet, "I, a single 27-year old living alone in New York City, can no longer find a reflection of my life anywhere on commercial television." She points out that for five years (1966–71) Marlo Thomas's portrayal of *That Girl* simply reinforced the idea that a single woman is endearing only insofar as she is incompetent. Thomas's role is that of a dizzy aspiring actress who depends on her father and her boyfriend for all advice and affection. Rosen credits this actress with having struggled with ABC executives for permission to play the part of a single woman who lives alone, and even implies that she may have helped *The Mary Tyler Moore Show* to appear in 1970. Although this article emphasizes the miraculous arrival of two unattached thirty-year-old working women in Mary and Rhoda, the author suggests that shows about single women remain rare and necessarily tokens to the modern woman's experience. Rosen notes that neither Sandy Duncan in *Funny Face* nor Shirley MacLaine in *Shirley's World,* both from the 1971 season, present unmarried women in convincing contexts. In fact neither of these shows lasted out the season, a further indication that *The Mary Tyler Moore Show* succeeded in part because it was the only one of its kind.[7]

In another *TV Guide* article that appeared in late 1973, Letty Cottin Pogrebin, a feminist columnist and author of *How To Make It in a Man's World,* writes an introductory essay to an upcoming ABC documentary entitled *Woman's Place.* Like Bird and Rosen, Pogrebin reinforces the feminist claim that "the personal is political" in a recollection of how television betrayed her as she was growing up in the 1950s. She develops a powerful argument for how she learned to lie as she became a well-socialized girl in this decade, and cites the many self-demeaning steps she took in an effort to imitate television's teenagers and to obey television's mothers. Pogrebin shows how the mass media, specifically TV, aligns itself with the interests of the nineteenth-century bourgeois family. Thus, women continue to uphold the myth of the patriarch. "In the constant search for male approval we were willing to lose ourselves," she laments. Her argument suggests that middle-class mothers who were learning to shape family life around the TV family in the 1950s saw themselves idealized by the medium, and because of that private bond created between mothering and televised representations of mothers, Pogrebin adds, "we [teenage daughters] never knew a girl had any other choice." Finally, the article exonerates network TV, for it turns the reader's attention to the possibilities within contemporary documentary to explore woman's place in American society. And insofar as "unlearning the lie" means rejecting the early decades of family-focused sitcom, her final lines affirm a determination apparently shared by television itself: "Now we are teaching the truth to our daughters so that growing up female can mean growing up free."[8]

It is interesting to note that, in some of the same ways *TV Guide* sought to reassure its viewer-readers that the network's new career woman show was really another, albeit more "responsive," commitment to family values, the determination of its coproducers Allan Burns and James Brooks to avoid social issues complemented what the publicity branch of the industry was promising. Burns and

Brooks have recently been interviewed in *The Producer's Medium,* and both make clear their commitment to "character comedy" rather than Lear-style comedy with its political tendency. When asked whether he felt that *The Mary Tyler Moore Show* addressed the question of women's rights, Brooks attributes to "good timing" the relationship that is established. Mary Richards's character and the women's movement "evolved" simultaneously, he claims, "but we did not espouse women's rights, we sought to show someone from Mary Richards's background being in a world where women's rights were being talked about and it was having an impact."[9]

But while these producers may have viewed the women's movement as "background" to their series, it is essential to note that they did hire women scriptwriters for *The Mary Tyler Moore Show.* The fact that Burns and Brooks bought more material from women writers than any other TV producers at that time is noted by Ellen Sherman in a 1974 *Ms.* magazine article on the long history of discrimination against women scriptwriters in the medium. Sherman remarks that it is one of *The Mary Tyler Moore Show* regulars, Gail Parent, who along with Renee Taylor, became the first woman to win an Emmy in 1973. In 1974 there were eight women awarded Emmys for a variety of categories in TV production, among them Treva Silverman, who received an award for Best Comedy Series Writer for *The Mary Tyler Moore Show.* Silverman, Parent, the team of Barbara Gallagher and Sybil Adelman, and Karyl Geld all worked for Burns and Brooks. In 1974 Silverman, then the only female head story editor in television, is quoted by Sherman: "Women on *The Mary Tyler Moore Show* are allowed to have a sense of their own intelligence. It's only then that the real breakthroughs for women can be made in television." The *Ms.* article mentions that fifty percent of the scripts accepted by the MTM producer team in 1973 were written by women, way above the typical percentages for other shows. During that same year, Sherman attests: "out of 63 series on television, 36 employed no women writers whatsoever."[10]

It remains important to explore how Burns and Brooks's commitment to character rather than social comedy occasionally collided with the political interests of female writers who had struggled for work in a sexist culture industry. What these producers say about politics as "background" and the ways in which they defend the primacy of individual characters as the basis for comedy confirm what we have seen as the historical and ideological mandate for keeping the familial intact through the presence in the workplace of the humane and accessible woman. There was surely a move away from the domestic sitcom where a private house provides the stage for all problem solving, but whether the TV newsroom as workplace marked a new environment for a new kind of women's work remains to be considered. Just as television audiences were comforted in the 1950s by the mirroring of their own lives in the screen's surface imagery of home spaces, it is arguable that the 1970s audience was wholly familiar with the look of a "newsroomfamily" and so was receptive to the position of the career woman in this context. The emphasis on character remains a powerful reminder of how the appeal of the familial includes its expansion at various times in history to encompass the sanctity and significance of human relationships in all aspects of daily life. And while there was an important concession to woman's new place in the postwar economy, we must also ask to what extent Mary Richards remained separated from the powers of authorship in the newsroom and from the policy-making work that is involved in editing and shaping television news.

The Mise-en-Scènes of Home and Work on *The Mary Tyler Moore Show*

The continuity that is achieved by character comedy is heightened by the use of limited sets and locations; we quickly learn to associate the three men and the three women who play major roles on *The Mary Tyler Moore Show* with specific rooms, doorways, and furniture. The men function primarily in the WJM newsroom, where each occupies a designated desk or separate office. The women who are Mary Richards's neighbors meet in her apartment, where they situate themselves in different areas, depending on whether they have been invited or have simply dropped in. Domestic and work spaces are thus quite rigidly distinguished and are marked according to gender by the kinds of social interactions that take place in each. Because we do not know what goes on between these two worlds, we are further reinforced in our perceptions about separate spheres. Although Mary alone is consistently comfortable in occupying both places, we never see her commuting between the two. And aside from the opening montage sequence that accompanies the titles for every episode, there is no city, no suburb, and no transportation to connect them. We thus view Mary's privileged role in both spheres as uniquely hers, perhaps coming to believe that she is afforded this mobility largely because others remain in their gender-determined places. Although there are significant instances when a woman from her house appears in the newsroom or when a newsman visits her apartment, these events mark irregularities in the narrative, small transgressions often associated with personal crises or more specifically with the needs of individuals to seek out Mary at such times.

The two principal interior sets provide contrasting mise-en-scènes, although they are similar in their obvious staginess and so remind us that both exist for a live studio audience as well as for us as home viewers. As a TV audience, we are established in relation to the live performance by the use of an editing pattern that cuts from full stage shots to tight shots on individuals or pairs. There are two long shots that recur: one of the whole set that is Mary's apartment and one that encompasses the entire newsroom. Both of these camera positions provide us with a strong sense of accessible space—space that may mirror or simply come to feel as familiar as the place of the viewer her/himself. Above all there is a symmetry in the composition of these two establishing shots. They function in similar ways to return us to "normal," a well-tried technique in sitcom. From having been moved about and around the verbally conflicting and sometimes physically colliding characters as they break from their places with such inevitable rhythms throughout any episode, these shots return us to a calm associated with spectator privilege, but, more important, they affirm our belief that resolution involves people-in-their-proper-roles-and places. They also affirm Mary Richards's power to mediate, so that a return to a full stage shot heightens our awareness of and even our investment in her social skills. Thus, the mise-en-scène of her apartment and that of her workplace gain a particular significance in relation to that True-Womanly aspect of her character. We see that she shapes and guides the interactions in both places, insuring that each remains separate but connected, by her own presence.

From the first episode ("Love is All Around," 1970), a number of clues to Mary's personality and to her social role are established by her relationship to her private living space. Some of the same efforts to legitimate modern womanhood by recalling old female attributes are intact through the very architecture of her home.[11] As she moves into a one-room "studio" apartment, from the quaint interior details and from an exterior shot that introduces the first scene as she arrives in the Minneapolis suburb, we also learn that Mary lives in a big Victorian house. Subdivided now for the modern one-child family or the "single" adult, the turreted mansion recalls an age when an extended family lived there with servants to care for its three generations of inhabitants. Its present state also reminds the audience of wartime changes and postwar realities: the middle-class family can no longer aspire to such palatial housing, and by the 1950s the suburban tract-home became the model for a more efficient nuclear family that could not afford to hire domestic help. Mary's apartment house thus represents the entire history of the American middle-class family home, and we are alerted to the ways in which she herself might embody one hundred years of good housekeeping. It will be her task to ensure that yesterday's family becomes today's familial. When Mary first enters the modernized space that will be hers, it is the empty but potential stage that will contain all her private life encounters for the first five years of the show. (Mary moves to a downtown highrise apartment toward the end of the series.) As an audience we are asked to identify with this moment of arriving and moving in, and while her first encounters at home and at her job all take place on Mary's first day in this new city, each meeting provides us with a brief dramatic introduction to the five characters who will become her familial friends and coworkers.

Phyllis Lindstrom is Mary's married friend from the past who lives on the first floor with her daughter Bess and husband Lars. She is landlady for the house and is the one who introduces Mary to her new apartment. While boasting about the clean paint and the new wall-to-wall carpet, Phyllis leads Mary toward the closed curtains, as if finally to display a view of suburbia through the three-part Victorian windows. She opens them with a dramatic gesture and what is revealed instead of the wooded landscape is the dark figure of a woman washing the windows from the outside ledge. Shrouded in an old-world kerchief and a big black coat is Rhoda, the other woman with whom Mary will share this house. She is disdained by Phyllis, and the reason for their animosity seems instantly apparent: Rhoda has challenged her neighbor's would-be gentility as hostess and even Phyllis's right to rent the apartment to Mary. As though from another world (and indeed as a Jew from the Bronx she is an invader to Mary and Phyllis's midwestern idyll), Rhoda enters her new neighbor's space through a window. She is dark and comical next to Phyllis Lindstrom, a recalcitrant city woman who transforms a polite discussion of decor to talk of salaries and property and upward mobility. Rhoda claims she put a whole month's paycheck into the new carpet because she planned to move from her upstairs garret into this more airy space. Phyllis characteristically runs for help from the building's owner and returns with the authority to "tell on" Rhoda and to inform Mary that she is lying. Mary registers shock at her crass invader: "You lied to me," she says to Rhoda, who answers with perfect equilibrium: "You betcha." Mary Richards must learn to mediate. From the first encounter with her opposing women neighbors, one from upstairs and one from downstairs, we find her in the middle, bending to negotiate the differences between an aggressive single working woman and a passive-aggressive married one. Throughout *The Mary Tyler Moore Show* she will bring Rhoda and Phyllis together, thus finding within herself and within her living space the room for difference. Mary's true work as mediator will depend very much on her apartment, situated as it is between these opposites and in a house that once contained a family. We will ask, throughout the series, as if to rework the words of daytime radio programs: "Can Mary Richards, girl-next-door, learn to live with and let live her antagonistic neighbors?"

There are three important parts to the set that is Mary's living space, and each area provides for different kinds of interactions between the residents of the big house and others who visit her there. At the extreme stage right is a door to the hallway on the second floor. This is Mary's front door, but it is also the meeting place for Phyllis and Rhoda, who frequently collide at this halfway point between their own apartments. They are always seeking out Mary's capacities to find equilibrium, and often they want both her spiritual and material provisions. This doorway also serves as a ministage for numerous goodnight kisses that become awkward goodbyes because, just as things get serious in Mary's private life, one of her "family" members rings the bell or just walks in. Mary's boyfriends become strangers when Lou, Murray, or Ted appear at her door. There is a passageway that leads from the door behind the sunken living-room center of the stage to the kitchen on the extreme left. This allows the characters who know and need Mary to proceed directly to her food supply or to her round dining table. It also distinguishes them from the "guests," outsiders who are motioned to the couch and stuffed chairs that constitute a "parlour." Because this more formal space often appears to dictate where people should sit and even what they should say, it functions to remind us of the differences between an old-fashioned hostess and a modern friend. Sometimes an establishing shot of the whole set reveals an agonized group staring out at us as though obedient to some decorous ideal that went out with horsehair furniture. But Mary's apartment as a whole does not have that kind of formality. Neither a fireplace nor a TV set provides a focus for her visitors. As a result it is Mary herself who is a center. Sometimes still and attentive with one other person, sometimes moving skillfully between several people, her apartment appears to facilitate her social skills.

Mary can stride like a long-legged runner across the span of her apartment in order to answer the doorbell, and she can provide for close community needs by settling people at her dining table, the third important area in her place. Innermost, and closest to the kitchen that is every True Woman's heartland, this space recalls the roundtable togetherness that included the Nelsons, the Goldbergs, and Mama's Norwegian family in the early years of TV. Mary gathers her feuding neighbors there for quiet meals, serves coffee and cookies to the newsmen who visit, and reminds us that she can still bring everyone together in old-fashioned ways. We also learn in the first episode that Mary's "open-house" modern lifestyle corresponds to the same lack of privacy that characterizes life in an old family house. In the first episode, when Rhoda returns for the tag to commiserate with Mary about the final visit and departure of her two-year-long "relationship," Mary marvels that her crass neighbor could be so attuned to her feelings of regret and resignation. The house itself provides an answer to this bond among sensitive women: Rhoda points to a low place on the wall near Mary's door and says, "I've got this tremendous intuition and you've got this heating duct that goes all the way up to my apartment." The script and the mise-en-scène thus confirm that both women's language and listening skills are dependent on their homelives. Here is the origin of the communications skills that Mary will take into the workplace.

In the WJM newsroom, Mary's desk situates her in a fixed position at the very center of the set. Her desk is next to Murray's, and their names and places suggest that "Mur" and "Mair" provide the newsroom "family" with its twins: the associate producer and the newswriter. The narrow space between their desks serves as a median line in the composition of the whole, with an entry door on the extreme right, a path across the open space behind Mary and Murray, and on the extreme left, usually offscreen (like Mary's kitchen), the private office of the boss, Lou Grant. Ted Baxter, the newscaster, appears frequently coming out of his dressing room or from the broadcast booth where he has been on camera. The booth is behind a curtained wall at the back of the set, placed in a relationship to the room that is similar to that of Mary's windows in her apartment. But the newsroom is painted blue and grey, and what is warm and colorful about Mary's room is cold and efficient here. Whereas we look directly out of Mary's big windows to see nature's changing seasons, the curtains to the broadcast booth are never opened, and the windowless newsroom is related to an outside world only by multiple clocks, wire-service machines, telephones, typewriters, and television sets. The lack of visual stimulation tells us that this is a "man's world," a bastion where man-made machines send and receive man-made information. There are large grey panels that make up the walls of the newsroom. They look as if they could be moved and resituated to provide for more efficient space modules as new machines replace the few humans that are left. We learn that Mary works here and that she is a central character among the men at WJM, but we also see that she will never conform to this space, never disappear into its hard surfaces.

Mary's clothes frequently provide a dazzling contrast to the grey neutrality of the newsroom (she never appears in the same outfit on different shows, perhaps to suggest that because, unlike her coworkers, we see her only once a week, we miss some aspects of her everyday presence). And in conjunction with her animated gestures, the higher pitch of her voice, and her capacities to move speedily from her desk to her boss's door, these brightly colored costumes mark her feminine presence at all times. Sometimes, too, Mary and Murray both dress in bright colors, as if bonded in an effort to be inconsistent in a consistently rationalized atmosphere. When these two match it is often because their allegiance as teamworkers is emphasized, or because Lou Grant's patriarchal postures make their tie more urgent. The self-serving vanity of Ted Baxter is also made obvious by occasional outrageously loud ties and handkerchiefs, and these function to keep him the ready target of his boss's anger. There are occasions when Ted's red ties seem to stimulate Lou's bullish disposition, confirming for us the differences between an old-time, shirt-sleeves-rolled-up newsman and a foppish anchorman.

Above all, the newsroom is a divided place. Unlike Mary's apartment it does not allow for the easy flow of people, nor does it provide access and intimacy. Its different parts suggest hierarchy among workers and competition between men and machines. In particular Lou Grant's office is a sealed-off, glassed-in private space where loud confrontations are audible only to specific victims on the inside but are visible to those who are on the outside. The ritual of knocking and waiting outside this door provides a vivid contrast to the way that people are welcomed into Mary's apartment. And because Lou's office corresponds to the space that is Mary's kitchen on that set, we also experience the sharp differences between her boss's desk-drawer liquor supply and Mary's kitchen coffee. When she is first interviewed for the job, Lou barks an invitation to her, hoping he has found a drinking partner. She completely misses his meaning, asks for a brandy alexander, and watches in silence as he drops his whiskey bottle back into his filing cabinet. Its metallic clank punctuates a meeting that is not what this newsman had expected from an office buddy. But Lou Grant remains intrigued by Mary, aware of a new kind of energy brought into his daily routine. In a three-part shot-reverse-shot sequence, he barks at her: "You know what? You've got spunk." Mary responds with a smile, and we cut to another medium close-up of her future boss: "I hate spunk." This nonconversation is followed by another in which the older man closes their deal: "If I don't like you, I'll fire you. If you don't like me, I'll fire you." Are these the words that men in power speak to women who have none? Mary listens. We listen. In this way and in many others she will provide this workplace with some humorous alternatives to its own deadlines and its own division of labor. She brings with her the playful flexibility of a modern woman and the sensitivities of a True Woman. Both are qualities much needed in an atmosphere where communication depends more on machines than people.

To what extent, we must now ask, does Mary's presence in these two locations grant *The Mary Tyler Moore Show* a critique of woman's place? The answer to this question will emerge in relation to the concept of family that is developed throughout the series. There are two directions in which these characters are pulled by Mary as a family-minded single woman. One is in the direction of community and cooperation, and the other is in the direction of a rigid social order that keeps men's and women's roles organized around opposing values and modes of behavior. This comedy series takes us both ways. We have observed how the mise-en-scènes of home and work mark the differences between these two aspects of the familial. And we have noted how it is Mary's capacity to move between the two spheres that keeps the comedy intact. On the one hand, she can go beyond her nineteenth-century domestic model to accept and combine all kinds of single and often separated characters in her one-room apartment, and similarly can enter the workplace to encourage more collectivity. On the other hand, Mary often appears to mediate between widely different people in order to send them all back into their narrowly defined roles as men and women who seem unchanged by and unable to challenge the social constraints that surround them.

Relationships and Roles at Home and at Work

Three kinds of relationships that have been the focus of much feminist debate provided *The Mary Tyler Moore Show* and *Rhoda* with some of their central themes and incidents. The first is mother-daughter relationships. There is perhaps no subject of more significance to the women's movement than this one: it raises historically and psychologically important questions about both kinds of women's roles, and more important, about the kinds of family bonds that are traditionally maintained through these relationships. Mary Richards has left her mother, but is placed decisively in the middle of Rhoda's relationship to her mother and Phyllis's relationship to her daughter. The second kind of relationship, related to the first, is "sisterhood": how does "sisterhood" become a new source of strength and community for women who seek alternatives to marriage and family-defined roles? The importance of Mary's familial friendships with Rhoda and Phyllis is central to her own show, and these friendships remain intact throughout both of these characters' spin-off series. These three women are bonded initially as neighbors but also because they are engaged in finding careers and male lovers, a combination long considered transgressive, if not impossible. The third set of relationship issues raised on *The Mary Tyler Moore Show* is those around women and work, more specifically Mary's relationships to both the men and the job in the TV newsroom. Feminist critics have long noted that women in journalism are frequently isolated or infantilized by their all-male coworkers, and it is most important to observe the ways in which Mary as a writer-producer appears to be a source for constant jokes, whereas in her role as a smoothing force of mediation within the newsroom she is a serious if not central character at WJM.

Although Mary has left her small Minnesota town to come to the big city (we see her making this break, with flowers and goodbyes, during the opening montage sequences that accompany the titles of each episode for the first two seasons), she remains a midwestern middle-class woman who lives alone on the middle floor of her apartment house. Separated from her parents, who occasionally visit in an episode, Mary appears to be a well-adjusted daughter who has successfully internalized her mother's homemaking and interpersonal skills, while having also moved toward the world of the father, where there is financial autonomy and a public presence. Her separation from the mother recalls Pogrebin's article on "Woman's Place" in a *TV Guide* from the early years of *The Mary Tyler Moore Show*. It was this feminist's argument that she could not separate from a web of girlhood lies until her father intervened to unfasten the glue that attached her own mother to the TV mother of the 1950s, and that had thus entrapped the adolescent author in the feminine mystique. Mary Richards does not discuss her own parenting, but her move from a small home town mirrors Mary Tyler Moore's own move from *The Dick Van Dyke Show* where she played a perfect wife and young mother. When Mary meets Lou Grant in the first episode of *The Mary Tyler Moore Show*, he affirms this many-leveled act of separation for her: he is the father-like boss who will take her away from her family past and will give her a job in the WJM newsroom. In this sense Mary Richards is beyond her family, but is still linked to familial needs and concerns. There is a marked difference between biological mother-daughter relationships in *The Mary Tyler Moore Show* and Mary's more mediated position as sisterly or daughterly in her friendships with women at home and men at work. Both Rhoda and Phyllis are still caught in mother-daughter dependencies, and it is Mary's task and trial to listen and often negotiate for her two best friends: one a daughter and one a mother.

Rhoda's relationship to her mother, Ida, is the central one in her life. Although she has moved to Minneapolis to work, it is immediately clear that Rhoda has not separated from her mother in any way but geographically. She enjoys some respite from Ida's Jewish mothering because, she tells Mary, talking on the telephone is less taxing: "I like her better person to person than in person." Later she will cling to the distance that the intercom provides when she is back in New York dealing with Ida on the *Rhoda* show in 1974. Rhoda refers to the double difficulty of meeting her mother after a long commute; "Ma and jet lag" seem an awful combination. In short, there is no separating from this kind of mother, and in addition to the temporary relief that Rhoda may find from short—and long-distance communication systems, she depends primarily on Mary's capacities to mediate when Ida is a visitor to Minneapolis. In the first two years of *The Mary Tyler Moore Show*, there are at least two such occasions: one episode in 1970 when Ida arrives with an immense present for Rhoda, with which she will attempt to guilt-trip her daughter, and another in 1971 when she will try to establish a "modern" mother-daughter bond around look-alike outfits. In both of these shows, Mary rescues Rhoda from two oppressive kinds of mothering: one Ida's own Jewish version (in which the note on the present says, "No one in the world will ever love you as much as I do"), and the second in which mothering as friendship is challenged as a miserable alternative to the first.

In both of these episodes, Rhoda clarifies for Mary the profound problems that are associated with Ida's mothering. In the first ("Support Your Local Mother," 1970), as Mary goes to read the card on what she sees as a most generous gift from mother to daughter, Rhoda cracks: "It's not a card, it's a curse." She can feel the ways that this attachment is not love, but *need*, and yet she cannot escape it. Mary must listen to her friend: "You're talking about midwestern love, I'm talking about Bronx love . . . My mother wants the people she loves to feel guilty." But it is not until she agrees to let Ida stay with her that Mary recognizes the no-win situation that Rhoda is in. In one of the more physical comic scenes between women, Mary and Ida chase each other around Mary's sofa trying to grab and give back the money that Rhoda's mother pretends-and-insists she wants to pay for her stay. Mary is exhausted and even frightened by this acted-out game, so that the next day when Ida moves to another level, demanding to be called "Mama," she becomes more determined to reunite Ida with her own daughter. We view Rhoda in the window of Hemple's department store fussing with a bridal couple, mannequins who are perfectly placed and dressed for the very event that Rhoda herself longingly anticipates. With the appearance of her mother outside the store window, and Mary on the inside urging her friend to talk with Ida, Rhoda is caught. As the unhappy daughter is reunited with her mother in a resigned embrace, we cut to Mary still standing in the store window. As if she wishes to be invisible, she assumes the pose of a mannequin well-wisher at the wedding. The comedy is thick with something serious, if not tragic, about Rhoda's life. While we may laugh to see the topic of predatory mothering as something that well-adjusted, midwestern Mary has to confront, at another level it is an essential part of every woman's experience in this culture. Feminist scholars have long noted the implications of women's tendencies to merge, relating them frequently to mother-daughter bonds. Questions of women's relationships to men and to work are skillfully integrated in this script, where Rhoda's mother is a deterrent to the sense of self that is required for both. It is in this way that we come to understand Mary's critical role for Rhoda, as a separated "sister" and a midwestern friend.

In "A Girl's Best Mother Is Not Her Friend," from the 1971 season, Ida visits and attempts to imitate Phyllis's relationship to her daughter, Bess. Because we know that Phyllis is a follower of trends and a consumer-wife and mother, her inane claim that mother-daughter matching dresses are a sign of "an easy, open relationship" falls into the comic realm of her character type. It is only when Ida hears this that it becomes the primary theme for this episode. This sometimes cruel mother has already, upon her arrival at the house in Minneapolis, begun to insult her daughter by comparing her to Mary: "Mary, you look so slim and trim, and Rhoda, you . . ." This comment is based on a sight gag created by a cut from the three women in a long shot to Ida's point-of-view shot of Rhoda's bottom as she bends over to pick something up. Mother's critical gaze thus becomes an invitation, if not an insistence, that the TV audience participate in the competitive exchange. Now we know that Ida is in control and will attempt to build a faddish mother-daughter friendship with the vulnerable Rhoda. Phyllis, the "expert" in this context, offers to lend Ida the books she has bought on the subject. The episode culminates with the unexpected appearance of Ida and Rhoda in the WJM newsroom, holding hands as they stand together in matching dresses. Ida's foolish plan has now become a comical performance for Mary and the newsmen. In a previous scene, Murray, the father of two, had responded to Mary's worried account of the mother-daughter plan: "Kids don't need parents for friends." So when the two look-alikes arrive, Ida's misconceived notion of modern mothering has been partially corrected by Murray's paternal wisdom to Mary. Now the dynamic shifts, and in the next scene Ida, Rhoda, and Mary are eating dinner at Mary's table. We learn that Ida is taking some desperate steps to identify with her daughter and has decided to stop wearing a bra in order to be "with it." Rhoda responds succinctly: "Ma, you're not 'with it', you're 'without it.' " By the end of this episode, perhaps because Mary has learned and mediated Murray's position and because Mary's table provides the necessary forum for exchange and clarification, Rhoda says to her mother: "You've been a swell friend, but I need a mother." This brief moment of equilibrium is soon lost, however, and in the tag we see Mary standing guard between mother and daughter. The feuding pair speak to each other through Mary: "Will you tell her . . ." "Will you tell her . . ." Mary mediates as the scene fades to black.

In this episode, there is a clear mockery of consumer-defined relationships between mothers and daughters, and of that postwar domestic ideal that implies that consuming is mothering and that shopping for matched outfits insures "togetherness." But at a deeper level, the attachment between Ida and Rhoda is also represented as a genuine longing on the older woman's part to be close to a "younger self." Even this sentiment is related to a critique that runs throughout *The Mary Tyler Moore Show* and *Rhoda* of the many ways that our culture privileges youth just as it idealizes motherhood and marriage. Perhaps Rhoda's constant talk of diets and makeup serve as reminders of how mothers' criticisms feed a marketplace that in turn profits from daughters' low esteem.

It is evident throughout all the MTM series that while character comedy remains foregrounded, what coproducers Brooks and Burns call "fortunate timing" in relation to the women's movement served scriptwriters, directors, and actors well. And although social issues surface largely through personality and family interactions, the critique—in this case of mother-daughter bonding—resonates with feminist concerns. As we have seen in other contexts, family relationships are often depicted as rigid and even harmful. Neither Ida nor Rhoda can separate enough to accept each other as different people. It is noteworthy, however, that these series do leave room for personal growth and change. In this way, there is an apparent response to some of the utopian aspects of feminism, and beyond providing "background" for static or stereotypic characters, there is movement implied by some developments in Ida and Rhoda's relationship. The *Rhoda* show continues to explore this same mother-daughter dynamic in considerably more detail, and although the gags about fat and age provide the necessary character-based continuity with *The Mary Tyler Moore Show,* the two women gain a new understanding of themselves as they become more separated. When Rhoda leaves her marriage to Joe after one year ("The Separation," 1976), Ida works through something for the first time: "In my day," she tells her newly separated daughter, "my mother would have said, 'make any adjustment to save the marriage . . . ;' that doesn't go now, does it?" Also for the first time in this episode, Ida realizes that although she would like to stay with Rhoda to comfort her at this lonely time, "That would have been good for me, but not for you, huh?" At this moment Rhoda can accept her mother's concern, and says "stick around, Ma." For viewers who have followed this painfully routinized relationship from its first appearance on *The Mary Tyler Moore Show* in 1970 to the moment when Ida in her old-world kerchief can listen to and embrace her daughter in the final seconds of the episode, this change has historical meaning. It is not that all family relationships are hopelessly entrenched, or that we can only sit back and laugh at the status quo. It is also that alternatives surface in these women-oriented comedies, and that the possibilities for new relationships among women seem to emerge, even within families, when there are possibilities for relationships between women and work.

In the case of Phyllis's relationship to her preteenage child, Bess, a very different dynamic is brought to light. Like Ida, Phyllis is a homebound parent, infantilized by Lars in the way that Ida is "taken care of" by Martin. Both women appear determined to prove their capacities for full-time mothering, whether in

an up-to-date mode or in a traditional sense. Phyllis has clearly read the latest literature, and she and Bess are on a first-name basis. Bess has been encouraged to
regard the All-American family mythos with distaste and to make precocious
comments whenever possible. The basis for comedy in this mother-daughter relationship lies in the fact that Phyllis herself is deeply committed to most of the
conventions and values upheld by the bourgeois family, and perpetuates myths
about the "creativity" of housework, a "pleasurable" marriage to Lars, and a "re-
warding" and "open" relationship to Bess. From the moment when she introduces Bess to her "Aunt Mary" and is unmasked for such family-mindedness
when Bess calls her antagonist "Aunt Rhoda," we know that Mary Richards will
be caught in many years of mediating another mother-daughter conflict. Her
rapport with Bess will be built on the fact that, for different reasons, both have
accepted family-togetherness as something of the past, perhaps as mass media
hype. In "Baby Sit-Com" (1971), Lou Grant is asked by Mary to take care of
Bess one night when Phyllis and Lars are away and Mary wants to go out on a
date. The young girl and the older man get along fine; she makes cookies and he
gets drunk. They end the evening playing poker with the cookies, having decided that there was nothing worth watching on TV, once Lou's much anticipated prizefight was over after a few seconds. Bess makes it clear that she has
better things to do than to watch *The Clancy Clan,* where "they have all these
kids, and everyone laughs a lot because they have all these kids." She is, like
Mary, one of the single female characters on *The Mary Tyler Moore Show* and on
its spin-offs who understands that family no longer means the redundant comedy generated by two parents and a lot of children. Her thinly veiled reference to
The Brady Bunch (1969–74), an ABC program about the marriage of two widowed parents with three children each, functions to provide *The Mary Tyler
Moore Show* viewer with some added encouragement to question that older
model. Treva Silverman is the scriptwriter for this episode, and her efforts to
place this series outside the family sitcom involve her pointed use of Bess, the
wise only child who "knows best" that friendship is more enduring than family,
and whose "old man" is too loaded to disagree.

   In another episode scripted by Silverman ("The Birds and—um—the Bees,"
1971), a different kind of commentary on family-ideology emerges. In the central plot, Phyllis begs Mary to tell Bess the facts of life. This plan has been trig-
gered by a subplot about a TV program that Mary has produced, entitled
"What's Your Sexual I.Q.?" While Phyllis found the documentary "informative,
enlightening, and mature" ("in other words, boring," says Rhoda), she does not
feel like enough of an expert to tell Bess about such matters. When Mary asks if
perhaps Bess's father Lars, a doctor, could do so, Phyllis notes that because he

slept through the program, he would do the same while talking about sex to his daughter. Rhoda supports Phyllis in this one instance and asks Mary to speak to Bess, recalling the absurdities of her own mother's explanation of the facts of life: "I thought I had to swim up the Columbia River." But before Mary agrees, she tries one more possible source of fatherly advice, for herself in this instance. She speaks to Lou Grant at the office, who explains to her that it was "perfectly natural" to educate his three daughters; he had simply told them that their mother had something to say to them about sex. After this extended buckpassing, itself a gentle mockery of how unmodern modern parents really are and of how much they may need to rely on a nonparent for this kind of interchange, Bess and Mary do begin to talk. Predictably, Bess takes over: "Are you leading up to telling me about love. . . ?" but unpredictably adds, "I already know about sex." Their conversation uncovers the greatest of family myths, and Bess asks for clarity: "Love and sex go together, right? So if you love someone, do you. . . ?" Mary is cornered as the only expert, a single woman and a TV producer-expert who must play the role of a parent. But she is honest and acknowledges to Bess that there is a difference. Perhaps for censorship reasons it is Rhoda who calls out her gratitude from the armchair where she has been listening in: "Thanks Mary, separating love and sex has changed my life." The tag supplies this episode with a last stab at family-based morality. Phyllis re-enters Mary's apartment to try to talk to Bess on her own, now that Mary has done the real work: "I'll make it sound spiritual and ethical . . . almost true." Silverman's script explores the comic side to the ways in which mothering means lying, and as is frequently the case, it is Mary's task to provide an alternative to that kind of female socialization.

The need to bypass and seek alternatives to family-defined relationships is nowhere more obvious than when we look at the ways in which Mary's female friendships are privileged in this series. Most particularly in the first four seasons, before Rhoda moves to New York and begins her spin-off in 1974 and Phyllis moves to San Francisco for her own show in the next year, these two neighbors are the subjects of every episode, central friendships in Mary's daily life as a career woman. We find that Phyllis and Rhoda provide her with more interesting interactions, conversations, and comradeship than do most of the dates with whom Mary shares some of her private life. While often these boyfriends are buffoons who make brief comic appearances, they also disrupt the primacy of her friendships at home and at work. The WJM newsmen are often depicted as jealous and petty about any "outside" man in Mary's life, and similarly her women friends are shown to be occasionally jealous but more often hurt when she ignores them for a stranger. While we are encouraged to admire Mary's capacities to keep everyone feeling cared-for, so that she can freely pursue her romantic interests, *The Mary Tyler Moore Show* is largely about the vitality of her friendships at home and at work. We too learn to take lightly the intruders. We are involved with Mary's own determination to live and work alone, among friends. Phyllis and Rhoda provide particularly significant alternatives to romantic or marital relations, and seem to affirm the feminist slogan of the period: "Sisterhood is Powerful."

By the early 1970s, consciousness-raising groups had begun to politicize many middle-class feminists. In these contexts they could practice another basic tenet of the women's movement: "The personal is political." Such groups allowed participants to acknowledge the isolation of their lives at home as well as the inadequacies of their social lives, where in "mixed company" they were isolated by gender. Consciousness-raising groups challenged the claim that women's talk was trivial, for they provided the safety wherein women could discuss both personal and political issues. Above all, women could come to understand that these two spheres are related and that there are similar needs for collectivity at home and at work. *The Mary Tyler Moore Show* reinforces the importance of women's talk by presenting small gatherings at Mary's apartment as a daily event in the lives of Mary, Rhoda, and Phyllis. In some ways, the old ideal of women's community in preindustrial times was behind the structuring of modern consciousness-raising groups: women had met regularly to talk, quilt, and share meals. At Mary's, women convene spontaneously for coffee, or to talk about problems associated with dieting. The simple repetitions of Rhoda's and Phyllis' entrances and exits reinforce for us the interconnectedness of their lives. In addition to these regulars, Mary is also visited by Ida and Bess and, after the *Rhoda* and *Phyllis* spin-offs, by Georgette and Sue Ann, two other friends whom she knows through connections at WJM. But all of these encounters, and the fluidity with which they occur, are associated with Mary's position as a single woman, and all of them serve to remind us that women's talk is neither trivial nor peripheral to women's lives. It is interesting to note that while Mary and her friends are often lured into alternative communities where lonely people meet, these excursions prove to be inadequate, if not farcical. There is no place like Mary's apartment where her circle of women friends feel at home.

Early in the first season of *The Mary Tyler Moore Show,* in a script written by Treva Silverman ("Divorce Isn't Everything," 1970), Mary and Rhoda are seen exercising together in Mary's apartment. The two seem aligned in their commitment to the new cult of aerobics, but only Mary is really moving her body. Rhoda stands still and waves her hands, for she is more interested in talking about joining the "Better Luck Next Time Club," where newly divorced people meet. She asks if Mary is often questioned about being single. Mary stops jog-

ging in place and gathers herself to answer in her most elegant way: "I could discover the secret of immortality, and still they'd say, 'look at that single girl, discovering the secret of immortality.'" With this comment Mary focuses the
entire episode on this absurd and painful truth about women's lives when they
remain unmarried. She first suggests that singles are forever "girls," a word that a
woman scriptwriter was surely sensitive to, and that no effort of imagination or
humane work can provide a meaningful identity in the face of this lack. It is with
this admission of anger that Mary is convinced to join Rhoda for an evening
among the divorcées. While Rhoda is usually willing to lie her way into such situations, Mary is humiliated into this activity. The group is pathetic, and Mary is
approached by a strange dentist who falls for her teeth. There is some irony here,
since of all the characteristics that make Mary insecure about her appearance,
her teeth are often the subject of comic exchange and some mockery about how
her eager smile makes her "likeable." Her encounter at the divorcées' club results
in Mary's being elected vice-president, at which point she admits that she has
never been married. Rhoda confesses at the same time, and so do all the people
assembled. All of them are single, and all of them live with the awareness of what
Mary had said about the onus of not being married.

In *Rhoda* there are many incidents devoted to similar efforts by the women
characters to join "groups" that provide encouragement and company for the
lonely and the overweight. In "An Elephant Never Forgets" (1976), Rhoda and
her sister Brenda, both single at this point, go to a "weight control center" in an
effort to find a way out of the fat-and-therefore-lonely rut they share. The first
segment of this episode is devoted to several comic exchanges between the instructor and the participants. Miss Fiske is thin and snippy, and we laugh at her
claim to control the situation with scales. The room is filled with men and
women who lie and confess, each with a mother-food story or a secret spaghetti-
popsicle recipe. The scene culminates with a physical fight between Rhoda and
Miss Fiske over Rhoda's weight. Each woman accuses the other of "jiggling the
beam" on the scales, and Rhoda takes most of her clothes off in an effort to
"win." But the lesson learned in this case is only presented after the sisters have
gone home (they share the same apartment building in much the way that Mary,
Rhoda, and Phyllis had on *The Mary Tyler Moore Show*), and Brenda is approached by a handsome male neighbor who "sees" her now that she is thinner.
He brings her flowers, but she is troubled: "Would you go out with me today if I
were fat?" she asks. He answers "no," and asks her, "Would you go out with me if
I were ugly?" To this she answers "yes," and sends him on his way. "You're the
best-looking guy I ever rejected . . . You're also the only guy I ever rejected." In
each of these episodes, the ways in which American culture conflates singleness

and loneliness are articulated. So too the ways in which marketing and promotion benefit from this profamily tendency within the society become the basis for many comic incidents.

But the most important critique of profamily ideology is shaped by Mary and her woman friends, whose meetings prove essential to the problem-solving that brings comic possibilities and calming resolution to every episode. In "Father's Day" (1973), the central plot revolves around a reunion between Ted and his long-separated father. Ted's anxiety about this encounter immediately involves Mary—for her own distance from family matters and for her compassion toward others who are less reconciled. She sympathizes with Ted's fears, and like his wife Georgette, who cares for him at home, Mary accepts this vain and infantile man in the workplace. With both women's encouragement, Ted is finally on his own, alone with his father, and we watch the two exchange life experiences: those of a pompous anchorman and those of a humble laundromat owner. It is Mary's clear thinking that enables Ted to meet his father, and as he does, so we also recognize something that Mary seems to know about Ted's unformed sense of self: there may be a connection between Ted's perpetual childishness and his unresolved status as a son without a father. Following the scene in which the two men talk in Ted's dressing room at WJM, we see Mary alone in her apartment cooking. Rhoda enters saying that she is bored, and Mary replies, "Tell him to go home." Rhoda responds, "Tell who? I'm alone." Mary concedes that she is also bored and the two sit down to share Mary's meal, as if to acknowledge that their friendship is an essential antidote to being bored with a man or by oneself. At this point Ted and Georgette enter, and Ted's proud reunion with his father is the subject: "Someday I'm going to look that way, like that little bald old man with a laundromat." Ted has agreed to loan his father the money he'd asked for, and Mary and Rhoda approve as he goes off to take the older man to the bus station. Thus, while families can pose problems for almost all the characters on *The Mary Tyler Moore Show*, Mary's single status and the alternative to parenting that she provides keeps her capable of helping others while she enjoys the friendships that they provide for her.

While Mary and Rhoda may complain about being bored and alone, the ways in which they consistently find each other and affirm their positions as single women is an important concession to the historical changes that have been shaping women's lives since the 1950s. Middle-class women in the 1970s were marrying later and were doing so after they had established careers. As we have observed in this discussion of *The Mary Tyler Moore Show*, the extent to which the single career woman can provide the center to a circle of people at home and at work is dependent on the fact that she cares for and mediates between people who are either married or are involved with family relationships. Mary does not proselytize against those who have families, but as an outsider to their worlds she can offer and sometimes advocate the new familial way of life. In a last example of how she recalls for us both the resilience of women's collectivity and the needs for people to make family-like commitments, we find that Mary promotes the more utopian aspects of the familial as she cultivates her dependencies on women friends. In "The Square-Shaped Room" (1971), written by Susan Silver, Mary, Phyllis, and Rhoda form a chain of interdependence as they appear to perpetuate the borrowing and returning of advice and things among themselves. At the outset of this episode, Mary is alone in her apartment talking with Phyllis about her latest problem: how to help Lou Grant choose the new decor for his house. Surprisingly, Phyllis recommends Rhoda's skills, perhaps because Rhoda is not present, but at this moment her sometimes adversary enters and good-heartedly suggests that Phyllis's talents be involved. Mary's feuding neighbors meet and cooperate to help her help her boss, but at another level they affirm a female pattern of sharing as they exchange suggestions. Rhoda's pretense for coming down to see Mary is to borrow an egg. Mary gives one to Rhoda who then gives the same egg to Phyllis from whom she had originally borrowed one. Phyllis recalls that she owes Mary an egg, and so gives it back to her. This circular game accompanies their three-way conversation about Lou's decorating problem, and through such cooperative words and gestures there is suggested a modern quilting bee. In the tradition of naming patterns for their specific documentary functions, this visual counterpart might have been called "Sister's Choice," or "Robbing Mary to Pay Rhoda." At Mary's home there is affirmed both the place for familial trust and the mutual exchange that has always characterized the daily lives of women. Theirs is not a competitive but a cooperative relationship, as long as Mary is in the middle. While some older gender-defined topics are central to this conversation, these women appear to be making and affirming a network for modern life, where being single can still mean belonging.

When Rhoda and Phyllis left *The Mary Tyler Moore Show* in 1974 and 1975, there was a shift in Mary's focus away from her women friends. In part because the two women who remained on the show were directly related to Mary's work life at WJM, and in part because there was no longer a communal house where Rhoda and Phyllis surrounded her, Mary's relationships with Sue Ann and Georgette were less integral to her daily life. These two had been peripheral characters from early on in the series, but after the departure of Mary's neighbors for opposite coasts in spin-off shows of their own, these two women were included in almost every episode. But they are profoundly different from the two women friends whom they replace. While Rhoda and Phyllis are somewhat rounded characters whom we knew to be engaged in their mother-daughter involvements and in their efforts to be separate people, Sue Ann and Georgette are caricatures of the male-defined woman. Perhaps because narrative continuity dictates, and because it is fully in keeping with Mary's character, these women also gain Mary's respect and acceptance. She establishes an allegiance to both the naïve newlywed Georgette and the seasoned marriage-wrecker Sue Ann. These two function in a different way from Mary's earlier friendships, and while they do not offer the same circle of trust and commitment that Phyllis and Rhoda provided, by comic contrasts to Mary's stability, Sue Ann and Georgette depend on and thus further motivate Mary's single lifestyle.

Georgette is helped by Mary in her efforts to marry Ted (these two characters' off-screen names are Georgia Engel and Ted Knight—surely another effort to integrate life and TV and a "perfect" marriage for Mary to mediate) and is counseled early on in *The Mary Tyler Moore Show* by both Rhoda and Mary to quit doing Ted's laundry and acting like a "professional victim." On "The Georgette Story" (1972), they teach Georgette to have some self-esteem. "Say something positive about yourself," Mary demands of the fluffy blonde dressed in pink. Georgette's response reveals her willingness to learn, an attribute that will soften her child bride stereotype. "I have good handwriting and I like animals. I like to think I'm a nice person. Very Nice. Damn nice!" Throughout the series Georgette will accompany her saccharine baby talk with tough talk, perhaps the vestiges of what she learned from the old days with Rhoda and Mary. We know from this episode on that Ted will not change and will remain a sexist, but that Mary's concern for and advice to Georgette will lead to their happy marriage. Ted tells Mary how pleased he is with Georgette's new self-esteem: "It's like being with a different woman. It's like being equal. I understand you're responsible. As long as I live, I'll never forgive you." This exchange characterizes Mary's friendship with Georgette; they will never be women who share the same commitment to a career and a single life, but Mary does not condemn Georgette, and she operates as a caring counselor to her throughout the show, finally even playing, with Lou Grant presiding, hostess and midwife at the birth of Georgette's and Ted's daughter, born during a party in Mary's apartment.

Sue Ann is Georgette's opposite, a bawdy TV personality who calls herself "The Happy Homemaker," while behind the scenes she is an outrageous vamp. Competitive and quick witted, Sue Ann needs Mary for some very different reasons. She is often led astray by men whom she believes that she has captivated, and because we see her almost exclusively in the WJM newsroom, on frequent breaks from her own show, Mary's role as Sue Anne's rescuer is also cultivated by Lou Grant's advice and fatherly concerns. Sue Ann is one of the family in this context, and when a seductive but deceitful woodsman seeks to enter into a business deal with her, it is Lou's request to Mary that she save Sue Ann from this fate. As they hug each other in a ladies' room, Sue Ann softens and admits to Mary: "I feel so alone." It is Mary's capacity to be alone that allows others to accept similar feelings. And even though she has lost her two best friends, both of whom are capable of living alone, Mary's continued bonding with Georgette and Sue Ann recalls for us that in being alone she is not a lonely woman.

Mary's relationship to the men at WJM confirms the pattern that we have seen emerging. Friendship is the enduring social bond, and as a single woman Mary is the one who demonstrates and teaches this truth. But while she seems to form a center for her closest women friends, Mary's work-related friendships with men are less convincingly "modern." It is in this sphere that far more rigid familial roles operate, and Mary seems to play the female parts necessary to maintain a traditional dynamic. Her same capacities to listen and mediate in this context are less directed toward a larger critique of woman's place in the society, and are consistently associated with her obedient "daughterly," admiring "sisterly," and her accepting "motherly" qualities. That is, the social model for the newsroom maintains the conservativism of the nuclear family, and some of Mary's resistant impulses that are shared with Phyllis and Rhoda are lost in this context. It is ironic, but perhaps historically predictable, that as we find her a competent career women in an all-male office (and a largely male profession), we also find her limited to female family stereotypes. We must ask if this is because our society has deeply cultivated a belief that women can only be mothers or whores, a dichotomy that leaves no place for a "good" career woman? Or does this tendency simply reflect ways in which patriarchy is the basis for institutional relationships that endure under capitalism, even when the traditional family has been challenged by women's new social and economic needs? A last consideration must include the fact that, until Mary arrives, WJM is a motherless-daughterless family, and that as Mary becomes an integral part of that group, she ultimately reveals her male coworkers as somewhat trapped in their own patriarchal world and clearly lacking some of the qualities and skills that are limited to women's roles in this culture. If there is a critique implicit in this aspect of the series, it lies in the fact that we see all three newsmen grow increasingly dependent on Mary in ways that they cannot admit or consciously accept.

In a 1976 episode entitled "Mary's Three Husbands," the fantasy lives of Lou, Ted, and Murray are enacted as dreams when each imagines his own version of a marriage to WJM's associate producer. The narrative begins as the three men sit in Lou's office drinking late into the night. Mary is conspicuously absent, on a date, and the somewhat inebriated men acknowledge their desires to possess her as a wife. Each one focuses on an aspect of Mary's personality and each reveals his own specific need to move her from the familial to the family—where his control is unchallenged. Murray's dream is the first: he situates himself as a struggling creative writer, impoverished but adored for his genius by his wife Mary. In this fantasy Mary appears as a flower-child bride, pregnant and absolutely selfless as she waits on Murray. When she feels the pains of labor, rather than disturb him, she retires quietly to a back room to give birth. Mary Richards's qualities of caring and competence are recognizable in Murray's imagining, as are her few familiar shouts of "Oh Boy!" as she acknowledges some pain. When she returns within seconds to show Murray the new baby, he looks up in awe and says, "What a woman," as his dream fades out. It is fitting to find that Murray, father of three and the newsroom's family man, sees a magic mommy in his coworker, but as viewers we have come to know and accept Mary's decision not to marry and mother. Thus, Murray's comical fantasy reveals a conflict that men cannot easily acknowledge but must feel as they learn to work with career women whose encouraging ways they need but whose lives they cannot control.

In the next sequence, Ted's dream envisions Mary as his new bride as they enter a lush honeymoon hotel suite. "You're mine," he tells her, and she answers, "Ted, darling, let's never leave this room." But as he sits on the bed's satin sheets and removes his shirt, his undershirt has an image of his own face on it. Trouble. Mary appears in a baby-doll nightie, and Ted says, adoringly, "You're even more beautiful than I am." Ted's cliché-ridden mind can find no more alluring way to imagine a wedding night with Mary, but what transpires is indicative of how truly limited this man really is, even in his own unconscious. Ted's Mary has no intention of being "his," and she tells him so as she leaves the room: "I will not get into that bed with you. Bye." Ted blubbers on alone until his fantasy with Mary fades. This man is such a narcissist that it is only in his dreams that he can picture Mary as anything but his mother. The role she plays with him in the newsroom is indeed that of a tolerant and often nurturant parent, who works to keep Ted's fragile ego intact when Murray and Lou cannot stop themselves from mocking him outright. That his dream should bring him close to a sexual relationship with this unconditional provider, a woman who gives him her home-made fried chicken for his office lunches, is indeed a comment on Ted's confused sense of self.

But it is Lou's fantasy about a marriage to Mary that shapes our final understanding of her role in the newsroom. In his dream, Lou and Mary have been married for fifty years. They are an old white-haired couple who are still putting the news together for Ted Baxter, an aged anchorman who cannot even remember his name. An old mustachioed Murray accuses Ted of being "as senile as you were fifty years ago," and Ted simply says "thanks," as he would have fifty years ago. But the comic sameness that Lou's dream implies shifts when Mary calls after her ancient boss and husband: "Mr. Grant, it's time we consummated our marriage." To this Lou replies from his beloved off-screen office: "Now you have to ruin it." But Mary demands an explanation in this flash forward, and Lou tells her: "When we were first married you were like a daughter to me, and it seemed unthinkable. Then you were like my sister, and now you're like my mother." At this point Mary Richards, done up in a white wig, unpins her hair and lets it fall to her shoulders, bats her eyes at Lou and waits for him to call her into his office. The dream fades to black and we return to the three newsmen, now quite drunk and tired from their storytelling. In the tag, Mary comes into the newsroom late in the evening and finds her three colleagues muttering to her about some future marriage. Each one gives her advice that is related to his own dream of desire, and as they leave her puzzled and alone, she stands for a minute, lifts the empty whiskey bottle and looks into it.

This curious episode is as tasteless as it is mythic, a script that seems not to fit the pattern of this series. But what it does do is to reveal, in perhaps the only way that is possible for such comedy, the underlying dynamics that operate to keep Mary in her job. "Mary's Three Husbands" touches on the nature of her relationship to the newsmen and makes an awkward effort to comment on the incest taboo that keeps this news family in working order.

There are numerous routines that occur frequently throughout *The Mary Tyler Moore Show* which further contribute to our understanding of this traditional family model. In the final pages of this discussion, let us turn to an examination of how this dynamic functions to keep Mary Richards's career as a newswoman in the shadow of her family-dictated role. There are several instances where Mary's efforts to define her job as a journalist conspire to humiliate her, in most cases returning her to the work she does as Lou's assistant, a role that suggests she is more secretary than producer.

From the first episode, when Mary arrives in the WJM newsroom to be interviewed for what she believes to be a secretarial job, there is the lurking possibility that this is what she has been hired to do. Murray calls out to Mary as she crosses the newsroom for the first time: "We've already hired a secretary," but when Lou Grants meets her in his office, Mary impresses him as someone whom he needs around. He negotiates with her for the salary and the title she will have: as associate producer he will be able to pay her ten dollars less per week than a secretary. She says that she cannot afford to be a producer when he goes on to offer that job for fifteen dollars less than a secretary per week. This comic exchange terminates when Mary delightedly agrees to be hired as an associate producer, but as she reaches across her boss's desk to shake hands, he doesn't budge, so she recovers in her most gesturally creative way and simply waves goodbye— like a little girl. In seven years, Mary will never call this man Lou, or will do so only when she is angry. In one instance, she defends her need to call him Mr. Grant. It is in her character to do so: "I call him Mr. Grant because I want to, not because I feel I have to. I started calling him Mr. Grant six years ago. It was comfortable then. It's comfortable now. It's what I want to call him. It's what I'm going to call him." Mary's history at WJM is the history of every woman who works in an all-male office. From the first day, they all call her Mary, and from the first day, she calls her boss Mr. Grant. This deference may be explained as part of Mary's nature, but it is also a feature of her job and of the hierarchy that remains intact through such means.

Mary asks for a raise on "Good Time News" (1972), and the central plot revolves around whether or not Lou Grant will agree to give her the fifty dollars more per week that she has found her male predecessor received. Before this issue surfaces, in a discussion at home with Rhoda, there are several indications that Mary is resentful of this and other inequities. She and Rhoda discuss the latter's recent date with a "stewardess." Mary corrects Rhoda, "They're called 'stewards' " and Rhoda responds, "I'm no sexist." Mary is working late a lot at the newsroom, and in the same conversation with Rhoda, she explains that she feels burdened by her token position. "This is our woman executive," Mary quotes as she describes the way in which she is presented by the station managers. Following this exchange at home, Mary complains to Lou about her needs for a higher salary. He brushes off her request as "one of those woman things," and until the end of the episode there is no more mention of Mary's right to equal pay. But it is the way in which she is finally granted this raise that is suspect from a feminist perspective, for Mary is "rewarded" by Lou mainly because she talks back to Ted Baxter while he is acting like an arrogant fool on the news show. Because he does not want to share the camera with anyone else, and because Lou has been told to add some "entertainment values" to help boost his ratings, it is Mary's responsibility to break Ted into this new format that will involve several different newscasters on each program. She does Lou's work for him, and in one of the few ways that an expressive and angry woman can be useful to a news producer. Because Ted actually interrupts Mary's editorial commentary while she is on the air, she shouts at him: "Shut up, Ted." This is Lou's own style, and he is delighted to see Mary on the screen doing what he could not do to humiliate Ted in public. It is a gesture that is not characteristic of Mary's way in the newsroom, but she is given her raise for this outburst. The question of equal pay for women is thus subverted by an interaction that ultimately reflects the boss's needs and his own power to get what he wants from his workers.

It is possible that the sexist nature of Mary's work as a producer of feature stories is occasionally mocked by a scriptwriter who titles her documentaries to suggest that she is stuck in the soft-news ghetto that is woman's place in journalism. There are some references to the names of her productions that perhaps serve as commentary on this phenomenon: "Chimps and What They Teach Us," or "Know Your Sexual I.Q." But the most explicit instances where Mary's opportunities as a journalist are shown to be limited are in the episodes where she attempts to become a writer, and fails each time. In "Room 223" (1971), by Susan Silver, Mary's lack of experience is first revealed when she must take over for Murray, and finds she cannot write up the fire story that comes over the wires. Lou hovers authoritatively over her as she tries to type this in time for the evening news, loses patience with Mary's bungling efforts, and writes the story himself in a few seconds. Mary is hurt by this incident, and in the next scene she, Rhoda, and Phyllis are found sitting in her apartment talking about what she should do. Phyllis suggests a college journalism course, which is what Mary tries. But the central plot in this episode soon forms around her relationship to her male professor, who is instantly both attracted to Mary and anxious about her authority as a full-time news producer. The conflict over her work-related skills and authorship thus becomes a romantic problem, somewhat complicated by the fact that Lou Grant is jealous of Mary's newfound authority figure. When Mary receives a C+ on her first assignment, she is reassured by her arrogant professor that he has "gone out with 'C' students before." She wonders why he gave her a "plus" because his comments had harshly criticized her writing for being too "flowery" and feminine, to which he quips: "I couldn't keep my personal feelings entirely out of it." Discouraged, Mary shows her first effort to Murray, her best-brotherly fan, and he is predictably enthusiastic about her work, calling it "terrific." Mary is caught between three men-who-write in this episode. She cannot get either genuine encouragement or fair criticism from any one of them, and this is because she is a woman. The issue of authority is here explicitly related to authorship, and Susan Silver's script seems to suggest that within the institution of journalism, a woman may mediate but not make the news.

In "Mary the Writer" (1976) she tries to affirm her skills as a journalist by producing a personal reminiscence about her grandfather. Once again, automatically Murray likes her work, and once again Lou does not even want to read it. She begs for his response, however, and after reading it he tells her, "It stinks." She stands tentatively in his office while he rants on about "what good writing is," and finally reads her a passage from Raymond Chandler. The prose is "masculine," a classic description of Los Angeles-style anxiety: "It was one of those hot dry Santa Anas that come down from the mountains and curl your hair and make your nerves jump." Lou Grant's effort to demonstrate "good writing" to Mary is obviously unrelated to her preferred subject or style. But she puts her boss and his favorite mystery author in their places with a deft and backhanded compliment: "He writes well about the weather." And from this brief rallying point she goes on to insist that her idea for a story is valid too: "Most people love reading about delightful, warm-hearted old men . . ." We respect Mary for her tenacity, but the battle is lost. Mr. Grant is no sentimentalist, and in this context "father knows best." Later in this same episode Mary again challenges him for his tough-mindedness and his refusal to compliment her on her writing efforts. She compares herself to Ted, saying that Lou Grant never treats him so meanly for his miserable writing skills. At this point her boss explains, "I respected you enough to tell the truth," and thus reveals to Mary his fatherly concern that she learn the trade like a "real man." What he cannot concede is that as a woman she might choose to write a different kind of prose, perhaps challenging the myth of objectivity that informs the form and content of news journalism. But the legitimacy of her position is completely eroded by the end of the episode, and although Lou Grant may be learning to be more sensitive to the feelings of a new writer, Mary's impulse is to retreat from the confrontation, having begged her boss to lie to her about the quality of her prose. Like a daughter who was briefly treated as a son, Mary recovers her girlishness as if to keep the familial order intact. As we have seen in other instances, an episode that begins by opening up a series of questions about authorship and authority ends with the recuperation of interfamilial relations and roles. In the context of the workplace, this tendency preserves the division between the sexes for the sake of the traditional division of labor. Mary will type the words and thoughts of the men who write the news at WJM.

In "The Last Show" (1977), a final goodbye scene takes place in the WJM newsroom where a sobbing, clinging collective of the three newsmen, Mary, Georgette, and Sue Ann bunch together in an enormous hug. With their arms intertwined, they pass around a box of tissues for their tears and move in unison toward the office door for the last time. The station manager has fired everyone but Ted, who never produced the news and who will remain behind as a showbiz personality, perhaps a last comment on the priorities of modern broadcast executives. Implied is the fact that an old-style journalist like Mr. Grant is no longer relevant for the production of today's TV news-as-entertainment. As this nostalgic group gropes its way across the floor, Mary steps aside to make her own farewell statement. As much as the past seven years may mark the end of an era for broadcast news, for Mary Richards they allowed a beginning and a new way to see herself as a working woman: "I just wanted you to know that sometimes I get concerned about being a career woman. I get to thinking my job is too important, and I tell myself that the people I work with are just the people I work with, and not my family. And last night I thought, 'What is a family anyway? They're just people who make you feel less alone and really loved.' And that's what you've done for me. Thank you for being my family." It is this message that explains in personal terms what is historically regressive about *The Mary Tyler Moore Show*, as well as indicating its innovative dimensions. In its seven years, the heroine, Mary Richards, remains separate from her own family, their small town, and the 1950s TV idyll in which women married and stayed home to raise big families. She continues throughout the series to grow up as a single woman, occasionally mentioning her age as if to remind us of her special authority and her increasing confidence that living alone is not lonely. Her friends at home and at work are her "family," she says, and we have seen how these dependencies provide the basis for what is most positive about family trust and cooperation, and for what is most confining about family roles and hierarchy.

In a brief but significant scene during "The Last Show," Mary is reunited with Rhoda and Phyllis. Lou Grant has arranged for them to surprise her with a visit to her apartment, and they arrive from opposite coasts to support and cajole their old friend as she adjusts to the loss of her job at WJM. It is reassuring and comical to see that Mary is still the stable center for these two, who scrap over which one she will visit and which one she will sit nearest to as they talk. All three women are single now, with Rhoda's divorce in the past and Phyllis recently widowed. Their appearance functions in part to recall for us the feminist concerns and hopes that had for so many years connected them as neighbors. During the first half of the series, these three shared lives that provided an alternative to family life, and Mary played an important part as she encouraged Rhoda and Phyllis to struggle within their individual families. Most particularly, she was a role model for these two friends as they sought to separate from a mother and a daughter. They also questioned consumer values and the place of woman as buyer and believer in the myths of transformation. And above all these women affirmed the interdependence and compatibility of a daily life that combined home and work. Thus Mary, Phyllis, and Rhoda formed a familial group, sustained by what is most necessary to modern life: community and critique.

What is clearly a more patriarchal notion of family relations appears to have shaped Mary's role among the newsmen and the nature of her work at WJM. In this sphere the problems raised around sex roles and the division of labor provide the basis for much comic conflict between the men and Mary, but narrative closure in each episode involves the return to a "working order" that affirms traditional family hierarchy. Problem solving in this context requires that Mary mediate less as a single woman friend and more as a daughter, sister or mother—and sometimes even as a forbidden wife-lover. In playing these roles, Mary functions as a nineteenth-century True Woman, this time "upholding the pillars" of the workplace with her willing hand. But while she thus humanizes the newsroom, we see that in many ways she must deny her role as a producer in that context. Like her counterpart from a previous era, when middle-class women were the angels of the home, Mary sacrifices with a smile at WJM, granting her coworkers a sense of individual worth and the capacity to form a caring collective. The increasingly rationalized and highly technical aspects of TV news production are thereby slowed for a resistant moment—those seven mythic years when Mary Richards brought her familial skills into the workplace.

10

I Love *Laverne and Shirley*

Lesbian Narratives, Queer Pleasures,

and Television Sitcoms

ALEXANDER DOTY

"At Last! Lost Memoirs of 'Lucy' Costar: 'Ethel' Tells All—Even Truth About Rumors She and Lucy Were Lesbian Lovers" screams the front-page headline of the August 29, 1989, *National Enquirer.* The story inside features pictures of Vivian Vance and Lucille Ball together off screen and in their *I Love Lucy* roles as Ethel Mertz and Lucy Ricardo, as well as the first installment of excerpts from Vance's "explosive secret autobiography," which begins:

> Lucille Ball and I were just like sisters. We adored each other's company. She and I had so many laughs on "I Love Lucy" that we could hardly get through filming without cracking up.
>
> Then I began hearing that Lucille and I were too close.
>
> My first husband disapproved of my closeness with Lucille. "People are talking about you two," he'd say. "You ought to be careful about the hugging and kissing you do on the show."
>
> The word in Pacific Palisades, where I lived, was that something was wrong with me, something my analyst wouldn't tell me about.[1]

This story of straight male hysteria breeding misogyny and homophobia in order to undermine close bonds between women is depressingly familiar. What is particularly interesting in this case is how the relations between actual women

A slightly different version of this chapter was originally published in Alexander Doty, *Making Things Perfectly Queer: Interpreting Mass Culture* (Minneapolis: Univ. of Minnesota Press, 1973), 39–62. It has been reprinted here by permission of the publisher.

(Ball and Vance) are mixed and conflated with those of two fictional characters (Lucy and Ethel) to create a narrative of lesbian desire. This lesbian narrative is constructed by male homophobes here: the husband, the analyst, and Vance's second husband's best friend, who found the autobiography and reports that this second husband told him "the hardest thing for Vivian to write about was the Hollywood rumors that she and Lucy had a lesbian relationship, but . . . she wanted to set the record straight."[2]

While Vance seems worried about the rumors, she also seems to consider lesbian desire a possible explanation of her feelings for Ball. When she begins to hear the gossip about herself and Ball, Vance visits her analyst to ask him, "Is there anything the matter with me that you've never told me?" After recording her analyst's assurances that she is fine, Vance puts aside the lesbian narrative in its patriarchal, homophobic form, only to pick it up immediately in another:

> Lucille and I used to watch our own shows and rock with laughter at what we'd done on camera. We thought we were knockouts in some routines.
>
> Before shooting, Lucille and I would do advance planning. We'd plot together: "What if I step on your head when I climb down from the upper berth? . . . Suppose we both get so busy crawling around on the floor that we back into each other under the table? . . ."
>
> But throughout the "Lucy" years I was in analysis, trying to sort out crossed wires in my life.
>
> I was married to a man, an actor, who liked to dominate and discipline me. I kept trying to please him, but nothing I did was right. There were times when I would literally beat my head against the bedroom wall in frustration. . . .
>
> Analysis finally helped me. And working with Lucille Ball, seeing all the strength she had, was good and healthy for me.[3]

Ultimately Vance also conflates herself and her feelings for Ball with her performance of Ethel and Ethel's relationship with Lucy. But this contraheterosexual, women-bonding narrative—this lesbian narrative—is cast in positive terms, finding its happy ending in the work, friendship, and love between two women.[4]

The ways in which Vance's and Ball's offscreen lives have been discussed in relation to their roles as Ethel and Lucy in order to express various discourses of lesbianism provide the background for analyzing other situation comedies in which the relationships between women are the raisons d'être of the series. It is no coincidence that the public and the press are concerned about monitoring on-the-set relationships as well as those offscreen between the main actors on these series, or that this news/gossip often influences how characters and narratives (individual episode narratives as well as a series' meganarrative) are read. Robert H. Deming, in *"Kate and Allie*: 'New Women' and the Audience's Television Archive,"* speaks briefly about how some of the "media discourses" surrounding these series "gave female characters a life-like dimension outside of the text," listing *TV Guide* articles such as "I'd Walk Through a Dark Alley with Cagney and Lacey Behind Me," "No Jiggles. No Scheming. Just Real Women as Friends," and "Are *Kate and Allie* Such Good Friends—Off Screen?" as examples.[5] Then there has been the extensively reported on-the-set feuding between Cindy Williams (Shirley) and Penny Marshall (Laverne), and, more recently, the estrangement of Delta Burke (Suzanne Sugarbaker) from her costars and from producer-writer Linda Bloodworth-Thomason on *Designing Women.*[6]

As these examples indicate, media and public interest in women-centered series is focused upon potential dissension among the actors. It is almost as if mass audience pleasure week after week in seeing pairs and groups of women characters in intense and enjoyable relationships must be tempered or undermined somehow by news about how the women who play these characters have problems with each other. These misogynistic and, I would contend, homophobic public discursive and media tactics are nothing new, of course. There were constant radio, newspaper, and magazine reports about the production of George Cukor's 1939 film *The Women,* depicting the filming as fraught with the jealousy and temperament of a cast of 135 women—and one "women's director." This type of publicity was featured at the time and has been quoted in relation to the production of the film ever since, even though Cukor repeatedly stated that all the actors behaved professionally and that they formed a "rather jolly bunch."[7]

Considering the interests of patriarchal heterosexual culture, it is not surprising most of its media should want to devalue any potential site of woman-centered pleasures in mass culture, particularly when these pleasures fundamentally rely on viewers assuming queer positions. What is so interesting about series such as *I Love Lucy* (and, later, *The Lucy Show* [1962–68]), *Laverne and Shirley* (1976–83), *Designing Women* (1986–93), *The Golden Girls* (1988–92), *Babes* (1990–91), *227* (1985–90), *The Mary Tyler Moore Show* (1970–77), *Kate and Allie* (1984–89), and *Alice* (1976–85) is their crucial investment in constructing narratives that connect an audience's pleasure to the activities and relationships of women—which results in situating most male characters as potential threats to the spectator's narrative pleasure.[8] It is this kind of narrative construction I am calling "lesbian." The spectator positions and pleasures that audiences take in relation to these lesbian sitcoms I call either "lesbian" (for self-identified lesbians) or "queer" (for anybody else).

The ideas behind Adrienne Rich's term "lesbian continuum" work well here, as this concept suggests that a wide range and degree of experience and emotion might be called "lesbian":

> I mean the term lesbian continuum to include a range . . . of woman-identified experience; not simply the fact that a woman has had or consciously desired genital sexual experience with another woman. If we expand it to embrace many more forms of primary intensity between and among women, including the sharing of a rich inner life, the bonding against male tyranny, the giving and receiving of practical and political support . . . we begin to grasp breadths of female history and psychology that have lain out of reach as a consequence of limited, mostly clinical, definitions of "lesbianism." [9]

In separating the concept of a lesbian continuum from Rich's notion of "lesbian existence" as the material, historical presence of lesbians and their "continuing creation of the meaning of [lesbian] existence," [10] I believe I am not taking anything away from the expressions of specifically lesbian cultures and identities. What I am suggesting here is that in mass culture reception, at least, the idea of a lesbian continuum might be adapted and expanded to include those situations in which anyone identifies with or takes pleasure in the "many . . . forms of primary intensity between and among women" elaborated in shows such as *Laverne and Shirley, The Mary Tyler Moore Show,* and *Designing Women.*

Within these terms, you don't need to be lesbian-identified to respond to the lesbian elements of narrative construction in these sitcoms. My approach in the following pages is not so much concerned with ways of reading and taking pleasure in these shows *as* a lesbian, but rather ways of queerly reading *with,* and taking queer pleasure *in,* the lesbian tenor or temper of these series. This approach does include specifically lesbian positions and pleasures insofar as self-identified lesbians share the readings I offer of these shows. [11]

As with spectators, so with the women characters in these sitcoms. The fundamentally lesbian foundations of narrative construction in these shows don't mean that the major characters need necessarily be read as subtextual or closeted lesbians. As Marilyn R. Farwell points out, borrowing "from Teresa de Laurens's distinction between character and narrative space we can conclude that a lesbian [character] can occupy heterosexual space and a heterosexual can occupy . . . lesbian narrative space." [12] I am more concerned here with how various lesbian narrative structures and spectator positions are developed and expressed in certain television situation comedies than in identifying isolated subtextual or queer cult lesbian characters or star personas (such as Sally Rogers/Rose Marie on *The*

Dick Van Dyke Show, Alice/Ann B. Davis on *The Brady Bunch,* and Aunt Bea/Frances Bavier on *The Andy Griffith Show*).

Because the sitcoms I discuss do present heterosexually marked characters in lesbian-charged spaces, however, they also allow for and even encourage readings of most of the women characters as "really" lesbian for viewers who use something like Rich's continuum to define "lesbian." My allegiance to the concepts of queerness and Rich's lesbian continuum in relation to understanding narrative construction and reception practices dispose me to read the dynamics between most of the women characters in the series mentioned in this section as lesbian in some way. From where I sit as a feminine gay, I will often see fundamentally lesbian bonding where others see straight homosocial bonding, or, perhaps, a homosocial bonding that jokingly plays with suggestions of lesbian desire.

Most frequently sitcoms such as *The Golden Girls, Kate and Allie,* and *Designing Women* point toward lesbian readings through double entendres; through oblique, displaced, or jokey references to lesbianism; or with "lesbian episodes." These "lesbian episodes" are those individual shows that feature characters clearly marked as "lesbian" in them, and whose project it is to raise and then to contain or deflect the lesbian charge—or the charge of lesbianism—that the series has accumulated around its regular cast. Typically these episodes encourage playful and comic connections between the "real" lesbians and the other women in the cast through jokes, double entendres, and cases of mistaken identity or misassumption. Yet these episodes are also particularly insistent about maintaining the idea of homosociality ("just friends") as fully distinct and apart from (as well as preferable to) the homosexual through another network of jokes that work to contain, disempower, or devalue visible representations of lesbianism.

Mimi White effectively summarizes the complex intersection of queer readers/queer cultures and women-centered sitcoms:

> Programs such as *The Golden Girls* and *Kate and Allie* offer the narrative premise of adult women living together as a family. The female characters in these shows—in couples or in groups—are firmly established as heterosexual, and episodes regularly deal with dating, the desire for male companionship, and past marriages. But at the same time, they validate women's bonding as a form of social stability, a viable and attractive alternative to the traditional family, and even hint at the possibility of lesbian lifestyles—at least as far as possible within dominant ideology. A subcultural reading would emphasize these aspects of the program . . . Indeed, such a reading might stress that on a week-to-week basis the

narrative privileges women's relations over their inadequate, transient dealings with men.[13]

The one point on which I would differ with White is her categorizing such readings as always subcultural, alternative, or "reading against the grain"—they are particular queer cultural readings of mass culture texts. Besides, as I have suggested, reading and enjoying mass culture texts such as *The Golden Girls* queerly in one way or another can be, and is, done by audiences of all sexual identities.[14] Indeed, the sitcoms I am concerned with encourage, and in many ways position, audiences to read and enjoy queerly, whether they would call it this or not. Specifically, they are positioned to take lesbian or queer pleasures in the development of women's relationships within situation comedy narratives.

But, as suggested earlier, this type of lesbian narrative construction and its attendant queer pleasures are not without their potential ideological problems. It is possible to see these sitcoms as performing certain homophobic cultural work as they construct and encourage pleasures that seek to have fundamentally lesbian narratives and enjoyments pass as straight or as "just friends" homosocial. With the surfaces of their characters, actions, and mise-en-scène insistently straight-coded, these sitcoms are allowed to present a wide range of intense women-bonding that straight audiences can safely enjoy because the codes of lesbian "femme-ininity" can also be read as representing the straight feminine. Christine Holmlund discusses this exploitation of the representational codes of femme-ininity in order to "sort of" treat lesbianism in films such as *Entre Nous* and *Personal Best*: "The unconscious deployment . . . of a cinematic lesbian continuum organized around the figure of the femme is politically and erotically ambiguous, both presenting and erasing lesbian identities and sexualities."[15] In relation to modern advertising, Danae Clark has also noted that "the sexual indeterminacy" found in attempts to target straights and lesbians simultaneously "allows a space for lesbian identification, but must necessarily deny the representation of lesbian identity politics."[16]

Clearly, the sitcoms I will discuss in this section do everything they can to assert a homosocial, "just friends" understanding of both the narrative camaraderie between their femme-inine characters and the audience's pleasure in this sight. As an April 1992 *TV Guide* ad promoting *Room for Two* (about a mother and daughter who work together) and *Sibs* (about three sisters) exclaims: "Grab Your Popcorn . . . It's a solid hour of *female* bonding!" But besides the (overly) insistent italicizing of "female" and the exclamation point, the ad offers a quote from the *Cleveland Plain Dealer* about *Sibs* that suggests another way of describing and understanding the appeal of these women-centered shows as "witty, sexy, adult" programs.[17] The project of the following analyses of *I Love Lucy, The Mary Tyler Moore Show, Laverne and Shirley,* and *Designing Women* is to discuss their "adult, sexy, witty" narratives and pleasures as fundamentally lesbian or queer, while acknowledging that my understanding and use of the term "lesbian" in relation to these narratives and characters works within the same broad definition that these very shows—like the films and advertising Holmlund and Clark critique—employ to simultaneously suggest and deny culturally and erotically specific forms of lesbianism. In the face of all this, I still maintain that these sitcoms' basic structuring principle can be called lesbian, even if these shows often seem to offer only hypothetically lesbian surfaces that encourage closeted queer enjoyment.[18]

One episode of *Kate and Allie* cleverly acknowledges the show's lesbian situation-comedy lineage when Allie falls asleep on the sofa and dreams that she and Kate are Lucy Ricardo and Ethel Mertz, and then Mary Richards and Rhoda Morgenstern. As the material at the beginning of this section implies, at some point in the run of *I Love Lucy* (1951–57), people began to read the closeness between Lucy and Ethel as encompassing the erotic. Recognizing that these erotics were the center of *I Love Lucy*'s narrative pleasures was not so clear during the show's initial run, perhaps, as it is in retrospect with the evidence of *The Lucy Show* (1962–68) and *Here's Lucy* (1968–74).[19] *The Lucy Show* was initially built around Lucille Carmichael (Lucille Ball) and Vivian Bagley (Vivian Vance), a widow and a divorcée living together with their children.[20] When Vance left the show, Ball recruited Ann Sothern, Joan Blondell, and Mary Jane Crofts to play her cohort for extended periods. The first *Lucy Show* after Vance's departure has a butched-up Lucy (in a grey suit and string tie) reading a letter from the just-married "Viv," who says the best thing about her marriage to a Mr. Burnside is that she won't have to change the initials on her luggage.

Looking back at *I Love Lucy,* the strength and dynamism of Lucy and Ethel's relationship are simultaneously the most consistent source of the show's pleasures and the source of the greatest threats to the narrative's maintaining some form of patriarchal heterosexual hegemony. While as a couple Lucy and Ethel only achieve partial or temporary disruptions of the status quo, the series depends on their lesbian comic energies to establish and propel most *I Love Lucy* narratives, thus encouraging a number of fascinating scenes and episodes during the show's long run. In "Vacation from Marriage" (October 27, 1952), the Ricardos and the Mertzes split up into same-sex couples after Lucy and Ethel decide their heterosexual relationships with Ricky and Fred are in "a rut." In an attempt to make their husbands envious, the women appear at the Ricardos' apartment (where the men are staying) dressed to go out nightclubbing. "I hope you two will have as gay an evening as we are," Lucy says to Ricky and Fred. But instead of going to the 21 Club, Lucy and Ethel return to the Mertzes' bedroom, where they have the following exchange:

> LUCY. How do you like it here at 21?
> ETHEL. *Très gay.*

Although the narrative motivation for all this is the women's attempts to get the men to call off the "vacation from marriage," the ultimate "gayness" of the show's female same-sex comradeship is established here as overtly as it ever can or will be.

In a more connotative or associative register, moments such as Lucy's imitating Tallulah Bankhead's gender-transgressing deep voice or her cross-dressing masculine or butch, and her butch-femme role-playing with Ethel (as reporters, as a male-female vaudeville team, Lucy as the writer-director of an operetta in which Ethel is the soprano star, as cowboys in a homemade Western film, Lucy as a baseball player) often work to reinforce those fundamental queer pleasures in the narrative for certain viewers by evoking lesbian cultural codes and references. Of Lucy and Ethel's comic teamwork, Patricia Mellencamp (chap. 2) notes that its "reliance on physical comedy rather than verbal comedy, with Lucy and Ethel as the lead performers, constituted another exclusion of Ricky." [21]

One of the most interesting episodes along these lines is "Lucy Is Envious" (March 29, 1954), in which Lucy and Ethel earn money by taking a stunt job publicizing the film *Women from Mars*. In their androgynizing Martian uniforms, Lucy and Ethel appear atop King Kong's phallic realm, the Empire State Building, and terrorize a group of tourists, as much by the strange language the pair have made up as by their looks. Frightened when a straight Earth woman screams after Lucy peers into her mouth, the alien women use their "paralyzing ray" to silence one of the men (the stunt's promoter), who threatens to warn the world. The stunt over, but still in their costumes, Lucy and Ethel return home. Joyfully leaping about as they count their wages, the women continue to speak to each other in "Martian." With their androgynous look and their incomprehensible language, Lucy and Ethel's difference is coded as dangerous and alien. Since they are set apart from straight Earth men and women here, there is little doubt as to what this difference is really all about. The sight (and sound) of Lucy and Ethel returning home as Martian women is so startling and weirdly funny that the rest of the episode's narrative works to completely reverse what has come before by having Ricky and Fred play men from Mars in order to scare "the girls" back into their roles as submissive housewives.

Integrating Lucille Ball's pregnancy into *I Love Lucy*'s text established a precedent, and a pattern, for having women-centered sitcoms use expectant motherhood to reinforce and expand the women-bonding aspects of their narratives. Far from shifting the series's emphasis toward heterosexual domestic concerns, as might be expected, the pregnancy and postpartum episodes of *I Love Lucy, Laverne and Shirley, Designing Women, The Golden Girls, The Mothers-in-Law,* and *Bewitched* are concerned with marginalizing and trivializing male characters while (re)establishing a network of supportive women around the mother(-to-be).[22] The famous "Lucy Is Enciente" episode (October 12, 1952) opens with Lucy and Ethel recalling their grandmothers, after which Ethel suggests Lucy's "dauncy" feeling might be a sign of pregnancy. Returning from the doctor's office, Lucy turns to Ethel in a blissful daze: "Ethel, we're going to have a baby." "We are?" Ethel exclaims, "Oh, isn't that wonderful, I never had a baby before." "You knew it even before I did," Lucy responds, adding, "This whole thing was practically your idea." In contrast, Lucy finds it nearly impossible to tell Ricky about her pregnancy—indeed, the episode is constructed so that he tells himself while a silent Lucy nods her assent. The episodes that follow this one would be good illustrations of feminist cultural and psychoanalytic theories about how motherhood establishes erotic bonds between women, including mothers and daughters.[23] Lucy's maternity, from being narratively conceived, in a manner of speaking, between her and Ethel, is developed to bring Lucy's mother (Mrs. McGillicuddy) and the upstairs neighbor/babysitter (Mrs. Trumbell) into the series as regulars to form a strong community of women. Besides this, these episodes remind us that there have always been strong mother-daughter elements in Ethel and Lucy's relationship, with Lucy the childish one who occasionally makes joking references to Ethel as a mother figure for her (as in "Lucy Writes a Novel," May 4, 1954).

The Mary Tyler Moore Show (1970–77) also worked out some of its lesbian narratives through the matrix of motherhood and mother-daughter relations. As if to indicate that the interactions among the women characters in the ensemble cast were the heart of the show's narrative appeal, only Mary Richards (Mary Tyler Moore) and her best friend Rhoda Morgenstern (Valerie Harper) were given mothers who were recurring characters (played by Nanette Fabray and Nancy Walker). Phyllis Lindstrom (Cloris Leachman), their landlady, is the mother of Bess, who in one episode leaves Phyllis and "adopts" Mary as her new mother. Another episode has Phyllis ask Mary to tell Bess all about sex. In addition, Mary's Aunt Flo (Eileen Heckart) makes a number of memorable appearances in which she outtalks and outdrinks Mary's gruff boss, Lou Grant. Fathers (Mary's, Rhoda's, Ted's) do appear on a number of episodes, but they are almost always narratively less important than mothers and mother-daughter pairs. Besides, the women are given most of the funniest lines and situations.[24]

Of course, local television news producer Lou Grant (who also functions as a father figure for Mary), head writer Murray Slaughter, and newscaster Ted Baxter do have their moments, as well as having entire shows built around them.[25] But many of the episodes ostensibly focused on Lou are concerned with his divorce or his dating, and both situations bring new women characters onto the show or involve established characters such as Aunt Flo, "Happy Homemaker" Sue Ann Nivens, and even Mary and Rhoda. As far as Ted and Murray are concerned, for a number of seasons many viewers (consciously or not) considered them gay or bisexual—or, in the words of Richard Corliss, audiences had "suspected" them of being "closet queens."[26] Viewers often read as effeminate, and therefore as gay, such things as Ted's overweening vanity about his looks and Murray's bitchy bon mot dialogue, which is usually directed at Ted in a tone of mixed irritation and affection. Thus (ef)feminized, Ted and Murray narratively become two more of "the girls," particularly when counterpoised with Lou, Gordy the weatherman, or one of Mary's dates.[27] Perhaps sensing these readings of Murray and Ted, the show's producers and writers made a concerted effort to heterosexualize the two men around the third season by bringing on Murray's wife as a recurring character and introducing Georgette Franklin (Georgia Engel) as Ted's girlfriend and later his wife.

But Georgette's addition to the cast in the middle of the show's third season, followed by that of Sue Ann Nivens (Betty White) at the beginning of the fourth season, was also a conscious effort by the show's creators to "build a second generation of supporting players . . . to keep the series strong over the long haul."[28] With Harper's departure at the end of the fourth season and Leachman's during the fifth (both to star in spin-off series named after their characters), Georgette and Sue Ann were developed as major characters to replace Rhoda and Phyllis.[29] However, with Rhoda and Phyllis (and Mrs. Morgenstern) gone, the show's last two seasons lost those all-women narratives about Mary's life at home. Her move from the old apartment building she shared with Rhoda, Bess, and Phyllis to an ultramodern apartment signaled the program's switch from lesbian narratives to more heterosexual(ized) ones.

Typical plots began to revolve around Ted and Georgette's marriage, their adoption of a boy genius, Mary's dates, her new steady boyfriend (played by *That Girl* beau, Ted Bessell), Lou's dates, his relationship with Mary's Aunt Flo, and Sue Ann's attempts to get Lou into bed. Indeed, the last two seasons become positively incestuous in their heterosexual plotting, with episodes in which Murray falls in love with Mary; Lou goes on a date with Mary; Mary dates Murray's father; Lou dates (and proposes to) Mary's aunt; and Lou, Murray, and Ted dream of what it would be like to be married to Mary. Only occasionally does the series attempt a return to the lesbian narratives that had made the show popular, as with episodes featuring Aunt Flo or Sue Ann's sister, or the one in which Georgette gives birth in Mary's apartment, with Sue Ann and Mary assisting. One indication of just how invested viewers were in the queer pleasures of the show's initial women-centered narratives is the series's precipitous slip in the Neilsen ratings to nineteenth and then to thirty-ninth place in its last two seasons after being ranked between seventh and eleventh place during the previous four seasons.[30]

I will let a detailed discussion of one episode stand in for the types of lesbian narratives/queer pleasures the series generated in its prime. This episode has Phyllis and Mary both seeing the same man, Mike (John Saxon), but its title, "Ménage-à-Phyllis," suggests that the power dynamics in this erotically charged trio lie with a woman, and that, therefore, the two other partners in Phyllis's ménage are Mike and Mary. Since it contains some obvious gay references, the narrative also seems willing to present certain aspects of women's relationships in a manner just barely this side of lesbian connotation. The episode's premise is that because Lars doesn't like to go to cultural events, Phyllis asks Mike, who has just broken his engagement, to be her escort. After Mary mentions Phyllis and Mike's arrangement, Ted remarks that it is "disgusting" to hear Phyllis is "running around." When Mary explains that Phyllis and Mike only go to the ballet and opera together as friends, Ted flips his wrist limply and says, "Oh, he's one of *those*!" Defending Mike against Ted's innuendo, Mary can't even say the term Ted implies: "No! Why does everyone think that just because a man likes ballet he's . . . No! He's not!" When Mike arrives in the newsroom to speak to Mary, Ted tries to be hiply tolerant, though after Mike leaves, he turns to Murray and says, "I just hope he's not using Mary to get to me."

On a night she is supposed to go out with Mike, Phyllis comes down with a cold, and Mary visits her with some ice cream and magazines. Lying on the sofa, Phyllis nostalgically recalls how her mother used to bring her ice cream when she was a little girl, and about how she told her mother she "wuved" everything: "I wuv my ice cream," "I wuv my teddy bear," "I wuv my mommy." When Mike arrives, Phyllis insists Mary take her place at the opera but asks her to bring back something—Mike. With Mary as the "mommy" as well as the rival for a man's affection, the show seems to be working itself out in straight "Electra complex" terms at this point, but the episode's second half moves the material firmly into the realm of lesbian narrative/queer pleasure by methodically downgrading, reducing, and eliminating the participation of men.

After a few more dates with Mike, Mary begins to feel confused about the situation. Lou and Murray cajole her into confiding in them with a pseudofeminist argument about women wanting men to be more sensitive and sharing but then not telling them anything personal. After Mary tells them she's been out with Mike two or three times and had fun but that he's never become romantic with her, Murray exclaims, "Maybe Ted *is* right about him!" To which Mary replies with some disgust, "*This* is why women don't confide in men!" Later, in her apartment, Mary and Phyllis attempt to discuss how they feel about their own and each other's interest in Mike. After Phyllis leaves, Mike arrives, but Phyllis returns in time for Mike to tell Mary and Phyllis that he's back with his former fiancée, Sharon. As the shots cross-cut between Mike alone in the frame and Mary and Phyllis sharing a frame, Mike suggests they all get together sometime. "Sure," Mary says dryly. "Sometime you and Sharon, and Phyllis and I can all go out dancing." With that, Mike exits, leaving Phyllis to console a not really upset Mary. "In your own peculiar way, Phyllis," Mary says, "you really care about me." Putting her head on Mary's shoulder, Phyllis replies, "Care about you, Mary? I 'wuv' you!" as the episode comes to a close. A coda finds Mary in the newsroom with Murray, asking him if he's "ever had a meaningful relationship with a woman that wasn't physical." "Yes," Murray says, "with my wife." In "Ménage-à-Phyllis," textual references to same-sex behavior and nonsexual relationships between men and women combine with the eroticized quasi-maternal interactions between two women to construct a narrative that passes through heterosexuality (Phyllis and Mary as rivals for the just-separated Mike) and bisexuality (Phyllis as being close to Mike and Mary simultaneously), to resolve itself as a lesbian domestic sitcom narrative with Mary and Phyllis reunited and declaring their affection for each other in Mary's kitchen.

In a similar way, *Laverne and Shirley* (1976–83) often developed its lesbian narratives and queer pleasures by "passing through" heterosexuality and other forms of relationships with men in order to reestablish the emotional and erotic status quo of two women living and working together. Much of the audience pleasure in this series is bound up in seeing how various threats to maintaining *Laverne and Shirley* as a couple are overcome. Set in the late 1950s and early 1960s in Milwaukee and then Burbank, the lesbian dynamics of this series often went beyond its narrative construction to include working-class lesbian cultural codes that positioned Laverne as the (unwitting) butch and Shirley as the (repressed) femme.[31]

Living in a basement apartment and working as bottle cappers for Shotz Brewery in Milwaukee, the pair often talked about men and their relationships with them in opposing terms: Laverne wanted lots of sex with lots of men, Shirley wanted to marry a professional and settle down in a middle-class suburb. But while Laverne's sexual aggressivity and voracity are frequently shown, Shirley's desire for a conventional marriage is consistently cast as a hopeless goal. This was for class-jumping reasons certainly, but I would also contend this was done in order to keep the narrative lesbian. Shirley often seems programmed to repeat the American Dream party line for women in her position at the time. Perhaps she has become fixated on this suburban dream, and will accept no substitute, because it allows her to stay with Laverne while providing her with an approved heterosexualizing cover: "I haven't found the right man/my 'prince' yet." Indeed, Shirley's favorite song is "High Hopes," from the film *A Hole in the Head.*

An episode involving the Shotz company psychiatrist literally analyzes and exposes Shirley's heterosexual cover-up. Entering the doctor's office with false bravado, Shirley flings around a scarf she clutches in her hand, as if to emphasize her femme-ininity: "All right Doctore [*sic*], do your worst to me! Sit up there in your ivory tower and pass judgment on me! But remember, down here life goes on, and we little people protect each other. So you can push us around all you like." Nervously and comically hyperdramatic, Shirley is already revealing her role-playing, her hiding something the doctor could "pass judgment on," and her need to be protected because of this.

Immediately, the doctor turns Shirley's attention to the picture of a house she drew as part of her psychiatric testing, telling her it's a "lovely house":

> SHIRLEY. Split level, colonial, flagstone driveway, doorbell that chimes "High Hopes."
> DOCTOR. And the dog you drew, is it a collie?
> SHIRLEY. Prince? Yes. It should be Princess, though. But I didn't find out she was a girl doggie until she had her puppies.
> DOCTOR. You know a lot about this house.
> SHIRLEY. Well yes. I've thought a lot about it, you know. It's my dream home.
> DOCTOR. I noticed one thing though—there's nobody in it.
> SHIRLEY. There's nobody in my house? [*takes the drawing from the doctor and frantically examines it*] There must be somebody here. [*laughs nervously*] So you're right. There's nobody in it! That doesn't mean anything, does it? Does it? . . . Of course it means something, doesn't it? Everything means something! [*starts to pound on her forehead with her fist*] Let me think. Why wouldn't there be people in my house? Why . . . wouldn't . . . there . . . be . . . people . . . in . . . my . . . house?

Although she first offers the weak explanation that there are no people in her house because they are all vacationing in Disneyland, she has to admit to the psychiatrist, "Gee, I just had a bad thought, you know. Maybe it's all just a pipe dream. Maybe I never will get married and have puppies. I don't know. Tell me, doctor do you think I'm doomed to a life of despair?" Desperately grasping the doctor's "it all depends" as "no," Shirley falls to her knees, thanks him profusely ("You don't know how relieved those words have made me feel"), and borrows his pencil so she can draw herself and her husband coming home from Disneyland onto her original picture.

The psychoanalytic setting for all this encourages us to see what is revealed here as fraught with hidden meanings. Even Shirley admits this: "Of course it means something, doesn't it? Everything means something." But the narrative cuts off the doctor's analysis with the suggestion that Shirley may or may not be "doomed to a life of despair" because she has constructed a fantasy of suburban life without a husband or children in it. The ambiguity here is provocative in light of the show's lesbian narrative structure and cultural coding. Shirley may be doomed to a life of despair if she continues to hold on to a heterosexual fantasy she clearly doesn't believe in or want. On the other hand, she may not be doomed, because this fantasy allows her to reject all men as somehow not good enough, so she can continue to live with Laverne—after all, her suburban "Prince" is really a "Princess."

Related to Shirley's gender confusion about the dog (the only figure she does draw in her house) is her slip of the tongue that connects her potential roles as (straight) wife and mother to a dog having puppies. Thus connected with both her unacknowledged desire for a lesbian "dream" household (just her and Princess), and the prospect of being the (doglike) mother of a straight household, the figure of the dog as articulated through Shirley's psychiatric test represents the dilemma both of her character and of the series' narrative: she/it *should* want to be heterosexual, she/it *tries* to be heterosexual, but the force of lesbian desire (of the character, in the text) is strong. It is strong enough to set in motion all manner of heterosexual cover-ups that seek to contain, defuse, redefine, or render invisible what would come out as undeniable lesbian desire in characters and queer pleasures in audiences. To take one example, Shirley is given a regular boyfriend, Carmine Ragusa, during the Milwaukee episodes, but he is generally kept at arm's length by the fantasy of a virginal and middle-class wedding that Shirley's episode with the psychiatrist calls into question. Perhaps tired of the pretense, the show's producers and writers decided to make Carmine Shirley's friend when she and Laverne move to California.

Like Shirley's fantasies of straight domestic bliss, Laverne's constant one-night stands might also be seen as a form of heterosexual cover-up, as they ultimately pose little threat to her living arrangement with Shirley. In the show's

1950s–60s context, there is no danger Laverne will go off to live with any of the men she sees for one or two dates. And although Laverne's sexual behavior can be read as hyperheterosexual, it is also linked to codes of masculinity and/or (stereo)typical codes of lesbian butchness. Frequently, Laverne's trysts begin with her making the first physical moves, often with an appalled Shirley looking on. While the men involved usually respond with pleased surprise to this sexual aggressivity, the number of Laverne's brief encounters during the run of the series comes to suggest that either the men don't come back for more or that Laverne doesn't want them to come back. Either way, Laverne is also narratively let off the ultimate straight hook of marriage and family because audiences are encouraged to enjoy how her masculinized sexual behavior scares men off, or how it is farcically rendered as "trampy" or "bad girl" behavior. Early in the series, Laverne's background as a high-school tough girl or "greaser" is often introduced in the form of members of her old girl gang, particularly Rosie Greenbaum. Episodes featuring Rosie explore the tensions that have developed between her and Laverne as a result of Rosie's pretentious behavior after she marries an upper-middle-class professional. Laverne sees Rosie's attitude as a betrayal of who she and Rosie were (and are), and the pair swiftly move from verbal insults to wrestling matches to express their frustrations. Most obviously, Rosie's betrayal is a class betrayal, but her girl-gang past with Laverne suggests her betrayal also concerns gender and sexuality: that is, heterosexual coupling in marriage versus women-bonding in pairs and groups.

Ultimately the series itself would place Shirley in Rosie's position, while providing Laverne with a steady boyfriend. But even these heterosexualizing narrative ploys were undercut by the accumulated force of the show's lesbian dynamics. As mentioned earlier, this lesbian atmosphere is established in *Laverne and Shirley* not only by how the program constructs the audience's emotional and erotic investment in its women-bonding narrative(s), but also by its frequent use of various cultural codes of lesbianism, which might be read as conventionally heterocentrist stereotyping, as lesbian culture-specific, or as some combination of both. The group of episodes that have *Laverne and Shirley* in the army, for example, play on codes of the butch sergeant and her troop of Amazons in a manner that allows straight-and queer-identified viewers, in their different ways, to enjoy the proceedings as lesbian comedy. These episodes also offer the spectacle of both Laverne and Shirley being transformed into masculinized women/butches during basic training, and then into hyperfeminized women/femmes when they are cast as prostitutes in an army hygiene film.

But most often, Laverne is the masculine/butch of the pair, while Shirley is the feminine/femme. The lesbianism linked to these positions comes very close to the series' narrative surface a few times during its seven-year run. In one episode, after the pair wins a plane trip for two in a Schotz Brewery lottery, Laverne admits she's afraid of flying. Shirley convinces her to face her fears, but Laverne panics once the plane takes off, accidentally knocking out the male copilot and pilot. Taking over for the pilot, Laverne puts on his cap while she follows the radio instructions of an air controller. As she clutches her trademark scarf, Shirley returns to the passenger cabin, pretending to be a volunteer stewardess ("Perhaps you've heard of us? Candy-stripers of the air.") in order to find a passenger who knows how to fly. When the real stewardess enters and tells everyone to prepare for a "crash landing," Shirley rushes to the cockpit, falls to her knees, says "Good-bye, Laverne," and gives her partner a passionate kiss. "We'll talk about that later, Shirl," replies a startled Laverne. But Shirley persists in expressing her deep feelings for Laverne as she squeezes into the pilot's seat so they can "die together." Touched by Shirley's sentiments, Laverne asks her if she remembers what she wrote in Laverne's high-school yearbook. As the plane descends, the pair recite in unison:

> If in heaven we don't meet,
> Hand-in-hand we'll bear the heat.
> And if it ever gets too hot,
> Pepsi-Cola hits the spot!

On the last line, the plane touches down while Laverne and Shirley scream and hold on to each other. As it turns out, the pilot has revived just in time to help with the landing, so the women's accomplishments are somewhat tarnished by male intervention, although the pilot calls what Laverne did "heroic." Of course, Laverne never does talk to Shirley about that kiss.

But she does "marry" her: twice, in fact. The first time is the result of another contest win. Shirley has entered a contest whose first prize is a wedding dress and a weekend at the Hotel Pfister. What she doesn't think through is how she'll be able to fulfill the contest requirement that the winner actually be married in the dress before enjoying her honeymoon at the Pfister. Enter Laverne, who is initially enthusiastic about spending the weekend with Shirley, and who only needs a little persuading to be talked into becoming her groom. What follows is a series of farcical situations that find Laverne and Shirley, in their wedding tuxedo and gown, trying to convince everyone they are indeed husband and wife.

More remarkable is Laverne's second "marriage" to Shirley, because it takes place during, and actually in the place of, Shirley's marriage to army surgeon Walter Meany. Coming near the end of Cindy Williams's participation in the show, this wedding also becomes the climax of Laverne and Shirley's long and loving relationship. Up to this point, the program found a number of narrative excuses not to show Walter Meany to the audience, that is, not to make incarnate a major threat to the show's lesbian narrative/queer pleasures. And we never do get to see Walter, because on the eve of the wedding he is involved in an accident that puts him in a head and body cast. Held in the intensive care ward of an army hospital and presided over by a uniformed army chaplain (which reminds viewers of Laverne and Shirley's stint as WACs), the wedding proceeds on schedule, with Laverne as both maid of honor and groom. Coming to the part of the service where rings are exchanged, Laverne stands behind the propped-up Walter, slips her hand through the crook of his arm, and places the ring on Shirley's finger. Still clasping hands as the chaplain says "I now pronounce you man and wife," Laverne and Shirley look tenderly at each other for a moment across Walter's immobilized body before realizing the implications and unclasping their hands. After kissing Walter, however, Shirley immediately turns to hug and kiss Laverne, as Walter is excluded from the shot.[32]

In spite of this marriage, *Laverne and Shirley* (and the program) were kept together a while longer by narrative ploys that had Walter constantly on special assignment.[33] When Cindy Williams became pregnant, the show looked as if it would follow *I Love Lucy*'s pattern and use a cast member's maternity to revitalize the bonds between women characters. As with Lucy and Ethel, Shirley first announces her pregnancy to Laverne. After this, the two of them go through various prenatal experiences together as a couple, something Laverne does again later when a somewhat feminized Sarge shows up pregnant and without a husband. But when Williams left to have her baby, she decided not to return to the show. With Williams/Shirley gone, the program became *Laverne and Company*. In a manner reminiscent of the last seasons of *The Mary Tyler Moore Show* and *Kate and Allie*, *Laverne and Company*'s narratives and characters are heterosexualized: Laverne is given a muscular stuntman for a boyfriend; the Monroesque starlet next door gets to drop by more often with news of her latest conquest; Carmine becomes engaged.[34]

Actually, Shirley's absence from the show left it with little hope of reviving the fundamental source of its audience appeal, since Shirley was always the character who most successfully negotiated the threatening lesbian narrative spaces between being a heterosexual character functioning within the structures of lesbian narrative, being a subtextual lesbian within the codes of straight and lesbian (sub)cultural connotation, and being denotatively marked as a "real" lesbian character by the text. In the army hygiene film episode, it is, significantly, Shirley's acting partner who makes a point of telling her he's gay after she warns him that she doesn't want any onscreen romance to continue offscreen. This being the case, it becomes clear that Shirley and her costar can only pantomime straight lust under their heterosexually pornographic stage names, "Shirley Love" and "Johnny Pulse." This sense of straight role-playing with its attempted repression of the queer is most intensely centered around Shirley, but this role-playing is also crucial to maintaining the queer pleasures of *Laverne and Shirley* for many viewers, as it camouflages what is lesbian about the program.

I will conclude this chapter with *Designing Women* (1986–93), not only because it is one of the most recent long-running lesbian sitcoms, but because its 1991–92 season clearly revealed an important point about these shows: the chemistry between the women characters/actors is ultimately more important to maintaining the lesbian dynamics in these shows than is the presence or absence of (straight) men. Going beyond the idea of men as potential threats to its community of women, *Designing Women* has been rather offhand about introducing, and then marginalizing or eliminating, the men who date or marry its women characters. Overall, this indifferent treatment of men and "compulsory heterosexuality" makes it clear that the narrative fact of straight romance and marriage does not necessarily heterosexualize lesbian sitcoms any more than being married makes actual lesbians straight.[35]

Until its 1991–92 season, *Designing Women* was popular with both critics and the public for having one of the most dynamic ensemble casts on American television: Dixie Carter (Julia Sugarbaker), Delta Burke (Suzanne Sugarbaker), Annie Potts (Mary Jo Shively), and Jean Smart (Charlene Stillfield). Even regular Meshach Taylor's Anthony Bouvier, the Sugarbaker interior design firm's delivery person and general assistant, was considered "one of the girls" (as Mary Jo puts it) and Suzanne's "girlfriend." Alice Ghostley, joining the cast later in the series run as the Sugarbakers' outrageous Aunt Bernice, rounded out the original ensemble of women and one (subtextual?) gay man.

With this cast, *Designing Women* ran through the entire spectrum of characteristic lesbian sitcom situations. Charlene's pregnancy and the birth of daughter Olivia largely took place in the absence of Charlene's air force officer husband, Bill, who was away on overseas duty. With the support of her coworkers/friends, Charlene has the child, returns to work, and finds a nanny to take care of Olivia on the floor above the firm's main office. With day nursery, offices, and stockrooms located in Julia's home, the series goes most other lesbian sitcoms one better by combining work and domestic spaces, and marking both as female, thereby intensifying the primacy of these women's relationships with each other. Indeed, *Designing Women* offers a matriarchal vision combining the spheres of work and home that patriarchal capitalism insists on keeping separate, gendered, and differently valued (male/work/important, female/home/trivial).

This matriarchal network of work and maternity expanded beyond biological mothers Charlene, Mary Jo, and Julia to include Suzanne, in an episode in which she accidentally puts some of Charlene's breast milk (stored in the office refrigerator for Olivia's feedings) into her coffee. Denying she used the milk, Suzanne yells, "What do you think I am—a pervert?" What "pervert" might mean here is taken up in a later sequence at a restaurant when Suzanne, photographed in two shots with Charlene, says she thinks their waiter Ian is "a homosexual." When Mary Jo returns from the bathroom, she overhears Ian's name and asks who he is. "Our homosexual waiter," Charlene answers, taking her cue from Suzanne. This suggestive pairing of Charlene and Suzanne occurs a number of times in the series, as does the coupling of Julia and Mary Jo. Among other things, Mary Jo and Julia have danced together while dressed as a (male) chef and a restaurant hostess, and while costumed as Bette Davis and Joan Crawford in *Whatever Happened to Baby Jane*? (the latter in the "The Strange Case of Clarence and Anita" episode).

Because Suzanne constantly comments about "homosexuals" during the series' run, it makes sense that she would be the character who is most immediately involved with the "real" lesbian character in *Designing Women*'s "lesbian episode." Mistaking the "coming out" of Eugenia Weeks, a friend from her beauty pageant days, as part of the Southern tradition of being presented as a straight, marriageable woman at a debutante ball, Suzanne agrees to go to a banquet with Eugenia. When the other women at the firm clarify matters, Suzanne is appalled, and asks them to come with her to a bar-restaurant where she is supposed to meet Eugenia. Certain it is a lesbian bar, the women attempt to play it cool, but end up acting awkward, particularly Mary Jo, who at one point asks Julia to hold her hand and pretend to be her girlfriend. Finally confronting each other in a health club sauna (where another woman understands their remarks as part of a lesbian love spat), Suzanne reconciles with Eugenia because she sees they have so much in common.

But while Suzanne was reconciling with Eugenia, Delta Burke found herself more and more at odds with her producers, writers, and costars. After a series of charges alleging that Burke's diva-like temperament and demands were disruptive to the atmosphere on the set, Burke countercharged that she was being badly treated (primarily because of weight gains) and was underappreciated. Many members of *Designing Women*'s cast, crew, and production staff felt Burke's new attitude was attributable to the influence of her husband, Gerald McRaney (star of the sitcom *Major Dad* (1989–93), in which he played a marine officer).[36] The situation came to a head during the 1990–91 season. Although the series achieved its highest Nielsen ratings ever (it was the ninth-ranked show), and Burke was nominated for an Emmy award for "best actress in a comedy series" (something no other cast member had achieved), *Designing Women* executives decided to fire Burke. Soon afterward Jean Smart announced that she would leave the show to pursue other acting projects and spend more time with her family.

Clearly hoping to retain the same type of family bonding between the women characters, the show's producers cast Julia Duffy as Suzanne and Julia's cousin Allison Sugarbaker, and Jan Hooks as Charlene's cousin Carlene. The hour-long 1991–92 season premiere to introduce the new characters left critics and audiences disappointed: Allison seemed shrill and aloof, and Carlene a colorless copy of Charlene.

Then, in what seemed an attempt to more quickly integrate the new characters into the existing ensemble, an episode was aired early in the season that made the "hidden" source of the series's narrative pleasures more overt through a "women marrying women" leitmotiv running throughout the episode. Carlene's gratitude to Mary Jo for helping her during her first weeks in Atlanta and at the firm touches off this theme. Rushing downstairs and into the combination living room-main office, Carlene excitedly says, "Mary Jo, you are just the best girlfriend I ever had. I mean it! If you were a man, I'd marry you." Then, as if seriously considering the issue, she looks offscreen, and her next line—"But, you know, Julia, I'd find you very attractive, too"—concludes over a shot of Julia smiling. Standing between Julia and Mary Jo, who are seated on a sofa, Carlene continues: "It would be a tough decision. Mary Jo or Julia? I can't decide! What do you think, Allison?" And although Allison sarcastically remarks, "I think you need a date—bad!" she then petulantly snaps, "Am not!" when Mary Jo advises Carlene not to pay attention to Allison because "she's just mad because none of us want to marry her." With no transition, Carlene replies, "Well, gosh, you know my divorce is just barely final. I don't think I'd be comfortable dating another man at this point." Given its context, Carlene's non sequitur implies she would, and does, feel comfortable dating (or marrying) another woman.

But since this cannot be expressed directly in the surface narrative except as a joke, Carlene finds herself constructing an elaborate scheme with Mary Jo in which they enlist Anthony as Carlene's date in order to thwart Carlene's ex-husband, who wants to remarry her. Although he skeptically views their plan as being "like something Lucy and Ethel would do,"[37] Anthony lowers his voice and plays his part, even in the face of a surprise encounter with Allison at the restaurant where he, Carlene, and her ex-husband are meeting:

> ANTHONY. Carlene and I have been dating for some time.
> ALLISON. I don't believe it.
> ANTHONY. It was a secret.
> ALLISON. I cannot believe that this woman blows into town five minutes ago and already she's got a best friend and a boyfriend. Not the ones I would choose, but still . . . I mean, I think I'm attractive, but I don't have a best friend. I don't have a boyfriend. And for some reason, none of the women at work want to marry me!

That the prospect of marrying a woman—or having a woman want to marry her—is finally more important to Allison than having a best friend or a boyfriend becomes clear in the last sequence of the episode. While the narrative works to have Carlene (re)place her semi-serious talk of marrying a woman within the terms of homosociality by having her tell Mary Jo, "You just got a little carried away with that female camaraderie. So what?" Allison remains in a less assimilable position. The frustration she expresses after discovering that Anthony is not Carlene's boyfriend goes beyond this specific case of being lied to by the other three women (and Anthony) to obliquely address certain bigger lies about the slippery straightness of characters and narratives on *Designing Women*: "Wait! Wait a minute! Are you telling me that you two are not going out? Oh, right. So first you weren't, then you were, and now you aren't. That's great. You know, you people are just messing with me. And I would like to tell you something: I wouldn't marry any of you girls if you begged me!"

As it turns out, both Allison and the audience are finally being "messed with" by the "first you weren't, then you were, now you aren't" presentation of the women (and Anthony, for that matter) on the show. Because although this episode's narrative tries to contain its lesbian dynamics by initially contextualizing the discussion of marriage in straight terms (Carlene's "If I was a man . . ."), Allison's obsessive returning to Mary Jo's remark (about how none of the other women at the firm want to marry her) takes the idea of women marrying women beyond its original jokey straight context and into a textual (rather than subtextual) queer space that links narrative, character, and audience pleasures. But perhaps Allison's moment of lesbian anger and frustration in the face of coy homosociality proved too much for the character and the newly recast series to bear. At the end of the 1991–92 season, executive producer Linda Bloodworth-

Thomason announced that Julia Duffy/Allison would not be returning for another season. Bloodworth-Thomason told the press that Duffy "did a spectacular job in a very difficult role," but that the character was being dropped from the series because "the network didn't feel the chemistry was right." [38]

I would contend that the chemistry wasn't right not only because Duffy/Allison wasn't able to establish a sisterly rapport with the rest of the cast but also because Allison was in danger of forcing *Designing Women* to "come out." [39] Duffy's Allison never really had a chance of connecting with women characters whose bonds are finally, if not permanently, heterosexualized by the end of each episode's narrative. But if the lesbian sentiments of characters such as Allison and the narratives built around them were to become more denotative and less connotative on series such as *Designing Women,* or if they were not explained as cases of women living, working, or otherwise banding together for basically economic or blood-relations reasons (as is the case with *Kate and Allie, Alice, The Golden Girls, Designing Women, Babes, Phyllis, It's a Living, Roseanne, Sugar 'n' Spice,* and *Laverne and Shirley*)—that is, if these sitcom narratives depicted women forming emotional, intellectual, and erotic relationships with each other out of choice rather than from necessity—what is threatening about these women-centered programs would be in danger of overwhelming the queer pleasures many audiences unwittingly experience as they watch women characters together.

Part Four | Television in the 1980s

As the 1980s began, many of the hit sitcoms of the 1970s were beginning to show signs of age. Although nine out of ten of the top rated programs in the 1978–79 season were sitcoms, by the 1983–84 season, only one sitcom, Kate and Allie *(1984–89), appeared in the Nielsen top ten. Yet, the sitcom genre was about to undergo a resurgence, propelled in part by enormous changes in the television industry. By the mid-1980s, almost half of all American homes were receiving cable. Independent stations, boosted by the improved reception made possible by cable, began to produce more of their own programs. In 1987 the emergence of a fourth network, Fox Television, further diminished the networks' control over viewers. The proliferation of VCRs and remote-control devices also changed how people watched television and what they watched. Viewers could choose from numerous programming options, and then switch at an instant. Videorecording meant that they could watch what they wanted when they wanted, or they could rent movies in lieu of watching television at all. The networks, faced with a decline in viewership, responded by defining audiences even more precisely in terms of race, class, and gender. They honed the art of narrowcasting—producing television shows for small but specific demographic segments of the viewing population.*

The conservative political climate, marked by efforts at de-regulation, also led to changes in programming. In this spirit, the Justice Department abolished the Television Production Code in 1982. The code, which broadcasters had voluntarily adopted in 1952 as a way to stave off government regulation, placed restrictions on the number of commercials that could be aired during a program, as well as on provocative program content. The result led to more advertisements per program, as well as to an increase in sexual language and themes. Relaxed censorship, though limited by the networks' fear of offending advertisers, was particularly well suited to the production of programs aimed at an urban, sophisticated audience. As the decade proceeded, the type of quality programming designed for a young, well-educated, socially liberal, affluent audience, initiated in the seventies with series such as The

Mary Tyler Moore Show, All in the Family, *and* M*A*S*H, *became more commonplace. "Quality" programs on the networks emulated the films and high-budget cable programs to which the upscale viewers coveted by advertisers were drawn. The fledgling Fox, in contrast, developed a different marketing strategy by pursuing the audiences abandoned by the networks: young, black, and urban.*

Lagging last in the ratings at the beginning of the decade, NBC began the trend to quality programming aimed at upscale viewers by adding Taxi *(1978–82 [ABC]; 1982–83 [NBC]), an award winning sitcom canceled by ABC, and by introducing* Cheers *(1982–93).* Cheers *was a workplace sitcom set in a Boston bar that became known for its literate writing and complex, evolving characters and storylines. Like many enduring sitcoms,* Cheers *started out slow in the ratings but entered the Nielsen top five in its fourth year and remained there for six more years.* Cheers *also demonstrated that a series could survive even after the departure of a main character; when Shelley Long left the series in 1987, she was replaced by Kirstie Alley, who became the bar's manager. The show remained a hit.*

Yet, the sitcom most responsible for the resurgence of the genre was a more traditional formula sitcom, The Cosby Show *(1984–92). The show, starring comedian Bill Cosby as a doctor with a lawyer wife and five children, marked both a return to and a twist on the traditional domestic family sitcom of the fifties. Like* Family Ties *(1982–89), it represented the socially conservative values of the Reagan era. After the somewhat dysfunctional television families of the 1970s, and in a culture where nearly half of all marriages ended in divorce, the tight nuclear Huxtable family harkened back to a simpler time. The show reiterated the simple moral lessons of the 1950s sitcoms, reinforcing traditional American values within the context of minor family conflicts. Like* Julia, The Cosby Show *took an assimiliationist position on race, leading to criticism while at the same time ensuring that a sitcom about a black American family became the most popular television program of the 1980s (even in aparteid South Africa). At the height of its popularity in 1986, half of the American viewing public was watching every Thursday night.* The Cosby Show *helped NBC secure first place in prime time ratings. It finished second in the Nielsen ratings in its first season, after which it remained number one for the next four years.*

Despite the success of The Cosby Show, *many of the other successful sitcoms of the 1980s featured alternative families:* Newhart *(1982–90) had no children,* Kate and Allie *were both divorced, and* Who's the Boss *(1984–92) featured a divorced woman and her widower housekeeper.* Full House *(1987–95) concerned a widower and his extended family, and* Webster *(1983–88) was about a black boy adopted by a white family. Yet, even these "aberrant" families were still defined by the norm of the middle-class nuclear family. All of these shows promoted the idea that family co-*

hesion and unity would help individuals overcome obstacles, an idea that has perme-
ated sitcoms throughout their history.

Toward the end of the decade, families became defined even more broadly as the
networks honed their appeals. Designing Women *(1986–93) and* Golden Girls
(1985–92) featured adult women working or living together, in an obvious attempt
to appeal to liberal, well-educated working women. Murphy Brown *(1988–98)*
was an updated version of The Mary Tyler Moore Show, *though Murphy, unlike*
her predecessor Mary Richards, played an assertive professional woman firmly en-
sconced in her role in the workplace. Like Mary Richards, however, Murphy Brown
was unable to achieve both a satisfying personal and professional life. While often
cited as a "femininist" show, her character was unable to balance the masculine de-
mands of the workplace with feminine characteristics, and thus her feminism re-
mained contained within traditional paradigms. The show is probably most
renowned because of its break from fiction into the real world of American politics.
When the unwed Murphy became pregnant during the 1990–91 season, then-Vice-
President Dan Quayle cited her pregnancy as an example of the lack of family values
in American culture. The subsequent media clamor was probably most remarkable
for the way that a fictional sitcom character became news, and for the way that the
substance of Quayle's speech, an attack on poor single parents, became lost in the
media shuffle.

The most significant sitcom to challenge the assumptions of the domestic formula
came as the decade near its end. In the midst of The Cosby Show's *recuperation of*
1950s harmony and sitcom conventions, the dramedy Frank's Place *was a generic*
innovation. Frank's Place *(1987–88) marked CBS's attempt to boost its ratings by*
airing a workplace dramedy with an ensemble all-black cast working in a
bar/restaurant in New Orleans. But Frank's Place *demonstrated the limits of de-*
parting from conventional formulas. The show was shot on film and had no laugh
track, characters spoke in authentic dialects, and lighting was dark and atmospheric.
The stories were often downbeat or resolved ambiguously. Unlike sitcoms where issues
of race and class were invisible, here they were foregrounded, typically serving as plot
dynamics. The show was moved six times in its first season as CBS desperately tried to
find it a place in the schedule. It was critically lauded for its diverse and complex por-
trayals of race and class relationships, but when it failed to secure an audience it was
cancelled after one season. After brief reappearances on the Black Entertainment
Network or on TV Land in the 1990s, it disappeared from the television landscape,
replaced by network sitcoms that adhered to formula.

The essays in this section demonstrate the move to the "quality" audience that de-
fined television in the 1980s.

J. M.

11

Where Everybody Knows Your Name

Cheers *and the Mediation of Cultures*

MICHELLE HILMES

The Institution in the Text

At the heart of contemporary critical practice lies the interface of structure and text, which post-structuralist theories approach from a number of perspectives. Textual analysis concerns itself with the semiotic, narrative, and ideological codes that operate within and around individual texts; reception studies concern themselves with the linguistic, psychoanalytic, and cultural codes that structure and guide the reception process. Yet necessarily coming before these steps, and establishing in some ways what Stuart Hall calls the "limits and parameters" that contain both the text and the decoding process, is the inscription of the structures of the institution upon the text: the process of *encoding*.[1]

The relationship of institution to text—whether referred to in terms of "power relations" by Michel Foucault or as the workings of "ideological state apparatuses" by Louis Althusser—has become a central concern for contemporary critical theory.[2] In the case of film and broadcast texts, where traditional notions of individual authorship have proven so problematic, the concept of the *institution* as producer of discourse holds particular validity. Yet, this connection remains difficult to make; its complexity and multiple articulations work against the posing of a generalizable, transcendent rule of correspondence. The critical interface might best be examined through a process of detailed, historically

A slightly different version of this chapter was originally published in *Wide Angle 12* (1990): 64–73. It has been reprinted here by permission of the publisher.

rooted analysis. An examination of ways in which specific media texts have been structured, determined, and set in place by media institutions can help us not only to detect the presence of codes operating within texts, but also to begin to assess their purposes and effects.[3]

In a broad sense, then, this chapter is concerned with the "institution in the text." It attempts to link specific historical and institutional conditions of production to the discourses thus produced. Television provides a particularly complex and fruitful ground for this sort of analysis. Its highly motivated and commercialized structures of expression and its commodified texts, multiple authors, and varied audiences combine to make TV "the great mediator"—the site at which cultural beliefs, values, and controversies meet daily to affirm our central core of ideology and myth. I will argue that the situation comedy *Cheers* occupies a unique position in the mediation structure of television, taking as its central premise a conflict that lies at the heart of the institution of television: "high" versus "low" culture, the tradition of the arts versus the tradition of entertainment, the academy versus the masses.

Despite the centrality of this particular set of oppositions to the discourse of television—as well as to popular discourses *about* television—it is one with which both traditional and critical theorists have had trouble coming to grips. As Terry Lovell points out in her analysis of marxist critical method, the traditional study of media, with its separation of sociology and aesthetics, works to keep the domains of elite and popular art distinct. "On the whole [sociologists] have gladly accepted an intellectual division of labor which reserves 'great art' for critics, and leaves 'mass art' to the sociologist[s]"—who have neglected the question. Unlike the study of religion, for example, the study of art as a social phenomenon has been marginalized, with high art given over to critical theory and low art virtually ignored. For marxist theories, the issue becomes more pressing. Since one task of such theories is to "plac[e] art within the structure of social relations," artistic expression—especially as it acts as a channel for ideology—is a central concern. But even within marxist theories, from the Frankfurt School to Althusser, "mass art, where it has been discussed at all, has been dismissed as the artistically worthless product and instrument of bourgeois ideology." Ideology itself becomes the central concern, leaving individual texts and the processes that produce them in obscurity.[4]

Yet, these texts are the common cultural experience for millions of people, both in the United States and worldwide. A program like *Cheers,* which was among the Nielsen top ten for six years, surely deserves more critical attention than *TV Guide, People,* and a handful of television anthologies can accord it. The program's success in drawing and keeping audiences suggests an ability to address topics, attitudes, and situations relevant in some way to millions of people. I would argue that part of that relevance has to do with the role of television itself—and the often conflicted and controversial act of watching television—in our culture today. I want to look at *Cheers* as a particularly explicit example of the mediation of the rhetoric, economics, and ideology of high versus low culture on television. I will examine the program along three parameters: (1) the utility of the "workplace family" as a situational premise in the mediation of cultural and ideological differences, (2) the representation of class and cultural backgrounds through characterization and conflict resolution, and (3) the placement of the viewer within the commodity relations of this program in particular and the institution of television in general.

Economics, Regulation, and Rhetoric

The scarcity of broadcasting channels and the relationship of the broadcast industry to government throughout its history have worked to give television a "protected" status unlike that of any other popular entertainment medium. The content of television has been regulated and restricted more than that of any other medium, at least until recently. At the same time, its economic interests have been protected against competition that appeared to threaten the "free TV" system. This extraordinary expenditure of government concern, based on the fact that television utilizes a public resource, created early expectations for the medium in excess of those placed on any other. If broadcasting were indeed to operate in the public interest, convenience, and necessity, then surely its programs should be held up to a higher standard than that of market appeal. This concept has an economic basis, in that broadcasters use the electromagnetic spectrum "for free." As former FCC commissioner Nicholas Johnson points out, broadcasting networks and stations were never envisioned as operating solely on a profit maximization basis; rather, it was expected that "operation in the public interest would preclude profit maximization by the spectrum user, and that the difference between a public service operating level of profits and a theoretical level of maximum profits would be the price exacted for the use of the spectrum." [5]

This combination of economics, technology, and regulation operated to create a kind of "utopian" rhetoric around television even more inflated than that produced by other technological innovations of the twentieth century. Television—especially "free television" of the kind purveyed by the networks—would usher in a new era of public education, information, and enlightenment, all at minimal cost to the consumer. Television would deliver high culture to the masses and rival public education in the elimination of social inequity—all this and *I Love Lucy*, too.[6] The contradictions between the rhetoric surrounding the young medium and the uses to which it would soon be put resulted in an ongoing state of tension between the actual content of television and the lofty expectations of critics and viewers alike. Reviewers such as Robert L. Shayon and Jack Gould of the *New York Times* as well as Lawrence Laurent of the *Washington Post* refused to let the high art/popular art problem die, constantly criticizing the medium for failing to live up to its potential. Their insistence on the greater mission of television—quite rightly predicated on its privileged and protected status—kept the issue of high versus low culture at the forefront of the discourse about television for years.

The Situation Comedy and the Workplace Family

In fact, of course, aside from a brief period of experimentation in the late 1940s and early 1950s, it was clear that the networks intended to build on the success of network radio, providing an entertainment service funded by advertising and based on the principle of maximum market share. And, as one of the aforementioned critics himself points out, the emphasis placed on the relatively infrequent cultural programs beloved of critics and reviewers—early live drama, in particular—led to the neglect of the ever increasing number of filmed series programs, except for bursts of scorn and dismissal.[7] One of these series was the situation comedy, whose enduring appeal indicates something of its utility in the television structure. The domestic sitcom, in particular, grew rapidly in popularity and number during the 1960s and 1970s, but a tension remained between the voice of conscience—mandating more "serious" programming—and the pull of market share.

Attempts were thus made to elevate the purpose of domestic comedy, from the middle-class wholesomeness of *Father Knows Best* (1954–62), *Donna Reed* (1958–66), and *Leave It to Beaver* (1957–63) to the outright moralizing of *The Jimmy Stewart Show* (1971–72) and the consideration of "serious" issues in the "new wave" of sitcoms in the early 1970s, such as *All in the Family* (1971–77), *Mary Tyler Moore* (1970–77), and *M*A*S*H* (1972–83). In the process, the nuclear family lost its hold on the domestic setting and the "workplace family" emerged. The workplace family consisted of a group of people occupying normal familial configurations but in the context of a place of employment—an ambulance unit, a newsroom, a police precinct, a hospital, even a bar. If the domestic sitcom family necessarily consisted of a group of people of the same class, race, education, and cultural background, the workplace family "opened up" the family environment, re-creating many of its structures but allowing a greater diversity of membership and a greater flexibility in the relationships among members. This in turn allowed different kinds of issues to be addressed—issues that went beyond the limited scope of the intrafamily conflict. As Jane Feuer remarks in her article on MTM Productions, "The work family is a solution to the problems of the nuclear family," integrating work and love within a framework freely chosen and open to all, ". . . a Utopian variation on the nuclear family more palatable to a new generation and to the quality audience."[8] However, the basic mandate of the domestic sitcom form remained: introduce a conflict that can be explored, maintained, and finally diffused. Whatever the composition of the family, it must not be allowed to fragment under pressure. Whatever the conflict, the family must finally remain together, unshaken.

The Situation at NBC

These two factors—the ongoing tension between high—and low-culture expectations and the workplace family format—came together in a unique form at NBC in the early 1980s. Network programming strategy itself had reached a crisis at this time. Increased competition from cable and videocassette recorders had resulted in a twelve percent drop in network share between 1979 and 1982, tending to draw away "upscale" viewers whose tastes—and pocketbooks—ran to theatrical films and "narrowcasted" cable services of a "high-culture" variety. Regular network schedules were in an uproar. Fred Silverman had just made his last stand at NBC, having hopped from ABC to CBS and raised both networks to the top of the ratings. He met his match at NBC; by 1981, the year the network brought on Grant Tinker from MTM Productions to head up programming, NBC was running a distant third in the ratings race.

Network schedules were shuffled at a desperate, frantic pace: regular shows were frequently preempted for specials, new programs were introduced randomly throughout the season, day and time slots were changed constantly, and new shows were often canceled after the briefest of tryouts.[9] Ironically, these negative factors account in part for the success over the next few years of NBC's new approach to programming. NBC simply could not afford to cancel new programs within a few weeks of their premieres; it could not afford replacements. This created a consistency of scheduling on NBC that contrasted with the jumbled programming on the other two networks, in turn giving the programs introduced during the 1982 and 1983 seasons time to build audiences. *Cheers,* though praised by critics, trailed dismally in the ratings through 1983 and 1984;

it was not until 1985 that the show began its climb to an eventual third place. *Family Ties, Hill Street Blues,* and *St. Elsewhere* followed a similar pattern.

With such shows as *Cheers, Family Ties, Hill Street Blues,* and *St. Elsewhere,* NBC demonstrated its new programming strategy: the network would compete with cable television and videocassette recorders; it would attempt to "win back" the younger, more affluent, highly educated, and high-culture oriented audience for network television. It is no coincidence, then, that NBC's rise from the depths of the Nielsen ratings began with MTM-inspired programming. When Grant Tinker took charge of NBC in 1981, he brought the MTM image of "quality TV" to the third place network—along with MTM "quality" demographics: "a liberal, sophisticated group of upwardly mobile professionals," as one writer describes them; "up-scale urbanites whose status as active consumers rendered them a desirable 'target market' for TV advertisers," in the words of another.[10] But this appeal to an "upscale" audience had to be made without alienating TV's "mass" audience; "high-culture" viewers had to be entertained, but not at the expense of "low-culture" fans. For a network television program with any aspirations above "least objectionable" status, this tension in network economics reaffirms and reinforces the tension in rhetoric and regulation. Just as the crisis in the television industry brought this issue to a head, NBC produced a program that dealt with the issue directly, though it was never billed as such. That program was *Cheers,* first seen on NBC in the fall of 1982.

Enter *Cheers*

Cheers was created by the production team now known as Charles/Burrows/Charles, made up of Glen and Les Charles, producers and writers, and director James Burrows. All three got their start in television under Grant Tinker at MTM Productions—"television university" as it was known—and worked together on *The Mary Tyler Moore Show, Phyllis, The Bob Newhart Show,* and *Taxi* (*Taxi* being one of the few successful sitcoms of the 1978–82 period). They must therefore be considered MTM alumni, employing stylistic elements and demonstrating thematic preoccupations similar to those prevalent at MTM.[11] *Taxi* represents the workplace drama at its most working class, and the concept for *Cheers* evolved out of a desire to work with a similar premise, only this time more "uptown." A hotel was considered as a possible setting—along the lines of *Fawlty Towers*—but ultimately rejected; the idea of making the bar owner a woman also got lost along the way.[12] Whatever the genesis, the central premise and characterization of *Cheers* reflects a desire to put high-culture and working-class types together in a neutral space and watch them interact.

But a bar is a bar, and the values of the academy can never finally win, given the centripetal force of the sitcom form. The show's premiere episode sets up the situation: Diane Chambers, graduate assistant in English literature and fiancée of an eminent professor, enters a bar, is ditched by her fiancé, and settles in to work for Sam Malone, ex-baseball player and recovering alcoholic bar owner. The show's other regular characters include Carla Tortelli, working-class "ethnic" waitress; Cliff Claven, blue collar postman and one of life's losers; Norm Peterson, down-and-out accountant; Coach, representing an extreme in naïveté; and later, Frasier Crane, a psychiatrist from the same cultural background as Diane.[13]

The basic mix is similar to that of *Taxi*, except that *Taxi*'s characters are all, on some level, "losers." Here, "winners" and "losers" compete on an even basis, and their fortunes go up and down in the course of the show. Class allegiance is never defined in terms of economics on *Cheers*; as the owner of the bar, Sam is the wealthiest character. Norm and Frasier, however, both lose or give up jobs in the course of the series, suggesting that mere income or occupation have little to do with class background. On *Cheers,* class is defined almost entirely in terms of allegiance or "taste."

Class allegiance is the central distinguishing trait of the characters as well as the device that motivates the various plots. Here, class allegiance is predicated not on economics or birth, but on attitudes; not on the hard facts of life, but on the ways in which those facts are interpreted and valued by the characters. The naming, or labeling and explanation of events and ideas thus forms the central conflict on *Cheers*: how will Sam respond to a night at the symphony or to educational public television? How does Diane's elaborate interpretation of an event differ from the common version we see on screen? How does accepted academic knowledge fit into the world view of the working-class members of the *Cheers* family, and how do they turn the concerns of such things as critical interpretation to their own areas of interest? In a typical episode, Diane or another representative of "high culture" attempts to explain something to the others: to give the "true" explanation, the "real" facts. But even though her facts may be right, their application often proves problematic.

The Characterization of Culture

The idea of knowledge itself, of what we know and how we know it, is called into question by the typical *Cheers* plot and is generally resolved to the detriment of the more academic version. This conflict may be expressed outright as a plot element, or simply employed as a device by which information is presented.

Moreover, it relies upon a certain complicity between the shows producers and the audience: we have to be able to understand the joke—and the references—when, for instance, Diane objects to Sam's decision to call in a con man to help Coach settle a debt with a card shark: "Oh, Sam, that's like calling in Spinoza to settle an argument between Nietzsche and Schopenhauer!" Those of us who get the joke are drawn into complicity with the show's terms. But those of us who do not are provided with an immediate face-saver in Coach's response to this remark: "She's got a point there, Sam." The hysterical laugh track assures us that at least we *know* we don't know, unlike Coach. The obvious disgust expressed by Carla and the rest of the cast over the pretentiousness of the remark also works to alleviate any discomfort we may feel.

Most frequently, Sam, the hero and main representative of "dirt under the fingernails" taste and values, reveals the inadequacy of his cultural definitions to an unseen but presumably better-informed audience: he does not know the right names, or how to pronounce them. For instance, one episode revolves around Sam's attempt to impress (read: seduce) an attractive reporter with his knowledge of high culture, in this case art. He determines to use Diane as his tutor, reveling in the idea of "using one woman's brain to get another woman's body." Overhearing their conversation on the impressionists—which begins with Diane correcting Sam's pronunciation of "Giverny"—Frasier Crane becomes suspicious of Sam's apparently sincere interest. Frasier's suspicions are confirmed (over Diane's protestations) when, at the end of the scene, Sam asks Diane one more question:

> SAM. OK, now, this Rubens guy—is this the same guy that invented that sandwich?
> DIANE. No, no, I'm afraid not . . .
> SAM. Well, OK, I was just wondering, boy, 'cause I'll tell you the women in his paintings look like they really tuck away the groceries.
> FRASIER. You're right . . . he'll be a curator in no time.

Meaningful critical interpretation is not limited to the realm of high art, however, as the following conversation, which begins with Woody referring to do-it-yourself kits, demonstrates:

> WOODY. . . . you know, like the coyote does on the *Roadrunner* cartoons? By the way, now I always wondered, if he can afford to buy all those kits to catch the roadrunner, why can't he afford to buy something to eat?

CLIFF. I think you're missing the point here. It's not that Wile E. Coyote wants to eat necessarily, or that he wants to eat a roadrunner. What he wants is to eat that particular roadrunner. It's very existential.

DIANE. We're trying to save a man's life here!

NORM. Yeah, Cliff, really . . . Besides, I'd have to disagree with you, you know? You never see the coyote eat anything else. When you think about it, you never see him eat anything at all . . . which may be why he's losing the damn bird all the time. I mean, the brain needs sugar, think about it . . .

CARLA. Yeah, yeah, yeah, but did you guys ever see the one where there were two roadrunners?

SAM. [*getting interested*] Two roadrunners?

Diane's perspective on knowledge usually allows her to win the battle, but frequently results in her losing the war. She is allowed to show Sam up for what he is, with explicit put-downs of his intelligence, as in a scene in which she and Sam attempt to concoct a story to make Frasier jealous.

SAM. "We were too hungry to eat" . . . aw, that's good, that's good.

DIANE. No, it's not good.

SAM. No, no, no, you see, hungry usually means food. Now, what I'm doing here is . . .

DIANE. No—I get it. It's just not good—erase that.

But Sam's attitudes are often subtly reinforced through a demonstrated consensus, even when those attitudes are directly critical of such high-culture totems as "quality" television. In one episode, Sam donates his old baseball jersey to be auctioned off on public TV, at Diane's request.

SAM. Aw, come, on . . . I just feel good to be able to do something to help out quality television. You know, I think maybe we should start watching this station more often.

TV. All right, now let's get back to our program, "Hydroemulsion: How Much, How Soon?"

SAM. [*reaching for remote control*] OK, wrestling.

Again, the audience is drawn into the terms of this conflict as well: we sit actively watching a show *not* on public TV even as Sam changes the channel.

One device frequently employed on *Cheers* to emphasize an "unrealistic" (read: overly refined) interpretation of events is that of disjunction between sound and image tracks: even as we are told one thing, the evidence before our eyes contradicts it. An example is Diane's account of her first meeting with Frasier on the grounds of a hospital to which she has retired after suffering a nervous breakdown. Diane offers an idyllic account of the meeting; what we actually see on the screen, however, includes cheating and recriminations that eventually lead to a fistfight between Diane and an elderly woman who tries to hit her with a mallet.

> I was playing croquet on the North Lawn one beautiful morning. It's a game I learned to play while I was there, and I got quite good at it. [Diane *accuses her elderly opponent of cheating.*] It was amazing to me how I could just lose myself in the flow of the game. I found that when I played with someone of equal ability that it gave me an appreciation for the nobler aspects of sport and competition. [*The elderly lady kicks* Diane *in the shins.*] Frasier happened by in the midst of this spirited contest and he stopped to correct a flaw in my swing. [Frasier *stops* Diane *as she is about to hit the elderly lady with her mallet, and gets an elbow in the stomach.*] My opponent on that particular day was as crafty a strategist as I. We really brought out the best in each other. [Diane *and the elderly lady square off and begin wrestling on the ground.*] Frasier remained not only to watch my game but to good-naturedly arbitrate a close call for us. [Frasier *pulls* Diane *kicking and screaming off the recumbent elderly lady.*] Who would ham guessed that a leisurely game of croquet would have provided me with such a trophy? [*Back to* Frasier *and* Diane *at bar.*]

However, this same device can also be used to show up the inadequacies of a low-culture aesthetic. In another episode Cliff brings us up to date on plot developments in a voice-over, but what we see on the screen are his slides from a trip to Florida, complete with out-of-focus "girls" in bikinis, palm trees off the vertical plane, and all the hallmarks of the most clichéd kind of vacation photography, including one of the lower half of Cliff's legs clad in white socks and black shoes propped on the hotel bed in front of him. And just as the *Roadrunner* debate defuses criticism of high-culture values by exaggerated popularism, the low-culture lack of academic knowledge is also parodied.

> CLIFF. [*Pointing to a sketch of a DNA molecule on a chalkboard*] So as we see, the roots of physical aggression in the male of the species is found right there in the old DNA molecule itself. Er, yeah, right here at about one o'clock, as I recall.
> DIANE. Fascinating, Cliff.
> CLIFF. Oh yes, Diane, fascinating. Hold on to your hat too, because the very letters DNA are an acronym for the words, "Dames are Not Aggressive."

DIANE. They stand for deoxyribonucleic acid.

CLIFF. Ah . . . yes, but parse that in the Latin declension, and my point is still moot.

Again, most of the audience will be able to laugh over the joke, secure in their own knowledge of Cliff's lack thereof.

"Quality Television"

I have argued that *Cheers* presents and balances high—and low-culture points of view, providing audiences with an opportunity both to take enjoyment in their ability to understand references to impressionists and philosophers, classical music, scientific fact, and public television—but also reassuring them that it's OK not to know. Knowledge of elite culture values is assumed—but not necessarily valorized and often made laughable. Just as each episode has a resolution, however, each resolution must always work to reaffirm the essential unity and family qualities of the *Cheers* group. In a typical *Cheers* plot, a character's aspirations to high culture (or low culture) threaten to separate him or her from the group, but in the end the group triumphs, demonstrating that allegiance to the group is more important than any interpretation or goal. Class and cultural allegiance become less important than the "workplace family" group, showing us that whatever our values, we are all the same under the skin.

And of course, according to *Cheers's* basic situation, high culture, personified by Diane, is always an intruder in a world dominated by the Sams, Carlas, and Cliffs of this world. Diane is only there on sufferance—Sam owns the place. And so, a neat twist is performed even on the idea of "quality TV": if critically acclaimed programs such as *Hill Street Blues* and *Lou Grant* allow the "quality audience [to] separate itself from the mass audience and . . . watch TV without guilt,"[14] then *Cheers* goes them one better. It invites us to laugh at our own "quality" aspirations, to revel in the very "mass-ness" of the TV experience. Television, rather than existing in a state of tension between high—and low-culture demands, becomes the very place where those differences are not only mediated but celebrated: by criticizing its own aspirations to high culture, *Cheers* frees us from having to choose. In the end, as the song goes, "everybody knows your name"—all allegiances are accommodated in an atmosphere of relaxation, escape, and acceptance.

12

Structuralist Analysis 1

Bill Cosby and Recoding Ethnicity

MICHAEL REAL

> In expressing love we belong among the undeveloped countries.
>
> —Saul Bellow

William H. Cosby, Jr., emerged in the last third of the twentieth century as one of the great popular artists of the age. His genius at tapping the popular sensibility placed him in the tradition of Charlie Chaplin, Walt Disney, Lucille Ball, Steven Spielberg, Monty Python, and precious few others. As both performer and producer, Cosby achieved the stature of an institution, eventually being featured on the cover of *Time* (September 28, 1987) as "Cosby, Inc." Considering that as a black American male, he was both heir to a strong entertainment tradition and victim of a stereotype, Cosby's achievement was especially interesting. From minstrel shows to *Birth of a Nation,* from Stepin Fetchit to *Amos 'n' Andy,* the black male in particular has been the subject of stereotyping. Even today representations of the black male in the mass media tend to be confined to comedy (Bill Cosby, Richard Pryor, Redd Foxx), sports (Michael Jordan, Dwight Gooden), and music (Lionel Ritchie, Michael Jackson, Prince), and to lack the full range of fictional and nonfictional roles available to white men and the different but restricted roles available to women.

Cosby's representation of ethnicity and gender, especially in his successful father role on prime-time television, occurs in a challenging context. Black schol-

A slightly different version of this chapter was originally published in Michael Real, *Super Media: A Cultural Studies Approach* (Newbury Park, Calif.: Sage, 1989), 106–31. It has been reprinted here by permission of the publisher.

arship, especially in film theory and practice, draws from semiotic and mythic analysis to describe and prescribe the black presence in the image industries of super media. Snead, Davis, and White articulate a call for new forms and techniques in the mythic media construction of African American experience.[1] The portrayal of black ethnicity in *The Cosby Show* contrasts with traditional stereotypes and, in the process, brings up for conscious consideration structures for coding and recoding the myth of blackness and all it stands for in super media today.

Icons, Formulas, and Genres in the Mythology of Super Media

Structuralist analysis, a technique employed in cultural studies, identifies the structure of linguistic and other sign systems used for expressing and communicating. *Codes* organize signs into systems—for example, when grammar organizes words into sentences. Certain structural features, such as binary oppositions of black and white or male and female, appear in the signs and codes of verbal expression, social relations, and mental categories. These structures exist as codes that relate the signifying practices of super media to the personal identity of members of the public. Myths tell a culture's stories through its signs and codes.

The Cosby Show, in its years atop American television ratings, managed to cleverly entertain as it carefully wound its way around and occasionally challenged the mythic stereotypical structuring of blackness that preceded it. Stereotypes, racial and otherwise, serve as shorthand codes of representation and social control. Myths construct narratives around types and stereotypes, and in the words of Kellner, "the myths of a society are the bearers of its ideologies."[2] In this sense the ideology of racism has been coded into American mythology from the earliest days of the republic. In the popular culture of Joel Chandler Harris, Stephen Foster, and many others, the dominant mythology about black Americans pictured slaves and ex-slaves on the plantation as happy-go-lucky singing and dancing servants.

The structure of myths of blackness, before and after *Cosby*, emerges from the psychology of American emotions and cultural life, in the same manner as all myths arise from and express collective emotions and culture.[3] For Ernst Cassirer, the key to explaining myth is the function of myth in human social and cultural life.[4] Myth is not merely an erroneous prescientific explanation of nature and life originating from faulty reasoning. For Cassirer, myth expresses something between our direct sense impressions and our logical rational thought, our *feelings*, centered especially in the human feeling for the unity of life. In addition, myth reflects and expresses *social*, not individual, life experiences and constitutes a collective representation. Through signs, codes, and myths, human society seeks to symbolize and control the environment. For Cassirer, the power of myth, and its place as ritual in culture and daily life, flows from its role as a system of personal and social representation and communication.

Television, more than any other super medium today, provides mythologies that play fundamental roles in expressing and representing human feelings and social life, including ethnicity, gender, and political ideology. The powerful dimensions of myth that make it omnipresent in contemporary television are summarized by Douglas Kellner:

> Television images and stories produce new mythologies for problems of everyday life. Myths are simply stories that explain, instruct, and justify practices and institutions; they are lived, and shape thought and action. Myths deal with the most significant phenomena in human life and enable people to come to terms with death, violence, love, sex, labor, and social conflict. Myths link together symbols, formula, plot, and characters in a pattern that is conventional, appealing, and gratifying.[5]

Unfortunately, for most of its history, and well before television, the dominant mythology in Western popular culture has included stereotypical symbols, formulas, and characters for virtually all nonwhites. Roland Barthes's famous description in *Mythologies* of the picture of a black African soldier saluting the French flag on the cover of *Paris Match* illustrates the subtleties of these representations. The picture conveys in a single image a mythology and an ideology of French imperialism, the integration of blacks, and the honor of the military, all of which were debated points at the time that *Paris Match,* without comment and in all likelihood without self-conscious intent, selected this mythically rich and biasing image. Even in news stories, the demands of storytelling constantly pull media beyond the transmission of information and toward mythically shared expectations and forms, a pull that easily leads to stereotypical coding.[6]

Literature and the arts have given rise to a form of interpretation that contrasts sharply with the traditional quantitative content analysis employed by empirical social scientists. Where content analysis, in the interest of quantification, takes many messages, shaves off the idiosyncrasies, and tallies the uniformities, the interpretation of popular esthetic codes, in the interest of qualitative analysis, zeroes in on the single expression, relishes its uniqueness and style, and explores meanings and parallels emanating outward. The former tells us how many karats a jewel has; the latter examines its luster and beauty. Quantitative content analysis tells us the ratio of blacks to whites in the events of the Huxtable household in *The Cosby Show.* Qualitative content analysis tells us what these blacks and whites are like.

Powerful elements at work through myth include icons, formulas, and genres. Signs and codes are primary structures always present in messages, whereas myth, icon, formula, and genre are secondary structures available to provide the standardized conventions of message content in super media texts. These secondary and aesthetic codes provide the well-recognized structures through which the popular arts are expressed and understood.

Bill Cosby personally, and his mythical television family collectively, have become icons of super media. Icon analysis is a form of message interpretation. Marshall Fishwick, drawing from Herbert Read and Erwin Panofsky, has described the place of contemporary icons.[7] The word icon, based on the Greek word for image, refers to "an object of uncritical devotion" and denotes medieval religious images painted on wooden panels. More generally, icons are external expressions of internal convictions tied to myths, legends, values, idols, and aspirations. Panovsky defined iconography as "the branch of art history that concerns itself with the subject matter or meaning of works of art, as opposed to their form." He distinguished surface data, which require identification, description, and authentication, from interior qualities, which call for deeper evaluation and interpretation.

"The mainstream of iconology in our time—because of its dissemination through mass media—is the popular stratum of our culture," according to Fishwick.[8] Media icons are as diverse as the superchild Shirley Temple, the Beatles, comic strip characters, the cowboy, and sports stars.[9] Icons are the static visual representations of our myths. Following Eliade, Gregor Goethals finds in both classical and popular icons the power to provide a sense of meaningful order and to integrate the personality of the viewer into that order.[10]

How did Bill Cosby become an icon of American popular culture? First emerging as a vivid and hilarious stand-up comic, Cosby developed routines about his boyhood friends, his brother and himself, his family and neighborhood, and sex and marriage, all delivered with vocal dramatics and masterful timing—they were nuanced and telling stories of everyday experience. These routines became popular records as well. With Robert Culp, Cosby costarred in a dramatic television series, *I Spy.* By the early 1970s, Cosby was providing voices and direction for the popular *Fat Albert* television cartoons, which also spun off two books, *The Wit and Wisdom of Fat Albert* (1973) and *Fat Albert's Survival Kit* (1975). As the commercial spokesman for Coca-Cola and Kodak, Cosby developed into one of the most credible pitchmen in the history of television, eventually registering the highest "Q Score" for audience appeal in history. As *The*

Cosby Show sat as the number-one rated television program from its beginnings in the fall of 1984 through the 1990s, Cosby also authored best-selling books. His first, *Fatherhood* (1986), sold 2.6 million in hardback, breaking the record held by *Iacocca*. At this point his annual earnings were the highest in the United States, averaging some fifty-seven million dollars. His iconic presence had become unavoidable in the super media.

The media icon may differ significantly from the real person. With a public persona as straightforward and comfortable as they come, Bill Cosby's actual persona was complex and almost contradictory. Relaxed and easy on stage, he could be intense and determined off it. In his chauffeured BMW, he preferred to ride in front next to the driver. Symbol and spokesperson for marriage and family, he was for years a regular at Hugh Hefner's Playboy mansion. Wearing a silver bracelet that proclaimed him "Camille's Husband," he nevertheless confessed to *Ladies Home Journal* (January 1988) that he had "never been a saint. I'm sure if anyone wanted to get me on my past, they very well could." Always best at reaching the popular, mass mainstream tastes, Cosby himself had personal tastes that were more elite. He developed an extensive art collection and, after going through college playing football, proceeded on to graduate school, despite a busy professional life, and was immensely proud of his doctorate. Carefully avoiding controversy in his prime-time program, Cosby was a generous supporter of Jesse Jackson, the antiapartheid movement, and other political causes. One-dimensional, Cosby was not.

The symbolic icon, Cosby, has chosen to use the genre of domestic situation comedy as his vehicle. A *genre* is a secondary code present in a creative work as a combination of setting, characters, dress, plot lines, and other elements regularly found in a widely recognized grouping of works.[11] By now a number of standard genres dominate super media films, television, books, and magazines: science fiction, westerns, gangster stories, detective mysteries, horror, combat, comedy, musicals, serial dramas (soap operas), romance, sports, and news. These and other genres have many subgenres as well. Westerns may be classical, contemporary, Samurai, or even, when made in Italy, spaghetti westerns. Comedy may be situation, stand-up, black, satirical, topical, or slapstick. Movies made for television have developed a tear-jerker, disease-of-the-week sub-subgenre featuring athletes, celebrities, and average people melodramatically dealing with trauma. Feature films from India may attempt to combine nearly every genre in a single film. Cosby, veteran of stand-up comedy, spy thrillers, and children's shows, found in the genre of situation comedy the perfect vehicle for his greatest success and for recoding black male ethnicity.

The genre of situation comedy employs standardized *formulas* for structuring its presentation. Myths and genres are universal forms, while formulas are limited; they represent "the way in which a particular culture has embodied both mythical archetypes and its own preoccupations in narrative form." [12] One safely knows that the Cosby domestic comedy will have humorous situations and clever lines, that it will present plot complications but always end well. The adventures of Cliff, Rudy, Theo, and the other Huxtables follow formulas. Popular formulas rely more heavily on convention than invention. *Conventions* are those parts of a cultural product that exist in similar products in the form of elements known to both author and audience beforehand. Since *All in the Family,* situation comedies have been taped before a live audience; *The Cosby Show* employed this convention. Conventions maintain a culture's stability. *Inventions* are those parts of a cultural product uniquely contributed by a particular artist; over time they may modify conventions. *The Cosby Show* offered a perfect opportunity to invent new definitions of the black male and the black family. Inventions enable a culture to respond to changing circumstances. *The Cosby Show* was prepared to take full advantage of television conventions distinguished by the intimacy of the small screen, the continuity of characters and series, and the use of contemporary concerns even in historical presentations. [13]

The coding of ethnicity in super media icons, formulas, and genres is complex and important, especially in humor. Asians today may be coded in the popular culture as exotic Orientals, overachieving competitors, ethnic gangsters, or stumbling intellectuals. Polish stereotypes run from the heights of the Solidarity movement to the depths of Polack jokes. The coding of Hispanics has "progressed" from lazy siestas under sombreros to Speedy Gonzales, from pistol-waving Zapatas to the Frito Bandito, from superstitious underachievers to undocumented "aliens," and finally to the excellence of *Stand and Deliver, The Milagro Beanfield War,* and *Zoot Suit.* A joke about three Jews and a blindfold illustrates the dangers of stereotypical humor. [14] Three Jews are about to be shot and are offered a blindfold by the captain of the firing squad. The first Jew takes the blindfold, the second takes it, but the third refuses it. The one next to him says, "Take the blindfold. Don't make trouble." This example of gallows humor has been cited as "liberating" in an internal Freudian way for Jews, but it may also serve to reinforce stereotypes of Jews as submitting too willingly to victimization. Commenting on this, Paul Lewis insists that "a good sense of humor refers not only to someone who laughs readily and often, not only to someone who creates humor easily, but also to someone whose creation and appreciation of humor is mediated by humanity." [15]

The Call for Recoding Blackness

An all-too-typical negative depiction of a black male occurred in a seemingly exemplary 1986 CBS documentary by Bill Moyers, "The Vanishing Family— Crisis in Black America." That documentary included a thirteen-minute segment featuring "Alice." Opposite her was "Timothy," the twenty-six-year-old father of her three children. In the course of following and interviewing Timothy, Moyers uncovers that he is also the father of three other children by different women, has not held a regular job in two and a half years, has been arrested several times, and does not contribute to the financial support of any of his six offspring. In an interview Moyers digs out of Timothy his pride in making children: "They're like artwork . . . I'm a babymaker. I guess I have strong sperm." Moyers elicits comments from Timothy that show no regrets that the six children are all supported by welfare. The representation of Timothy is absolutely everything that a welfare abolitionist and racist could ask.

This portrayal of Timothy is not merely information; it shares in the restricted codes of a historical mythology. What mythic dimension does Timothy take on? The question is not whether the picture is true; apparently Timothy is all too real. The question is, rather, what this single case generalizes to, mythically and iconically, in the imagination of the viewer. How does Timothy code and image black maleness, and what reinforcing or conflicting codes and images surround this representation? Unfortunately, for the health of the popular imagination, steeped as it is in past stereotypical conventions of the image industries, the positive alternatives are restricted and the negative reinforcements numerous and readily available.

Painfully aware of such mythological frames, black critiques look to create not only new images but a new sensibility about blacks in film and television. Armond White observes, "How black characters might be presented in a politically correct, emotionally resonant situation depends on the filmmaker's mythic or visionary sense of his subject."[16] Negative myths, stereotypes, and ways of seeing that have shackled Hollywood are to be stripped away and recoded by those who share the subject's own ethnic experience and vision.

In a perceptive analysis, "Recoding Blackness: The Visual Rhetoric of Black Independent Film," James Snead of Yale remarks,

> Recoding blackness means revising visual codes surrounding black skin on screen and the public realm. In the traditional dialectic of film and audience, the spectator takes pleasure in recognizing what "everyone knows" to be obviously

true. Stereotyped images, most notoriously of women and blacks, hide real para-
doxes, contradictions, and inequities in society underneath the unthinking
pleasure of filmic recognition. Particularly in Hollywood's early character repertoire, black skin signified "subhuman, simpleminded, superstitious, and submissive." Continuous association has fixed and transmitted this falsification, and
the repetition of codes seems to validate the first coding as correct and the later
versions as obviously true.[17]

Drawing on Umberto Eco and Jacque Lacan, Snead points to underlying
psychological problems in the need to feel authoritative, the same emotional
level of existence where Cassirer places myth. Snead says, "The spectator-subject
codes the black as servile or absent in order to code himself as masterful and present. The black serves, in other words, as an 'Imaginary' remedy for the spectator-
subject's lack of authority."[18]

Snead takes Roland Barthes's famous concept of "writing degree zero" as a
starting point for a strategy to counteract and replace the repetition of the
pseudovalidated falsification. He reasons, "Recoding can arise from the very nature of film language, rupturing previous significations in unexpected ways.
Where black skin is already framed, or coded into place, montage might be the
only realm of freedom. Semioclasm, the 'smashing of codes,' does not return the
lack to the [b]lack as coding does, but returns the sign to zero, where it begins
afresh, mounted in a new context."[19]

A black esthetic of film calls for new content and form, new film style as well
as new film subjects and judgments. Predictability diminishes as Snead applies
the work of Christian Metz: "The black filmmaker exercises the freedom to recode blackness. The 'other place' on the filmstrip comes after the coded past and
present, no longer addressing the dominant 'I,' but redressing codes in the unknown shot to come."[20]

Codes of Ethnicity in *The Cosby Show*

The centerpiece of Cosby's contribution to super media has been the weekly
television program *The Cosby Show*. As a prominent social force, can the show
"resolve cultural conflict and contradictions" in the way that Levi-Strauss describes myth's structural power? Or does the show "suppress contradictions and
idealize existing conditions" in the way that Roland Barthes identifies myth's
masking powers? A cultural studies reading of the show's texts over the years

sheds light on this question and on the show's self-conscious techniques for re-coding blackness.

The Cosby Show as a standard televised situation comedy is centered in the living room and kitchen of the residence of Dr. and Mrs. Cliff Huxtable. He, Cliff, is a obstetrician-gynecologist, and she, Clair, is a lawyer. Their family in the beginning consists of a college student daughter, Sandra; two teenagers, Denise and Theo; a preteen, Vanessa; and a preschool girl, Rudy. As actors aged, so do their characters and the family life as a whole. Each show opens with a lively jazz score over an introduction to the ensemble cast. Each cast member is shown dancing to the score. Cosby himself is shown first and last in this se-quence and sometimes dancing with each of the other cast members. In this in-troductory montage, as in the shows themselves, each family member is given his or her relatively balanced screen time, but it is clear that Cosby is the focal point. The family emphasis and the centrality of Cosby are among the principal sym-bolic contributions of the show.

The Father Figure

As a result of antifamily practices during slavery and subsequent discrimina-tory employment practices, black families have had a larger-than-average num-ber of single-parent households with female heads. Timothy, in the CBS documentary described above, represents the epitome of the black male stereo-type as absentee father out of the household. The Cosby character of Cliff Huxtable, M.D., the loving, caring, and incredibly *present* father of five, is the antithesis to this stereotype. He shares decisions with his wife but is in charge. He shows unwavering understanding, perceptive advice, and good-humored charm in all his dealings with his children. His character is unquestionably es-tablished as a well-employed breadwinner, and yet he is present at home and in-volved with his children to an unusual degree for a working male of any race. When he takes responsibility—along with his protégé in training for responsible maleness, Theo—for finding and removing the snake in the cellar, or carving the Thanksgiving turkey, or any of a thousand other duties, Cosby is the incarnation of the perfect father figure.

The Strong Nuclear Family Unit

Consisting of two loving parents, five clever and achieving children, and grandparents who visit its solid house, the Huxtable family seems to have moved right out of texts on the sociology of the nuclear family and into our living rooms. The parents have a stable union; they frequently reminisce about when they first met and dated in college, even about failing to tell their parents about everything they did. The children are intelligent and well adjusted; when they have problems with grades or siblings or boyfriends or girlfriends or behavior, they always respond quickly to parental attention and reintegrate into the closely knit family unit. The children have predictable conflicts, as in wearing each other's clothes or demanding the privileges granted another, but they always wind up reinforcing and assisting each other as well as their parents. Against the stereotype of black families as unstable, full of unwanted pregnancies, and rife with street talk, conflict, and drugs, this family is as stable as the Rock of Gibraltar and as nuclear as anything Einstein ever conceived.

The Professionals

Allegedly, Cosby's real-life wife, Camille, was the one who insisted that Cosby be cast not as a chauffeur, as planned, but as a doctor. Added to this high-status male role is the female role of a wife who is a lawyer. This couple is about as stereotypically upwardly mobile and yuppie as can be imagined. While Ozzie Nelson never had an occupation in that family show, and Archie Bunker was almost never shown working at his, both Cliff and Clair are actually shown from time-to-time in scenes at their work. Cliff instructs and counsels young parents-to-be, and Clair negotiates with her law partners. When Theo gets them arguing over his punishment, Cliff calls from his doctor's office to Clair's law office, and their professional personas are overlaid on their family roles. *The Cosby Show* presents the antithesis to the stereotype of blacks on welfare and without professional training or gainful employment. Those who object that the Huxtables are "atypical" never seem to raise the same objection against Redd Foxx's portrayal of a junk dealer on prime time (*Sanford and Son*), although being a junk dealer is no more typical of blacks than being a doctor or a lawyer. In fact, very few portrayals on television are "typical."

Affluence and Fiscal Responsibility

The Cosby Show offers no apologies for the obvious affluence that it portrays. The Huxtables own a nice home, two or more cars, excellent wardrobes for parents and children, and the full range of home appliances; they appear to lack for no material goods. They go to nice dinners and nightclubs, take vacations, and send their children to college with no apparent financial strain. Lest their children become financially reckless, however, they instruct them carefully on the realities of living expenses. When Denise wishes to spend all her savings to buy an expensive, attractive, and untested used car, Cliff dissuades her by speaking of costs of gas, insurance, and maintenance. When Theo wants to skip college, get a job, and buy a motorcycle, Cliff gets out Monopoly money to explain to him the hard facts of rent, food, clothing, transportation, entertainment, and other costs when matched against income. All this, of course, counters the black stereotype of indigent spendthrifts who throw away their last dollars on Cadillacs, clothes, and drink. This black family's enviable affluence has come from planning, hard work, and fiscal common sense.

The Value of Education

Against stereotypes of school dropouts and poorly educated unemployables, the Huxtable household seems to ooze with affirmations of education and the value of school. Cliff and Clair refer periodically to their years in college and professional school; the children often deal with school issues of homework assignments and grades; everyone plans for college; and the Cosby spinoff *A Different World* is set in a racially mixed but predominantly black college. The Huxtables' eldest daughter, Sandra, was a success at Princeton, but Denise, after intense lobbying by her father, chose to attend his traditional black college, Hillman. Consistent with the program's validation, Cosby has personally contributed more than a million dollars to black college funds. *The Cosby Show* has featured episodes set at college, as when Denise and her grandfather wind up collaborating in stealing the bear's head that is the symbol of their rival college. The show has even showcased a professor as "the master teacher" and commencement ceremonies complete with educational rhetoric and ceremonial music. Cosby's own credit at the end reads: "William Cosby, Jr., Ed.D."

The Multigenerational Family

Although the Huxtables are a nuclear family, they are not without the older generation, since Cliff's father and mother are frequent and good-humored visitors. In addition, Sandra married her likable but slow-witted boyfriend, Alvin, and a new generation can begin. The grandparents are also upscale and articulate, making the program a portrait of three generations of a stable, successful black family. Any stereotype of blacks as isolated into discontinuous generations finds its opposite here.

Multiracialism

Although the emphasis is black, the show is carefully inclusive of a variety of ethnic representations. Rudy has a chubby white playmate, Peter, as well as her black friend Bud. When the experienced black actor Roscoe Lee Browne plays a Hillman professor of literature, the equally experienced white actor Christopher Plummer enters as a professor of drama at Columbia. Cliff borrows a saw from a white neighbor, and Rudy, feared lost at the plaza, is found at a Chinese restaurant playing with her friend, the daughter of the owner. Clair collaborates with her white law partners and Cliff counsels a pregnant Latino woman. All this helps to counter any charge that blacks or others live with and care about only "their own."

Racial Pride

Despite its appeal to a broad cross-section of the American television audience, *The Cosby Show* makes deft and frequent reference to elements of black history and culture. Student essays for school, Black History Week, pictures on the walls in the background, references in conversations, and other opportunities are seized on to refer to historical personages and events in black American history and culture. Black jazz receives especially prominent endorsement through the taste and conversations of Cliff and his father, and through an occasional guest appearance by a black musician. Singer Lena Horne is the focus of one episode, when Cliff arranges a family celebration to attend her show and she graciously shares dinner with the family afterward. Another episode is built around Martin Luther King, Jr., when to write an essay for school, Theo interviews his parents and grandparents, who describe the March on Washington. The episode concludes with the soundtrack of King's voice delivering his incomparable "I Have a Dream" speech as the family watches a television documentary. Participation in sports is affirmed as Cliff inspires Theo with tales of his old gridiron conquests, but obsession with them is avoided, in keeping with the falseness of their career promise for most black youths. Family members never speak in jive or nonstandard black dialect; although, for example, Theo does perform with his buddy "Cockroach" a rap version of Mark Antony's speech from Shakespeare's *Julius Caesar*. Given the show's popularity in South Africa, NBC was uncomfortable with an antiapartheid poster on Theo's wall, but Cosby insisted it stay in. All in all, the show manages to affirm black pride but not in a heavy-handed way.

Racial discrimination and conflict are never directly raised, despite the emphasis on black pride.

Humor Mediated by Humanity

Of course, what makes the show successful is its humor. The Huxtable family, despite their ideal circumstances and values, is still very funny. Bill Cosby personally is something of a comic genius. His nonverbal skills are marvelous. The bell rings, he lifts his eyes, and he does a very subtle dance move across the room to "charmingly" open the door. Nothing has been said, but the live audience responds with genuine laughter. As Cosby does it, it is funny! He can make taking care of a sick child the most delightful experience in the world. In one episode the germs in the patient Rudy become live characters acted out by Cosby. He makes a tight, prissy little face and mincingly articulates, "Party, party. We're going to party." Then when Cosby gives the spoon with medicine to the child, it is a major nonverbal experience. The airplane roars in carrying the medicine. Rudy sits up in bed transfixed, beginning to smile and giggle contagiously. Cosby continues clowning cleverly and easily with the airplane-spoon. He's got Rudy going, and he's got the live audience going and, one can only assume, he's got the home audience going. It's laughing time. In that moment *The Cosby Show* has created classic Aristotelian humor by surprise. It is the common seen in an uncommon way. There is a shock of recognition as audience members say to themselves, "I've been there!" A basic human experience is created fresh on television, cleverly and as if new.

Cosby's artistic restraint and control strengthen the entire effect. Cosby does not embarrass himself or anyone else with his clowning. It is quite the opposite of the problem depicted so bitingly in Robert Townsend's low budget success *The Hollywood Shuffle* (1986): the negative, insulting "black" roles to be performed in Hollywood by using bad grammar and hyperactive mannerisms. Cosby will not demean himself for a laugh, as a Stepin Fetchit character was forced to. He does not mock others, as an insulting stand-up comic working the Borscht Belt might. One laughs "with" Cosby, not at him; he knows and intends what is funny.

Broad Popular Appeal

Bill Cosby's comic and naturalistic acting abilities have been central to the appeal of *The Cosby Show*. Through these entertainment skills, backed by restless ambition and calculating foresight, Bill Cosby has become extremely successful, to a degree rare for a person of any ethnic background. There is, in his ability to entertain, an echo of the ultimate and absolute genius of nonverbal humor, Charlie Chaplin. There is in all Cosby's work an element one saw in Walt Disney: an immediate sense of what the largest portions of the public will respond to, an ability to operate in the middle register between the heights of elite culture and the depths of brutal culture.[21] For Cosby this means a sense of "popular taste" perceptively and humorously presented in books, records, television, and live appearances. He is obviously a maestro of modern super media.

Achievements and Limitations in the Cosby Recoding of "Black"

Does *The Cosby Show* serve to (1) "suppress" or (2) "resolve" the social contradictions that surround it? It recodes black ethnicity around the father figure and the strong nuclear family, an affirmation of the value of education, a sense of affluence with fiscal responsibility, and a population that is multigenerational and multiracial. Does this recoding merely mask and obscure problems through ideological manipulation—one function of Barthes's mythologies or does this television program actually initiate or reinforce needed catharsis and resolution, as Levi-Strauss saw myths doing? Obviously the question is a false opposition. To some degree the Cosby show does both. First, let us look at the negative "masking" function.

Critics of *The Cosby Show* tend to be cynical about the material comfort and security of two wealthy professionals and their children. Are these "typical" blacks, or is this not some kind of fairy tale that, in the best Bettelheim tradition, lulls children and adults into believing the myth "Be good and you'll live happily ever after"? Is this not a conformist compromise whose principal ideological function is to convince subordinate groups that they should conform to this society's rules? The answer is a partial yes; this program does not in any overt way attempt to rearrange the power structure in the United States. Many harsher realities of black existence are ignored or obscured. High unemployment, especially among the young, finds no echoes in *The Cosby Show.* Racial discrimination in housing, education, and other areas is not confronted. Police harassment of minority populations receives no attention. What is omitted from the show is significant. The show carefully avoids antagonizing any members of the audience. In this sense, as the saying goes, it "comforts the afflicted" far more than it "afflicts the comfortable." Relative to the dominant ideology, *The Cosby Show* is clearly "reformist conservative" in the manner of a subordinate recoding that attempts to change only one dimension, and not an oppositional recoding that challenges the larger system.

But *The Cosby Show* does have a positive role in the class struggle in precisely the way Stuart Hall, a Jamaican by birth, speaks of that struggle. In his well-known essay, "The Rediscovery of 'Ideology': Return of the Repressed in Media Studies," Hall describes the political and ideological battle over the principal descriptor to go with the term *black*.[22] Hall speaks of the class struggle in language that "took the form of a different accenting of the same term: e.g., the process by means of which the derogatory colour 'black' became the enhanced value 'Black' (as in 'Black is Beautiful'). . . . The struggle was not over the term itself but over its connotative meaning."[23] In discussing Bernstein, Bourdieu, and Volosinov, Hall explains further:

> Of course, the same term, e.g., "black," belonged in both the vocabularies of the oppressed and the oppressors. What was being struggled over was not the "class belongingness" of the term, but the inflection it could be given, its connotative field of reference. In the discourse of the Black movement, the denigratory connotation "black = the despised race" could be inverted into its opposite: "black = beautiful." There was thus a "class struggle in language."[24]

Hall also referred to this as "an ideological struggle to disarticulate a signifier from one, preferred or dominant meaning-system, and rearticulate it within another, different chain of connotations."[25] Hall argued for action: " 'Black' could not be converted into 'black = beautiful' simply by wishing it were so. It had to become part of an organized practice of struggles requiring the building up of collective forms of black resistance as well as the development of new forms of black consciousness."[26]

Here, at precisely this point in Hall's description of the coding of black ethnicity, is where *The Cosby Show* has been most active. It has had potentially decisive effects in convincing middle Americans that a black man and his family can be their most favored weekly guest. Reversing the tradition of *Amos 'n' Andy*, in which blacks were funny because they were different and even inferior linguistically.[27] Cosby establishes very firmly a strong, positive role model for father, family, education, career, and pride.

The Cosby Show shifts the connotation of *black* decisively, following on the widespread influence that the historic miniseries *Roots* had on American consciousness. After sitting through a week with Alex Haley's enslaved family tree, as part of the largest American week-long television audience in history, mass-mediated America had reason to be sympathetic to a black attempting to survive and succeed in America. Leslie Fishbein's definitive history of that remarkable American television docudrama, based on Haley's somewhat mythical genealogy, explains the popular style and emphasis in what was subtitled and advertised as "the saga of an American family." [28] Note the two descriptors: *American* and *family*. Fishbein recounts how dramatically influential the series was in focusing national attention on a long-distorted segment of American history and mythology. And she suggests that Haley and ABC provided a valuable learning experience for both blacks and whites. She judges they deserved their many awards even though they significantly distorted historical facts. The distortions were secondary: "The facts were far less significant than the myths *Roots* wished to generate." [29] And here, like Cosby later, *Roots* centered on family and on America, although its myths were historical and heroic, whereas Cosby's are contemporary and domestic. Both were movements to correct history and recode popular understanding of *black*.

Before the 1960s, black Americans were commonly called "Negro." The first mass-media use of black as a term of pride came in the declaration of the late 1960s civil rights movement: "I'm Black and I'm proud!" Since that time no individual has done as much as Bill Cosby to engineer symbolically a shift in the connotation of *black* from the negative one imposed by the historic oppressors to the positive one sought by self-respecting and proud African Americans.

There is evidence that both Cosby and the show's "production consultant," his friend Alvin F. Poussaint, M.D., of Harvard, understand and intend this recoding. A more racially militant Bill Cosby has appeared on television, but rarely. In a memorable sequence in a 1969 segment of CBS's *Of Black America* series, Cosby narrates and comments on the crucial relationship between media images and children's self-perceptions. Speaking from a quiet classroom filled with elementary students, Cosby draws on psychological data to indicate in children's drawings of themselves what weak and inadequate self-concepts some black children evidence compared with white children. He then flips off the lights and flicks on a film projector to show a series of stereotypical black portrayals from Hollywood movies of the 1920s and 1930s. The black males are slow and dumb. They are superstitious, and they scare easily, with bulging eyes and quaking knees. Cosby points out that the nasty Negroes in a segment from *Birth of a Nation* are actually whites wearing blackface. The segments show actors playing dim-witted black children, women, and men in various roles as Cosby notes that virtually no other roles were available to blacks in movies at the time. In one segment even the little white girl, Shirley Temple, is smarter, braver, and more mature than the adult black servants, who can barely speak and who move gingerly except when they break into a happy dance to entertain the white children at a birthday party. Stepin Fetchit, Willie Best, Bill "Mr. Bojangles" Robinson, and others were hired in films only to play stereotypes. From these vivid segments, Cosby moves into a discussion of a few pioneer black inventors and leaders and remarks how their achievements "got lost in the history books." This observation is supported by a passage he then reads from the leading American history text, by Harvard professors Samuel Eliot Morison and Henry Steele Commager. They characterize slavery by writing, "As for Sambo [at this Cosby lifts his eyes from the text and says quietly and sarcastically, "Sambo, Professor Morison? Sambo, Professor Commager?"], there is reason to believe his lot was not an unhappy one," or words to that effect. Cosby's part of the program concludes with more examples of black achievement and his final comment, "You've got to give us credit for more than rhythm." This *Of Black America* episode is partly a remnant of a more militant time but also a reminder that "the Coz" is far from unaware of the importance of media stereotypes, images, and labels.

Cosby's emphasis on positive values, of course, goes beyond issues of race as well. The popular priest-sociologist-novelist Andrew Greeley calls Cosby the most popular preacher in America, ahead of any priest, minister, rabbi, or tele-vangelist. Speaking of the quality situation comedies such as *Family Ties* and *The Cosby Show,* Greeley notes, "His program and the others are based on the insight that implicit ethics and religion in a matrix of humor are highly commercial in a country where meaning and belonging are as important as they have ever been, and where those institutions traditionally charged with meaning and belonging—churches and schools—are failing to deliver sufficient amounts of either." [30]

In Gerbner's sense of television as "the new religion," [31] a new religion that anchors our values and identities, Bill Cosby and others with television influence have a unique power to serve society in profound and meaningful ways. Cosby's *awareness* of this power, as shown in various ways, including his arguments with Eddie Murphy as Murphy recounts these in his film *Raw* (1987), sets him off almost as much as does the success with which he exercises that power.

Cultural studies can affirm *The Cosby Show* for its historic contribution to re-coding *black* and for its other positive services, but, confined to prime-time formulas in a situation comedy genre, the show was subject to constraints and goals that prevented it from taking the struggle to a deeper level of coding. The primary criticism here has to do with the high expectations for recoding established by Snead, White, and Davis as described above. They demand not only a recoding of black but also a remaking of the code itself—a more radical task than prime-time entertainment genres and formulas permit. The code of environment and image through which good or bad *black* is expressed is also posed as part of the problem. Armond White charges, "The classical filmmaking style, which developed synchronically with the generic myths of Hollywood, never included a realistic or truthful appreciation of black American experience." [32] This absence has created a basic problem for the "black filmmakers' difficult, awestruck efforts to join the general discourse of American films." He warns, "Although blacks and whites have shared the myths of Hollywood-dreaming at the same icons and projecting fantasies into a common pool—it has been an anomalous activity and a deeply superficial relationship."[33]

The challenge of an African American sensibility has also drawn the attention of black folklorist and filmmaker Gerald Davis.[34] He calls for "the development of a visual product consistent with African-American interior and exterior world views and expressive systems, and visually and conceptually 'different' from the products modeled after the standard and inadequate Hollywood vocabulary" (p. 101). Insiders can do what outsiders, however well intentioned, cannot do. Davis reasons that "if the producer, camera person, and editor consciously understand . . . characteristic emotional, psychic, and intellectual response to African-American existence, . . .the media imager begins to approach a cinematic or video product closely tied to the particular historical matrix we identify as African-American culture."[35] A new black film esthetic under the control of the black filmmaker makes it possible, in the words of Davis, "to produce an African-American cinematic way of looking at both African-American phenomena and the workings of the wide world, without the self-consciousness and embarrassment that frequently attends watching a film on African-American materials produced from another perspective."[36]

This task and others lie well beyond the possibilities of what a network prime-time entertainment program can hope to tackle, no matter how well intentioned and forward thinking the creators and producers. This is, in fact, probably not a task approachable through popular or mass culture but only through the more rarefied atmosphere of elite culture, in much the way that feminist films have evolved in specialized circles in recent decades. But this distinction takes us from *The Cosby Show* to complex questions of class and power.

Class, Group Identity, and Decoding Culture

The Cosby Show recodes blackness, but it fails to address directly class and group conflict within American society. In super media culture and daily life, social class is one form of subordination alongside patriarchy, racial and ethnic separation, regionalism, nationalism, religious discrimination, and more. Members of the upper-, middle-, and lower-income groups clearly exhibit distinct tastes in much of their selection and appreciation of super media. Social class affects super media because media are decoded by class membership, media products are identified with class taste levels, and hegemony occurs through ruling class influence over media products.

In Great Britain, where awareness of class differences is significantly higher than in the United States, research has established that members of different classes decode media messages in different ways, often consistent with their class membership. Graham Murdock notes that these studies "have reconnected studies of consumption to the sociology of stratification." [37] For example, a working-class laborer has access to social experience and interpretive schemata consistent with his or her place in the stratified social order. If the worker is particularly frustrated, he or she may interpret a story of conflict between Theo Huxtable in *The Cosby Show* and the police in favor of Theo rather than the representatives of law and order, even though the show clearly portrays Theo as in the wrong. A more contented member of the upper class will, in contrast, identify with and favor the forces of established law and order, the police. The Glasgow University Media Group has established that conflicts between owners and trade unions are interpreted in broadcast and press coverage in such a way that the interests of the ownership class are more favorably portrayed than those of the working class. [38]

Does Cosby's show favor the interests of the dominant over the subordinate? The degree and manner in which the interests of the dominant class influence popular culture raise difficult questions. Tony Bennett suggests that Gramsci's notion of hegemony offers a solid middle ground for answering this. [39] On one side, rigid structuralism charges that the popular culture is an "ideological machine" that dictates the thoughts of the people, while on the other side, populist culturalism romantically views the popular culture as the authentic voice of subordinate classes. Bennett emphasizes Gramsci's contribution to resolving this conflict: "in Gramsci's conspectus, popular culture is viewed neither as the site of the people's cultural deformation nor as that of their cultural self-affirmation . . . ; rather, it is viewed as a force field of relations shaped, precisely, by these contradictory pressures and tendencies." [40] Gramsci contended that the antagonistic relation between ruling and subordinate classes was less one of direct "domination" than one of negotiated "hegemony." The interests of the ruling class must contend with a set of opposing class cultures and values rising from the subordinate classes. Ruling-class hegemony is effective to the extent that it is articulated to and incorporates such divergences. Thus members of subordinate classes do not encounter ruling-class culture interests directly but, rather, in this negotiated version of ruling-class culture and ideology. Robert Gray notes that "certain aspects of the behavior and consciousness of the subordinate classes may reproduce a version of the values of the ruling class. But in the process value systems are modified."[41] At the same time, potentially dissident values in the subordinate-class culture are transformed as they are articulated to ruling-class ideology, which prevents the working through of their full dissident implications. The result is a compromise familiar to students of the popular media. Figure 12.1 illustrates this dynamic.

Hegemony can now be seen as the greater power of the dominant against the dissident values in Figure 12.1. Compared to that of England, membership in the American ruling class has been less defined and discussed, but the cultural studies distinction between dominant and subordinate groups raises questions about *The Cosby Show.* Is it not convenient that America's most popular television programs do not raise issues of disparity and inequality? Redd Foxx in *Sanford and Son* (1972–77) played a junk dealer who seemed no more deprived or unhappy than the affluent, professional Huxtables. Entertainment television meticulously avoids problematic portrayals of class and social conflict except in those rare adventurous shows from Norman Lear and Tandem Productions.

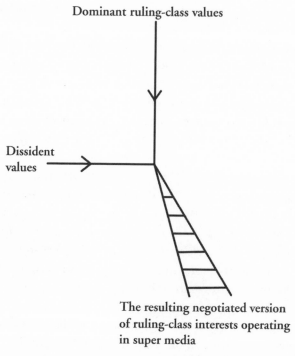

Dominant ruling-class values

Dissident
values

The resulting negotiated version
of ruling-class interests operating
in super media

Figure 12.1. Dissident Value Conflict in Super Media

Even *Miami Vice* (1984–89) and *Hill Street Blues* (1981–87), for all their ethnic and criminal conflict, do not draw attention to possibilities for social structural change. Why?

The answer lies with control of the television text. Do audiences really determine programming? Recent American sociology questions the absoluteness of programmers' claims about this. Ball-Rokeach and Cantor note that, despite communicators' claims to be answering to an audience, "most research shows that the audience's input remains indirect and obscure." [42] Special interest groups, such as gays [43] or Action for Children's Television, can over time make inroads against unwanted media portrayals. But, among groups trying to affect media content, "some have greater access to the media due to their higher class or status, as, for example, economic and political elites," in the words of Ball-Rokeach and Cantor. [44]

Do creative artists determine television programming? The sociology of organizations that produce culture reveals the importance of group membership within the media organizations. This membership produces a narrowed frame of "professionalism" that is inhibiting [45] and ideologically restricting. [46] More generally, Ball-Rokeach and Cantor note that recent sociology confirms "power over what is shown rests finally with those who own or finance the media, rather than with individual creators." [47] They also note that "usually there is general agreement within an editorial staff or on a set because both the creative people and the decision makers subscribe to the same basic values and norms." This belief consensus becomes tighter toward the top. The same authors observe that only media workers who subscribe to "the values and beliefs of those who control the organization are likely to be offered elite positions within those organizations." [48] These restrictive filters are the mechanisms of "ruling class negotiated domination" in *The Cosby Show* and other American television.

In "The Political Economy of the Television (Super) Text," Nick Brown explains "the direct role of economy in shaping the form of American television texts. [49] The "supertext" of television includes all programs, commercials, announcements, and so on. He finds that serial forms, such as *The Cosby Show,* "serve to continue the subject along the itinerary of habituated consumption." [50] Ultimately, "in the television age, consumption and social control have become linked." [51] Diversity and change are unlikely against the "megatext" of the television schedule and history.

This control, however, is negotiated, not absolute. Horace Newcomb points this out by applying the notion of "semiotic excess" proposed by Hartley and Fiske. [52] The idea of semiotic excess is that "once the ideological, hegemonic work has been performed, there is still excess meaning that escapes the control of the dominant and is thus available for the culturally subordinate to use for their own cultural-political interests."[53] When meanings proposed by television conflict with viewers' beliefs, the possibility for aberrant decoding and dissent arises. Similar to the notion of polysemic readings of a text, Bakhtin's notion of "heteroglossia,"[54] or multiple speaking in a text, emphasizes ideological struggle and the possibility of freedom even where the forces of domination are apparent.

Television is constrained by the demands of its own "consensus narratives" as much as by dominant ideology. David Thorburn finds a consensus narrative has "the ambition or desire to speak for and to the whole of its culture, or as much of 'the whole' as the governing forces in society will permit."[55] Its task is "to articulate the culture's central mythologies in a widely accessible 'language,' an inheritance of shared stories, plots, character types, cultural symbols, narrative conventions."[56] This it does by storytelling in a popular language legible to the common understanding of a majority of the culture. The communal and collaborative nature of such storytelling confines it to the "dominant pieties of the culture." As the chief carrier of the lore and inherited understanding of its culture, consensus narrative is essentially conservative, but it is not closed. A continual testing, rehearsal, and revision of cultural experience and values takes place within consensus narratives.

Within the negotiated dominant ideology and consensus narratives, there is yet a semiotic excess through which *The Cosby Show* attempts to bring about limited but real change. The change is real in recoding blackness, particularly in inserting a positive icon to replace negatives stereotypes of black males in family life. But the change is limited, given the centrist demands of prime time, to inventions of recoding blackness while accepting the framing conventions of situation comedy formulas and genres. Recoding blackness in this manner serves liberal progress but does not directly threaten any of the protected interests of super media ownership and the dominant class. It is, in the classic phrase of Daniel Hallin, "reformist conservatism."[57]

Placed in the context of theories of codes, myths, icons, genres, class, and ideology, the positive and negative portrayals of black males, from Stepin Fetchit to Bill Cosby, serve to illustrate the mechanisms on a broad cultural level through which super media as a whole create, sustain, and reflect meanings and the interpretation and structuring of existence. Pro and con, the conflicting portrayals become differently refracting prisms through which current cultural struggles are expressed.

In its general implications, *The Cosby Show* does serve to "resolve" America's racial failures by powerfully recoding *black* and effectively countering generations of negative stereotypes. At the same time, the show "suppresses" other problems and solutions by omission through the program's own choices and, especially, through the limitations imposed in subject and style by the political economy of mainstream popular super media.

Bill Cosby's role in super media illustrates structures of subordination and struggle within the symbolic world of super media. As women and ethnic minorities seek better employment and portrayals, they will continually challenge inherited practices and values in super media and make those challenges larger than any one individual or any one group. Media are an essential component of "self-determination" today, and restricted media access and control for any group is a social deficiency doing a disservice to all. If it is true that the absence of freedom for anyone diminishes the freedom of all, then efforts toward gender and ethnic parity in super media deserve universal support and gratitude.

Part Five | Television in the 1990s and Beyond

If anything differentiated television in the 1990s from the previous decades, it was the increasing fragmentation of the television audience. Digital cable, satellite dishes, Fox and independent channels, and the even the Internet all vied for the attention of the media viewer, and all eroded the traditional base upon which the networks relied. Cable networks also made headway into sitcom territory, with original offerings that were not bound to the same standards as the networks.

As the decade began, ABC was the top-rated network, with an array of successful family-oriented sitcoms such as Full House *(1987–95),* Family Matters *(1989–97), and* Home Improvement *(1991–99), as well as somewhat darker sitcoms such as* Roseanne *(1988–97) and* Grace under Fire *(1993–98). The networks continued to attempt to draw the upscale television viewer with the greatest level of disposable income by narrowcasting, a strategy that involved emulating the Fox network's sitcoms geared to younger, more cynical audiences.*

As the decade proceeded, three sitcoms that critiqued the idealized nuclear family epitomized by The Cosby Show *and other family sitcoms became representative of the 1990s sitcom. ABC's* Roseanne *was a realistic, slice-of-life portrayal of a working-class family, one of the most positive portrayals of a working-class sitcom family ever on network television. The show, conceived by comedian Roseanne Barr, was a deliberate attempt to show the underside of the harmonious nuclear family portrayed in typical domestic sitcoms.* Roseanne *depicted a family marked by conflict, struggle, and pain, yet one where setbacks were overcome by humor. Roseanne was a strong female character who overturned many stereotypes of the television sitcom mother, and the show addressed many controversial issues.* Roseanne *was in the Nielsen top ten until its final season, when it fell from fifth to thirty-fourth in the ratings.*

Married . . . with Children (1987–97) was the first hit sitcom to air on the Fox Network. It was conceived as a counter to The Cosby Show *and other sitcoms featuring idealized nuclear families. The Bundy family was defined by its dysfunctionality. Al Bundy was a shoe salesman who hated his job, barely tolerated his wife and children, and commanded none of the authority and respect accorded the middle-class television father. The crass humor deliberately inverted the bounds of "good taste." While the well-educated and morally grounded Huxtable family had virtually limitless opportunities, the Bundys remained on the bottom of the socioeconomic ladder. Fox, not available in all markets, did not achieve the ratings numbers of the networks, but* Married . . . with Children *had a sizable following.*

Married . . . with Children *was followed by* The Simpsons *in 1989, an animated sitcom.* The Simpsons, *concerning the travails of another working-class family, featured an inept father, ditzy mother, rebellious son, and smart daughter (along with an infant who didn't speak). Like* Married . . . with Children, *it parodied the nuclear family, although it also served as social commentary as it satirized contemporary American culture.*

The Simpsons' enduring success, coupled with the cheap production costs of animated sitcoms, led to a plethora of adult-oriented animated sitcoms on Fox, cable networks such as the Comedy Channel, and the three major networks. Yet, even in these shows about dysfunctional families, the nuclear unit remained cohesive and committed. While this norm was satirized, it was not challenged, nor were the consumerist and corporate values that grounded American culture.

By the early 1990s, NBC, lagging third in the ratings, and with an eye on the successes of the fledgling Fox network, abandoned its long-term strategy of airing child-oriented programs early in the evening (with the hope that the children would bring their parents to the set). As more families owned two or more television sets, it was becoming more common for family members to watch separately, and thus designing shows aimed at particular audience segments became even more pragmatic. NBC began to aggressively pursue the young, hip, urban, professional audience so successfully courted by Fox. Beginning with the hit Seinfeld *(1990–98), NBC aired a slew of sitcoms featuring young, white, unmarried, urban and upscale characters:* Mad about You *(1992–99),* Frasier *(1993–),* Friends *(1994–),* Caroline in the City *(1995–99),* Suddenly Susan *(1996–2000), and* Veronica's Closet *(1997–2000) propelled NBC to number one in the ratings. These were followed by a spate of workplace sitcoms such as* Just Shoot Me *(1997–),* News Radio *(1995–99), and* Spin City *(1996–), all of which, in contrast to their predecessors, featured dysfunctional workplace families (though, like nuclear families of earlier days, they were cohesive and committed at the core).*

By 1995, ABC dropped the family-oriented Full House *and added* Ellen *(1994–98),* The Naked Truth *(1995–98), and* The Drew Carey Show *(1995–) in an attempt to combat NBC's success.* Ellen, *often referred to as* Seinfeld *with women, became infamous as the first sitcom whose main character was openly gay; yet, despite major controversy and high ratings surrounding Ellen's "coming out" on the program, the show failed to maintain its audience and was canceled soon after. Yet,* Will and Grace, *about the relationship of a gay man and straight woman, came on the air without major controversy in 1998 and became a hit soon after.*

None of these sitcoms addressed the standard preoccupations of the domestic family sitcom, nor did they reflect the interests of rural, conservative, working-class or African American viewers. The majority of 1990s sitcoms on the major networks took place in urban, rather than suburban environments, and most featured either young professionals or dysfunctional nuclear families. The Fox network, with shows such as Martin *(1992),* The Fresh Prince of Bel Air *(1990–96),* Sinbad *(1993–94),* Roc *(1991–94), and* Living Single *(1993–), dominated with African American viewers. When, in the mid-1990s, Fox opted to focus on sports and dramas that would appeal to white viewers, the independent networks WB and UPN picked up the slack. These networks also began to focus on the teen audiences, with sitcoms such as* Sabrina the Teenage Witch *(1997–) and* Boy Meets World *(1998–) further eroding the networks' control over television viewers. Cable stations such as HBO and Showtime also began to produce their own sitcoms. HBO's* Larry Sanders Show *(1992–98) and* Sex and the City *(1999–) were two of the most popular. These sitcoms were known for adult themes and content, without any restriction on language or nudity.*

Overall, sitcoms in the 1990s and 2000s reflect attempts to reach the desirable demographic: young, sophisticated, urban viewers weaned on television, who appreciate parody and complexity of representations but who are potentially lured away from television by new media forms. Many successful sitcoms such as The Simpsons *thrive on intertextuality: references to other forms of media or popular culture that the savvy viewer will "get."* Seinfeld *creator Larry David's sitcom* Curb Your Enthusiasm *(2000–), an HBO sitcom, even goes so far as to star the main character as himself, interacting with his real life famous friends in an improvised fashion. Characters on sitcoms often refer to other television shows or even make guest appearances in character. While the television audience becomes more fragmented, the television world becomes more self-contained.*

As the new millenium approached, it appeared that the sitcom was on the wane, with few new concepts or ideas to capture elusive television viewers. The networks had some moderate successes with Will and Grace *(1998–),* Everybody Loves Raymond *(1997–), and, for a time,* Dharma and Greg *(1997–2002). The Fox network challenged network dominance with its hit* Malcolm in the Middle *(1999–), and HBO showed that it was a force with its unconventional comedy* Sex and the City *(1998–). (In 2001,* Sex and the City *won an Emmy for best comedy, the first time a cable network won in this category.) Only* Everybody Loves Raymond *featured a middle-class nuclear family that was not dysfunctional. In a social context marked by cynicism and disillusion regarding "family values," and in a viewing environment where families rarely watched television together, it seemed that the middle-class family sitcom, historically the mainstay of the genre, had run its course. Even long-running non-nuclear family sitcoms such as* Friends *(1994–2002) and* Frasier *(1993–) were winding down, and there were few new hits to take their place.*

Yet, it appears that in the aftermath of September 11, 2001, the sitcom began to reclaim its place at the heart of television programming. In the weeks following the ordeal, ratings for familiar sitcoms such as Friends *and* Will and Grace *soared as viewers seemed to seek solace in familiar rituals. The ensuing months, marked by an economic recession, prompted the television industry to repeat familiar formulas. In a statement that indicated the prevailing sentiment within the industry, Bruce Helford, executive producer of ABC's* George Lopez Show *(2002–), remarked, "People don't want to be alienated. They are looking for something safer."[1] The 2002–3 television schedule reflected perceptions of the public's need for nostalgia, and for what yet another television executive referred to as "a post-September 11 longing for comfort and safety."[2] As a result, several new sitcoms that harkened back to the past were introduced in the 2002–3 season, including a remake of* Family Affair *(1966–71) on the WB network, and two shows based upon* The Wonder Years *(1988–93): WB's* Do Over, *about a thirty-four-year old who returns to live in his high school body, and Fox's* Oliver Beene, *about an adult whose voice-over narration recounts his childhood growing up in the Cold War period. Two other new network sitcoms featured men who gave up successful careers to spend time with their families (NBC's* It's Not about Me *and ABC's* My Second Chance*). NBC, citing the public's desire for stability, only offered five new shows, three of which were sitcoms.[3] Although NBC was the top-rated network and thus did not need many new offerings, two of its three new sitcoms—*In-Laws *and* Hidden Hills*—featured suburban nuclear families, representing a departure from its urban, child-free comedies of years past. It appears that the cycle is shifting once more, and the sitcom will remain one of television's most durable forms.*

The essays in this section reflect the increasing fragmentation of the television audience while demarcating the shifting cultural landscape of television in the 1990s and beyond.

J. M.

13

Roseanne

Unruly Woman as Domestic Goddess

KATHLEEN ROWE KARLYN

> Sometime after I was born in Salt Lake City, Utah, all the little babies were sleeping
> soundly in the nursery except for me, who would scream at the top of my lungs, trying to
> shove my whole fist into my mouth, wearing all the skin off on the end of my nose. I was
> put in a tiny restraining jacket. . . . My mother is fond of this story because to her it illus-
> trates what she regards as my gargantuan appetites and excess anger. I think I was proba-
> bly just bored.
>
> —Roseanne Barr, *Roseanne: My Life as a Woman*

Questions about television celebrities often center on a comparison with cinematic stars—on whether television turns celebrities into what various critics
have called "degenerate symbols" who are "slouching toward stardom" and en-
gaging in "dialogues of the living dead."[1] Roseanne Barr is a television celebrity
who has not only slouched but whined, wisecracked, munched, mooned, and
sprawled her way to a curious and contradictory status in our culture explained
only partially by the concept of stardom, either televisual or cinematic. Indeed,
the metaphor of decay such critics invoke, while consistent with a strain of the
grotesque associated with Barr, seems inappropriate to her equally compelling
vitality and *jouissance*. In this chapter, I use the name "Roseanne" to refer to
Roseanne Barr-as-sign, a person we know only through her various roles and
performances in the popular discourse. My use follows Barr's lead in effacing the

A slightly different version of this chapter was originally written under the name Kathleen K.
Rowe and published in *Screen* 31 (1990): 408–19. It has been reprinted here by permission of the
author and the publisher. The author thanks Ellen Seiter for her helpful comments on an earlier
draft of this chapter.

251

lines among her roles: Her show, after all, bears her name, and in interviews she describes her "act" as "who she is."

Nearing the end of its second season, her sitcom *Roseanne* (1988–97) securely replaced *The Cosby Show* at the top of the ratings. The readers of *People Weekly* identified her as their favorite female television star, and she took similar prizes in the People's Choice award show this spring. Yet Roseanne, both person and show, has been snubbed by the Emmys, condescended to by media critics, and trashed by the tabloids (never mind the establishment press). Consider *Esquire's* solution of how to contain Roseanne. In an issue on its favorite (and least favorite) women, it ran two stories by two men, side by side, one called "Roseanne—Yay," the other "Roseanne—Nay." And consider this from the *Star*: "ROSEANNE'S SHOTGUN 'WEDDING FROM HELL'"—"Dad refuses to give pregnant bride away—'Don't wed that druggie bum!' "; "Maids of honor are lesbians—best man is groom's detox pal"; "Ex-hubby makes last-ditch bid to block ceremony"; "Rosie and Tom wolf two out of three tiers of wedding cake" (6 February 1990). Granted that tabloids are *about* excess, there's often an edge of cruelty to that excess in Roseanne's case and an effort to wrest her definition of herself from the comic to the melodramatic.

Such ambivalence is the product of several phenomena. Richard Dyer might explain it in terms of the ideological contradictions Roseanne plays upon—how, for example, the body of Roseanne-as-star magically reconciles the conflict women experience in a society that says, "consume, but look as if you don't." Janet Woollacott might discuss the clash of discourses inherent in situation comedy—how our pleasure in *Roseanne's* show arises not so much from narrative suspense about her actions as hero, nor from her one-liners, but from the economy or wit by which the show brings together two discourses on family life: one based on traditional liberalism and the other on feminism and social class. Patricia Mellencamp might apply Freud's analysis of wit to Roseanne as she did to Lucille Ball and Gracie Allen, suggesting that Roseanne ventures farther than her comic foremothers into the masculine terrain of the tendentious joke.[2]

All of these explanations would be apt, but none would fully explain the ambivalence surrounding Roseanne. Such an explanation demands a closer look at gender and at the historical representations of female figures similar to Roseanne. These figures, I believe, can be found in the tradition of the "unruly woman," a topos of female outrageousness and transgression from literary and social history. Roseanne uses a "semiotics of the unruly" to expose the gap she sees between the ideals of the New Left and the Women's Movement of the late 1960s and early 1970s on the one hand, and the realities of working class family life two decades later on the other.

Because female unruliness carries a strongly ambivalent charge, Roseanne's use of it both intensifies and undermines her popularity. Perhaps her greatest unruliness lies in the presentation of herself as *author* rather than actor and, indeed, as author of a self over which she claims control. Her insistence on her "authority" to create and control the meaning of *Roseanne* is an unruly act par excellence, triggering derision or dismissal much like Jane Fonda's earlier attempts to "write" her self (but in the genre of melodrama rather than comedy). I will explain this in three parts: the first takes a brief look at the tradition of the unruly woman; the second, at the unruly qualities of *excess* and *looseness* that Roseanne embodies; and the third, at an episode of her sitcom that dramatizes the conflict between female unruliness and the ideology of True Womanhood.

The Unruly Woman

The unruly woman is often associated with sexual inversion—"the woman on top"—according to social historian Natalie Zemon Davis, who first identified her fifteen years ago in her book *Society and Culture in Early Modern France*. The sexual inversion she represents, Davis writes, is less about gender confusion than about larger issues of social and political order that come into play when what belongs "below" (either women themselves, or their images appropriated by men in drag) usurps the position of what belongs "above."[3] This topos isn't limited to early modern Europe but reverberates whenever women, especially women's bodies, are considered excessive—too fat, too mouthy, too old, too dirty, too pregnant, too sexual (or not sexual enough) for the norms of conventional gender representation. For women, excessive fatness carries associations with excessive wilfulness and excessive speech ("fat texts," as Patricia Parker explains in *Literary Fat Ladies,* a study of rhetoric, gender, and property that traces literary examples of this connection from the Old Testament to the twentieth century).[4] Through body and speech, the unruly woman violates the unspoken feminine sanction against "making a spectacle" of herself. I see the unruly woman as prototype of woman as subject—transgressive above all when she lays claim to her own desire.

The unruly woman is multivalent, her social power unclear. She has reinforced traditional structures, as Natalie Davis acknowledges.[5] But she has also helped sanction political disobedience for men and women alike by making such disobedience thinkable. She can signify the radical utopianism of undoing all hierarchy. She can also signify pollution (dirt or "matter out of place," as Mary Douglas might explain). As such she becomes a source of danger for threatening the conceptual categories that organize our lives. For these reasons—for the power she derives from her liminality, her associations with boundaries and taboo—she evokes not only delight but disgust and fear. Her ambivalence, which is the source of her oppositional power, is usually contained within the license accorded to the comic and the carnivalesque. But not always.

The unruly woman has gossiped and cackled in the margins of history for millennia, from Sarah of the Old Testament, who laughed at God (and figures in Roseanne's tribute to her grandmother in her autobiography), to the obstinate and garrulous Mrs. Noah of the medieval Miracle Plays (who would not board the Ark until she was good and ready), to the folk figure "Mère Folle" and the subject of Erasmus's *Praise of Folly*. Her more recent incarnations include such figures as the screwball heroine of the 1930s film, Miss Piggy, and a pantheon of current female grotesques and sacred monsters: Tammy Faye Bakker, Leona Helmsley, Imelda Marcos, and Zsa Zsa Gabor. The media discourse around these women reveals the same mixed bag of emotions I see attached to Roseanne, the same cruelty and tendency to carnivalize by pushing them into parodies of melodrama, a genre which, unlike much comedy, punishes the unruly woman for asserting her desire. Such parodies of melodrama make the unruly woman the target of our laughter, while denying her the power and pleasure of her own.

The disruptive power of these women—carnivalesque and carnivalized—contains much potential for feminist appropriation. Such an appropriation could enable us to problematize two areas critical to feminist theories of spectatorship and the subject: the social and cultural norms of femininity, and our understanding of how we are constructed as gendered subjects in the language of spectacle and the visual. In her essay "Female Grotesques," Mary Russo asks: "In what sense can women really produce or make spectacles out of themselves? . . . The figure of female transgressor as public spectacle is still powerfully resonant, and the possibilities of redeploying this representation as a demystifying or utopian model have not been exhausted." [6] She suggests that the parodic excesses of the unruly woman and the comic conventions surrounding her provide a space to act out the dilemmas of femininity, to *make visible* and *laughable* what Mary Ann Doane describes as the "tropes of femininity." [7]

Such a sense of spectacle differs from Laura Mulvey's. It accepts the relation between power and visual pleasure but argues for an understanding of that relation as more historically determined, its terms more mutable. More Foucaultian than Freudian, it suggests that visual power flows in multiple directions and that the position of spectacle isn't entirely one of weakness. Because public power is predicated largely on visibility, men have traditionally understood the need to secure their power not only by looking but by being seen—or rather, by fashioning, as author, a spectacle of themselves. Already bound in a web of visual power, women might begin to renegotiate its terms. Such a move would be similar to what Teresa de Lauretis advocates when she calls for the strategic use of narrative to "construct other forms of coherence, to shift the terms of representation, to produce the conditions of representability of another—and gendered social subject." [8] By returning the male gaze, we might expose (make a spectacle of) the gazer. And by utilizing the power already invested in us as image, we might begin to negate our own "invisibility" in the public sphere.

Roseanne as Spectacle

The spectacle *Roseanne* creates is for herself, produced *by* herself from a consciously developed perspective on ethnicity, gender, and social class. This spectacle derives much of its power from her construction of it as her "self"—an entity which, in turn, she has knowingly fashioned through interviews, public performances, and perhaps most unambiguously her autobiography. This book, by its very existence, enhances the potency of Roseanne-as-sign because it grants a historicity to her "self" and a materiality to her claims for authorship. The autobiography describes key moments in the development of "Roseanne"—how she learned about female strength when for the first time in her life she saw a woman (her grandmother) stand up to a man, her father; how she learned about marginality and fear from her childhood as a Jew in Utah under the shadow of the Holocaust, and from her own experience of madness and institutionalization. Madness is a leitmotif both in her autobiography and in the tabloid talk about her. [9] Roseanne's eventual discovery of feminism and counterculture politics led to disillusionment when the women's movement was taken over by women unlike her, "handpicked," she writes, to be acceptable to the establishment.

Coexisting with the pain of her childhood and early adulthood was a love of laughter, the bizarre, a good joke. She always wanted to be a writer, not an actor. Performance, however, was the only "place" where she felt safe and because, since her childhood, she could always say what she wanted to as long as it was funny; *comic* performance allowed her to be a writer, to "write" herself. While her decision to be a comedian was hampered by a difficulty in finding a female tradition in which to locate her own voice, she discovered her stance (or "attitude") when she realized that she could take up the issue of female oppression by adopting its language. Helen Andelin's *Fascinating Womanhood* (1974) was one of the most popular manuals of femininity for the women of her mother's generation. [10] It taught women to manipulate men by becoming "domestic goddesses." Yet, Roseanne discovered, such terms might also be used for "self-definition, rebellion, truthtelling," for telling a truth that in her case is both ironic and affirmative. And so she built her act and her success on an exposure of the "tropes of femininity" (the ideology of True Womanhood, the perfect wife and mother) by cultivating the opposite (an image of the unruly woman).

Roseanne's disruptiveness is more clearly paradigmatic than syntagmatic, less visible in the stories her series dramatizes than in the image cultivated around her body: Roseanne-the-person who tattooed her buttocks and mooned her fans. Roseanne-the-character for whom farting and nose picking are as much a reality as dirty dishes and obnoxious boy bosses. Both in body and speech, Roseanne is defined by *excess* and by *looseness*—qualities that mark her in opposition to bourgeois and feminine standards of decorum.

Of all of Roseanne's excesses, none seems more potent than her weight. Indeed, the very appearance of a two-hundred-plus-pound woman in a weekly prime-time sitcom is significant in itself. Her body epitomizes the grotesque body of Bakhtin, the body that exaggerates its processes, its bulges and orifices, rather than concealing them as the monumental, static "classical" or "bourgeois" body does. Implicit in Bakhtin's analysis is the privileging of the female body— above all the *maternal* body which, through pregnancy and childbirth, participates uniquely in the carnivalesque drama of inside-out and outside-in, death-in-life and life-in-death. Roseanne's affinity with the grotesque body is evident in the first paragraph of *Roseanne: My Life as a Woman,* where her description of her "gargantuan appetites" even as a newborn brings to mind Bakhtin's study of Rabelais.[11] Roseanne compounds her fatness with a "looseness" of body language and speech—she sprawls, slouches, flops on furniture. Her speech— even apart from its content—is loose (in its sloppy enunciation and grammar) and excessive (in tone and volume). She laughs loudly, screams shrilly, and speaks in a nasal whine.

In our culture, both fatness and looseness are violations of codes of feminine posture and behavior. Women of "ill-repute" are described as loose, their bodies, especially their sexuality, seen as out of control. Fatness, of course, is an especially significant issue for women, and perhaps patriarchy nowhere inscribes itself more insidiously and viciously on female bodies than in the cult of thinness. Fat females are stigmatized as unfeminine, rebellious, and sexually deviant (under— or oversexed). Women who are too fat or move too loosely appropriate too much space, and femininity is gauged by how little space women take up.[12] It is also gauged by the intrusiveness of women's utterances. As Henley notes, voices in any culture that are not meant to be heard are perceived as loud when they do speak, regardless of their decibel level ("shrill" feminists, for example). Farting, belching, and nose picking likewise betray a failure to restrain the body. Such "extreme looseness of body-focused functions" is generally not available to women as an avenue of revolt but, as Nancy Henley suggests, "if it should ever come into women's repertoire, it will carry great power" (p. 91).

Expanding that repertoire is entirely consistent with Roseanne's professed mission.[13] She writes of wanting "to break every social norm . . . and see that it is laughed at. I chuckle with glee if I know I have offended someone, because the people I intend to insult offend me horribly."[14] In an interview in *People Weekly,* Roseanne describes how Matt Williams, a former producer on her show, tried to get her fired: "He compiled a list of every offensive thing I did. And I do offensive things. . . . *That's who I am. That's my act.* So Matt was in his office making a list of how gross I was, how many times I farted and belched—taking it to the network to show I was out of control" (emphasis added). Of course she was out of control—*his* control. He wanted to base the show on castration jokes, she says, recasting it from the point of view of the little boy. She wanted something else—something different from what she sees as the norm of television: a "male point of view coming out of women's mouths . . . particularly around families."[15]

Roseanne's ease with her body, signified by her looseness, triggers much of the *unease* surrounding her. Such ease reveals what Pierre Bourdieu describes as "a sort of indifference to the objectifying gaze of others which neutralizes its powers" and "appropriates its appropriation."[16] It marks Roseanne's rebellion against not only the codes of gender but of class, for ease with one's body is the prerogative of the upper classes. For the working classes, the body is more likely to be a source of embarrassment, timidity, and alienation, because the norms of the "legitimate" body—beauty, fitness, and so on—are accepted across class boundaries whereas the ability to achieve them is not. In a culture that defines nature negatively as "sloppiness," physical beauty bears value that is not only aesthetic but moral, reinforcing a sense of superiority in those who put some effort into enhancing their "natural" beauty (p. 206).

Roseanne's indifference to conventional readings of her body exposes the ideology underlying those readings. Concerning her fatness, she resists the culture's efforts to define and judge her by her weight. Publicly celebrating the libidinal pleasure of food, she argues that women need to take up more space in the world, not less. And her comments about menstruation similarly attack the "legitimate" female body, which does not menstruate in public. On an award show she announced that she had "cramps that could kill a horse." She startled Oprah Winfrey on her talk show by describing the special pleasure she took from the fact that she and her sister were "on their period"—unclean, according to Orthodox law—when they were allowed to bear their grandmother's coffin. And in her autobiography she writes about putting a woman (her) in the White

House: "My campaign motto will be 'Let's vote for Rosie and put some new blood in the White House—every 28 days' " (p. 117). Rather than accepting the barrage of ads that tell women they can never be young, thin, or beautiful enough and that their houses—an extension of their bodies—can never be immaculate enough, she rejects the "pollution taboos" that foster silence, shame, and self-hatred in women by urging them to keep their genitals, like their kitchen appliances, deodorized, anticepticized, and "April fresh." Instead she reveals the social causes of female fatness, irritability, and messiness in the strains of working class family life, where junk food late at night may be a sensible choice for comfort after a day punching out plastic forks on an assembly line.

Demonic Desires

The November 7, 1989, episode of *Roseanne* is in some ways atypical because of its stylistic excess and reflexivity. Yet I've chosen to examine it because it so clearly defines female unruliness and its opposite, the ideology of the self-sacrificing wife and mother. It does so by drawing on and juxtaposing three styles: a realist sitcom style for the arena of ideology in the world of the working class wife and mother; a surreal dream sequence for female unruliness; and a musical sequence within the dream to reconcile the "real" with the unruly. Dream sequences invariably signal the eruption of unconscious desire. In this episode, the dream is linked clearly with the eruption of *female* desire, the defining mark of the unruly woman.

The episode begins as the show does every week, in the normal world of broken plumbing, incessant demands, job troubles. Roseanne wants ten minutes alone in a hot bath after what she describes as "the worst week in her life" (she just quit her job at the Wellman factory). But between her husband, Dan, and her kids, she can't get into the bathroom. She falls asleep while she's waiting. At this point, all the marks of the sitcom disappear. The music and lighting signal "dream." Roseanne walks into her bathroom, but it's been transformed into an opulent, Romanesque pleasure spa where she is pampered by two bare-chested male attendants ("the pec twins," as Dan later calls them). She's become a glamorous redhead.

Even within this dream, however, she's haunted by her family and the institution that stands most firmly behind it—the law. One by one, her family appears and continues to nag her for attention and interfere with her bath. And one by one, without hesitation, she kills them off with tidy and appropriate means. (In one instance, she twitches her nose before working her magic, alluding to the unruly women of the late 1960s-early 1970s sitcom *Bewitched*

[1964–72]). Revenge and revenge fantasies are of course a staple in the feminist imagination, especially in films such as Marleen Gorris's *A Question of Silence* (1982), Nelly Kaplan's *A Very Curious Girl* (1969), Cecilia Condit's *Possibly in Michigan* (1985), and Karen Arthur's *Lady Beware* (1987). In this case, however, Roseanne doesn't murder for revenge but for a bath.

Roseanne's unruliness is further challenged, ideology reasserts itself, and the dream threatens to become a nightmare when she is arrested for murder and brought to court. Her family really *isn't* dead, and with her friends they testify against her, implying that because of her shortcomings as a wife and mother she's been murdering them all along. Her friend Crystal says: "She's loud, she's bossy, she talks with her mouth full. She feeds her kids frozen fish sticks and high calorie sodas. She doesn't have proper grooming habits." And she doesn't treat her husband right even though, as Roseanne explains, "The only way to keep a man happy is to treat him like dirt once in a while." The trial, like the dream itself, dramatizes a struggle over interpretation of the frame story that preceded it: the court judges her desire for the bath as narcissistic and hedonistic, and her barely suppressed frustration as murderous. Such desires are taboo for good self-sacrificing mothers. For Roseanne, the bath (and the "murders" it *requires*) are quite pleasurable for reasons both sensuous and righteous. Everyone gets what they deserve. Coincidentally, ABC was running ads during this episode for the docudrama *Small Sacrifices* (November 12–14, 1989), about a real mother, Diane Downs, who murdered one of her children.

Barely into the trial, it becomes apparent that Roseanne severely strains the court's power to impose its order on her. The rigid oppositions it tries to enforce begin to blur, and alliances shift. Roseanne defends her kids when the judge— Judge Wapner from *The People's Court*—yells at them. Roseanne, defended by her sister, turns the tables on the kids and they repent for the pain they've caused her. With Dan's abrupt change from prosecutor to crooner and character witness, the courtroom becomes the stage for a musical. He breaks into song, and soon the judge, jury, and entire cast are dancing and singing Roseanne's praises in a bizarre production number. Female desire *isn't* monstrous; acting on it "ain't misbehavin'," her friend Vanda sings. This celebration of Roseanne in effect vindicates her, although the judge remains unconvinced, finding her not only guilty but in contempt of court. Dreamwork done, she awakens, the sound of the judge's gavel becoming Dan's hammer on the plumbing. Dan's job is over too, but the kids still want her attention. Dan jokes that there's no place like home but Roseanne answers, "Bull." On her way, at last, to her bath, she closes the door to the bathroom to the strains of the chorus singing "We Love Roseanne."

The requirements for bringing this fantasy to an end are important. First, what ultimately satisfies Roseanne isn't an escape from her family but an ac-knowledgment from them of *her* needs and an expression of their feeling for her—"We love you, Roseanne." I am not suggesting that Roseanne's series miraculously transcends the limitations of prime-time television. To a certain degree this ending does represent a sentimental co-opting of her power, a shift from the potentially radical to the liberal. But it also indicates a refusal to flatten contradictions. Much of Roseanne's appeal lies in the delicate balance she main-tains between individual and institution and in the impersonal nature of her anger and humor, which are targeted not so much at the people she lives with as at what makes them the way they are. What Roseanne *really* murders here is the ideology of "perfect wife and mother," which she reveals to be murderous in itself.

The structuring—and limits—of Roseanne's vindication are also important. Although the law is made ludicrous, it retains its power and remains ultimately indifferent and immovable. Roseanne's "contempt" seems her greatest crime. More important, whatever vindication Roseanne does enjoy can happen only within a dream. It cannot be sustained in real life. The realism of the frame story inevitably reasserts itself, and even within the dream, the reconciliation between unruly fantasy and ideology can be brought about only deploying the heavy ar-tillery of the musical and its conventions. As Rick Altman has shown, few forms embody the utopian impulse of popular culture more insistently than the musi-cal, and within musicals, contradictions difficult to resolve otherwise are acted out in production numbers.[17] That is what happens here. The production num-ber gives a fleeting resolution to the problem Roseanne typically plays with: rep-resenting the unrepresentable. A fat woman who is also sexual; a sloppy housewife who is a good mother; a "loose" woman who is also tidy, who hates matrimony but loves her husband, who hates the ideology of True Womanhood yet considers herself a domestic goddess.

There is much more to be said about Roseanne and the unruly woman: about her fights to maintain authorial control over (and credit for) her show; her use of the grotesque in the film *She-Devil* (1989); her performance as a standup comic; the nature of her humor, which she calls "funny womanness"; her iden-tity as a Jew and the suppression of ethnicity in her series; the series' move toward melodrama and its treatment of social class. A more sweeping look at the unruly woman would find much of interest in the Hollywood screwball comedy as well as feminist avant-garde film and video. It would take up questions about the re-lation between gender, anger, and Medusan laughter—about the links Hélène Cixous establishes between laughing, writing, and the body and their implica-tions for theories of female spectatorship.[18] And while this chapter has emphasized the oppositional potential of female unruliness, it is equally important to expose its misogynistic uses, as in, for example, the Fox sitcom *Married . . . with Children* (1987–97). Unlike Roseanne, who uses female unruliness to push at the limits of acceptable female behavior, Peg Bundy embraces the unruly woman stereotype, embodying the "male point of view" Roseanne sees in so much television about family.

Roseanne points to alternatives. Just as "domestic goddess" can become a term of self-definition and rebellion, so can spectacle-making—when used to seize the visibility that is, after all, a precondition for existence in the public sphere. The ambivalence I've tried to explain regarding Roseanne is evoked above all, perhaps, because she demonstrates how the enormous apparatus of televisual star-making can be put to such a use.

14

The Triumph of Popular Culture

Situation Comedy, Postmodernism, and The Simpsons

MATTHEW HENRY

> Good art that reaches thirty million people and makes them feel connected may have more to offer us now than great art that reaches three thousand and makes them feel more or less alone. In our time the standards for art have changed, expanded. The future belongs to Bart Simpson.
>
> —Tad Friend, 1993

Ars Pro Multis

Art is currently in a conceptual crisis, and its status is now one of the most contentiously debated issues in academe. This is a debate inclusive of all disciplines (painting, sculpture, architecture, photography, film, music, and literature); a debate embodied by discussions of the difference (or loss of difference, to paraphrase Leslie Fiedler) between traditionally high and low art forms; and a debate haunted by the imprecision of the concept of postmodernism in relation to modernism, both artistically and historically. The modernists' insistence upon the separateness of the artist and the autonomous nature of art as a closed "object" yielded a concept of art that has had dominion for much of the twentieth century. The implication of Tad Friend's statement above is that this "great" art, the canonized art of high culture, has less meaning for us now: it is an art of isolation, for it maintains a distance between object and viewer, and an art accessible only to the elite.

However, the popular art of mass culture, or "good" art, has great signifi-

A slightly different version of this chapter was originally published in *Studies in Popular Culture* 17, no. 1 (1994): 85–100. It has been reprinted here by permission of the publisher.

cance for us now: it is art that questions the need for critical distance; it is art that, instead of making people feel isolated, makes them feel connected to society. Many of the traditional art forms are not capable of this contemporarily, but many of the predominant new art forms are, especially film and television. Television, in particular, offers strong societal connections: it has created a new form of tribalism, for it is a "shared cultural experience" in which important issues are addressed and through which the viewer is engaged.[1]

Friend is then correct in asserting that the standards for art have "changed, expanded."[2] A radical alteration has been, and still is, taking place. Art is not dead in our age, as some critics have been hasty to assert; it has simply been transformed.

Nevertheless, Friend's bold statement that the "future belongs to Bart Simpson" poses some difficult questions for the academic: how, exactly, does the future belong to Bart Simpson? why should it belong to him? and if so, what are the social and political implications of such dominance? I hope to answer these questions by examining *The Simpsons* in numerous contexts, but I am most interested in viewing this show with regard to postmodernism. Linda Hutcheon asserts postmodernism is a phenomenon "unavoidably political"[3]; it is critical of power and domination but also involved in it, unable to "escape implication in that which it nevertheless still wants to analyze and maybe even undermine."[4] This is true of *The Simpsons,* which incorporates into the sitcom format many of the techniques of postmodernism with the result of paradoxically both critiquing and creating American popular culture. In short, *The Simpsons* is involved in the production of the very "culture" it satirizes: it is at once a hilarious situation comedy, a biting social commentary, and a monumental merchandising phenomenon. Hence the primary foci of my discussion: the primacy of the family sitcom today, its manifestation in *The Simpsons,* and the methods by which this show influences and is influenced by contemporary American culture.

The Rise of the Sitcom

Situation comedies have become the preferred mode of television; they are "our most pervasive, powerful and cherished form of media output."[5] And a look at the statistics affirms this: in terms of viewership, of the ten top-rated television shows in 1952, shortly after the introduction of television, only one was a sitcom; by 1972, three of the top ten were sitcoms; and in 1992 an incredible seven of the ten most watched shows were sitcoms.[6] What is the appeal of sitcoms? Foremost, being simultaneously more ridiculous and more realistic than the viewer imagines his own life to be, sitcoms imbue the banal with "potent allegorical force.[7] They offer viewers the myth that all problems can be resolved with wit and humor within a short period of time. More significantly, the rise in popularity of the sitcom has coincided with the rise of television shows based on blue-collar families, a tradition begun in the 1950s with *The Honeymooners*, continued with great success in the 1970s with *All in the Family*, and continuing into the 1990s with popularity in shows like *Roseanne* and *Married . . . with Children*.[8]

The Simpsons was, therefore, inevitable, the next logical step in the blue-collar tradition; its enormous success, however, was quite unexpected. Less than a year after its premier in December 1989, the show was "a breakaway ratings hit, industry trendsetter, cultural template, and a viewing experience verging on the religious for its most fanatical followers."[9] The appeal of *The Simpsons* lies in the fact that it is a cartoon and blue-collar sitcom all in one. Though it has strong appeal for (and is thus quite successfully marketed to) a youth audience, *The Simpsons* is also a show for adults, baby boomer adults in particular: it plays upon their sense of nostalgia for similar shows, especially *The Flintstones* and *The Jetsons*, tapping into a desire for lost youth, the childlike enjoyment of watching cartoons, and the comedic surrogate family. But *The Simpsons* is also packed with witty jokes, sophisticated satire, and numerous references, both obvious and obscure, drawn from both "high" and "low" culture. This latter quality signals the intertextuality of *The Simpsons*, which works on one level as a form of postmodern pastiche, a collage of (seemingly) unrelated surfaces. In this sense the show operates like a "mobile game of trivia" for its adult fans,[10] and trivia, as David Marc has noted, is "the most salient form of sitcom appreciation.[11]

Secondarily, *The Simpsons* functions at a level similar to other sitcoms based on the working class, such as *Roseanne*, in that it allows an identification with characters who are somewhat more "real" and whose lives more closely resemble those of its viewers. Thus, all members of the audience can identify with the Simpsons on some level: with the Simpsons' struggle to make ends meet, with Homer's difficulties as both provider and role model, with Marge's attempts to be "supermom," with Lisa's desire to find a place where her intelligence will be "an asset instead of a liability," or with Bart's antiestablishment, bad-boy posture. Though the members of the Simpson family are far from the media-constructed norm represented on television by shows like *Leave It to Beaver, Father Knows Best,* or even *The Flintstones,* they are perhaps closer to the actual norm. This distinction was well displayed in the debate over "family values" during the 1992 presidential election, during which George Bush made his infamous call for "a nation closer to the Waltons than *The Simpsons*."[12] Bush's comment was a lament for the loss of an idealized past and concept of family. What Bush failed to see is that these were only *images* of self and family, only media-constructed identities intended to further a capitalistic philosophy: in short, advertisers and the media gave the masses the life they desired. Thus, Bush's call for the past was a call for a return to falsity, to unreality. *The Simpsons* are more akin to what we are today, more representative of the American family and more attuned to the realities of contemporary life. They live in a society "loosed from its moorings," full of corruption, voracious consumerism, and moral decay.[13] Their America is our America. They are as dedicated to family values as the Waltons ever were but, in such a society, find it increasingly hard to live up to them.

Working Against the Tradition

Television's tradition for the family sitcom was defined by the middle-class lifestyle represented on shows like *The Adventures of Ozzie and Harriet* (1952–66), *Father Knows Best* (1954–62), *Leave It to Beaver* (1957–63) and *Dick Van Dyke* (1961–66). Foremost, these sitcoms offered visions of intact nuclear families, which have been "the fundamental unit of organization in urban industrial America."[14] Atop the nuclear family was posited a patriarchy in which the father was portrayed as knowing, correct, and superior to his wife and children, a structure that worked to reinforce the prevalent sexual stereotypes. Primarily concerned with the high jinks of one or more of its characters (plots usually centered on some form of miscommunication or misunderstanding), these shows also posited a sheltered environment dissociated from the "real world": economic or social problems did not penetrate the fictional world and impact upon the characters. Moreover, traditional family sitcoms established and perpetuated the myth of the happy family. No matter the conflict, resolution and a return to happiness were guaranteed: each week the narrative would return the characters to the same situation and frame of mind with which they began—they would learn nothing new, and would neither change nor grow.[15] With the exception of the working-class sitcom *The Honeymooners* (a ratings bomb that ran only one season, from 1955–56), such middle-class family sitcoms dominated the airwaves in the 1950s and 1960s; after *The Flintstones* left the air in 1966, no other working-class family series appeared on television until *All in the Family* in January 1971.[16]

However, after the success of *All in the Family* (1971–83), working-class family sitcoms began to emerge and rapidly supplant the traditional middle-class family sitcom. The decade of the 1970s was thus a highpoint for working-class sitcoms. One reason for this stands clear: the sitcom needed to add to its "mimetic agenda" the complex social and political issues of the day in order to retain its credibility as "chronicler and salesman of the American family." [17] Nevertheless, during the 1980s there was a strong shift back towards the genre's conventional family center and its hermetic, middle-class lifestyle, a movement that coincided with the conservative zeitgeist of the Reagan years. Although its heyday was past, the myth-tradition was largely carried on in a number of sitcoms during this period: *Family Ties* (1982–89), *Growing Pains* (1985–92), and the wildly successful *Cosby Show* (1984–92) all offered a return to the secure ground of middle-class suburbia and the stable nuclear family.

The 1990s saw a return to shows based in the working class, and these types of sitcoms became predominant. Both critically and economically, the most popular sitcoms of the decade were *Roseanne, Married . . . with Children,* and *The Simpsons.* What set these three sitcoms apart from their predecessors most distinctly is that they incorporated real-world problems into their stories, thereby problematizing the traditionally hermetic nature of family sitcoms. Moreover, these shows are a revolt against the idealized images of domestic life portrayed by sitcoms like *Leave It to Beaver* or *Father Knows Best.* But, unlike many of their contemporaries, they did not attempt to reflect the changing family structure in America. Instead, *Roseanne, Married . . . with Children,* and *The Simpsons* each revived the domestic sitcom, using the traditional nuclear family construct (mom, dad, kids, dog and a house in the suburbs) in order to skewer its conventions. In these shows, the patriarchy is shattered, the universal authority and correctness of both the mother and the father are undermined, and the dominant values systems are rigorously questioned. Thus, by including contemporary realities and subverting the myth-traditions of the family sitcom, these three shows significantly changed the face and nature of the television sitcom. [18]

Complicitous Comedy

Like all forms of popular media in a postindustrial economy, sitcoms are vital modes of image production, and *The Simpsons* is a premier example. Above all, the sitcom is a corporate product. It is a mass consumption commodity and an expression of the underlying assumptions of the corporate culture that has come to dominate American society. [19] It is a vehicle for bringing consumers to advertisers in the marketplace. Demographically, sitcoms appeal to the largest buying audience—teenagers and young working adults with disposable income. *The Simpsons* succeeds as a business because it bridges the gap between these groups and an older, established audience with even more spending power: it has multi-generational appeal, attracting "boomers" and "busters" alike. Thus, *The Simp-*

sons is an industry that, by capitalizing upon the immaterial, upon the image, is able to sell phenomenal amounts of merchandise—both its advertisers' and its own.

The initial success of *The Simpsons* was due to the willful manipulation of the image of Bart Simpson, which capitalized upon the archetype of the adolescent rebel. The sitcom also skyrocketed to fame on the commodification of language: Bart's instantly reproducible phrases "Don't have a cow, man," "Eat my shorts," and "Ay, caramba!" were decontextualized, packaged, and sold to the public en masse. Bart's image and words appeared on T-shirts, bumper stickers, baseball caps, beach towels, coffee mugs, and dozens of other items. The ubiquity of Bart's image has had great influence on consumers, to the delight of merchandisers to be sure. But, more significantly, Bart's ubiquity has also had profound societal ramifications: school officials in a number of states (Ohio and California were the first) quickly condemned the cartoon show and singled out Bart Simpson as a poor role model for school children, going so far as to ban the wearing of a T-shirt bearing Bart's image and the slogan "Underachiever and Proud of It!" [20]

An episode of *The Simpsons* speaks tellingly of both the rampant commodification and the postmodern qualities of the show. In "Bart Gets Famous" (February 3, 1994), Bart, already a commodity in our world, becomes a commodity in the alternate "real" world of the television show when he appears as a fill-in on the variety show of his hero, Krusty the Clown. Frightened by the scrutiny of the audience, Bart is unable to speak his single line and accidentally destroys the set. His instant reply, "I didn't do it," is merely a conditioned response, an excuse derived from years of delinquent behavior. But it is accepted as part of the act, deemed hilarious, and instantly reproduced. Thus, Bart inadvertently becomes a pop culture icon. His commodification is compounded by the rapid production of a cheap biography, a recording contract and hit song, a Bart-Chat hotline, and a Bart Simpson doll.

The irony of this episode is that quite similar things happened in the exterior, "real" world after the initial success of *The Simpsons*: in addition to the aforementioned capitalization upon Bartspeak and the distribution of his image, *The Simpsons* have given us a newsletter, an "uncensored" family album, four separate comic book series, and a hit record, *The Simpsons Sing the Blues*. The show's producers are obviously aware of the strong parallels between the commodification of Bart's image in the fictional world of the television show and the real world of its viewers, and they self-consciously, blatantly play upon this. They know that the irony in *The Simpsons* depends upon a certain degree of cynicism on the part of the audience regarding commercial television and its mission of providing advertisers with a market. The episode cited here thus ends on a tellingly self-reflexive note. Having found himself suddenly unpopular, Bart is gathered at home with his family taking consolation. His sister Lisa says, "Now you can go back to being you instead of a one-dimensional character with a silly catch-phrase," which, in one sense, is what he is. We then get a rundown of the major characters' own catchphrases. Lisa however, refuses to cooperate: with a look of disdain for those identified by surface and image, willing to participate in their own commodification, Lisa says, "I'll be in my room." Homer then asks, "What kind of a catchphrase is that?" Thus, we can see that *The Simpsons* is simultaneously complicitous in and critical of its role in the production of popular culture.

Patricia Waugh states that postmodern texts "flaunt their implication in and complicity with Late Capitalism by deliberately incorporating aspects of mass culture."[21] Such complicity is evident in *The Simpsons'* intertextuality: the show includes material from all aspects of the cultural terrain, from film, television, literature, science fiction, and other comics, to name a few. Such intertextual incorporations, blatant transgressions of real-world boundaries, problematize the ontological status of the cartoon's fictional world by acknowledging its artifice. This self-conscious blurring of boundaries is, in fact, one of the ways in which *The Simpsons* most effectively comments upon itself and the culture of which it is a part, and I will speak more in the next section on the use of these as a means of critiquing American culture. Let me point out here that the use of other forms and "texts" in *The Simpsons* underscores both its complicity in popular culture and its intertextual nature, and these characteristics further distinguish it as a postmodern sitcom. I have also argued here for the status of *The Simpsons* as a producer of popular culture. Fredric Jameson notes, in defining pastiche, that with the collapse of "the high-modernist ideology of style . . . the producers of culture have nowhere to turn but to the past."[22] The pastiche or, as Jameson says, the "cannibalizing" of the past is a primary practice of postmodernism, and this is eminently displayed in *The Simpsons*. However, as I will argue next, the "neutral practice" of pastiche is merely one aspect of this cartoon's agenda, and it is inextricably bound with the more active practice of parody. As a postmodern text, *The Simpsons* does indeed have an "ulterior motive": to critique contemporary American society, using the past as well as the present with a strong satirical impulse.

Critical Comedy

According to Linda Hutcheon, "most television, in its unproblematized reliance on realist narrative and transparent representational conventions, is pure commodified complicity, without the critique needed to define the postmodern paradox." [23] This critique is crucial to the definition of postmodernism. It is also what sets *The Simpsons* apart from the sitcoms defined by the myth-tradition. Those who have criticized *The Simpsons* have missed the point. Above all else, the show is a satire, one fundamentally involved with a critique of American society. Foremost, *The Simpsons* is a satire upon the idealized images of family life depicted in the mythic traditional sitcom; but it is also a knowing and sharp satire upon the excessive, complex, hypocritical, and often idiotic state of contemporary American culture.

As noted earlier, *The Simpsons* works against the tradition of the family sitcom by deconstructing the myth of the happy family. *The Simpsons* highlights the superficiality of the myth (exposing the falseness of tension-free relationships), decenters its authority (radically removing it from the traditional realm of the father), and undermines its conventions (subverting concepts such as the "moral" and the "happy ending"). *The Simpsons* refuses to be complicitous in the perpetuation of the myth-tradition; its refutation is founded upon a more pragmatic, realistic approach to representations of the family today, as Victoria Rebeck has accurately stated: "Rather than engage in the pretentious misrepresentation of family life that one finds in the 'model family' shows (from *The Donna Reed Show* to *The Cosby Show*), [*The Simpsons*] admits that most parents aren't perfect. They haven't worked out their own childhood confusion, and they don't have the answers to all their children's problems." [24]

It is important to point out here Rebeck's deceptively casual use of *The Cosby Show* as an example of the "model family." As noted previously, *The Cosby Show* embodies the myth-tradition of the sitcom in numerous ways; in short, it sums up a great deal of television sitcom history. In the media-hyped showdown between *The Simpsons* and *The Cosby Show*, when Fox moved *The Simpsons* to Thursday nights, the weaknesses of the traditional family sitcom were made abundantly clear. It was a stroke of genius for Fox to put the cartoon up against what Jerry Herron calls "NBCs 2-D paterfamilias," for it exposed *Cosby*'s "informational nullity" and forced a visual showdown that demonstrated "the impoverishment of historically constituted forms." [25] The ratings triumph of *The Simpsons* (and subsequent cancellation of *Cosby*) underscored the fact that the family sitcom in its traditional structure and conventional trappings was null and void.

Although *The Simpsons* is critical of the myth of the happy family, it nevertheless utilizes some of its conceits in order to strengthen its position as a viable family sitcom: the genius of *The Simpsons* is that it "leaves what is real and valuable about the myth unscathed." [26] That is, in the Simpson family, behind all the confusion and bickering, there is always an underlying sense of commitment and caring that does not appear artificial or prefabricated; ultimately, the affection here is sincere, all the more so for the problems that confound it and complicated manner in which it is finally exposed. The traditional sitcoms were less problematic regarding familial affection—it was a given at the onset of each episode, exemplified by the plot, and reinforced by the conventional happy ending.

It was stated previously that one of the most pervasive conventions of the myth of the happy family was the assurance that in each episode resolution was guaranteed, and that each week the narrative would return the characters to the same situation and frame of mind with which they began. This is not to say that in countering the tradition *The Simpsons* offers characters who learn from their mistakes and, as a result, change or grow. Instead, *The Simpsons* satirizes this convention by self-consciously acknowledging it as such.

The finest example of this comes from the episode "Homer Loves Flanders" (March 17, 1994). Homer and Ned Flanders, Homer's fundamental Christian neighbor, become close friends when Ned does Homer a kindly deed. Within the context of the show, this is surprising, for Ned has been Homer's object of both ridicule and indifference for the eight years they have been neighbors. When Bart expresses concern over the continuation of this friendship, Lisa assures him that "every week something odd happens to *The Simpsons* . . . [but] by next week we'll be back to where we started from, ready for another wacky adventure." When Ned tires of Homer's irritating presence and coldly shuns him, it appears this is the case; but there is a subsequent reunion, and it now appears the episode will end with them still friends, thereby undermining the convention that would return the characters to an original blank status. This worries Bart; he says to his sister: "I don't get it. You said everything would be back to normal, but Homer and Flanders are still friends." She sadly replies: "Yeah, maybe this means the end of our wacky adventures." Cut to: the Simpson living room and the caption "The Following Thursday, 8:00 P.M." As Homer is pitching the concept of *The Simpsons'* latest "wacky adventure" (aptly, a stay at a haunted house), Ned stops by. "Get lost, Flanders," Homer shouts. Bart and Lisa look at one another and heave a sigh of relief, happy that the convention has been maintained. Thus, the convention is exposed for what it is: an artificial structure superimposed upon the sitcom to appease the audience with the myth of easy resolution and a circulation back to happiness.

The Simpsons also uses techniques associated with postmodernism in order to subvert and critique traditional sitcom notions such as the "warm moment," wherein everyone embraces, all problems are (re)solved and we learn a valuable moral lesson. This is most emphatically displayed in the episode titled "Blood

Feud," in which Bart donates blood to save the life of Homer's boss, Mr. Burns. Hoping to ingratiate himself, and thereby receive a generous reward, Homer forces Bart to donate. When the family receives nothing more than a "thank you," Homer dashes off a sarcastic note, thus reaping the ire of Mr. Burns, who immediately decides to have Homer killed. But Burns has a change of heart and decides to give *The Simpsons* a gift after all: a stone head, an ancient Olmec Indian carving so large it completely fills their living room. With *The Simpsons* gathered round the head, staring at it, eating dinner on trays, this episode denies us closure and any sense of a lesson by self-consciously ending with a debate on the moral of the show:

> MARGE. The moral of this story is "A good deed is its own reward."
>
> BART. Hey, we got a reward. The head is cool!
>
> MARGE. Well, then, I guess the moral is "No good deed goes unrewarded."
>
> HOMER. Wait a minute. If I hadn't written that nasty letter, we wouldn't have gotten anything.
>
> MARGE. Well, I guess the moral is "The squeaky wheel gets the grease."
>
> LISA. Perhaps there is no moral to this story.
>
> HOMER. Exactly. It's just a bunch of stuff that happened.

Such self-consciousness is abundant on *The Simpsons*. In addition to being a means for exposing its intertextual nature, as outlined in the previous section, it is a method by which the show highlights its refusal to take either the myth-tradition or itself seriously and through which the show calls attention to itself as artifice. Within the scope of this paper, it would be impossible to do justice to the self-reflexive quality of *The Simpsons,* for there are innumerable examples. I will offer only a few, beginning at the beginning. In the aforementioned title sequence of the show, three distinct features are self-consciously altered each week. First, Bart's chalkboard missives almost invariably begin "I will not. . . ," but they are changed for each episode to accommodate his most recent misbehavior (e.g., "I will not teach others to fly," "I will not make flatulent noises in class," "I will not yell 'she's dead' during roll call"). Second, Lisa's saxophone solo, with which she disrupts her band practice, is noticeably different each week. But the feature that plays most upon this conceit is the sequence's final moment, when the family gathers in the living room. Two particular episodes of *The Simpsons* speak most tellingly of its self-conscious stance: in one, *The Simpsons* arrive to confront themselves already seated on the couch—confused glances all around; in the other, as *The Simpsons* dash into the room from one side, they dash out of the frame on the other (filmic frames are drawn to acknowledge this), turn momentarily in empty white space, and then dash back into the living room again.

Marguerite Alexander states that among the prerequisites for postmodernism is a "shattering of the fictional illusion."[27] As is obvious from the examples just cited concerning the opening sequence of the show, *The Simpsons* accomplishes a shattering of the fictional illusion, self-consciously and confrontationally flaunting its status as artifice. This accomplishment is facilitated by the fact that *The Simpsons* is a cartoon, which allows the show to also revel in the realm of the absurd, and this further sets it apart from its predecessors and its contemporaries. Instead of dealing with probabilities, *The Simpsons* often deals with improbabilities. *The Honeymooners,* for example, dealt with the former: Ralph was always trying to rise above the level of the exploited working class through a series of get-rich-quick schemes. *The Simpsons,* however, deals in the latter: Homer easily rises (and as easily falls) to any social and/or economic level—witness the episode in which Homer becomes a Colonel Tom-like manager of a country-western singer or the episode in which Homer becomes an astronaut. Such a self-conscious pose is one of the key methods for conveying satire on *The Simpsons.* To effect this, the members of the Simpson family, as well as the entire cast of the show, are continually put into unlikely and/or absurd situations—witness the episode in which *The Simpsons* are kidnapped by aliens or the one in which Homer and friends form a wildly successful pop music group, The B-Sharps. However, the satire on *The Simpsons* is most effective when it is rooted in contemporary realities. Among other things, *The Simpsons* mercilessly exposes the hypocrisy and ineptitude of pop psychology, modern child-rearing, commercialism, consumerism, fundamental religion, environmental abuse, corporate greed, and the deceits of American education. Considering its great success, both commercially and critically, David Berkman rightly forces us to question whether it is only in the cartoon, the "visually unreal," that can we accept the harsh realities that satire shows us.[28] Perhaps this is so. Since the satire of *The Simpsons* is so pervasive and its targets so widespread, it would be impossible to discuss it in total within this paper. We have already seen numerous examples, both direct and implied. For the sake of brevity, then, let me deal with only one already mentioned instrument of the show's satire: *The Itchy and Scratchy Show.*

The Itchy and Scratchy Show details the exploits of a cat and mouse comedy team modeled on Tom and Jerry. But this cartoon goes its model one better: we are shown every gruesome detail of the ways in which this cat and mouse team seek to destroy each other. They are forever being sliced, diced, disemboweled, de-skinned, beheaded, impaled, and exploded, all with gratuitous amounts of blood. Of the violence in cartoons and live-action shows, Matt Groening has said: "My problem . . . is that there's an anticipation of cruelty which I find really repugnant." [29]

Groening satirizes America's desire for cruelty by offering it up in spades: *The Itchy and Scratchy Show* takes the violence associated with contemporary cartoons to the extreme, thus confrontationally exposing the powerful appeal of violence, its ubiquity today, the crass manner in which it is marketed to children, and the blasé attitude towards it that parents adopt.

The Itchy and Scratchy Show appears on *The Simpsons* with great regularity, offering up its doses of extremely violent and bloody images for the sheer entertainment of its viewers, meaning both the Simpson children and us, the viewers of *The Simpsons*. These images were always shown without any overt commentary at the sitcom's diegetic level the satire was allowed to speak for itself. But in one episode, the show finally addressed its own complicity in the controversial issue of cartoon violence, likely in response to the controversy over censorship raging at that time in the media. In "Itchy and Scratchy and Marge," Marge is disturbed by the amount of time her children spend indoors watching television, especially *Itchy and Scratchy*, and the amount of violence to which they are thus exposed. She organizes a moral watchdog group that campaigns to ban the *Itchy and Scratchy* cartoon. They win the case, and the kids lose their show. We are then given a scene wherein the children emerge from their homes into the sun-filled outdoors to the sounds of Beethoven's Pastoral Symphony. It appears to be the first time their stunted existences have been freed of consumer society's traps. But this traditional happy ending is quickly subverted; it is an ironic and mock-glorious ending, for a new problem arises: Marge's watchdog group now wants to ban the appearance of Michelangelo's *David*. Marge is opposed to this idea and thus realizes that if "great art" is to be protected from censorship, popular art must be as well. At the end of the episode, Bart and Lisa are again watching *The Itchy and Scratchy Show*, and Marge helplessly looks on, wondering if she has done the right thing. Gerard Jones states that the effectiveness of the point about censorship is "undercut by the deep, queasy ambivalence it evokes about the value of television, the impoverishment of life, and the effectiveness of social action." [30] I find no such ambivalence. *Itchy and Scratchy* is back on the Simpsons' television, and *The Simpsons* is still on ours: It is the triumph of popular culture.

15

Sitcoms Say Good-bye

The Cultural Spectacle of Seinfeld*'s Last Episode*

JOANNE MORREALE

Sitcoms rarely say good-bye. Most simply disappear at a stroke, the victims of poor ratings that force their cancellation. Increasingly, however, sitcoms call attention to their departure and invite the entire nation to witness their farewell. The hype surrounding the closing episode of *Seinfeld* (May 14, 1998), in particular, elevated it to the status of cultural spectacle. As columnist Caryn James noted, " 'Seinfeld' has been at the center of the longest, most carefully orchestrated good-bye in television history."[1]

We can begin to illuminate the frenzy surrounding the end of Seinfeld by placing it within its televisual context. The show was conceived and written by Larry David and Jerry Seinfeld, primarily as a vehicle to get comedian Jerry Seinfeld's act on television. Their conceit was that the show would be, like Seinfeld's act, about "the spaces between life,"[2] or, as it has come to be known, about nothing . . . that is, a comedy of manners about "life's minutiae, people's foibles, and mankind's quotidian moments of angst."[3] Self-reflexivity was embedded within its premise: Jerry Seinfeld played himself as a stand-up comic who used his own experiences as the basis for his onstage performances, in much the same way that the real comedian bases his act on acute observations of the small moments of his own offstage life. The show was primarily set either in Seinfeld's apartment or in Monk's Coffee Shop, where the characters' paths would intersect along with the multiple plotlines that structured the show.

According to lore, NBC executives originally rejected the pilot of what was

A slightly different version of this chapter was originally published in the *Journal of Popular Film and Television* (fall 2000): 108–15. It has been reprinted here by permission of the author and the publisher.

then known as *The Seinfeld Chronicles* (an event that became the basis for the self-referential 1993 season closer, "The Pilot," as well as the series finale). Head of NBC programming Brandon Tartikoff dismissed the show as "too New York, too Jewish."[4] But at the insistence of one executive, *The Seinfeld Chronicles* went on the air as a summer replacement show. It did well enough so that a slightly altered version, renamed *Seinfeld,* debuted in January 1990, and went on to become one of the most successful sitcoms in television history. It was one of the top five Nielsen rated shows for six consecutive years and became the cornerstone of NBC's "Must See TV" campaign, helping the network to record profits of nearly one billion dollars in 1998 alone.[5] It was one of very few sitcoms to consistently deliver audiences of more than thirty million viewers each week to the network, and more important, they consisted of the demographic most valued by advertisers—young, urban, upscale viewers who typically did not watch much television.[6] Consequently, *Seinfeld* charged advertisers a million dollars per minute, and for the last episode, watched by an estimated seventy-six million viewers (many of whom were in the desirable eighteen—to forty-nine-year old age group), thirty-second commercials cost nearly two million dollars—an unprecedented figure.[7] *Seinfeld*'s economic clout mirrored its cultural capital.

This chapter offers a reading of *Seinfeld* as a cultural spectacle, using the closing episode as an illustrative case study. *Seinfeld* flouted many of the conventional rules for sitcom success, yet remained in the Nielsen top ten until Jerry Seinfeld decided to end the series after a nine-season run. Above all, the collective "mourning" ritual over the last episode was a pseudo-event whose very existence was predicated upon its construction as such. The final episode became a unifying national moment, as manufactured by the media. To a large extent, the endless hype that turned the final episode into a cultural spectacle was a ploy to boost ratings and thus revenues. Yet, public fascination with both *Seinfeld* and its closing episode deserves deeper scrutiny. Both the intertexts that surrounded the end of *Seinfeld* and the episode itself demonstrated the blurring of fiction and reality that characterized *Seinfeld* as a postmodern text. This essay posits that *Seinfeld*'s postmodern stylistic devices: self-referentiality, intertextuality, parody, and play with the sitcom form, called attention to its discourse, or mode of addressing viewers, as much as its narrative. The last episode of *Seinfeld,* emblematic of the series as a whole, magnified the discursive relationship constructed between text and viewer; in so doing, it illustrated the way that hypermediated relationships serve as the locus of community in contemporary culture.

Although very few sitcoms have formal conclusions, those that do demonstrate the way that texts address viewers through the use of self-referentiality. As Michael Dunne writes, ". . . we must recognize that self-referentiality has become more common and elaborate in today's popular culture. Because of the increasing immersion of Americans in all forms of mediation, moreover, the rhetorical intention of the self-references has shifted considerably, away from the artist's self-expression and toward an affirmation of the mediated community that is embracing both creator and audience."[8]

Sitcoms with planned endings typically include self-referential stylistic devices in their last scenes, as a final nod to viewers before the series leaves the air. These moments highlight the relationship between text and viewer by enabling the viewer to read multiple levels of meaning. *The Dick Van Dyke Show*, for example, ended on a self-reflexive note, with Rob Petrie writing an autobiography that would be turned into a television show starring Alan Brady. (This was the exact inverse of the premise of the show, which was actually written by Carl Reiner, who played television star Alan Brady.) In *The Mary Tyler Moore Show*, the newsroom staff lost their jobs when the television station was sold, just as the cast lost their jobs when the series left the air; similarly, both actors and characters in *Cheers* were out of work when bartender Sam Malone uttered his last words, "Sorry, we're closed." *Newhart* finished by implying that the entire series had been a dream; in the last scene he woke up in bed next to Suzanne Pleshette, his wife from the earlier *Bob Newhart Show*. "I dreamt I was an innkeeper in a crazy little town in Vermont," he told her. Similarly, *Roseanne* concluded by claiming that the entire last season (where the Connors won the lottery) had been an extended fantasy, written by Roseanne in the form of a novel after Dan died. *The Cosby Show* ended with Cliff and Claire Huxtable holding hands and dancing off the set and out the studio door, dismantling the fiction of the show for the first and last time. The final episode of *M*A*S*H*, which received the highest Nielsen rating of any episode in television history,[9] celebrated the end of the Korean War. Its last scene depicted an aerial view of B. J. Hunnicut's enormous stone sculpture of the words "Good-bye"—both his salute to Hawkeye, who looks down as he is departing in a helicopter, and a final good-bye to the viewers of *M*A*S*H*.

As television in general has become increasingly postmodern, so have many final episodes. They are no longer simply self-referential, but they also incorporate intertextuality, parody, and play with the sitcom form, indicating an even greater emphasis upon the discursive relationship set up between text and viewer. The 1998 season saw the close of *Murphy Brown, Ellen, The Larry Sanders Show*, and *Seinfeld*, all finishing with aesthetically complex episodes that blurred the lines between fiction and reality. Only *Seinfeld*, however, had the ratings and audience to enable its additional construction as a cultural spectacle.

Seinfeld's final episode was written and produced by Larry David, who had left at the end of the seventh season but returned for the finale. The ending was shrouded in secrecy, spurring special editions of magazines, conversations on Internet chat groups, television interviews with principal and subsidiary characters, topics for talk shows, and even subjects for news stories. These intertexts enabled *Seinfeld* to become a definitive cultural moment. Critics and fans alike, fueled by the media barrage, speculated on the ending, typically expressing their desire for a sense of closure. The final episode then responded to the proliferation of media coverage, both by addressing the rumors that abounded concerning the show's conclusion, and by putting *Seinfeld,* its characters, and by implication, its viewers, on "trial." Its ironic message suggested that doing nothing is itself an act with repercussions and thus the characters were indeed without redeeming social value.

    Seinfeld closed in a recursive loop, in an episode that was replete with self-referential and intertextual references that rewarded viewers' knowledge of both the text and discourse about the text. The final episode responded to "The Pilot," the hour-long 1993 season closer where Jerry and George sell a show about "nothing," called *Jerry,* to NBC network executives. *Jerry* aired on NBC, with Seinfeld playing himself, and look-alike actors playing George, Elaine, and Kramer. The pilot did not get optioned, but in the final episode new executives call Jerry and George into the NBC offices to discuss the show.[10] The executives immediately begin to describe *Jerry* in a way that parodies the way *Seinfeld* was often discussed in the media: "It's something that will have people talking at the water coolers. We call it a water-cooler show." Jerry adds, "Because the next day at the offices people gather around the water cooler to talk about it, right?" George sardonically retorts that a more apt metaphor might be to call it a coffee-machine show, because no one really talks around the water cooler. The executives also suggest that Jerry and Elaine have a romantic relationship. Initially, NBC executives made a similar request for *Seinfeld,* an idea which both Larry David and Jerry Seinfeld vetoed.[11] Here, George and Jerry object as well ("This is not a relationship show," George protests), but they rapidly agree when the executives threaten not to produce the show. Then, as George and Jerry leave the office, there is an intertextual reference to the ending of *The Mary Tyler Moore Show,* evoking what David Marc calls "the electronic shadow memory" of the past.[12] As George and Jerry gloat over their good fortune, they almost hug but back off at the last minute. The scene recalls the ending of *Mary Tyler Moore,* where the characters embraced in a giant group hug as they huddled off the set. It simultaneously refers to Larry David's "No hugging, no learning" credo, which was a deliberate rebuke both of the "warmedies" of the 1970s, where caring and camaraderie in the workplace replaced the nuclear family, and of the domestic family sitcoms of the 1950s, where every narrative resolved with a lesson learned.

Jerry then informs Elaine that he and George are moving to Los Angeles, lending credence to a popular rumor regarding one possible ending of *Seinfeld* (because the actual show was produced there). When Jerry tells his parents about his good fortune, his father both mocks television and refers to another television icon. "It's all crap on television," he says. "The only thing I watch is *Xena: Warrior Princess* . . . do you ever watch that?"

To celebrate their good fortune, George and Jerry decide to take Elaine and Kramer to Paris on a chartered NBC jet. When Jerry's detested neighbor Newman finds out, he begs Jerry to include him. When Jerry declines, Newman threatens him by shouting, "Your day of reckoning will come." His remark both foreshadows the plot and plays upon another rumor that *Seinfeld* would end with the eccentric mailman Newman "going postal."

As they bicker on the plane (with George grousing that Ted Danson's private jet must be better), the "pilot" literally fails when Kramer stumbles into the cockpit. As the plane begins to fall, Seinfeld screams, "Is this how it ends? It can't end like this!" He is talking both to the other characters and viewers at home, referring both to the fictional life of the character and to the series. Then Elaine clutches Jerry's arm and states, "I've always loved . . ." She doesn't get to finish, teasing viewers (and NBC executives) who hoped for Jerry and Elaine to get together after all. However, at the show's end, she revealed that the object of her affection was United Airlines.

The plane lands for repairs, and the four are stranded in a small town called Latham, Massachusetts. As they stand on a street corner, they not only "do nothing" while a carjacking crime takes place, but they poke fun at the overweight man behind the wheel while Kramer videotapes the scene. In consequence, they are charged with breaking the "Good Samaritan Law" and are put on trial for "criminal indifference." They hire lawyer Jackie Chiles (a parody of Johnny Cochran who first appeared as Kramer's lawyer in "The Maestro"). He pointedly remarks, "You don't have to help anybody. That's what this country's all about." The scene then cuts to the prosecutor, who makes a comment that refers to both the program and the trial, "This place is going to be swarming with media. The whole country is going to be watching. The big issue in this trial is going to be character." In fact, the trial becomes a self-reflexive look at the attention the final episode of Seinfeld has received. In an homage to schlockmeister Geraldo Rivera, whose own daytime talk show had gone off the air a few weeks before, the trial is covered as a story on *Geraldo Live,* his evening news program. The opening credits appear, followed by Rivera's doubly articulated commentary,

"We're here to talk about what you've probably been discussing in your homes and around the water coolers in your offices . . . I'm talking about the controversial 'Good Samaritan' trial that gets underway Thursday in Latham, Massachusetts." There is a cut to on-the-scene reporter Jane Wells, whose conversation with Rivera regarding the "Seinfeld Four" makes a reference to another of the rumors regarding the ending of *Seinfeld*. She says, "There's no love lost with that group. There seems to be some friction between Jerry Seinfeld and Elaine Benis. The rumor is that they once dated and that it ended badly." Rivera responds, "Maybe this trial will end up bringing them closer together. Maybe they'll end up getting married."

The rest of the episode relies upon viewers' knowledge of earlier seasons of *Seinfeld*. Both regulars and guests from previous episodes attend the trial, whether as observers or character witnesses. The assemblage of characters further indicates *Seinfeld*'s ability to blur fiction and reality. The real Keith Hernandez, the fictional J. Peterman (who plays the actual owner of a mail-order catalog company), and a body double of George Steinbrenner (the latter always shot from the back, with Larry David's voice) all appear in court. Other witnesses accuse the Seinfeld Four of all manner of indignities, in a simple reiteration of the plots of classic episodes. As they speak, flashbacks to the episodes verify their words. For example, the virgin whom Jerry dated reports on the infamous "contest," a disabled woman accuses Kramer of selling her a deficient wheelchair, the Bubble boy relates the story of George bursting his protective bubble, and the Soup Nazi accuses Elaine of disrupting his store and selling his recipes.

In addition to knowledge of the text and intertexts, *Seinfeld* relied on viewers' awareness of sitcom conventions in order to play with and parody the form. Up until the last episode, *Seinfeld* obeyed the sitcom formula based on familiarity, repetition, and unchanging characters and locations. But the final episode rendered place unfamiliar. The characters were stripped of their place; they were decontextualized and taken out of the Manhattan setting that made them familiar. As they arrive in Latham, the familiar, edgy, electronic *Seinfeld* music is momentarily replaced by a hillbilly twang. Latham, a rural small town, is the opposite of Manhattan. The New Yorkers in *Seinfeld* (and implicitly, the "urban" audience of *Seinfeld*) share the self-indulgent and self-absorbed characteristics of the four main characters. For instance, back in Manhattan when George asks a fellow diner in Monk's Restaurant if he can use her ketchup, she refuses, and only surrenders it when it is empty. In Latham, however, refusing to help is a crime; its inhabitants are not like the characters or the audience of *Seinfeld*. The Seinfeld Four, and their fans, are completely out of place.

Without their place, all that was left is their characters, which are deemed irredeemable. At the beginning of the episode, George complains about the service at Monk's Restaurant; in the jail cell, he repeats his complaint about the service, virtually word for word. As they wait for their trial, they eat cereal and debate how much milk to use given their new need for conservation. Discussion of "milk estimation skills" for cereal was one of comedian Jerry Seinfeld's signature routines, and his love of cereal was a constant theme in the show. But in other words, they talked about nothing. Despite a radical shift in context, their characters did not alter.

In the end, they are found guilty and sentenced to a year in jail. Still, they refuse to change. They worry about having to wear uniforms in prison. As they walk to their cell, the ever-inventive Kramer comes up an idea for a prison show. Once inside, Elaine obsesses about cell phone propriety, and Jerry critiques the buttons on George's shirt. George asks, "Haven't we had this conversation before?" And of course, they have. This was the first conversation of *The Seinfeld Chronicles.* The characters have become parodies of the sitcom convention that requires a static situation where characters do not change. As Mick Eaton notes, "The necessity for the continuity of character and situation from week to week allows for the possibility of comedy being generated by the fact that the characters are somehow stuck with each other."[13] Here the characters were literally stuck with each other, imprisoned in a small square box with nowhere to go. Similarly, Barry Took remarks that "the 'perfect situation' for a sitcom is 'a little enclosed world where you have to live by the rules.'"[14] In *Seinfeld,* the boundaried settings that typically define the sitcom form became a literal prison. The characters had always been confined, whether in Jerry's apartment or squeezed into a booth in Monk's Coffee Shop, but here their confinement became both explicit and literal. The next-to-last shot of the series depicted the camera slowly panning back from a close-up to a long-shot of the four inmates. The flat lighting, gray walls and vertical bars of the cell emphasize the sense of enclosure and entrapment. But the characters remained untransformed by their experience in the same way that their characters remained unchanged throughout the course of the series. Meaning was irrevocably closed down, providing an unsatisfying conclusion for viewers who wanted resolution if not redemption. *Seinfeld* finished by destroying its central premise that it was a show about nothing. Instead, it became about *something*—about the nature of the sitcom and sitcom characters, articulated in a manner that afforded the audience the pleasure of recognition of extra-, intra-, and intertextual references, but none of the pleasure of a happy ending. Ironically, many viewers whose enjoyment had come from recognizing the disruptions of narrative conventions were dismayed by the fact that the final episode refused to provide conventional narrative closure.

Seinfeld generated such heated emotions because it was so integrally related to viewers' identities as both individual subjects and members of a cultural community. According to Steve Neale and Frank Krutnik, sitcoms are important to us precisely because of their "consolidatory" function;[15] that is, their mode of addressing viewers is a means of communalization and consolidation. They note that sitcoms are extensions of the bonding activity that is at the basis of all jokes; in making sense of the sitcom world, in "getting it," the viewer is interpolated by the text. The pleasure derived from sitcoms is integrally related to the viewer's sense of inclusion, to the affirmation of communal bonds between text and reader. There is a demarcation between those viewers on the inside, who get the joke, and those on the outside who are excluded. The entire final episode of *Seinfeld* was an extended in-joke, as was the series itself. Even minor moments were ways of addressing insiders. For instance, the judge in the trial was named Vandelay, George's all-purpose fake name throughout the series. Over the course of the series, *Seinfeld* even created a new lexicon among insiders, with phrases such as "Yadda, yadda, yadda," "Not that there's anything wrong with it," "spongeworthy," and "master of your domain" becoming the social glue that bound together members of a cultural community.

Thus *Seinfeld,* like television in general, was concerned with reaffirming cultural identities by demarcating an "inside" that consisted of those with similar interests and values, as opposed to those marginalized on the "outside." *Seinfeld* constructed a community of insiders, those who knew the often implicit rules of television sitcoms, as well as the social rules that the *Seinfeld* characters disregarded. *Seinfeld* addressed these viewers by simultaneously acceding to and altering the implicit conventions of television sitcoms.

As in conventional sitcoms, *Seinfeld*'s narrative structure was based on an inside/outside dichotomy. The disruptions that provided the motor for individual plots came mainly from intrusions from the "outside" that were rejected (most classically exemplified when George planned to marry at the end of the 1996 season, but was "saved" when his fiancée, Susan, died). Also, in most sitcoms, the "inside" situation either takes place in the home or workplace or some combination of both (as in *The Dick Van Dyke Show*). The basic "inside" setting in *Seinfeld* was Jerry's Manhattan apartment, although *Seinfeld* was one of the first sitcoms to present a "family" of friends who did not live together and were unrelated by kinship or work. The other stock setting was Monk's Coffee Shop, a place connoting leisure and consumption. Elaine was the only main character who held a steady job (and she job-switched several times), but none of the characters ever seemed in want of money. Rather, the characters' tenuous connection to the world of work reflected their marginal relationship to the stable social order, just as the location in the coffee shop reflected the show's emphasis on consumption, whether of food, sex, or commodities. The characters had no productive relationships; like true creatures of television, they were constantly ingesting, using, and buying.

As Larry David explained when he was still writing for the show, "I've never watched a lot of sitcoms, nor has Jerry. We're not following any kind of formula—no rules or anything—its just our sensibility."[16] Thus *Seinfeld* was neither a domestic family nor a workplace sitcom; nor did its characters form an "inside" core of mutually supportive members of a (surrogate) family. Similarly, Jane Feuer writes that the recurring situation in sitcoms is such that the unity of the "family" takes precedence over all other values.[17] *Seinfeld*, however, mocked the principles of group unity and loyalty that typically bind together either the nuclear or surrogate family in sitcoms. The *Seinfeld* characters were bound together merely by convenience. Their bonds were largely utilitarian, as evidenced by Elaine and Jerry's casual sexual relationship that was devoid of emotional connection. For example, in "The Deal" (May 2, 1991) they devise a set of rules to allow them to revive their sexual relationship without feeling obligated to one another. Yet, they derived little satisfaction from their relationships, whether with each other or with the endless stream of partners who provided the basis for plotlines. Because of their deviation from "normal" sitcom relationships, and from the "rule" that sitcom characters must be likable, they are put on trial. As Judge Vandelay states when he sentences the four, "Your utter disregard for everything that is good and decent has rocked the very foundation upon which our society is built." He might have substituted the word "sitcom" for society.

In effect, *Seinfeld* inverted the conventional inside/outside dichotomy with regard to the characters. Rather than the "inside" consisting of a cohesive, normative group, the four main characters were themselves marginalized. They were single adults unable or unwilling to form lasting relationships, whose selfishness and self-absorption challenged standards of middle-class behavior and decorum. The stable "inside" situation in *Seinfeld* was in fact unstable, indicated by the constant conflict that marked the internal dynamic of the group, and by their sneering refusal to help a stranger in need in the final episode. Yet, the "unstable" inside situation of the narrative, where *Seinfeld* parodied the setting, characters, and relationships of conventional sitcoms, helped to create the "stable" community of insiders. The richer the narrative play with sitcom rules and conventions, the more there was for viewers to "get" on the discursive level.

In the final episode, the refusal to act becomes a crime. "Have you ever heard of a *guilty* bystander?" lawyer Jackie Chiles asks rhetorically. The characters did nothing except make cynical comments while videotaping a carjacking. They remained aloof and uninvolved as they turned real life into a movie, in a more extreme version of the way that the show about nothing routinely transformed mundane experiences into sources of humor. "Nothing" was sacred in *Seinfeld*; "nothing" defined the moral center of the show. The characters remained self-absorbed, oblivious to conventional morality or the pieties of political correctness.

As the series progressed, *Seinfeld* increasingly rendered the conventional relationship of viewer identification with characters problematic. Mikhail Bakhtin's distinction between two types of bodies, the classical and the grotesque, provides a useful lens through which to consider the representation of characters on *Seinfeld*.[18] The grotesque body, personified in the figure of the clown, is one marked by excess, unruliness, and celebration of the lower body stratum. Apart from Seinfeld, the three main characters embodied the grotesque: Kramer, the physical clown who made every entrance a gymnastic exercise; George, overweight and avaricious, characterized by a pathological toilet obsession; or Elaine, the bizarre dancer, with excessive appetites for food and sex. The themes of individual texts were often grotesque, with several "bodily" topics such as nose-picking, bared nipples, breast implants, penis size, urinating in public, diarrhea, and regular references to sexual subject matter. The "performance" of *Seinfeld* was often a celebration of the taboo, a reveling in the unmasking of social proprieties. Yet, clowns are always bifurcated figures who create laughter by incorporating fears; viewers who identified with them were installed into uneasy subject positions.

Alternatively, Seinfeld himself was the controlled classical body, excessive in its own compulsive need for cleanliness and order. In the final episode, he objects to George urinating with the bathroom door open. In another episode, he throws away a shoelace because it trailed on the bathroom floor. He is horrified when Kramer doesn't wear underwear. He rejects a woman because she dropped her toothbrush in the toilet bowl. And, in fact, the final episode reveals that he actually won the contest to see who could exert the most self-control by refraining from masturbation. ("I cheated in the contest," George informs him as the plane is going down.) But unlike the clowns who performed, his character did not "act" in the show; he served as the straight man who reacted to the events around him. *Seinfeld* accommodated real-life comedian Jerry Seinfeld's act to the demands of the form. His character was often the bemused bystander, observing and noting the foibles of his hapless friends. Yet unlike other comedic straight men, such as George Burns (who also played a fictionalized version of himself), Seinfeld lacked the narrative authority that is typically associated with the classical body. His character was obsessed *with* control, but was not *in* control. (Control, discussed via the metaphor of "having hand," was a recurrent theme in

Seinfeld). In some instances, Seinfeld even manifested his lack of control by breaking out of character, most famously when he stole a loaf of marble rye bread from an elderly woman.

Overall, the representations of classical and grotesque bodies in *Seinfeld* reflected tensions within the culture that remained unresolved. As with all clowns, their celebration of (and in Seinfeld's case, disdain for) the vulgar and the mundane was a way to stave off fear of the cosmos as well as death.[19] (Ironically, the chaotic Kramer's first name was Cosmo.) The characters represented the cultural ideal of perpetual youth, unconstrained by the demands of the social order. The fact that George and Jerry's parents were semiregulars on the show attests to the adolescent positioning of the characters. At the same time, they expressed contemporary malaise, in the form of fear of intimacy, manifested in their inability to form lasting commitments. In the end, the text's discourse mimicked its narrative. *Seinfeld* maintained its own illusion of perpetual youth by never growing old, by reappearing endlessly in syndication, just as it exhibited the same fear of intimacy demonstrated by the characters in the narrative. Jerry Seinfeld the comedian seemed to acknowledge this when he said *"Seinfeld*'s all about break-ups. And ultimately the show had to break up with America. In the end, it just couldn't commit.[20]

It is here, too, that one of the contradictions that marks *Seinfeld* becomes apparent: viewers who mourned the end of *Seinfeld* were themselves committed to the text; they were intimately involved with the text, the characters, and their fictional lives. Identification and commitment, however, occurred with the discourse of the text, perhaps more so than the characters within it. The fundamental play of the narrative—the inversion of typical sitcom conventions of place, characters, and relationships, along with the plethora of self-referential and intertextual references, served to "consolidate" the discourse. It was precisely the consolidary function of *Seinfeld*'s discourse, its mode of address, that lured viewers. The discourse of *Seinfeld* created a pseudo-intimacy with viewers by "speaking" to them, by creating a mediated community "in the know." The intertexts that surrounded the last episode, and the episode itself, magnified the construction of this community of insiders.

Sitcoms are all about relationships. In *Seinfeld,* the most important relationship was between text and reader. In a show about characters who were shallow, self-centered, neurotic, and afraid of intimacy, the text's discourse created a pseudo-intimacy with the viewer, one that ultimately formed the basis for social relationships. The closing episode became a cultural marker, a basis for "real" discussions with friends and colleagues. Ultimately, it suggested that mediated relationships have become the ground for actual ones, that virtual participation in a media event has become the basis for community, that television viewers are all, like the characters in *Seinfeld,* guilty as charged. *Seinfeld*'s final episode parodied the superficiality and self-absorption of its audience. At the same time, the cultural spectacle surrounding *Seinfeld*'s departure created a deep sense of nostalgia. Viewers mourned the loss of *Seinfeld* even before the last episode aired. They felt nostalgia for *Seinfeld* because, like all commodities, it reminded them of a past moment when they "imagined possession would bring happiness but which, now that it has arrived, is experienced only as the ache of unfulfilled expectations."[21] The disconcerting closing episode made apparent that there would be no future, no fulfillment, and no redemption for the Seinfeld Four, nor for the viewers who watched the show. The characters showed no remorse, and the final shot depicted Jerry, clad in orange uniform, conducting his opening monologue from within a prison of his own making. According to Jerry Seinfeld, "The stage experience is very pure. It's very empirical. An authentic moment in your life."[22] Thus *Seinfeld* ended the way it began, with a stand-up comedian performing his act, stripped of all of the artifice of the sitcom form.

Notes
Bibliography
Index

Notes

Introduction

1. Paul Wells, "Where Everybody Knows Your Name: Open Convictions in Closed Contexts in the American Situation Comedy," in *Because I Tell a Joke or Two: Comedy, Politics, and Social Difference,* ed. Stephen Wagg (New York: Routledge, 1998), 180–81.

2. Jane Feuer, "Genre Study and Television," in *Channels of Discourse, Reassembled,* 2d ed., ed. Robert C. Allen (Chapel Hill: Univ. of North Carolina Press, 1992) 138–60.

1. Why Remember Mama? The Changing Face of a Woman's Narrative

1. Elizabeth Meehan and Bradford Ropes, "Mama's Birthday" (episode), Theater Arts Collection, University Research Library, Univ. of California, Los Angeles.

2. Rick Mitz, *The Great TV Sitcom Book* (New York: Richard Marek, 1980), 458.

3. Rosemary Rice, Dick Van Patten, and Robin Morgan, *I Remember Mama* Symposium, Museum of Broadcasting, New York, N.Y., Dec. 17, 1985, author's notes. Ralph Nelson, private conversation with author, Dec. 17, 1985; repeated during interview with author, Monteceito, Calif., Jan. 11, 1986,

4. Ralph Nelson, interview by George Lipsitz, Monteceito, Calif., Jan. 11, 1986.

5. Rosemary Rice, *I Remember Mama* Symposium.

6. Robin Morgan, *I Remember Mama* Symposium.

7. Kathryn Forbes, *Mama's Bank Account* (New York: Harcourt, 1943).

8. *Current Biography,* 1945, 102. John Van Druten, *I Remember Mama* (New York: Dramatists Play Service Incorporated, 1944).

9. *New York Times,* May 17, 1966.

10. Stefan Kanfer, *A Journal of the Plague Years* (New York: Atheneum, 1973), 154.

11. Andrea Walsh, *Women's Film and Female Experience* (New York: Praeger, 1984), 104.

12. Quoted in Walsh, *Women's Film,* 106–7.

13. Dewitt Bodeen screenplay, *I Remember Mama,* Fred Guiol Collection, California State Univ. at Fullerton, #4–87.

14. Dewitt Bodeen screenplay, *I Remember Mama.*

15. Ralph Nelson Papers, Special Collection 875, University Research Library, Univ. of California, Los Angeles, Box 78, Scripts #1, 13, 20, 6. "T. R.'s New Home" and "Mama's Bad Day," Academy of Television Arts Collection, Univ. of California, Los Angeles, Calif.

16. Ralph Nelson Papers, Box 78, Scripts #9, 2. Frank Gabrielson Papers, Sudbury, Mass., "Mama and the Magic Lantern," "The Pet Show," "Nels and the Girl with the Lively Eyes."

17. "Tricycles Last," T86 1142, Museum of Broadcasting, New York.

18. "Nels and the Train Set," T86 0092, Museum of Broadcasting, New York.

19. "The Hansens Rise in the World," T86 1128, Museum of Broadcasting, New York.

20. Ralph Nelson Papers, Box 45.

21. Ralph Nelson Papers, Box 44 (Memo from Doris Quinlan to Carol Irwin, Frank Gabrielson, and Ralph Nelson, Dec. 8, 1954).

22. Ralph Nelson Papers, Box 44 (CBS Press Release), 1949.

23. "T. R.'s New Home," Academy of Television Arts Collection.

24. Ernest Dichter, *The Strategy of Desire* (Garden City, N.Y.: Doubleday, 1960), 209.

25. Tania Modleski, "Femininity as Mas(s)querade: A Feminist Approach to Mass Culture," in *High Theory/Low Culture,* ed. Colin McCabe (New York: St. Martin's, 1986), 42.

26. Ralph Nelson Papers, Box 78, Script #13.

27. Ralph Nelson Papers, Box 78, Script #2.

28. Ralph Nelson Papers, Box 78, Script #15.

29. Hale Lamont Havers, interview with author, Sudbury, Mass., May 15, 1987.

30. Murray Schumach, "Writing for Video," *New York Times,* Feb. 18, 1951, x9.

31. Ralph Nelson, interview with author, Monteceito, Calif., Jan. 11, 1986.

32. Ibid.

2. *Amos 'n' Andy* and the Debate over American Racial Integration

1. Black middle-class values are taken up in David G. Nielson, *Black Ethos* (Westport, Conn.: Greenwood, 1980), and August Meier, *Negro Thought in the Age of Booker T. Washington, 1885–1915* (Ann Arbor: Univ. of Michigan Press, 1965).

2. The quotations are from Estelle Edmerson, "A Descriptive Study of the American Negro in United States Professional Radio, 1922–1953" (master's thesis, Univ. of California, Los Angeles, 1954), 115, 87, 94. NAACP activities are recorded in that organization's files in the Library of Congress.

3. H. B. Alexander, "Negro Opinion Regarding *Amos 'n' Andy,*" *Sociology and Social Research* 16 (Mar. 1932): 345–54; Bishop J. Walls, "What about *Amos 'n' Andy?*" *Abbott's Monthly,* Dec. 1930, 38–40, 72, in James Weldon Johnson Memorial Collection, Beineke Library, Yale Univ., Hartford, Conn.; *Los Angeles Sentinel,* Mar. 18, 1948.

4. The Enoch Pratt Free Library of Baltimore reported that especially among "older" patrons demand was so heavy "you could hardly get hold of" some tapes. (Florence Connor and Carolyn Houck, telephone interviews with author, Pratt Library). Tapes also available in Afro-American Studies Program, Univ. of Maryland, College Park, Md. See also James Wolcott, "Holy Mack'ell: Amos 'n' Andy Videotapes Are Hot Items on the Nostalgia Market," *Esquire,* Jan. 1981, 11–12.

5. President's Committee on Civil Rights, *To Secure These Rights* (Washington, D.C., 1947). A good essay and bibliography on the period is Richard Polenberg's *One Nation Divisible: Class, Race and Ethnicity in the United States since 1938* (New York: Penguin, 1980), chap. 3, 330.

6. David Freeman, Jaffe Agency, to Hugh Wiley, Mar. 26, 1952, Apr. 21, 1952, Wiley Papers, Bancroft Library, Berkeley, Calif.

7. L. S. Cottrell quoted in Paul F. Lazarsfeld, *Radio and the Printed Page* (New York: Arno, 1940), 56–57, and in Edmerson, "Descriptive Study," 195.

8. J. Fred MacDonald, "Stride Toward Freedom—Blacks in Radio Programming," paper loaned by MacDonald to author, 7–14, later a chapter in his *Don't Touch That Dial!* (Chicago: Nelson-Hall, 1979).

9. Sample of Benny-Anderson dialogue in MacDonald, "Stride Toward Freedom," 11a. Black ambivalence toward Rochester can be seen in Edmerson, "Descriptive Study," 185–87 (newspapers and *The Negro Yearbook* cited), and in Anderson himself, telephone interview by author, June 1970, in which he claimed never to have crossed boundaries of bad taste nor depicted unreal characters.

10. See *Pittsburgh Courier,* Mar. 4, 1942, for an example. A rich literature includes John B. Kirby, *Black Americans in the Roosevelt Era: Liberalism and Race* (Knoxville: Univ. of Tennessee Press, 1980).

11. For a sample of reviews of local and prime time network programs see *Variety,* Oct. 7, 1942, 26; Mar. 11, 1942, 18, 35; May 13, 1942, 32–33; May 20, 1942, 36; Feb. 10, 1943, 30; Feb. 17, 1943, 28; Mar. 3, 1943, 33; Apr. 8, 1942, 30; Mar. 15, 1944, 53; May 3, 1944, 1; Mar. 22, 1944, 3; Feb. 16, 1944, 43; see also MacDonald, "Stride Toward Freedom," 25–33.

12. *Sponsor,* Dec. 1949, 44, on Robinson, cited in Edmerson, "Descriptive Study," 12, 45; synopsis of *Story of a Drum,* CBS Feb. 15, 1946, in Katherine Dunham Collection, Morris Library, Southern Illinois Univ., Carbondale, Ill., Box 7.

13. Documents from *Destination Freedom* Collection, Institute for Popular Culture Studies, Northeastern Illinois Univ., cited in J. Fred MacDonald, "Radio's Black Heritage: *Destination Freedom,* 1948–1950," *Phylon* 39 (Mar. 1978): 66–73

14. Edmerson, "Descriptive Study," 165, and conversations between Barnouw and Cripps, 1975–76. Edmerson's informants ("Descriptive Study," 350–59), cited sponsors who feared pejorative associations with blacks ("nigger flour") and "a mixed reception from Negroes themselves." Thus civil rights groups inquired into broadcasting as a weapon. Ann Tanneyhill of the National Urban League (NUL), for example, argued: "I do hope we will be able to move into the fields of motion pictures and radio in 1948. We 'scooped' other race relations agencies on the comic book but I fear they will beat us to the draw on motion pictures and radio" *(Morning for Jimmy* File, NUL Records, Library of Congress, Washington, D.C.).

15. "The Forgotten 15,000,000," *Sponsor,* Oct. 1949, 24–25, 54–55; Edmerson, "Descriptive Study," 350–54; "Selling the Negro Market," cover story in *Tide,* Jul. 20, 1951, in NAACP records; "Can TV Crack America's Color Line?" *Ebony,* May 1951, 58. From 1948 through 1952, *Ebony* gave heavy coverage to television as though believing its own assertion that "television has supplied ten-league boots to the Negro in his fight to win what the Constitution of this country guarantees."

16. *Variety,* Jan. 9, 1952, 32; Sep. 3, 1952, 26; Feb. 6, 1951, 31; Jan. 11, 1950, 28 (in which George S. Schuyler's talk show is seen as "in line with a new policy of cultivating the Negro audience").

17. *Amsterdam News* (New York City), Aug. 12, 1939.

18. *Variety,* May 3, 1950, 30, 40.

19. On programming, see *Variety,* Feb. 8, 1950, 58; Apr. 19, 1950, 24; "Television," *Ebony,* June 1950, 22–25; *Variety,* Jan. 11, 1951, 28; Sep. 10, 1952, 30; Oct. 22, 1952, 27; Nov. 26, 1952, 30. On policies of executives, *Variety,* Nov. 8, 1950, 26; Jan. 17, 1951, 26; Jul. 18, 1951, 1.

20. Edith Tedesca, CBS personnel, quoted in Edmerson, "Descriptive Study," 103.

21. Glucksman-Barnett correspondence in Barnett Papers, Chicago Historical Society, NUL interceded for blacks seeking entry into broadcasting, as in placing lyricist Joe Lutcher as a prospective writer of Camel cigarette commercials, thereby providing another crack in the white monopoly. Wesley R. Brazier to Guichard Parris, Dec. 5, 1952, NUL Records, Series 5, Los Angeles, 1944–61 file, Box 42.

22. Reels are scattered among Clark College, Atlanta; Library of Congress; and Kit Parket, Carmel, Calif.; Glucksman to Barnett, Aug. 25, 1954; *Variety,* Aug. 11, 1954, 41.

23. *Amos 'n' Andy* began in 1929 on Chicago radio, moving eventually to network broadcasting, recordings, two RKO films in 1930, and animated cartoons (cartoon in Library of Congress, films on KDKA-TV (Pittsburgh); *Variety,* Oct. 9, 1930, 31; Aug. 20, 1930, 4; Oct. 8, 1930, 22. See also Norman Kagan, "Amos 'n' Andy: Twenty Years Late, or Two Decades Early?" *Journal of Popular Culture* 6 (summer 1972): 71–75.

24. Quoted in Kagan, "Amos 'n' Andy," 71–75.

25. *Los Angeles Sentinel,* Mar. 18, 1948; *Variety,* Feb. 1, 1950; Apr. 28, 1948, 1; Oct. 4, 1950, 30; Nov. 5, 1950, 1, the latter for a report of the national post-prime-time sneak preview.

26. Nick Stewart, Bill Walker, Ernest Anderson, Jester Hairston, Alvin Childress, Sig Mickelson, and Charles Barton, interviews with author, June 1970 and the summers of 1976 and 1977.

27. *Variety,* Oct. 4, 1950, 30; C. L. Dellums to Walter White, Dec. 6, 1950, NAACP Records.

28. *Ebony,* May 1951, 21; *Variety,* Oct. 4, 1950, 30; Color, clipping; Dellums to White, Dec. 6, 1950; Lindsay II White et al. to Lewis S. Rosenstiel, Schenley Distillers, copy, Jun. 27, 1951 (all but *Ebony* and *Variety* in "*Amos 'n' Andy*" file, NAACP Records).

29. *Pittsburgh Courier,* Jul. 7, 1951; *Variety,* Jul. 4, 1951, 1; Walter White to Committee, copy, Jul. 10, 1951; White, memorandum for file, Jul. 11, 1951, and on Jul. 10, 1951 marked "not to be given out," in NAACP Records. The committee included the topmost rank of the national NAACP, along with Ralph Bunche, journalists Norman Cousins and Lewis Gannett, Louis T. Wright, Charming Tobias of the YMCA, and Algernon Black of the National Council of Churches.

30. *New York Times,* Sep. 22, 1951; Walter White to "subscribing newspapers," copy, Jul. 12, 1951; Gloster B. Current to "NAACP branches and state conferences," copy, Jul. 16, 1951; NAACP press release, "Why the Amos 'n' Andy TV Show Should Be Taken Off the Air," Aug. 15, 1951; press release, "New Protests Mark 4th Week . . . July 26, 1951"; Ardie A. Halyard, Milwaukee Branch, to *Current,* 27 Jul. 27, 1951, NAACP Records.

31. Walter White to newspapers, Aug. 2, 1951; White to Billy Rowe, Jul. 27, 1951, NAACP Records, in which White argued that the shows affected society to the point of causing a riot, and demanded proof of Rowe's linkage of the NAACP with the Communist Party.

32. For the mixed black response see *Chicago Defender,* Jun. 23, 1951 (Fred O'Neal), Jul. 7, 14, 28, 1951, and Aug. 18, 1951 (CCNP); *Variety,* Jan. 28, 1953, 1 (NBC defense), Jun. 24, 1953 (sponsors); *Defender,* Sep. 29, 1951 (UAW), Aug. 18 (anti-NAACP actors), 25, 1951, Sep. 8, 1951 (Negro Masons' split), Sep. 29, 1951 (clerical protest); *Variety,* Aug. 8, 1951, 1 (statements by Lester Walton and Noble Sisle); *Negro Achievement,* Nov. 9, 1952, 40, latter in James Weldon Johnson Memorial Collection, Beineke Library, Yale University, Hartford, Conn.

33. W. Richard Bruner, "Amos 'n' Andy Hassle Won't Stop TV Show," *Printers' Ink,* Aug. 13, 1951; Arnold M. Rose, "TV Bumps into the Negro Problem," *Printers' Ink,* Jul. 2, 1951, 36; Walter White, "Negro Leader Looks at TV Race Problem," *Printers' Ink,* Aug. 24, 1951, 31; *New York*

World Telegram and Sun, Jul. 27, 1951; *Interracial Review,* Sep. 1951; *New Leader* Oct. 15, 1951; Gosden and Correll quoted in *Advertising Age,* Aug. 13, 1951; Harold Doman and Thelma Eastman, draft petition on "integration," Jul. 31, 1951; Lindsay H. White and James E. Allen, NAACP, to Lewis S. Rosenstiel, Schenley, copy, Jun. 27, 1951; Walter White to newspapers, copy, Aug. 2, 1951, all in NAACP Records.

34. *Variety,* Aug. 23, 1950, 28, Sep. 24, 1952, 30 (Luigi); Oct. 1, 1952, 101 *(Cellini)*; Sep. 16, 1953, 31 *(Bonino)*; Walter White memorandum, Jul. 10, 1951, recounting the role of Edward J. Lukas, American Jewish Committee, in influencing the content of *The Goldbergs,* NAACP Records.

35. "Happy Stevens," "The Kingfish's Secretary," and "The Rare Coin" in Enoch Pratt Free Library; scripts in Library of Congress and in Special Collections Department, Research Library, Univ. of California, Los Angeles.

36. "The Jewel Store Robbery," in Pratt Library, script in Library of Congress, Motion Picture, Broadcasting, and Recorded Sound Division.

37. "Happy Stevens," "The Kingfish's Secretary," and "The Rare Coin" in Enoch Pratt Free Library.

38. "The Christmas Show," viewed courtesy of Professor Al-Tony Gilmore, chairman, Afro-American Studies, Univ. of Maryland, College Park, Md.

39. *Variety,* Dec. 31, 1952, 18.

40. Edmerson, "Descriptive Study," 89, 117, 126–29, 192, 391–93, 396, 403.

41. Hampton quoted, *Pittsburgh Courier,* Aug. 4, 1951, in Edmerson, "Descriptive Study," 391; Blatz sample in *California Eagle,* Aug. 23, 1951, also in Edmerson, "Descriptive Study," 393. Edmerson's other interviews derived from pages cited in note 40.

42. George Norford, interview by author, Oct. 29, 1970, in which Norford recalled a tension between feeling that the shows were "funny as hell" and his opposition to network exclusivity that denied blacks access to the air; conversations with Professor Emeritus G. James Fleming of Morgan State University, especially one on Oct. 31, 1975. On the National Urban League campaign, see Ann Tanneyhill, NUL, to Frank Stanton, CBS, Aug. 10, 1951; Tanneyhill to Bill Chase, Aug. 10, 1951; Tanneyhill to Lewis S. Rosenstiel, Aug. 10, 1951, NUL Records, Series 7, Box 1. On the NAACP's inquiry into a "National Negro Broadcasting Council" and some form of "network-calibre" programming for blacks, see Harry Novik, WLIB, to Walter White, Jan. 10, 1951, Jul. 7, 1954; and David D. Osborn et al. to White, Jul. 1954, 19, in NAACP Records.

43. *Chicago Defender,* Jul. 7, 14, 28, 1951; *Variety,* Jun. 18, 1952 (Blatz's withdrawal); Mar. 11, 1953, 2, 5 *(Four Star* and also the outsized "nut" of *Amos 'n' Andy)*; *Variety,* Aug. 8, 1951 (a page-one story on the threats of Lester Walton, a veteran black drama critic, and Noble Sissle, a famous bandleader, to picket NAACP offices as a means of dramatizing black opposition).

44. In the decade following the suspension of production, *Amos 'n' Andy* remained a staple of the syndication market, generally in a pattern of good solid ratings in southern states and through the West to Bakersfield, and in smaller markets. Thus, in the same summer week in 1955, it finished first among syndicated shows in Little Rock but ninth in Washington. Where it was possible to measure, it seemed to play equally well in northern towns such as Evansville and southern towns like Shreveport, but also in large markets where heavy black populations resided such as Detroit. One week in 1956, it was number one in New Orleans with a rating of more than 50 and an audience share of more than 80, while one month later in New York, in keeping with its pattern of flopping in large markets, it finished tenth, with a rating of 7.5, against *Looney Tunes.* This trend

also included less clearly measurable traits, among them the possibility that when *Amos 'n' Andy* was opposed by programs that were slanted toward children, the adults in the family overrode the tastes of the young. In Shreveport in the summer of 1961, for example, *Huckleberry Hound* finished fourth with a rating of 16 as against the 22 posted by *Amos 'n' Andy*. Gradually, through the early 1960s, even though the same viewing patterns persisted, the size of the figures tailed off. Ratings consistently fell below 20, even in southern and small-town markets, and even in towns such as Dayton, Bakersfield, Atlanta, Charlotte, and New Orleans the show regularly finished ninth or tenth in the local race for hegemony in syndication. Sample made by Alma Taliaferro Cripps and Paul Hagan Cripps for the years 1954–63.

45. *Variety* continued to cover the story even as the combative elements of it diminished. See Jul. 2, 1952, 24; Dec. 31, 1952, 18; May 13, 1953, 38–39; Sep. 16, 1953, 21; Jun. 3, 1953, 25; Jan. 13, 1954, 25. For postmortems in addition to Wolcott, "Holy Mack'ell," see "The Case of the Missing Roast Beef," *Ebony,* Apr. 1958, 143; "Requiem for the Kingfish," *Ebony,* Jul. 1959, 57–64; Edward T. Clayton, "The Tragedy of *Amos 'n' Andy*," *Ebony,* Oct. 1961, 66–73 (which reported that "no other Negro show has been able to find a national sponsor"); and Thomas Cripps, "The Films of Spencer Williams," *Black American Literatuare Forum* 12 (winter 1978): 128–34.

3. Situation Comedy, Feminism, and Freud: Discourses of Gracie and Lucy

1. Eric Goldman, *The Crucial Decade and After: America, 1945–1960* (New York: Vintage Books, 1960).

2. Jean Baudrillard, "Requiem for the Media," in *For a Critique of the Political Economy of the Sign,* trans. Charles Levin (St. Louis, Mo.: Telos, 1981), 184.

3. The transcription was taken from tape.

4. See Patricia Mellencamp, "Jokes and Their Relation to the Marx Brothers," in *Cinema and Language,* ed. Stephen Heath and Patricia Mellencamp (Frederick, Md.: University Publications of America, 1983), for further explication of jokes and the comic within the wacky male world of the Marx brothers.

5. Roland Barthes, "Writers, Intellectuals, Teachers," in *Image-Music-Text,* ed. Stephen Heath (London: Fontana/Collins, 1977), 205–6.

6. Samuel Weber, *The Legend of Freud* (Minneapolis: Univ. of Minnesota Press, 1982), 114.

7. Ibid., 114.

8. Ibid., 116.

9. Bart Andrews, *Lucy and Ricky and Fred and Ethel* (New York: E. P. Dutton, 1976). This book contains a synopsis of shows by air date and title that helped me to organize my textual analysis.

10. Hayden White, "The Value of Narrativity in the Representation of Reality," *Critical Inquiry* 7, no. 1 (1980): 10.

11. Sigmund Freud, *Jokes and Their Relation to the Unconscious,* trans. James Strachey (New York: Norton, 1960), 196.

12. Ibid., 231

13. Ibid., 235.

14. Sigmund Freud, "Humour," in *The Standard Edition of the Complete Psychological Works of Sigmund Freud,* vol. XXI (London: Hogarth, 1964), 162–63.

4. Returning from the Moon: Jackie Gleason and the Carnivalesque

1. Sarah Ruth Kozloff, "Narrative Theory and Television," in *Channels of Discourse,* ed. Robert C. Allen (Chapel Hill: Univ. of North Carolina Press, 1987), 53.

2. John Fiske, *Television Culture* (New York: Methuen, 1987), 151.

3. *Cavalcade of Stars* was originally aired on the now-defunct DuMont network. The program moved to CBS in 1952, where it was renamed *The Jackie Gleason Show* and occupied the Saturday evening eight-to-nine slot for several years. A complete history of the show, along with descriptions of all the extant episodes, appears in Donna McCrohan, *The Honeymooners' Companion: The Kramdens and the Nortons Revisited* (New York: Workman, 1978). A more recent popular compendium of "Honeymooners" lore can be found in Peter Crescenti and Bob Columbe, *The Official Honeymooners Treasury* (New York: Perigee, 1985). The only book-length biographical studies of Gleason to have thus far appeared are James Bacon, *How Sweet It Is: The Jackie Gleason Story* (New York: St. Martin's, 1986) and Jim Bishop, *The Golden Ham: A Candid Biography of Jackie Gleason* (New York: Simon and Schuster, 1956).

4. M. M. Bakhtin, *Rabelais and His World,* trans. Helene Iswolsky (Bloomington: Indiana Univ. Press, 1984); Mary Douglas, *Purity and Danger: An Analysis of the Concept of Pollution and Taboo* (London: Routledge, 1984); Michel Foucault, *The History of Sexuality: Volume I: An Introduction,* trans. Robert Hurley (New York: Vintage, 1980); Elaine Scarry, *The Body in Pain: The Making and Unmaking of the World* (New York: Oxford Univ. Press, 1985); Klaus Theweleit, *Male Fantasies: Volume I: Women, Floods, Bodies, History,* trans. Stephen Conway et al. (Minneapolis: Univ. of Minnesota Press, 1987); Klaus Theweleit, *Male Fantasies: Volume II: Male Bodies: Psychoanalyzing the White Terror,* trans. Erica Carter et al. (Minneapolis: Univ. of Minnesota Press, 1989); Henri Bergson, "Laughter," in *Comedy,* ed. Wylie Sypher, trans. Fred Rothwell (New York: Doubleday, 1956); Jean-Paul Sartre, "The Comic Actor," in *Sartre on Theater,* trans. Frank Jellink (New York: Pantheon, 1976); Sigmund Freud, *Jokes and Their Relation to the Unconscious,* ed. and trans. James Strachey (New York: Norton, 1960).

5. David Marc, *Demographic Vistas* (Philadelphia: Univ. of Pennsylvania Press, 1984), 99–100. Marc's analysis of performance modes represents a variation of distinctions made in relation to cinematic acting by James Naremore's concept of the performance frame (cited in Naremore, *Acting in the Cinema* [Berkeley: Univ. of California Press, 1988]) and Stephen Heath's divisions among agent, character, person, image, and figure (cited in Heath, "Body, Voice," in *Questions of Cinema* [Bloomington: Univ. of Indiana Press, 1981], 176–93). Such a characterization of Gleason's multifaceted persona differs from Richard Dyer's concept of structured polysemy in that Dyer's notion posits a loose relationship between various parts of an actor's image, which may be activated by different audiences at different times ("what the range of things was that [a star] could be read as meaning by different audience members" [Dyer, *Stars* (London: British Film Insitute, 1979), 72]). By contrast, my discussion of Gleason's persona is predicated on the supposition that each part of his image contributes to the whole because such a part is read in terms of its relation to the others.

6. Both John Bryant and Darrell Y. Hamamoto have analyzed the Gleason persona in similarly class-related terms: John Bryant, "Emma, Lucy, and the American Situation Comedy of Manners," *Journal of Popular Culture* 13, no. 2 (fall 1979): 248–56; Darrell Y. Hamamoto, *Nervous Laughter: Television Situation Comedy and Liberal Democratic Ideology* (New York: Praeger, 1989).

7. Barbara Ehrenreich, *The Hearts of Men: American Dreams and the Flight from Commitment* (Garden City, N.Y.: Anchor Press, 1983); Benita Eisler, *Private Lives: Men and Women of the Fifties* (New York: Franklin Watts, 1986).

8. Joseph L. Pleck, *The Myth of Masculinity* (Cambridge, Mass.: MIT Press, 1981).

9. John D'Emilio and Estelle B. Freedman, *Intimate Matters: A History of Sexuality in America* (New York: Harper, 1988).

10. The "Glea Girls" appeared only during the 1950–57 season, though their presence reflected an attitude toward women that pervaded the show throughout its run.

11. The effectiveness of this contrast between Gleason and Kramden is attested to by the fact that *The Honeymooners* ranked significantly lower in the ratings when it was broadcast independently of the context created for it by the larger variety format presided over by the "real" Gleason. In more recent years the success of "Honeymooners" reruns must be viewed in the context of Gleason's unchallenged status as a larger-than-life television legend.

12. Bakhtin, *Rableais.* The Bakhtinian framework lends itself to a variety of applications. Bakhtin himself develops his conceptual scheme in terms of class rather than gender divisions, and it has been elaborated in these terms by Peter Stallybrass and Allon White. Its potential as a framework for delineating issues of gender has been explored by Mary Russo and Judith Mayne, both of whom focus on Bakhtin's discussion of popular images of the grotesque body as a pregnant hag to explore the misogyny of patriarchal texts. In a Bakhtinian analysis of pornography, Robert Stam has emphasized the implications of the concept of the grotesque body in terms of the depiction of sexuality. Yet another application of the Bakhtinian model has been carried by John Fiske in his exploration of the relationship between consumer culture and the grotesque body images represented in the phenomenon of television wrestling. My own use of Bakhtin differs from these others in its emphasis on the contrast between grotesque and classical bodies rather than on the analysis of grotesquery alone.

13. Over the years various sources on *The Honeymooners* have been suggested. Donald F. Glut and Jim Harmon, in *The Great Television Heroes* (Garden City, N.Y.: Doubleday, 1975), state that the series was based on an old burlesque routine entitled "Friendly Neighbors," presumably performed by Laurel and Hardy (148).

Bacon *(How Sweet It Is,* 92) quotes Gleason as citing the George Kelly play *The Show Off* as a further source for the show. Steve Allen's ("Jackie Gleason," in *Funny Men* [New York: Simon and Schuster, 1956], 161) excellent early appraisal of the comedian suggests yet another source in the radio show *The Bickersons.* Gleason's own earlier television incarnation as Chester B. Riley (a role later identified with William Bendix) may also have played a part in the creation of the Ralph Kramden character.

14. Bakhtin, *Rabelais,* 395.

15. David Grote, *The End of Comedy: The Sit-Com and the Comedic Tradition* (Hamden, Conn.: Archon, 1983); Mick Eaton, "Television Situation Comedy," in *Popular Film and Television,* ed. Tony Bennet et al. (London: British Film Institute, 1981), 25–26; Roger Rollin, "In the Family: Television's Re-Formulation of Comedy," *Psychocultural Review* 2, no. 4 (fall 1978).

16. Jane Feuer, "Narrative Form in American Network Television," in *High Theory/Low Culture: Analyzing Popular Culture,* ed. Colin MacCabe (Manchester: Manchester Univ. Press, 1988): 104–14.

17. Robert C. Allen, *Speaking of Soap Operas* (Chapel Hill: Univ. of North Carolina Press, 1985); John Ellis, *Visible Fictions: Cinema: Television: Video* (London: Routledge, 1982).

18. The role of Alice was originally played by Pert Kelton, who was replaced early in the series because of illness.

19. J. Hoberman (in "Ralph and Alice and Ed and Trixie," *Film Comment* 21, no. 5 [Oct. 1985]: 62–68) has argued that the kitchen setting of *The Honeymooners* represents an avoidance of the bedroom and thus sexuality. My own analysis emphasizes the kitchen as a room in which Alice rather than Ralph is in a position to exercise complete control of the surroundings.

20. Rick Altman, "Dickens, Griffith, and Film Theory Today," *South Atlantic Quarterly* 88, no. 2 (spring 1989): 321–60.

21. Peter Brooks, "Freud's Masterplot: A Model for Narrative," in *Reading for the Plot: Design and Intention in Narrative* (New York: Vintage, 1985), 17

22. Ibid., 101.

5. Sitcoms and Suburbs: Positioning the 1950s Homemaker

1. In *Women: The Longest Revolution* (London: Virago, 1984), 18, Juliet Mitchell argues that women are bound up in this contradiction: "[Women) are fundamental to the human condition, yet in their economic, social, and political roles, they are marginal. It is precisely this combination—fundamental and marginal at one and the same time—that has been fatal to them."

2. Stuart Ewen and Elizabeth Ewen, *Channels of Desire: Mass Images and the Shaping of American Consciousness* (New York: McGraw-Hill, 1982), 235.

3. Graham Murdock and Peter Golding, "Capitalism, Communication, and Class Relations," and Stuart Hall, "Culture, Media, and the 'Ideological Effect,' " in *Mass Communication and Society*, eds. James Curran, Michael Gurevitch, and Janet Woollacott (Beverly Hills: Sage, 1979), 12, 36, 336–39.

4. I began this study by considering prime-time network sitcoms with runs of three seasons or more from 1948 through 1960. Fourteen of these thirty-five sitcoms were structured around middle-class families living in suburban single-family dwellings. Eight of these fourteen defined the family unit as a breadwinner father, a homemaker mother, and children growing into adults: *The Ruggles* (1949–52), *The Aldrich Family* (1949–53), *The Stu Erwin Show* (1950–55), *The Adventures of Ozzie and Harriet* (1952–66), *Father Knows Best* (1954–62), *Leave It to Beaver* (1957–63), *The Donna Reed Show* (1958–66), and *Dennis the Menace* (1959–63).

The other six suburban family sitcoms shared some of these traits, but centered their narratives on situations or characters other than the family ensemble: *Beulah* (1950–53) focused on a black maid to an apparently broadly caricatured white middle-class family; *December Bride* (1954–61) concerned an attractive, dating widow living with her daughter's family; *The Bob Cummings Show* (1955–59) concentrated on the adventures of a playboy photographer living with his widowed sister and nephew in a suburban home; *I Married Joan* (1952–55) focused on the zany adventures of the wife of a domestic court judge; *My Favorite Husband* (1953–57) had a couple working for social status in the suburbs; and *Bachelor Father* (1957–62) featured an attorney who cared for his young niece in Beverly Hills.

This information was derived from the following sources: Tim Brooks and Earle Marsh, *The Complete Directory of Prime Time Network Television Shows, 1946-Present* (New York: Ballantine Books, 1981); Les Brown, *The New York Times Encyclopedia of Television* (New York: Times Books, 1977); Henry Castleman and Walter J. Podrazik, *The TV Schedule Book* (New York: McGraw-Hill, 1984).

5. Kenneth Rhodes, "Father of Two Families," *Cosmopolitan* Apr. 1956, 125.

6. Rhodes, "Father of Two," 125; Bob Eddy, "Private Life of a Perfect Papa," *Saturday Evening Post*, Apr. 27, 1957, 29; Brooks and Marsh, *Complete Directory*, 245–46.

7. Rhodes, "Father of Two," 125; Eddy, "Private Life," 29.

8. Newspaper critic John Crosby, quoted in Eddy, "Private Life," 29.

9. "TV's Eager Beaver," *Look*, May 27, 1958, 68.

10. Brooks and Marsh, *Complete Directory*, 340–41, 352–53.

11. Eddy, "Private Life," 29; Rhodes, "Father of Two," 126.

12. Eddy, "Private Life," 29; Rhodes, "Father of Two," 127.

13. "Jane Wyatt's Triple Threat," *Good Housekeeping*, Oct. 1959, 48.

14. Eddy, "Private Life," 176; Dolores Hayden, *Redesigning the American Dream: The Future of Housing, Work, and Family Life* (New York: Norton, 1984), 17.

15. Hayden, *Redesigning*, 40; see also Gwendolyn Wright, *Building the Dream: A Social History of Housing in America* (Cambridge: MIT Press, 1981).

16. Hayden, *Redesigning*, 35, 38, 55; Wright, *Building the Dream*, 246, 248.

17. Hayden, *Redesigning*, 41–42; Wright, *Building the Dream*, 247.

18. Wright, *Building the Dream*, 247–48.

19. Ibid., 248.

20. Hayden, *Redesigning*, 55–56; Wright, *Building the Dream*, 256.

21. Hayden, *Redesigning*, 63, 109.

22. Ibid., 17–18; Wright, 254–55.

23. "Jane Wyatt's Triple Threat," 48.

24. Danny Peary, "Remembering *Father Knows Best*," in *TV Book*, ed. Judy Fireman (New York: Workman, 1977), 173–75.

25. Long-running suburban family sitcoms that ran on network prime time during the early years of the women's movement were *Father Knows Best* (1954–62), *Leave It to Beaver* (1957–63), *The Donna Reed Show* (1958–66), *The Dick Van Dyke Show* (1961–66), *Hazel* (1961–66), *Dennis the Menace* (1959–63), and *The Adventures of Ozzie and Harriet* (1952–66). This information was obtained from Brooks and Marsh, *Complete Directory*, 15–16, 193, 199–200, 211, 245–46, 322, 423–24.

6. The Unworthy Discourse: Situation Comedy in Television

1. Mick Eaton, "Television Situation Comedy," in *Popular Film and Television*, eds. Tony Bennett, Susan Boyd-Bowman, Colin Mercer, and Janet Woollacott (London: William Collins and Sons, 1981), 26.

2. Raymond Williams, *Television: Technology and Cultural Form* (London: William Collins and Sons, 1974).

3. Rick Mitz, *The Great TV Sitcom Book* (New York: Richard Marek, 1980).

4. For a few preliminary exceptions, one might consider various essays in Richard Adler and Douglas Cater, eds., *Television as a Cultural Form* (New York: Praeger, 1976); Horace Newcomb, ed. *Television: The Critical View* (New York: Oxford Univ. Press, 1982); Horace Newcomb, *TV: The Most Popular Art* (Garden City, N.Y.: Doubleday, 1974).

5. Stephen Neale, *Genre* (London: British Film Institute, 1980).

6. See Mitz, *Great TV Sitcom Book*.

7. Will Wright, *Six Guns and Society: A Structural Analysis of the Western* (Berkeley: Univ. of California Press, 1977); Gary Gerani with Paul H. Schulman, *Fantastic Television* (New York: Harmony Books, 1977).

8. Mitz, *Great TV Sitcom Book,* 3.

9. Andre Bazin, "Qu'est-ce que le cinéma? III," in *Cinema et Sociologie* (Paris: Les Editions du Cerf, Collection 7e Art, 1961), 147.

10. Christian Metz, *Le signifiant imaginaire* (Paris: UGE, 1977). Reprinted as "Le signifiant imaginaire," *Communications* 23 (Paris: Seuil, 1977).

11. Neale, *Genre,* 19.

12. Ibid., 20.

13. Ibid.

14. Ibid., 21.

15. Ibid., 24.

16. Newcomb, *Most Popular Art,* 57–58.

17. Neale, *Genre,* 24–25.

18. Ibid., 27.

7. From Gauguin to *Gilligan's Island*

1. Original airing May 22, 1965.

2. The literature on the lure of the primitive is expansive and ever-growing. For two good introductions see Christian Marouby, *Utopie et Primitivisme* (Paris: Editions du Seuil, 1990); and Bernard Smith, *European Vision and the South Pacific: 1768–1850,* (New York/London: Oxford Univ. Press, 1960).

3. Alexander Selkirk was marooned on Mas a Tierra in 1704 and served as inspiration for countless fictional characters.

4. Jules Verne, *The Mysterious Island* (1875; reprint New York: Dodd, Mean, 1958).

5. See Pierre Macherey, "Jules Verne: The Faulty Narrative," in *A Theory of Literary Production,* trans. Geoffrey Wall (New York: Routledge, 1985). I am indebted to Macherey for his brilliant analysis of how the "instruments of production" and the formal unfolding of the novel express the content: the exhaustion of bourgeois ideology.

6. Verne, *Mysterious Island,* 341.

7. Recent literature on Gauguin explores these themes in great detail. See Abigail Solomon-Godeau, "Going Native," *Art in America* 77 (Jul. 1989): 8–29; and Griselda Pollock, *Avant-garde Gambits: Race and the Gender of Art History* (London: Thames and Hudson, 1992). For the most recent examination of the issues see Stephen Eisenman, *Gauguin's Skirt* (London: Thames and Hudson, 1996).

8. For Gauguin's quest for escape, see Griselda Pollock and Fred Orton, "Les données Bretonnantes: La prairie de répresentation," *Art History* (Sept. 1980): 314–45; and Gill Perry, "The 'Going Away': A Preparation for the Modern," in *Primitivism, Cubism, Abstraction: The Early Twentieth Century,* ed. Charles Harrison, Francis Frascina, and Gill Perry (New Haven, Conn.: Yale Univ. Press/Open Univ., 1993).

9. Abigail Solomon-Godeau, "Going Native," *Art in America* 77 (Jul. 1989): 18–29.

10. From a letter to J. F. Willumsen, Pont Aven, autumn 1890 (in Herschel Chipp, *Theories of*

Modern Art [Berkeley: Univ. of California Press, 1968], 79). For the origins of this view in the travel literature of exploration, see Smith, *European Vision.*

11. "Le rêve qui m'emmenait â Tahiti était cruellement démenti par le présent. C'est la Tahiti d'autrefois que j'amais. . . . Ma résolution vite prise: partir de Papeete, m'eloigner du centre européen" (Gauguin qtd. in George Beauté, *Paul Gauguin vu par les photographes* [N.p., 1988], 74; my translation).

12. The vast expansion of the television market in this period is well documented. For a concise overview see "The Global Impact of Television: An Overview" in Frank Coppa, *Screen and Society: The Impact of Television upon Aspects of Contemporary Civilization* (Chicago: Nelson Hall, 1979).

13. See Lawrence Murray's "Universality and Uniformity in the Popular Arts: The Impact of Television in Popular Culture" in *Screen and Society,* ed. Frank Coppa (Chicago: Nelson Hall, 1979).

14. By the 1970s, the rural havens would be replaced by the decidedly urban spaces of the "reality comedies" such as *Good Times* and *All in the Family.*

15. If the shows allow room for subversive intent, their radicalness is compromised by the characters' desires to master bourgeois values *(The Addams Family* excepted).

16. Two books are indispensable for anyone seeking information on the conception, production, and history of *Gilligan's Island*: see Sherwood Schwartz, *Inside Gilligan's Island: From Creation to Syndication* (Jefferson, N.C.: McFarland, 1988); and Sylvia Stoddard, *TV Treasures: A Companion Guide to Gilligan's Island* (New York: St. Martin's Paperback, 1990). Stoddard includes brief synopses of every script that aired from the series. Episodes of the series are available from the Turner Broadcasting System, distributed by Columbia House Video Library.

17. Stoddard, *TV Treasures.*

18. See, for example, Ram Nath, *Smoking: Third World Alert* (New York: Oxford Univ. Press 1986).

19. Schwartz, *Inside Gilligan's Island.*

20. See Schwartz, *Inside Gilligan's Island,* 1; Stoddard, *TV Treasures,* 5.

21. Schwartz, quoted in Stoddard, *TV Treasures,* 5.

22. Schwartz, *Inside Gilligan's Island,* 3.

23. The original or "lost" pilot of the show (which would have established the "pre-castaway" life of the characters) was not aired during the production of the series, much to the chagrin of Schwartz. On Oct. 16, 1992 it was aired on the Turner Network. However, the original calypso title song may be heard on the first aired episode, "Two on a Raft" (original airing Sept. 26, 1964) (see Stoddard, *TV Treasures,* 36).

24. In fact, the original episode was actually shot in Kauai, Hawaii, where the film *South Pacific* had earlier been shot (Stoddard, *TV Treasures,* 9; Schwartz, *Inside Gilligan's Island,* 47).

25. Episode no. 18, "X Marks the Spot" (original airing Jan. 31, 1965) (Stoddard, *TV Treasures,* 74). In episode no. 96, "The Pigeon" (original airing Apr. 3, 1967), we can induce that the island is "300 miles S.E. of Honolulu."

26. Verne, *Mysterious Island,* 62.

27. Macherey, "Jules Verne," 189.

28. "The light and active boy then sprang on the first branches, the arrangement of which made the ascent of the Kauri [tree] easy, and in a few minutes he arrived at the summit, which emerged from the immense plain of verdure" (Verne, *Mysterious Island,* 175).

29. On the ahistorical realm of the native, see James Clifford, "Histories of the Tribal and the Modern," in *The Predicament of Culture* (Cambridge: Harvard Univ. Press, 1988).

30. I am grateful to Lori Weintrob for suggesting this term.

31. Stoddard, *TV Treasures,* 122.

32. Episode no. 40, "Smile You're on Mars Camera" (original airing Oct. 14, 1965) (Stoddard, *TV Treasures,* 136).

33. We should bear in mind the French occupation of colonies such as Tahiti and Madagascar during the lifetimes of Gauguin and Verne, for example.

34. See Stanley D. Reid and Laurel J. Reid, "Tourism Marketing Management in Small Island Nations: A Tale of MicroDestinations," in *Global Tourist Behavior,* ed. Muzalfer Uysal (London/New York: Haworth, 1994); Brian Goodall and Gregory Ashworth, *Marketing the Tourism Industry: The Promotion of Destination Regions* (Crock Helm: 1998); John Urry, *The Tourist Gaze: Leisure and Travel in Contemporary Societies* (Thousand Oaks, Calif.: Sage, 1990).

35. See Reid and Reid, "Tourism Marketing."

36. Episode no. 51, "Erika Tiffany Smith to the Rescue" (original airing Dec. 30, 1965) (Stoddard, *TV Treasures,* 169).

37. In the original screenplay and pilot, Mary Anne is replaced by a character named "Bunny." As many viewers have observed, the early opening sequences of the show refer to the Professor and Mary Anne as "the rest," the result of a billing dispute settled later in the series.

38. See episode no. 3, "Voodoo Something to Me" (Stoddard, *TV Treasures,* 161).

39. I am grateful to Jessica Falvo for pointing out the anachronisms of the Ginger character.

40. For literature on primitivism, see Christian Marouby, *Utopie et Primitivisme* (Paris: Editions du Seuil, 1990); and Clifford, "Histories."

41. Episode no. 91, "High Man on the Totem Pole" (original airing Feb. 27, 1967) (Stoddard, *TV Treasures,* 292).

42. Episode no. 10, "Waiting for Watubi" (original airing Dec. 5, 1964) (Stoddard, *TV Treasures,* 52).

43. Only the character Jungleboy (played by the Anglo-American actor Kurt Russell) is assumed to be a friendly native. See episode no. 19, "Gilligan Meets Jungle-boy" (original airing Feb. 6, 1965) (Stoddard, *TV Treasures,* 76).

44. Episode no. 78, "Topsy Turvy" (original airing Nov. 14, 1966) (Stoddard, *TV Treasures,* 251).

45. For a fascinating account of this issue, see Annie E. Combes, *Re-inventing Africa* (New Haven, Conn.: Yale Univ. Press, 1995).

46. Episode no. 37, "Gilligan's Mother-in-Law" (original airing Sept. 16, 1965) (Stoddard, *TV Treasures,* 131).

47. Episode no. 98, "Gilligan, the Goddess" (original airing Apr. 17, 1967) (Stoddard, *TV Treasures,* 304).

48. Episode no. 5, "Wrongway Feldman" (original airing Oct. 24, 1964) (Stoddard, *TV Treasures,* 42). See also episode no. 24, "The Return of Wrongway Feldman."

49. Stoddard, *TV Treasures,* 40

50. Episode no. 15, "So Sorry My Island Now" (original airing Jan. 9, 1965) (Stoddard, *TV Treasures,* 62).

51. Episode no. 30, "Forget Me Not" (original airing Apr. 24, 1964) (Stoddard, *TV Treasures,* 96).

302 | Notes to Pages 127–134

52. In Episode no. 39, "The Little Dictator" (original airing Sept. 30, 1965), the ex-president of the Republica Ecuario lands on the island with aggressive intentions. In Episode no. 70, "Gilligan vs. Gilligan" (original airing Sept. 12, 1966), the danger comes in the form of a Russian spy altered by plastic surgery to resemble Gilligan.

53. Episode no. 68, "Meet the Meteor" (original airing Apr. 28, 1966) (Stoddard, *TV Treasures,* 210).

54. Episode no. 71, "Pass the Vegetables, Please" (original airing Sept. 26, 1966) (Stoddard, *TV Treasures,* 238).

55. Stoddard, *TV Treasures,* 327–41.

8. "Is This What You Mean by Color TV?" Race, Gender, and Contested Meanings in *Julia*

1. David Caute, *The Year of the Barricades: A Journey Through 1968* (New York: Harper and Row, 1988).

2. *Amos 'n' Andy* remained in syndication until 1966. NBC attempted a short-lived variety show with Nat King Cole in 1957.

3. Les Brown, *Television: The Business Behind the Box* (New York: Harcourt Brace Jovanovich, 1971), 78–79.

4. J. Fred MacDonald, *Blacks and White TV: Afro-Americans in Television since 1948* (Chicago: Nelson-Hall Publishers, 1983), 116.

5. MacDonald, *Blacks and White TV,* 117. *Julia* was also criticized by the U.S. Commission on Civil Rights in its influential publication *Window Dressing on the Set: Women and Minorities in Television* (Washington, D.C.: U.S. Commission on Civil Rights, Aug. 1977).

6. The Hal Kanter Papers are located at the Wisconsin Center Historical Archives, State Historical Society, Madison, Wisc. The Kanter papers contain primarily final draft scripts for all the *Julia* episodes; Kanter's personal correspondence, production materials for the series, and ratings information; and a large selection of viewer letters. Most of the letters to which I will be referring later in this paper are filed in folders labeled "fan letters, favorable" and "fan letters, unfavorable." Some viewer letters are also scattered among Kanter's correspondence folders.

7. This script is filed in the Hal Kanter papers, Box 18.

8. This script is filed in the Hal Kanter papers, Box 19.

9. This script is filed in the Hal Kanter papers, Box 18.

10. Stuart Hall, "Encoding/ Decoding," in *Culture, Media, Language,* ed. Stuart Hall, Dorothy Hobson, Andrew Lowe, and Paul Willis (London: Hutchinson, 1980), 128–38.

11. Sixty-one of the letters came from married women and twenty-three from single women or those whose marital status was unidentifiable. Thirty-three letters came from men. The rest were either unidentifiable by gender or were from children and young people. The preponderance of women viewers is mirrored in ratings materials located in a ratings folder in Hal Kanter papers, Box 18. A breakdown of the *Julia* audience for a two-week period ending Sept. 28, 1969, showed that women between the ages of eighteen and forty-nine formed the largest bulk of the audience, followed by female teens. Men between the ages of eighteen and forty-nine formed the smallest share of the audience.

12. Carlo Ginzburg, "Morelli, Freud, and Sherlock Holmes: Clues and Scientific Method," *History Workshop* 9 (spring 1980): 5–36. Ginzburg argues that for historians a conjectural approach (the analysis of clues) "holds the potential for understanding society. In a social structure of

ever-increasing complexity like that of advanced capitalism, befogged by ideological murk, any claim to systematic knowledge appears as a flight of foolish fancy. To acknowledge this is not to abandon the idea of totality. On the contrary; the existence of deep connection which explains superficial phenomena can be confirmed when it is acknowledged that direct knowledge of such a connection is impossible. Reality is opaque; but there are certain points—clues, signs—which allow us to decipher it" (27).

13. All of the following viewer letters, unless marked otherwise, are in the Hal Kanter papers, Box 18.

14. The writers of these letters are, respectively, a male viewer from DuBois, Penn., a female viewer from Colton, Calif., and a female viewer from New York City.

15. "Wonderful World of Color," *Time,* Dec. 13, 1968, 70.

16. Robert Lewis Shayon, " 'Julia': Breakthrough or Letdown?" *Saturday Review,* Apr. 20, 1968, 49.

17. Robert Lewis Shayon, " 'Julia' Symposium: An Opportunity Lost," *Saturday Review,* May 25, 1968, 36.

18. Shayon, " 'Julia' Symposium," 36.

19. Ibid.

20. Robert Lewis Shayon, " 'Julia': A Political Relevance?" *Saturday Review,* Jul. 20, 1968, 37.

21. For an examination of white as norm see Richard Dyer's "White," *Screen* 29, no. 4 (autumn 1988): 44–64. Dyer observes, "In the realm of categories, black is always marked as a colour . . . and is always particularising; whereas white is not anything really, not an identity, not a particularising quality, because it is everything—white is no colour because it is all colours" (45).

22. Richard Warren Lewis, "The Importance of Being Julia," *TV Guide,* Dec. 14, 1968, 26.

23. Mrs. Medgar Evers, "A Tale of Two Julias," *Ladies' Home Journal,* May 1970, 60–65.

24. "Diahann Carroll's Juggling Act," *Good Housekeeping,* May 1969, 38–51.

25. Betty Friedan's groundbreaking text of second-wave feminism, *The Feminine Mystique* (New York: Dell, 1963), analyzed the discontented housewife stories that began to crop up in women's magazines in the early 1960s. Despite her enormously influential work, Friedan's analysis did not appear to affect the type of stories published in magazines such as *Ladies' Home Journal.* The blindness of this particular magazine to the emergent women's liberation movement was made plain in March 1970, when over a hundred feminists occupied the magazine's offices demanding sweeping editorial and policy changes. See Alice Echols, *Daring to Be Bad: Radical Feminism in America, 1967–1975* (Minneapolis: Univ. of Minnesota Press, 1989), 195–97.

26. See, for instance, John Fiske, *Television Culture* (London and New York; Methuen, 1987) and *Understanding Popular Culture* (Boston: Unwin Hyman, 1989).

27. MacDonald, *Blacks and White TV,* 138–39.

28. Thirteen women, one man, and three children or young people identified themselves as black. There was also a group of thirteen letters from an inner-city grade school writing class. From the tone of the letters, I suspect the class was predominantly made up of black children.

29. Jacqueline Bobo, "The Color Purple: Black Women as Cultural Readers," in *Female Spectators: Looking at Film and Television,* ed. E. Deidre Pribram (London and New York: Verso, 1988), 90–109.

30. David Morley, *The Nationwide Audience* (Chapel Hill and London: Univ. of North Carolina Press, 1985), 14.

31. This letter is located in the Hal Kanter papers, Box 1, among Kanter's general correspon-

dence. A significant number of letters from self-identifying black viewers can be found in this general correspondence rather than in the fan letter files.

32. Hal Kanter papers, Box 1.

33. Ibid.

34. *Ebony* (Nov. 1968), 56–58.

35. *Saturday Review,* Apr. 20, 1968, 49.

36. Marilyn Diane Fife, "Black Images in American TV: The First Two Decades," *The Black Scholar,* Nov. 1974: 13–14.

37. For an overview of this debate see Linda Gordon, "On Difference," in *Women, the State, and Welfare,* ed. Linda Gordon (Madison: Univ. of Wisconsin Press, 1990).

38. See Angela Y. Davis, *Women, Race, and Class* (New York: Vintage Books, 1981), and Jacqueline Jones, *Labor of Love, Labor of Sorrow: Black Women, Work, and the Family, from Slavery to the Present* (New York: Vintage Books, 1985).

39. See E. Franklin Frazier, *The Family: Its Function and Destiny* (New York: Harper and Row, 1959), and his classic statement on black families, *The Negro Family in the United States* (Chicago: Univ. of Chicago Press, 1939). For a good introduction to the various debates about the black family in the 1960s and early 1970s, see John H. Bracey, Jr., August Meier, and Elliott Rudwick, eds., *Black Matriarchy: Myth or Reality?* (Belmont, Calif.: Wadsworth, 1971).

40. Daniel P. Moynihan, *The Negro Family: The Case for National Action* (Washington, D.C.: U.S. Department of Labor, Office of Planning and Research, Mar. 1965).

41. Moynihan in Bracey, Meier, and Rudwick, *Black Matriarchy,* 140.

42. See, for instance, noted black sociologist Andrew Billingsley's book *Black Families in White America* (Englewood Cliffs, N.J.: Prentice-Hall, Inc., 1968), 199–202.

43. Black feminists have more recently begun to explode this myth. For a critique of Frazier, Moynihan, and other discourses on the black family, see Bonnie Thornton Dill, "The Dialectics of Black Womanhood," in *Feminism and Methodology,* ed. Sandra Harding (Bloomington and Indianapolis: Indiana Univ. Press, 1984), 97–108.

44. Todd Gitlin discusses the "turn toward relevance" in network programming in the wake of the social movements of the 1960s in his book, *Inside Prime Time* (New York: Pantheon Books, 1983), 203–20.

Part Three: Television in the 1970s

1. See Jane Feuer, "Melodrama, Serial Form, and Television Today," *Screen* 25, no. 1 (1984): 4–16.

9. *The Mary Tyler Moore Show*: Women at Home and at Work

1. Michèle Barrett and Mary McIntosh, *The Anti-Social Family* (London: Verso, 1982), 31.

2. Barbara Welter, "The Cult of True Womanhood: 1820–60," *American Quarterly* 18, no. 162 (1966), 152.

3. Fabian Linden, *Women: A Demographic Social and Economic Presentation* (New York: The Conference Board, 1973), 22–23.

4. Dwight Whitney, "You've Come a Long Way, Baby: Happy Hotpoint Is Now Mary Tyler Moviestar," *TV Guide,* Sep. 19, 1970, 34.

5. Dick Adler, "The Writer Wore Hotpants," *TV Guide*, Jul. 15, 1972; Joseph Finnigan, "Cameraperson in Hotpants," *TV Guide*, Sep. 9, 1972.

6. Caroline Bird, "What's Television Doing for Fifty Percent of Americans?" *TV Guide*, Feb. 27, 1971.

7. Diane Rosen, "TV and the Single Girl," *TV Guide*, Nov. 6, 1971, 12.

8. Letty Cottin Pogrebin, "Woman's Place: A Personal View of What It's Like to Grow Up Female," *TV Guide*, Sep. 1, 1973.

9. Horace Newcomb and Robert S. Alley, eds., *The Producer's Medium: Conversations with Creators of American TV* (New York: Oxford Univ. Press, 1983), 216.

10. Ellen Sherman, "Femme Scribes Cop Top Jobs," *Ms.*, Dec. 1974.

11. Most of the episodes cited in this essay are from the collection that was donated to the Wisconsin Center for Film and Theater Research in Madison, Wisconsin. I am grateful for the permission granted to study these tapes and films, and thank Ms. Lynn Dietrich at MTM Enterprises. I am also most grateful to Ms Maxine Fleckner, the director of the Wisconsin Film Archive, for her resourcefulness and guidance. The episodes are titled in the MTM collection and I have used these throughout the essay. But the reader may note that these titles do not appear in *TV Guide* for the weekly listings and are not included in the credits of the shows as televised.

10. I Love *Laverne and Shirley*: Lesbian Narratives, Queer Pleasures, and Television Sitcoms

1. Vivian Vance, "Lucy and I Adored Each Other—Then People Began to Whisper That We Were Lovers," *National Enquirer*, Aug. 29, 1989, 20. There is background commentary in this article by an anonymous *Enquirer* staff writer that Vance clearly did not write.

2. Ibid.

3. Ibid., 20–21.

4. One of the more recent uses of Lucy and Ethel that capitalizes upon their lesbian aura (as well as their gay cult status) is an ad for AIDS Project Los Angeles, which features a still of the pair looking at each other as they struggle to carry a large fish (from the "Deep-Sea Fishing" episode, Nov. 19, 1956). The main caption, "Be a Buddy and Help Someone Out," is followed by copy beginning: "What makes life so much better is sharing it with a Buddy. Laughing. Crying. Talking. Holding. Going to dinner. Taking in a movie. Having fun." This public service ad has been featured in issues of the gay magazine *Genre* (the Apr./May 1991 issue, for example), as well as in other gay and lesbian publications.

5. Robert H. Deming, *"Kate and Allie*: 'New Women' and the Audience's Television Archive," *Camera Obscura* 16 (Jan. 1988): 157.

6. Representative of the publicity accorded Burke's "feud" with *Designing Women*'s cast and crew, and her subsequent firing, is *People* magazine's coverage by Elizabeth Sporkin, Lois Armstrong, Tom Cunnett, and Jack Kelly (36, no. 3 [Jul. 29, 1991], 46–51), which uses "Why They Dumped Delta" as the front-page headline for its "Odd Woman Out" story—a title evoking that of Ann Bannon's famous lesbian novel *Odd Girl Out*.

7. Quoted in Charles Higham and Joel Greenberg, *The Celluloid Muse: Hollywood Directors Speak* (New York: Signet/New American Library, 1972), 63.

8. The following is a partial list of American situation comedies I would consider lesbian sitcoms: *The Girls*, 1950, CBS; *I Love Lucy*, 1951–57, CBS; *My Friend Irma*, 1952–54, CBS; *It's Always Jan*, 1955–56, CBS; *Those Whiting Girls*, 1955–57, CBS; *The Gale Storm Show*, 1956–60,

CBS/ABC; *How to Marry a Millionaire,* 1957–59, syndicated; *My Sister Eileen,* 1960–61, CBS; *The Lucy Show,* 1962–68, CBS; *The Patty Duke Show,* 1963–66, ABC; *Petticoat Junction,* 1963–70, CBS; *Bewitched,* 1964–72, ABC; *The Flying Nun,* 1967–70, ABC; *The Mothers-in-Law,* 1967–69, NBC; *Here's Lucy,* 1968–74, CBS; *The Mary Tyler Moore Show,* 1970–77, CBS; *Rhoda,* 1974–78, CBS; *Phyllis,* 1975–77, CBS; *Alice,* 1976–85, CBS; *Laverne and Shirley,* 1976–83, ABC; *The Betty White Show,* 1977–78, CBS; *Sugar Time!,* 1977–78, ABC; *The Roller Girls,* 1978, NBC; *Goodtime Girls,* 1980, ABC; *It's a Living,* 1980–82, ABC and syndicated; *Private Benjamin,* 1981–83, CBS; *Square Pegs,* 1982–83, CBS; *Kate and Allie* 1984–89, CBS; *The Golden Girls,* 1985–92, NBC; 227, 1986–89, NBC; *Designing Women,* 1986–93, CBS; *Roseanne,* 1988–97, ABC; *Sugar 'n' Spice,* 1990, NBC; *Babes,* 1990–91, Fox; *Princesses,* 1991, CBS; *Sibs,* 1991–92, ABC; *Good and Evil,* 1991, ABC; *Nurses,* 1991–94, NBC; *Room for Two,* 1992–93, ABC; *Golden Palace,* 1992–93, CBS.

9. Adrienne Rich, "Compulsory Heterosexuality and Lesbian Existence," in *Powers of Desire: The Politics of Sexuality,* ed. Ann Sitnow, Christine Stansell, and Sharon Thompson (New York: Monthly Review Press, 1983), 192. To a certain extent, queer rhetorical-political strategies have led me to adopt and adapt Rich's lesbian continuum in this section, particularly because it rejects the idea that what is called "homosocial" is really fully distinct from what is called "homosexual." At present, straight culture's careful maintenance of the line between homosociality and homosexuality only encourages homophobia and heterocentrism, as the homosocial is always considered preferable to the homosexual. If there wasn't some problem about being labeled "homosexual," straight culture wouldn't care if certain straight personal relationships and cultural representations were misperceived as being queer. As this clearly is not the case until there are pervasive signs that queer labels have ceased to be hysteria-inducing to straights, any same-sex intensities in life or in cultural representation I will call "homosexual," "lesbian," "gay," "bisexual," or "queer." Lesbian and gay maintenance of the homosexual/heterosexual line is another matter, as this is concerned with keeping same-sex sex as the central definer of queerness in order to prevent the cultural and political neutralization and domestication of lesbianism and gayness by straight culture.

10. Ibid., 192.

11. Another aspect of specifically lesbian cultural spectatorship practices I will not directly address here is readings of characters and shows developed around erotic attraction and desire. Gail Sausser, in the "Movie and T.V. Heart-Throbs" section of *Lesbian Etiquette* (Trumansburg, N.Y.: Crossing, 1986), includes some brief comments that highlight these types of lesbian pleasures in television situation comedies: "I also had a crush on Morticia Addams (Carolyn Jones) of The Addams Family. You've got to love a woman who has pet man-eating plants and only lets her husband kiss her hand. . . . Do you remember *The Patty Duke Show*? Patty's charms never overwhelmed me, but I do know certain lesbians who were in love with her. I loved Elizabeth Montgomery on *Bewitched,* but like her mother, Endora, I never could understand what she saw in 'Der-wood.' Barbara Eden on *I Dream of Jeannie* was another crush of mine, no matter how politically incorrect her role was. It's amazing to think of the latter two women's roles: both had incredible magical powers, but chose to be subservient to humbling men who ordered them around. And speaking of politically incorrect, I won't mention the name of the person who had a crush on Tina Louise a. k. a. 'Ginger' on *Gilligan's Island,* but I do see it as a forerunner to her current crush on Joan Collins" (59). It is clear from Sausser's list that lesbian erotic pleasures in situation comedies are not necessarily focused on those programs I am calling "lesbian sitcoms," whose women-centered narrative

construction encourages other types of queer audience positioning and pleasure in nonlesbian audiences.

12. Marilyn R. Farwell, "Heterosexual Plots and Lesbian Subtexts: Toward a Theory of Lesbian Narrative Space," in *Lesbian Texts and Contexts: Radical Revisions,* ed. Karla Jay and Joanne Glasgow (New York and London: New York Univ. Press, 1990), 95.

13. Mimi White, "Ideological Analysis and Television," in *Channels of Discourse,* ed. Robert Allen (Chapel Hill: Univ. of North Carolina Press, 1987), 162.

14. Not mentioned in this section are those gay readings of many of these sitcoms which interpret the women characters as gay men. Developed within cultural contexts that foster (imposed or chosen) cross-gender identification, these "women-as-gay men" readings of mass culture have been, and still are, common in gay culture.

15. Christine Holmlund, "When Is a Lesbian Not a Lesbian?: The Lesbian Continuum and the Mainstream Femme Film," *Camera Obscura* 25/26 (Jan.-May 1991): 145–46.

16. Danae Clark, "Commodity Lesbianism," *Camera Obscura* 25/26 (Jan.-May 1991): 192.

17. Promotional advertisement. *TV Guide* (Central Pennsylvania edition), Apr. 11–17, 1992, 148–49.

18. I borrow the term "hypothetical lesbian" from Chris Straayer's "Voyage en douce, entre nous: The Hypothetical Lesbian Heroine," *Jump Cut* 35 (1990): 50.

19. Between *I Love Lucy* and *The Lucy Show, The Lucy-Desi Comedy Hour* ran for three seasons (1957–60) and thirteen episodes. These shows most often relegated Ethel (and Fred) to the sidelines, while featuring guest stars, often celebrity couples: Ida Lupino/Howard Duff, June Haver/Fred MacMurray, Betty Grable/Harry James. While their narratives were more straight-couple oriented, these programs occasionally recalled *I Love Lucy*'s Lucy-Ethel lesbian narrative and performative dynamics, as when Lucy forms temporary alliances with her women guest stars in order to get around their husbands. In the "Lucy Wins a Racehorse" episode (Feb. 3, 1958), for example, Betty Grable lends Lucy the money she needs to care for a horse Little Ricky wants, but which "Big" Ricky wants to get rid of. "Betty, you're just what I've been looking for," a grateful Lucy exclaims, "an Ethel Mertz with money!"

20. During the run of *The Lucy Show,* Viv and/or Lucy were involved in many activities that could be read in specifically lesbian cultural terms: playing softball, coaching sports teams, doing home repair work, volunteer firefighting, playing competitive pool, and being WAVES in World War II. Viv also played Antony to Lucy's Cleopatra in an all-woman, volunteer firefighter production of Shakespeare's Antony and Cleopatra. A 1992 promotional ad for reruns of *The Lucy Show* on the Nickelodeon cable channel had an announcer intoning "Lucy . . . Vivian . . . Two single women, living on the edge—together" over a shot of Vivian tumbling on top of Lucy. It makes a person wonder if the "double pink triangle" diamond Nickelodeon used as part of its "Nick at Night" logo during this ad was just a coincidence.

21. Patricia Mellencamp, "Situation Comedy, Feminism, and Freud: Discourses of Gracie and Lucy," in *Studies in Entertainment: Critical Approaches to Mass Culture,* ed. Tania Modleski (Bloomington: Indiana Univ. Press, 1986), 90. (See also chap. 3 of this book.) (Ball often remarked that her favorite impersonation was of Tallulah Bankhead. She even hired Bankhead for an episode of *The Lucy-Desi Comedy Hour* titled "The Celebrity Next Door" (Dec. 3, 1957). This identification with Bankhead through imitating her voice is interesting as it suggests something of what is covered up in the narratives and major women characters of *I Love Lucy, The Lucy Show,*

and *Here's Lucy.* In her discussion of the narrativization of the female voice in films as a process that carefully contains that voice by synchronizing it with and suturing it to the body, Kaja Silverman mentions certain transgressions from this patriarchal auditory regime: "This vocal corporalization is to be distinguished from that which gives the sounds emitted by Mae West, Marlene Dietrich, or Lauren Bacall their distinctive quality, since in each of these last instances it is a 'male' rather than 'female' body which is deposited in the voice. Otherwise stated, the lowness and huskiness of each of these three voices connote masculinity rather than femininity, so that the voice seems to exceed the gender of the body from which it proceeds. That excess confers upon it a privileged status vis-à-vis both language and sexuality" *(The Acoustic Mirror* [Bloomington: Indiana Univ. Press, 1988], 61). Of course, Tallulah Bankhead could be added to this list of vocally "masculine" transgressors. Her well-documented private life was also marked by "excess," much of it relating to her bisexuality and her affinity for queers and queer cultures. Ball's penchant for imitating Bankhead finds outlets on her series, as in one episode of *I Love Lucy,* "Lucy Fakes Illness" (Jan. 28, 1952), where Bankhead's is one personality that emerges when Lucy pretends to have amnesia (another is Katharine Hepburn). Pretense or not, however, the Bankhead model, with its subversive implications for gender and sexuality, is revealed as being inside Lucy.

22. This narrative pattern of marginalizing men and emphasizing women-bonding in these situation comedies' maternity and birth episodes reflects existing Western cultural practices which, until recently, have confined men (apart from doctors and their assistants) to the "waiting room." *I Love Lucy* acknowledges this male marginalization and alienation, with its attendant woman-envy, in the "Ricky Has Labor Pains" episode (May 1, 1953). During Lucy's sixth month, Ricky develops periods of nausea, dizzy spells, and stomach cramps. A doctor tells Lucy that Ricky's symptoms are psychosomatic, and suggests she make him the "center of attention" for a while. So Lucy arranges a "daddy shower" with the help of Ethel's husband, Fred. But, disguised as male reporters, Lucy and Ethel invade the all-male space of the "daddy shower," reminding us that in lesbian sitcom narratives, men can become the "center of attention" only temporarily.

23. Adrienne Rich has some provocative thoughts about maternal erotics: "If women are the earliest sources of emotional caring and physical nurture for both female and male children, it would seem logical, from a feminist perspective at least, to pose the following questions: whether the search for love and tenderness in both sexes does not originally lead toward women; *why in fact women would ever redirect that search.* . . . I doubt that enough feminist scholars and theorists have taken the pains to acknowledge the societal forces that wrench women's emotional and erotic energies away from themselves and other women and from women-identified values" (183). Implicit in Rich's words here is the question of why more, if not all, women aren't lesbian. The comedies I am treating here create situations in which the women all are, in a manner of speaking, lesbian, if not "actually," then in the way their relationships develop, and are developed by, narratives that position audiences to take queer pleasures in the series.

24. Serafina Bathrick, "The Mary Tyler Moore Show: Women at Home and at Work," in *MTM: 'Quality Television',* ed. Jane Feuer, Paul Kerr, and Tise Vahimagi (London: British Film Institute, 1984), 99–131, provides an excellent straight feminist analysis of the series. While Bathrick sees Mary as a character who moves between an all-woman "family" at home and a male-dominated patriarchal "family" at work, she consistently emphasizes "the ways in which Mary's female friendships are privileged in this series," with Phyllis and Rhoda providing "particularly significant alternatives to romantic or marital relations" (118).

25. One male character on *The Mary Tyler Moore Show* who is referred to constantly, but

whom the audience never sees, is Phyllis's husband, Dr. Lars Lindstrom. This narrative decision makes Mary's home life totally women-centered, with dates and male coworkers becoming only temporary visitors.

26. Richard Corliss, "Happy Days Are Here Again," in *Television: The Critical View*, ed. Horace Newcomb (New York: Oxford Univ. Press, 1982), 70.

27. The narrative use of gays and gayness as markers of another queer agenda is common in lesbian sitcoms. Perhaps this reflects the ways in which lesbianism has been more persistently rendered invisible in straight culture than gayness has been. As a result, mass culture texts often have gays and gayness stand in for all queer identities and all forms of queerness. From *The Mary Tyler Moore Show* onward, it is a rare lesbian sitcom that doesn't invoke or represent gayness regularly, while repressing any unmistakable codes of lesbianism entirely, relegating lesbianism to suggestive jokes, or containing it in those special "lesbian episodes" referred to earlier in this section. Perhaps more frequent lesbian innuendo or more overt lesbian representation on these shows would threaten many viewers by making manifest the queerness of their pleasures in these shows.

As for specific examples of gayness also representing a show's more fundamental lesbian queerness, besides those connotative readings of Ted and Murray as gay, *The Mary Tyler Moore Show* plays with gay innuendo in the "Menage-à-Phyllis" episode (discussed in this chapter), and provides Phyllis with a gay brother who becomes fast friends with Rhoda, which is perhaps the program's acknowledgment of Rhoda's status as a cult figure for the show's gay audience. *Laverne and Shirley* has gay characters appear in various episodes—the actor in the army training film, a snooty boutique salesman to whom Shirley says, "We girls wouldn't want to buy something from a man who smells like the inside of my grandmother's purse." Many viewers also read upstairs neighbors Lenny and Squiggy as a gay pair. *The Golden Girls* has a gay houseboy on its pilot episode, and Blanche's gay brother appears on two shows, once with his future male spouse. Anthony Bouvier, the one regular male character on *Designing Women*, besides being black, is also heavily gay-coded, with most of the innuendo centering on his time in prison.

During its 1990–91 season, *Roseanne* gives the title character a gay boss in a long-term relationship (the character was dropped after the 1991–92 season). Predictably enough, in terms of lesbian sitcom narrative repression and substitution, these men are introduced on an episode that takes great pains to heterosexualize Roseanne's tomboy-butch, baseball-playing daughter Darlene by having her tell her mother that she likes boys, but she refuses to go to a formal dance because all the fuss involved in dressing feminine makes her feel strange. Roseanne's police officer (and, later, truck driver) sister, Jackie, had already undergone some heterosexualizing in the previous season, but Roseanne's comment to Darlene in response to her decision not to go to the dance reminds us of what is being repressed: "I think you've been hanging out with Aunt Jackie too much!"

Intertexual events have been at work since the series' premiere that both reveal and support the lesbian charge of *Roseanne*. For example, Laurie Metcalf, who plays Jackie, was cast as a (sympathetic) lesbian police officer in *Internal Affairs* (1990, Paramount, Mike Figgis), a film that also has a gay erotic text. Then there are two pieces that appeared in issues of *Parade* magazine (a Sunday supplement in many local American newspapers). In the Sep. 15, 1991, section "Personality Parade," a reader asks columnist Walter Scott, "With all the concern about AIDS, I was surprised when two gay characters turned up on the 'Roseanne' show. My husband says this proves what he's always suspected—that Roseanne is gay. I don't believe it. Who's right?" Scott's answer, in part, is: "You are. Roseanne Barr Arnold's real-life brother and sister are homosexuals, however, and she says, 'My show seeks to portray various slices of life, and homosexuals are a reality' " (2). Lynn

Minton's Jan. 26, 1992, "What We Care About," a feature column in *Parade*'s "Fresh Voices," devoted to teenagers' questions and viewpoints, asks Sara Gilbert, who plays Darlene, "Are you a
tomboy?" While Gilbert answers "no," she admits "most of my friends are guys . . . with them I
feel comfortable. If one of them shows up, I can, like, roll out of bed and not have to take a shower"
(4). This sounds just like something Darlene would say—and reflects the character's general attitude toward boys on the show, which is friendly but not romantic. Later in 1992 Gilbert was featured in the film *Poison Ivy* (New Line, Kati Shea Ruben), which places her character in a
lesbian-suggestive relationship with Drew Barrymore.

28. Vince Waldron, *Classic Sitcoms* (New York: Macmillan, 1987), 151.

29. *Mary Tyler Moore* spinoffs *Rhoda, Phyllis,* and *The Betty White Show* each developed lesbian
narratives. *Rhoda* is particularly interesting because the first show simultaneously establishes the
series' potential narrative center as the relationship between Rhoda, her sister Brenda (whom she
lives with), and their mother, while it also introduces a steady romantic interest for Rhoda in the
form of Joe Gerard, the owner of a wrecking company. Joe and Rhoda marry in the first season,
and episodes in the next two seasons reflect the tensions between the demands of lesbian narrative
construction and the requirements of a heterosexual-couple sitcom. After a short, frustrating period as a housewife, Rhoda begins her own window-dressing business with an old school friend,
Myrna Morgenstein. And she still maintains close ties with her sister (they live in the same building) and with her mother.

However, it soon became apparent to the show's creators that Rhoda (and actress Valerie
Harper) wasn't the only one frustrated with the character's married life. CBS president Fred Silverman felt that the idea of Rhoda marrying was "the worst programming idea ever . . . the moment
she fell in love and got married the whole series lost its bite. The source of all the comedic conflict
on the show was gone. The stunt hurt the show" (quoted in Feuer, Kerr, and Vahimagi, *MTM*,
209). While the show was initially popular with audiences, second thoughts among Rhoda's producers and writers convinced them to gradually move the show back to its (lesbian) roots. Joe and
Rhoda separate, then divorce. During Joe and Rhoda's estrangement, airline stewardess Sally Gallagher is introduced as Rhoda's new friend. But Rhoda's last two seasons reveal a series only uncer-
tainly committed to developing its lesbian narrative space, as Las Vegas entertainer Johnny
Venture becomes Rhoda's sometime boyfriend, Sally and Brenda begin going out on regular dates
with Gary Levy, and Brenda develops a steady relationship with an accordion player.

30. Waldron, *Classic Sitcoms,* 141, 147, 153, 159, 166, 173.

31. For anyone interested in exploring butch and femme cultures, styles, and attitudes, a good
place to start is Joan Nestle, ed., *The Persistent Desire: A Butch-Femme Reader* (Boston: Alyson,
1992). In addition, three valuable articles are Joan Nesde's "The Fem Question," in *Pleasures and
Dangers: Exploring Female Sexuality,* ed. Carole Vance (London: Pandora, 1989), 232–41; Sue-
Ellen Case's "Toward a Butch-Femme Aesthetic," *Discourse* 11, no. 1 (fall-winter 1988–89):
55–71; and Madeline Davis and Elizabeth Lapovsky Kennedy's "Oral History and the Study of
Sexuality in the Lesbian Community: Buffalo, New York, 1940–1960," in *Hidden from History:
Reclaiming the Lesbian and Gay Past,* ed. Martin Bauml Duberman, Martha Vicinus, and George
Chauncey, Jr. (New York: New American Library, 1989), 426–40. Joan Nestle's autobiographical
A Restricted Country (Ithaca, N.Y.: Firebrand, 1987) also contains a wealth of observations and in-
sights regarding butch and femme identities and relationships.

A production history note by Richard Corliss in "Happy Days" suggests that a heterosexualized version of butch-femme dynamics may have been in the minds of *Laverne and Shirley* cocreators Garry Marshall and Mark Rothman as they devised Cindy Williams's Shirley Feeney as a character "who could express both slapstick and sentiment, who was both Lucille Ball and Mary Tyler Moore. The idea here was to put a Mary Richards character into Lucy situations, and to play her adorable fastidiousness against a more pragmatic good-time-Charlotte colleague: Penny Marshall's Laverne DeFazio" (72). This quote also makes it clear that Marshall and Rothman understood the sitcom lineage of their show and its characters.

32. A similar moment occurs at the end of *Gentlemen Prefer Blondes* (1953, Twentieth Century-Fox, Howard Hawks) when, after a double wedding, the camera tracks in from a shot of the two male-female couples to frame a tight two shot of best friends Lorelei Lee (Marilyn Monroe) and Dorothy Shaw (Jane Russell) exchanging tender looks as the film fades to black. For a good lesbian-feminist reading of this film, see Lucy Arbuthnot and Gail Seneca's "Pre-text and Text in *Gentlemen Prefer Blondes*," *Film Reader* 5 (1982): 13–23, reprinted in *Issues in Feminist Film Criticism,* ed. Patricia Erens (Bloomington and Indianapolis: Indiana Univ. Press, 1990), 112–25.

33. Marriage is usually a threat to the narrative pleasures of lesbian sitcoms. This holds true even if the major women characters are already married when the series debuts. The comic high points on *I Love Lucy* occur when Ethel and Lucy ignore, resist, or temporarily escape the demands of being wives. On lesbian sitcoms featuring unmarried women, the marriage of one of them often signals that a series will end in a season or two, as was the case with *Laverne and Shirley, Kate and Allie,* and even *Rhoda,* in a way. Perhaps learning from its predecessors, *The Golden Girls* ended its seven-year run with Dorothy's wedding, about which Bea Arthur (who plays Dorothy) commented, "That's the way they're going to get rid of me—which is better, I guess, than having me killed off in a flaming car wreck or something" *(Entertainment Tonight,* Apr. 15, 1992, ABC).

Even talk of an engagement on these sitcoms becomes a narrative crisis for the women characters and a source of anxiety for viewers, who consciously or not realize an engagement or a marriage would change these women's relationships to each other, and therefore their own relationship to the show—and not for the better. When it comes down to it, any sort of romantic or sexual situation with a man on these programs, including dating, is disruptive. Appearances by ex-husbands are different because they usually strengthen the bonds between women by reinforcing the undesirability of heterosexual unions, as *Kate and Allie, The Golden Girls,* and *Designing Women* have shown.

34. Since Laverne's "company" on the last years of the show is almost exclusively male, the series develops an interesting gay text, with the characters Lenny and Squiggy (already read as a gay pair by some viewers), Carmine, and Mr. De Fazio taking up more and more narrative space. A number of episodes feature these male characters while marginalizing Laverne, or positioning her as "one of the boys" butchly performing comic stunt work and rough physical comedy. There are a few episodes during the final seasons that attempt to recreate the butch-femme dynamics of *Laverne and Shirley* by substituting Rhonda, the blonde starlet-next-door, for Shirley. One episode has Laverne possessed by the spirit of a man during a seance. While in this cross-gender mental state, Laverne kisses Rhonda.

35. The term "compulsory heterosexuality" is from Adrienne Rich's "Compulsory Heterosexuality."

36. For typical popular press coverage of the Burke–*Designing Women* situation, see articles such as Sporkin et al., "Odd Woman Out"; Mary Murphy and Frank Swertlow, "Delta Re-

designed," *TV Guide,* Jul. 4–10, 1992, 10–16; Susan Littwin, "Not Just Whistlin' Dixie," *TV Guide,* Dec. 15, 1990, 4–5, 7, 9–10; Elaine Warren, "Shake-Up at the Sugarbakers: It's Now Re-Designing Women," *TV Guide,* Sep. 21, 1991, 10–17.

37. This reference to Lucy and Ethel is only one of a number of allusions in *Designing Women* to the series' lesbian sitcom predecessors. For example, the end of one episode finds Mary Jo, Charlene, and Julia deciding to protect Suzanne from possible arrest by saying they were with her when a fire broke out at the Design House exhibit. When Mary Jo says they are like the Four Musketeers, "all for one and one for all," everyone emotionally embraces each other in a big circle. "Isn't this sweet," Charlene comments from within the circle, "I feel like we're on the last episode of *The Mary Tyler Moore Show.*"

Another episode begins with Charlene ordering videos from the *I Love Lucy* fan club. "I love Lucy!" Charlene exclaims. Julia replies, "I love Ethel, too," after which she admits she wouldn't mind watching the videotapes with Charlene when they arrive. Later in the same episode, the cast wonders how they can stop an unscrupulous photographer from printing some racy pictures for which he's flattered them into posing. Charlene comments that if the photographer had taken "pictures of Lucy and Ethel, they'd find a way to get the film back." This remark inspires the photographer's assistant, Estelle, to help the women: "Of course, Lucy and Ethel would steal the film!" Deciding to substitute her own photographs of "The Women of Atlanta" (the episode's title) for those of the male photographer, Estelle tells Mary Jo, Charlene, Julia, and Suzanne she didn't know she liked Southern women, and that they "should get together more often." The episode ends with Estelle's pictures shown in a montage, followed by a still of Lucy dressed as a hillbilly, which acts both as an homage to Lucy and as a reference to Charlene, who is from the mountains of Missouri.

38. "Julia Duffy Leaving '*Designing Women,*' " *New York Daily News,* reprinted in *The Morning Call* (Allentown, Pa.), Mar. 27, 1992, D2.

39. Even after Duffy's departure, however, *Designing Women*'s (pseudo?) dyke saga continued. In its seventh season opener (Sep. 25, 1992), the series introduced new regular Judith Ivey as B. J. Poteet, a rich widow who hires the Sugarbaker firm to redecorate her mansion. A late-night business meeting at B. J.'s home quickly turns into a drunken party, with Julia playing cards and smoking cigars, Mary Jo sitting on Julia's lap, and the whole cast partying in the mansion's hidden sexual bondage room.

11. Where Everybody Knows Your Name: *Cheers* and the Mediation of Cultures

1. Stuart Hall, "Encoding/Decoding," in *Culture, Media, Language,* ed. Stuart Hall, Dorothy Hobson, Andrew Lowe, and Paul Willis (London: Hutchinson, 1980), 128–38.

2. Louis Althusser, "Ideology and Ideological State Apparatuses," in *Lenin and Philosophy and Other Essays* (London: New Left Books, 1971), 127–86; Michel Foucault, *Power/Knowledge: Selected Interviews and Other Writings, 1972–77,* ed. Colin Gordon (Brighton, England: Harvester, 1980).

3. Examples of works that address these issues include Robert C. Allen's examination of soap opera production, text, and reception *(Speaking of Soap Operas* [Chapel Hill: Univ. of North Carolina Press, 1985]) and Ellen Seiter's "Promise and Contradiction: The Daytime Television Serials," *Screen* 23 (1982): 150–63. In general, the work of Stuart Hall and those associated with the Media, Culture, and Society group frequently deal with the relationship of media texts and insti-

tutions and provide useful models for analysis. See *Culture, Media, Language,* ed. Stuart Hall, Dorothy Hobson, Andrew Lowe, and Paul Willis (London: Hutchinson, 1980).

4. Terry Lovell, *Pictures of Reality* (London: British Film Institute, 1983), 1–3.

5. Nicholas Johnson, "Towers of Babel: The Chaos in Radio Spectrum Utilization and Allocation," *Law and Contemporary Problems,* summer 1969: 533.

6. See Chapter 1, "Responses to Television," in Horace Newcomb, *TV: The Most Popular Art* (New York: Anchor Books, 1974), 1–24.

7. Lawrence Laurent, "Wanted: The Complete Television Critic," in *The Eighth Art,* ed. Robert L. Shayon (New York: Holt, Rinehart, and Winston, 1962), 155–71; see also William Boddy, "Loving a Nineteen Inch Motorola," in *Regarding Television,* ed. E. Ann Kaplan (New York: The American Film Institute, 1983), 2, 3.

8. Jane Feuer, "The MTM Style," in *Television: The Critical View,* ed. Horace Newcomb (New York: Oxford Univ. Press, 1987), 81, 83; Lawrence E. Mintz, "Situation Comedy," in *TV Genres: A Handbook and Reference Guide,* ed. Brian G. Rose and Robert S. Alley (Westport, Conn.: Greenwood, 1985), 107–29.

9. Jane Mayer, "The High Road: NBC's Grant Tinker Wins Critical Acclaim but Not Big Audiences," *New York Times,* Dec. 16, 1982, A1; Tony Schwartz, "Why the TV Season Went Wrong," *New York Times,* May 9, 1982, sec. II, p. 1.

10. Feuer, "MTM Style," 52; Thomas Schatz, *"St. Elsewhere:* Evolution of the Ensemble Series," in *Television: The Critical View,* ed. Horace Newcomb (New York: Oxford Univ. Press, 1987), 89; Cameron Stauth, *"Cheers:* The Hit That Almost Missed," *Esquire,* Feb. 1984, 85+; Karen Stabiner, "For Bob Newhart, Affection Is Still the Essence of Successful Comedy," *New York Times,* Dec. 26, 1982, sec. II, p. 25.

11. Both *Taxi* and *Cheers,* along with *Family Ties,* were distributed by Paramount Television under the aegis of Gary Nardino (Aljean Harmetz, "He Stars as a Salesman of Shows to the Networks," *New York Times,* Jun. 27, 1982, 27, 28). The executive producers of *Cheers* were Charles H Joffe, Larry Brezner, and Buddy Morra. Besides the Charles brothers, producers include James Burrows, Ken Levine, and David Isaacs. Several of *Taxi's* writers also moved to *Cheers,* among them, Ken Estin, Earl Pomerantz, David Lloyd, and Sam Simon, all of whom more frequently produced than wrote for the show in later seasons. Other regular writers include Tom Reeder, Ken Levine, David Isaacs, Catherine Greene, Heidi Perlman, David Angell, Cheri Eichen, and Bill Steinkellner.

12. One story has director James Burrows's father, noted theater director Abe Burrows, making the key suggestion that Sam should be a more "downtown," "dirt under the fingernail" type (Neal Koch, "Bartenders with Class," *Channels,* Nov. 1988, 59+).

13. This entire analysis is based on the now "old" *Cheers,* before the departure of Shelley Long from the cast. The later seasons of *Cheers,* while maintaining ratings just as high as the original show, were considerably different in their central source of tension: no longer so much about culture as about its late 1980s equivalent, simple wealth—the Yuppie agonistes. As the audience changed, so did *Cheers,* and some of my specific observations about the show's narrative and ideological mechanisms may not apply to later seasons. The basic principles of institution/text linkage, however, remain the same.

14. Feuer, "MTM Style," 80.

12. Structuralist Analysis 1: Bill Cosby and Recoding Ethnicity

1. J. Snead, *Recoding Blackness: The Visual Rhetoric of Black Independent Film,* speech given at "The New American Filmmakers Series: Exhibitions of Independent Film and Video," no. 23, Whitney Museum of American Art, New York, Jun. 20, 1985; G. Davis, "Trusting the Culture: A Commentary on the Translation of African-American Cultural Systems to Media Imaging Technology," in *Black American Culture and Scholarship: Contemporary Issues,* ed. B. Reagon (Washington, D.C.: Smithsonian Institution, 1985), 99–105; A. White, "Telling It on the Mountain," *Film Comment* Oct. 1985: 39–41.

2. Douglas Kellner, "Television, Mythology, and Ritual," *Praxis* 6 (1982): 133–55

3. The power of myth in accounting for significant dimensions of contemporary media has received increasing attention from communication scholars, most notably Roger Silverstone, *The Message of Television: Myth and Narrative in Contemporary Culture* (London: Heinemann Educational Books, 1981); James Carey, ed., *Media, Myths, and Narratives: Television and the Press* (Newbury Park, Calif.: Sage, 1988); Douglas Kellner, "TV, Ideology, and Emancipatory Popular Culture," *Socialist Review,* May-Jun. 1979: 13–53; Douglas Kellner, "Television, Mythology, and Ritual," *Praxis* 6 (1982): 133–55; Hal Himmelstein, *Television Myth and American Mind* (New York: Praeger, 1984); Gaye Tuchman, *Making News: A Study in the Construction of Reality* (New York: Free Press, 1978); and Len Masterman, *Television Mythologies: Stars, Shows, and Signs,* ed. Len Masterman (New York: Marion Boyers, 1984). The writings of Ernst Cassirer on myth as a symbolic form in all human life (especially *The Myth of the State* [New Haven: Yale Univ. Press, 1946], and *An Essay on Man* [New Haven: Yale Univ. Press, 1944]) provided the first detailed explanation of the role of the psychology of emotions in myth.

4. Cassirer, *Myth of the State.*

5. Kellner, "TV, Ideology," 22. See also Douglas Kellner, "Television Images, Codes, and Messages," *Television* 7 (1980), 1–19; Douglas Kellner, "Network Television and American Society: Introduction to a Critical Theory of Television," *Theory and Society* 10 (1981): 31–62, also in in E. Wartella and C. Whitney, eds., *Mass Communication Yearbooks* (Beverly Hills, Calif.: Sage, 1982), 411–42; Kellner, "Television, Mythology"; Douglas Kellner, *Herbert Marcuse and the Crisis of Marxism* (London: Macmillan, 1984); Douglas Kellner, "Postmodernism as Social Theory: Some Challenges and Problems," *Theory, Culture and Society* 5 (1988): 2–3.

6. See, for example Tuchman, *Making News;* Lance Bennett and Murray Edelman, "Toward a New Political Narrative," *Journal of Communication* 45, no. 4 (1985): 156–71.

7. Marshall Fishwick, "Icons of America," in *Icons of America,* ed. Ray Browne and Marshall Fishwick (Bowling Green, Ohio: Bowling Green State Univ. Popular Press, 1978); Marshall Fishwick, "Entrance," in *Icons of Popular Culture,* ed. M. Fishwick and R. Browne (Bowling Green, Ohio: Bowling Green State Univ. Popular Press, 1970).

8. Fishwick, "Entrance," 6.

9. Fishwick, "Entrance"; Fishwick, "Icons of America."

10. Gregor Goethals, *The TV Ritual: Worship at the Video Altar* (Boston: Beacon, 1981).

11. John Cawelti, *Adventure, Mystery, and Romance* (Chicago: Univ. of Chicago Press, 1976).

12. Ibid., 6.

13. Horace Newcomb, ed., *Television: The Critical View,* 4th ed. (New York: Oxford Univ. Press, 1987); Horace Newcomb, *TV: The Most Popular Art* (New York: Anchor Books, 1974).

14. P. Lewis, "Joke and Anti-Joke: Three Jews and a Blindfold," *Journal of Popular Culture* 21, no. 1 (1987): 63–74.

15. Ibid., 71.

16. White, "Telling It," 40.

17. Snead, *Recoding Blackness,* 1.

18. Ibid.

19. Ibid., 2.

20. Ibid.

21. Michael Real, *Mass-Mediated Culture* (Englewood Cliffs, NJ: Prentice-Hall, 1977).

22. Stuart Hall, "The Re-discovery of 'Ideology': Return of the Repressed in Media Studies," in *Culture, Society, and the Media,* ed. M. Gurevitch et al. (London: Methuen, 1982), 56–90.

23. Ibid., 78–79.

24. Ibid., 79.

25. Ibid., 80.

26. Ibid., 82.

27. See Thomas Cripps, "Amos 'n' Andy and the Debate over American Racial Integration," in *American History, American Television: Interpreting the Video Past,* ed. John E. O'Connor (New York: Ungar, 1983), 33–54 (see also chap. 2 of this book).

28. L. Fishbein, "Roots: Docudrama and the Interpretation of History," in *American History, American Television: Interpreting the Video Past,* ed. John E. O'Connor (New York: Ungar, 1983), 279–305.

29. Ibid., 295.

30. See P. Paulsen, "Sit-com Sermons Preach Loving Lessons," *Media and Values,* summer/fall 1987: 26–27.

31. George Gerbner, "Mass Media and Human Communication Theory," in *Human Communication Theory,* ed. Frank Dance (New York: Holt, Rinehart, and Winston, 1967). Also in Dennis McQuail, ed., *Sociology of Mass Communications* (Harmondsworth, England: Penguin, 1972). See also Goethals, *TV Ritual;* Tony Schwartz, *Media: The Second God* (New York: Doubleday, 1984).

32. White, "Telling It," 40.

33. Ibid., 34.

34. Davis, "Trusting the Culture," 101.

35. Ibid., 102.

36. Ibid., 103.

37. Graham Murdock, "Misrepresenting Media Sociology: A Reply to Anderson and Sharrock," in *Mass Communication Review Yearbook,* vol. 3, ed. D. Whitney et al. (Beverly Hills, Calif.: Sage, 1982), 755–66.

38. Glasgow University Media Group, *Bad News* (London: Routledge and Kegan Paul, 1976); Glasgow University Media Group, *More Bad News* (London: Routledge and Kegan Paul, 1980).

39. Tony Bennett, Colin Mercer, and Janet Woollacott, eds., *Popular Culture and Social Relations* (Milton Keynes, England: Open Univ. Press, 1986).

40. Ibid., 11.

41. Robert Gray, 1976, cited Bennett, Mercer, and Woollacott, eds., *Popular Culture,* 6.

42. S. Ball-Rokeach, and M. Cantor, eds. *Media, Audience, and Social Structure* (Newbury Park, Calif.: Sage, 1986), 18.

43. K. Montgomery, K. "Gay Activists and the Networks," *Journal of Communication* 31 (1981): 49–57.

44. Ball-Rokeach and Cantor, eds., *Media, Audience,* 18.

45. Tuchman, *Making News.*

46. Golding, P. "Media Professionalism in the Third World: The Transfer of an Ideology," in *Mass Communication and Society,* ed. J. Curran et al. (London: Edward Arnold, 1977), 291–308, reprinted by Newbury Park, Calif.: Sage, 1979.

47. Ball-Rokeach and Cantor, eds., *Media, Audience,* 15.

48. Ibid., 16.

49. Nick Brown, "The Political Economy of the Television (Super) Text," *Quarterly Journal of Film Studies,* summer 1984: 175.

50. Ibid., 178.

51. Ibid., 181.

52. Horace Newcomb, "One Night of Prime-time: An Analysis of Television's Multiple Voices," in *Media, Myths, and Narratives: Television and the Press,* ed. James Carey (Newbury Park, Calif.: Sage, 1988), 88–112; John Hartley "Encouraging Signs: Television and the Power of Dirt, Speech, and Scandalous Categories," in *Interpreting Television: Current Research Perspectives,* ed. W. Rowland and B. Watkins (Newbury Park, Calif.: Sage, 1984), 119–41; John Fiske, "Television: Polysemy and Popularity," *Critical Studies in Mass Communication* 3, no. 4 (1986): 391–405.

53. Fiske, "Polysemy and Popularity," 401.

54. M. M. Bakhtin, *The Dialogic Imagination: Four Essays,* trans. C. Emerson and M. Holquist (Austin: Univ. of Texas Press, 1981).

55. David Thorburn, "Television as an Aesthetic Medium," in *Media, Myths, and Narratives: Television and the Press,* ed. James Carey (Newbury Park, Calif.: Sage, 1988), 56.

56. Ibid., 57.

57. D. Hallin, "We Keep America on Top of the World," in *Watching Television,* ed. Todd Gitlin (New York: Pantheon, 1986), 9–41.

Part Five: Television in the 1990s and Beyond

1. Alessandra Stanley, "Wearied by Reality, Television Returns to a 1980's Mindset," *New York Times,* July 24, 2002, B7.

2. Caryn James, "For Fall, TV Looks Back, and Back," *New York Times,* May 18, 2002, B7; Suzanne C. Ryan, "Prime-Time Develops a Conscience: New TV Shows Echo Post-Sept. 11 Themes," *Boston Globe,* May 22, 2002, E1.

3. Bill Carter, "NBC Is Adding Only Five New Shows to Its Prime-Time Fall Line-up, and Moving the Successful 'Scrubs,' " *New York Times,* May 14, 2002, C8.

13. *Roseanne*: Unruly Woman as Domestic Goddess

1. The phrase "slouching toward stardom" is Jeremy Butler's.

2. Janet Woollacott, "Fictions and Ideologies: The Case of the Situation Comedy," in Tony Bennett, Colin Mercer, and Janet Woollacott, *Popular Culture and Social Relations* (Philadelphia:

Open Univ. Press, 1986), 196–218; Patricia Mellencamp, "Situation Comedy, Feminism, and Freud," in *Studies in Entertainment: Critical Approaches to Mass Culture*, ed. Tania Modleski (Bloomington: Indiana Univ. Press, 1986), 80–95 (see also chap. 3 of this book).

3. Natalie Zemon Davis, *Society and Culture in Early Modern France* (Standford, Calif.: Standford Univ. Press, 1975).

4. Patricia Parker, *Literary Fat Ladies: Rhetoric, Gender, Property* (New York: Methuen, 1987).

5. Natalie Zemon Davis, *Society and Culture,* 124–51.

6. Mary Russo, "Female Grotesques: Carnival and Theory," in *Feminist Studies, Critical Studies,* ed. Teresa de Lauretis (Bloomington: Indiana Univ. Press, 1986), 217.

7. Mary Ann Doane, *The Desire to Desire: The Woman's Film of the 1940s* (Bloomington: Univ. of Indiana Press, 1987).

8. Teresa de Lauretis, *Technologies of Gender* (Bloomington: Indiana Univ. Press, 1987), 109.

9. For example "Roseanne Goes Nuts," *Enquirer,* Apr. 9, 1989, and "My Insane Year," *People Weekly,* Oct. 9, 1989, 85–86. Like other labels of deviancy, madness is often attached to the unruly woman.

10. Helen Andelin, *Fascinating Womanhood* (Santa Barbara, Calif.: Pacific Press Santa Barbara, 1974).

11. Mikhail Bakhtin, *Rabelais and His World,* trans. Helene Iswolsky (Bloomington: Indiana Univ. Press, 1984).

12. Nancy M. Henley, *Body Politics: Power, Sex, and Non-verbal Communication* (Englewood Cliffs, N.J.: Prentice-Hall, 1977), 38.

13. In "What Am I Anyway, a Zoo?" *New York Times,* Jul. 31, 1989, she enumerates the ways people have interpreted what she stands for—the regular housewife, the mother, the postfeminist, the "Little Guy," fat people, the "Queen of Tabloid America," "the body politic," sex, "angry womankind herself," "the notorious and sensationalistic La Luna madness of an ovulating Abzugienne woman run wild," etc.

14. Roseanne Barr, *Roseanne: My Life as a Woman* (New York: Harper and Row, 1989), 51.

15. "My Insane Year," 85–86.

16. Pierre Bourdieu, *Distinction: A Social Critique of the Judgement of Taste,* trans. Richard Nice (Cambridge: Harvard Univ. Press, 1984), 208.

17. Rick Altman, *The American Film Musical* (Bloomington: Univ. of Indiana Press, 1987).

18. See Hélène Cixous (with Catherine Clément), *The Newly Born Woman,* vol. 24 of *Theory and History of Literature,* trans. Betsy Wing (Minneapolis: University of Minnesota Press, 1984).

14. The Triumph of Popular Culture: Situation Comedy, Postmodernism, and *The Simpsons*

1. Stuart M. Kaminski, *American Television Genres* (Chicago: Nelson Hall, 1985), 8

2. Tad Friend, "Sitcoms, Seriously," *Esquire,* Mar. 1993, 124.

3. Linda Hutcheon, *The Politics of Postmodernism* (New York: Routledge, 1989), 1

4. Ibid., 4

5. Friend, "Sitcoms, Seriously," 114

6. Ibid., 115.

7. David Marc, *Comic Visions: Television Comedy and American Culture* (Boston: Unwin Hyman, 1989), 161.

8. Harry Waters, "Family Feuds," *Newsweek,* Apr. 23, 1990, 60.

9. Ibid., 58

10. Lawrence Grossberg 1987. "The In-Difference of Television," *Screen* 28, no. 2 (1987): 30.

11. David Marc, *Demographic Vistas: Television in American Culture* (Philadelphia: Univ. of Pennsylvania Press, 1984), 12.

12. Harry Stein, "Our Times," *TV Guide,* May 23–29, 1992, 31.

13. Ibid.

14. Darrell Y. Hamamoto, *Nervous Laughter: Television Situation Comedy and Liberal Democratic Ideology* (New York: Praeger, 1989), 17.

15. John Ellis, *Visible Fictions Cinema: Television: Video* (London: Routledge and Kegan Paul, 1982), 125.

16. Richard Butsch, "Class and Gender in Four Decades of Television Comedy: Plus ca Change . . ." *Critical Studies in Mass Communications* 9 (1992), 392.

17. Marc, *Demographic Vistas,* 13.

18. David Berkman, "Sitcom Reality," *Television Quarterly* 26, no. 4 (1993): 64.

19. Gerard Jones, *Honey, I'm Home! Sitcoms: Selling the American Dream* (New York: Grove, 1992), 4.

20. Rebeck, Victoria A. "Recognizing Ourselves in the Simpsons," *The Christian Century,* Jun. 27, 1990, 622.

21. Patricia Waugh, ed. *Postmodernism: A Reader* (London: Edward Arnold, 1992), 191.

22. Frederic Jameson, "Postmodernism, or, The Logic of Late Capitalism," *New Left Review,* 146 (1984): 65.

23. Hutcheon, *Politics of Postmodernism,* 10

24. Rebeck, "Recognizing Ourselves," 622.

25. Jerry Herron, "Homer Simpson's Eyes and the Culture of Late Nostalgia," *Representations* 43 (1993): 18.

26. Frank McConnell, " 'Real' Cartoon Characters," *Commonweal,* Jun. 15, 1990, 390.

27. Marguerite Alexander, *Flights from Realism* (London: Edward Arnold, 1990), 4.

28. Berkman, "Sitcom Reality," 69.

29. Sean Elder, "Is TV the Coolest Invention Ever Invented?" *Mother Jones,* Dec. 1989, 30.

30. Jones, *Honey, I'm Home!* 268

15. Sitcoms Say Good-bye: The Cultural Spectacle of *Seinfeld*'s Last Episode

1. Caryn James, "Good-bye Already! For *Seinfeld* and Others, Parting Is Such Sweet Sitcom," *New York Times Online,* May 12, 1998, 1.

2. Lynn Hirschberg, "So What's to Become of Our Jerry?" *Vanity Fair,* May 1998, 246.

3. Glen Collins, "How Does Seinfeld Define Comedy? Reluctantly," *New York Times Online,* Sep. 29, 1991, 2

4. Critics have noted the predominance of Jewish humor and stereotypes, despite the fact that Jerry was ostensibly the only Jewish character. See, for example, Albert Auster, "Much Ado about Nothing: Some Final Thoughts on *Seinfeld,*" *Television Quarterly* 29, no. 4 (May 1998): 24–33; and Carla Johnson, "The Schlemiel and the Schlimazl in *Seinfeld,*" *Journal of Popular Film and Television,* fall 1994, 117–24.

5. Don Aucoin, "How 'A Show about Nothing' Changed the Whole TV Industry, *Boston Globe,* May 10, 1998, N9.

6. This audience consists of what Ron Becker has called slumpies (an acronym for socially liberal, urban-minded professionals): hip, sophisticated, "urban-minded" white, college-educated, upscale eighteen to forty-nine year olds with liberal attitudes, disposable incomes, and a distinctly edgy and ironic sensibility, a group basically comprised of the aging yet still socially progressive and upwardly mobile baby boomers and the youthful twenty—and thirty-somethings that follow in their wake. See Ron Becker, "Prime Time Television in the Gay Nineties: Network Television, Quality Audiences, and Gay Politics," *The Velvet Light Trap,* fall 1998: 36–47.

7. Bill Carter, "Seinfeld Ratings Grazed Superbowl," *New York Times Online,* May 16, 1998. See also Matthew Gilbert, "Trivial Pursuit," *New York Times,* May 10, 1998, N8.

8. Michael Dunne, *Metapop: Self-referentiality in Contemporary American Popular Culture* (Univ. Press of Mississippi, 1992), 11.

9. The much hyped "secret" ending of *M*A*S*H* was watched by an unprecedented 125 million viewers—nearly half of the U.S. population at the time. This record will probably remain unbroken because of the proliferation of new technologies (cable, VCRs, pay-per-view, satellite dishes, and the Internet) which fragment contemporary television audiences. See Steven Stark, *Glued to the Set* (New York: Delta, 1997).

10. As Jerry and George wait for their meeting, posters of two moderate NBC hits, *Suddenly Susan* and *Third Rock from the Sun,* prominently frame them. There was no such blatant attempt at network cross promotion in "The Pilot," although the opportunity certainly afforded itself. But with the megahit *Seinfeld* ending, NBC may have felt more of a need to promote its other sitcoms.

11. Rob Long, "Jerry Built: The Success of 'Seinfeld' was an Implicit Rebuke to PC Pieties," *National Review Online,* Feb. 9, 1998.

12. David Marc, *Demographic Vistas: Television in American Culture* (Philadelphia: Univ. of Pennsylvania Press, 1984), 165.

13. Mick Eaton, "Television Situation Comedy," in *Popular Film and Television,* ed. Tony Bennett, Susan Boyd-Bowman, Colin Mercer, and Janet Woollacott (London: British Film Institute, 1981), 37.

14. Barry Took, quoted Steve Neale and Frank Krutnik, eds., "Broadcast Comedy and Sitcom," *Popular Film and Television Comedy* (New York: Routledge, 1990), 253.

15. Ibid., 242.

16. Collins, "How Does Seinfeld," 3.

17. Jane Feuer, "Narrative Form in American Network Television," in *High Theory/Low Culture: Analyzing Popular Culture and Film,* ed. Colin MacCabe (Manchester: Manchester Univ. Press, 1998), 108.

18. See M. M. Bahktin, *Rabelais and His World,* trans. Helene Iswolsky (Bloomington: Indiana Univ. Press, 1984); Virginia Wright Wexman, "Returning from the Moon: Jackie Gleason, the Carnivalesque, and Television Comedy," *Journal of Film and Video* 42, no. 4 (winter 1990): 20–31 (see also chap. 4 in this book).

19. Wexman, "Returning," 24.

20. A. J. Jacobs, "You've Been a Great Audience! Good Night!" *Entertainment Weekly,* May 4, 1998, 5.

21. Jerry Herron, "Homer Simpson's Eyes and the Culture of Late Nostalgia," *Representations* 43 (1993): 2.

22. Collins, "How Does Seinfeld," 4.

Bibliography

Archives

Academy of Television Arts Collection, Univ. of California, Los Angeles, Calif.

Barnett Papers, Chicago Historical Society, Chicago, Ill.

Fred Guiol Collection, California State University at Fullerton, Fullerton, Calif.

Hal Kanter Papers, Wisconsin Center Historical Archives, State Historical Society, Madison, Wisc.

James Weldon Johnson Memorial Collection, Beineke Library, Yale Univ., Hartford, Conn.

Katherine Dunham Collection, Morris Library, Southern Illinois Univ., Carbondale, Ill.

Motion Picture, Broadcasting, and Sound Division, Library of Congress, Washington, D.C.

Museum of Broadcasting, New York, N.Y.

National Urban League (NUL) Records, Library of Congress, Washington, D.C.

Ralph Nelson Papers, Special Collection 875, University Research Library, Univ. of California, Los Angeles, Calif.

Special Collections Department, Research Library, University of California, Los Angeles, Los Angeles, Calif.

Wisconsin Film Archive, Wisconsin Center for Film and Theater Research, Madison, Wisc.

Books and Articles

Adler, Dick. "The Writer Wore Hotpants." *TV Guide,* Jul. 15, 1972.

Adler, Richard, and Douglas Cater, eds. *Television as a Cultural Form.* New York: Praeger, 1976.

Alexander, H. B. "Negro Opinion Regarding Amos 'n' Andy." *Sociology and Social Research* 16 (Mar. 1932): 345–54.

Alexander, Marguerite. *Flights from Realism.* London: Edward Arnold, 1990.

Allen, Robert C. *Speaking of Soap Operas.* Chapel Hill: U. of North Carolina Press, 1985.

Allen, Steve. "Jackie Gleason." In *Funny Men,* 145–63. New York: Simon and Schuster, 1956.

Althusser, Louis. "Ideology and Ideological State Apparatuses." In *Lenin and Philosophy and Other Essays,* 128–38. London: New Left Books, 1971.

Altman, Rick. *The American Film Musical.* Bloomington: Univ. of Indiana Press, 1987.

———. "Dickens, Griffith, and Film Theory Today." *South Atlantic Quarterly* 88, no. 2 (spring 1989): 321–60.

Andelin, Helen. *Fascinating Womanhood.* Santa Barbara, Calif.: Pacific Press Santa Barbara, 1974.

Andrews, Bart. *Lucy and Ricky and Fred and Ethel.* New York: E.P. Dutton, 1976.

Ang, Ian. *Watching Dallas.* London: Methuen, 1985.

Arbuthnot, Lucy, and Gail Seneca. "Pre-Text and Text in *Gentlemen Prefer Blondes*." *Film Reader* 5 (1982): 13–23. Reprinted in *Issues in Feminist Film Criticism,* edited by Patricia Erens, 112–25. Bloomington: Indiana Univ. Press, 1990.

Arlen, Michael. "The Media Drama of Norman Lear." In *The View from Highway One: Essays on Television,* 53–66. New York: Farrar, Straus, and Giroux, 1976.

Aucoin, Don. "How 'A Show about Nothing' Changed the Whole TV Industry." *Boston Globe,* May 10, 1998, N9.

Auster, Albert. "Much Ado about Nothing: Some Final Thoughts on *Seinfeld*." *Television Quarterly* 29, no. 4 (May 1998): 24–33.

Bacon, James. *How Sweet It Is: The Jackie Gleason Story.* New York: St. Martin's, 1986.

Bakhtin, M. M. *The Dialogic Imagination: Four Essays.* Translated by C. Emerson and M. Holquist. Austin: Univ. of Texas Press, 1981.

———. *Rabelais and His World.* Translated by Helene Iswolsky. Bloomington: Indiana Univ. Press, 1984.

Ball-Rokeach, S., and M. Cantor, eds. *Media, Audience, and Social Structure.* Newbury Park, Calif.: Sage, 1986.

Barnouw, Erik. *Tube of Plenty.* New York: Oxford Univ. Press, 1975.

Barr, Roseanne. *Roseanne: My Life as a Woman.* New York: Harper and Row, 1989.

Barrett, Michèle, and Mary McIntosh. *The Anti-Social Family.* London: Verso, 1982.

Barthes, Roland. *Mythologies.* Translated by A. Lavers. New York: Hill and Wang, 1972.

———. *S/Z.* Paris: Seuil, 1970.

———. "Writers, Intellectuals, Teachers." In *Image-Music-Text,* edited by Stephen Heath. London: Fontana/Collins, 1977.

Bathrick, Serafina. "The Mary Tyler Moore Show: Women at Home and at Work." In *MTM: "Quality Television,"* edited by Jane Feuer, Paul Kerr, and Tise Vahimagi, 99–131. London: British Film Institute, 1984.

Baudrillard, Jean. "The Evil Demon of Images and the Precession of Simulacra." In *Postmodernism: A Reader,* edited by Thomas Docherty, 194–99. New York: Columbia Univ. Press, 1993.

———. "Requiem for the Media." In *For a Critique of the Political Economy of the Sign,* translated by Charles Levin. St. Louis, Mo.: Telos, 1981.

Bazin, Andre. "Qu'est-ce que le cinéma? III." In *Cinema et Sociologie.* Paris: Les Editions du Cerf, Collection 7e Art, 1961.

Beauté, George. *Paul Gauguin vu par les photographes.* N.p., 1988.

Becker, Ron. "Prime Time Television in the Gay Nineties: Network Television, Quality Audiences, and Gay Politics." *The Velvet Light Trap* (fall 1998): 36–47.

Bennett, Lance, and Murray Edelman. "Toward a New Political Narrative. *Journal of Communication* 45, no. 4 (1985): 156–71.

Bennett, Tony. "Gramscian Ideology and Popular Culture." In *Popular Culture and Social Relations,* edited by T. Bennett, Colin Mercer, and Janet Woollacott, 6–21. Milton Keynes, England: Open Univ. Press, 1986.

Bennett, Tony, Susan Boyd-Bowman, Colin Mercer, and Janet Woollacott, eds. *Popular Television and Film.* London: William Collins and Sons, 1981.

Bennett, Tony, Colin Mercer, and Janet Woollacott, eds. *Popular Culture and Social Relations.* Milton Keynes, England: Open Univ. Press, 1986.

Bergreen, Lawrence. *Look Now, Pay Later.* New York: New American Library, 1981.

Bergson, Henri. "Laughter." In *Comedy,* edited by Wylie Sypher, translated by Fred Rothwell. New York: Doubleday, 1956.

Berkman, David. "Sitcom Reality." *Television Quarterly* 26, no.4 (1993): 63–69.

Billen, Andrew. "Seinfeld." *New Statesman,* Aug. 21, 1998, 43.

Billingsley, Andrew. *Black Families in White America.* Englewood Cliffs, N.J.: Prentice-Hall, 1968.

Bird, Caroline. "What's Television Doing for Fifty Percent of Americans?" *TV Guide,* Feb. 27, 1971.

Bishop, Jim. *The Golden Ham: A Candid Biography of Jackie Gleason.* New York: Simon and Schuster, 1956.

Bobo, Jacqueline. "The Color Purple: Black Women as Cultural Readers." In *Female Spectators: Looking at Film and Television,* edited by E. Deidre Pribram, 90–109. London and New York: Verso, 1988.

Boddy, William. "Loving a Nineteen Inch Motorola." In *Regarding Television,* edited by E. Ann Kaplan. New York: American Film Institute, 1983.

Bourdieu, Pierre. *Distinction: A Social Critique of the Judgement of Taste.* Translated by Richard Nice. Cambridge: Harvard Univ. Press, 1984.

Bracey, John H., Jr., August Meier, and Elliott Rudwick, eds. *Black Matriarchy: Myth or Reality?* Belmont, Calif.: Wadsworth, 1971.

Brooks, Peter. "Freud's Masterplot: A Model for Narrative." In *Reading for the Plot: Design and Intention in Narrative,* 90–112. New York: Vintage, 1985.

Brooks, Tim, and Earle Marsh. *The Complete Directory to Prime Time Network Television Shows, 1946-Present.* New York: Ballantine, 1981.

Brown, Les. *The New York Times Encyclopedia of Television.* New York: Times Books, 1977.

———. *Television: The Business Behind the Box.* New York: Harcourt Brace Jovanovich, 1971.

Brown, Nick. "The Political Economy of the Television (Super) Text." *Quarterly Journal of Film Studies* (summer 1984): 174–82.

Bruner, W. Richard. "Amos 'n' Andy Hassle Won't Stop TV Show." *Printers' Ink,* Aug. 13, 1951.

Brunsdon, Charlotte. "Television: Aesthetics and Audiences." In *Logics of Television: Essays in Cultural Criticism,* edited by Patricia Mellencamp, 59–72. Bloomington: Indiana Univ. Press, 1990.

Brunsdon, Charlotte, and David Morley. *Everyday Television: "Nationwide."* London: British Film Institute, 1978.

Bryant, John. "Emma, Lucy, and the American Situation Comedy of Manners." *Journal of Popular Culture* 13, no. 2 (fall 1979): 248–56.

Butsch, Richard. "Class and Gender in Four Decades of Television Comedy: Plus ca Change . . ." *Critical Studies in Mass Communications* 9 (1992): 387–99.

Cahiers du cinéma. "Television." Special issue, fall 1981.

"Can TV Crack America's Color Line?" *Ebony,* May 1951, 58.

Carey, James, ed. *Media, Myths, and Narratives: Television and the Press.* Newbury Park, Calif.: Sage, 1988.

Carter, Bill. "NBC Is Adding Only Five New Shows to Its Prime-Time Fall Line-up, and Moving the Successful 'Scrubs.' " *New York Times,* May 14, 1998, C8.

———. "Seinfeld Ratings Grazed Superbowl." *New York Times Online,* May 16, 1998.

Case, Sue Ellen. "Toward a Butch-Femme Aesthetic." *Discourse* 11, no. 1 (fall-winter 1988–89): 55–71.

Cassirer, Ernst. *An Essay on Man.* New Haven: Yale Univ. Press, 1944.

———. *The Myth of the State.* New Haven: Yale Univ. Press, 1946.

Castleman, Harry, and Walter J. Podrazik. *The TV Schedule Book.* New York: McGraw-Hill, 1984.

———. *Watching TV: Four Decades of American Television.* New York: McGraw-Hill, 1982.

Caute, David. *The Year of the Barricades: A Journey Through 1968.* New York: Harper and Row, 1988.

Cawelti, John. *Adventure, Mystery, and Romance.* Chicago: Univ. of Chicago Press, 1976.

———. *The Six-Gun Mystique.* Bowling Green, Ohio: Bowling Green Univ. Popular Press, 1970.

Chatman, Seymour. *Story and Discourse: Narrative Structure in Fiction and Film.* Ithaca, N.Y.: Cornell Univ. Press, 1978.

Chipp, Herschel. *Theories of Modern Art.* Berkeley: Univ. of California Press, 1968.

Cixous, Hélène, with Catherine Clément. *The Newly Born Woman.* Vol. 24 of *Theory and History of Literature.* Translated by Betsy Wing. Minneapolis: University of Minnesota Press, 1984.

Clark, Danae. "Commodity Lesbianism." *Camera Obscura* 25/26 (Jan.-May 1991).

Clayton, Edward T. "The Tragedy of Amos 'n' Andy." *Ebony,* Oct. 1961, 66–73.

Clifford, James. "Histories of the Tribal and the Modern." In *The Predicament of Culture.* Cambridge: Harvard Univ. Press, 1988.

Collins, Glen. "How Does Seinfeld Define Comedy? Reluctantly." *New York Times Online,* Sep. 29, 1991, 1–5.

Collins, R., et al., eds. *Media, Culture, and Society: A Critical Reader.* Newbury Park, Calif.: Sage, 1986.

Combes, Annie E. *Re-inventing Africa.* New Haven, Conn.: Yale Univ. Press, 1995.

Conner, Steven. *Postmodernist Culture.* Oxford: Basil Blackwell, 1989.

Coppa, Frank. *Screen and Society: The Impact of Television upon Aspects of Contemporary Civilization.* Chicago: Nelson Hall, 1979.

Corliss, Richard. "Happy Days Are Here Again." In *Television: The Critical View,* edited by Horace Newcomb. New York: Oxford Univ. Press, 1982.

Cosby, William. *Fat Albert's Survival Kit.* New York: Windmill Books, 1975.

———.*Fatherhood.* New York: Doubleday, 1986.

———. *The Wit and Wisdom of Fat Albert.* New York: Windmill Books, 1973.

Crescenti, Peter, and Bob Columbe. *The Official Honeymooners Treasury.* New York: Perigee, 1985.

Cripps, Thomas. "Amos 'n' Andy and the Debate Over American Racial Integration." In *American History, American Television: Interpreting the Video Past,* edited by John. E. O'Connor. New York: Ungar, 1983.

———. "The Films of Spencer Williams." *Black American Literature Forum* 12 (winter 1978): 128–34.

Davis, Angela Y. *Women, Race, and Class.* New York: Vintage Books, 1981.

Davis, G. "Trusting the Culture: A Commentary on the Translation of African-American Cultural Systems to Media Imaging Technology." In *Black American Culture and Scholarship: Contemporary Issues,* edited by B. Reagon, 99–105. Washington, DC: Smithsonian Institution, 1985.

Davis, Madeline, and Elizabeth Lapovsky Kennedy. "Oral History and the Study of Sexuality in the Lesbian Community: Buffalo, N.Y., 1940–1960." In *Hidden from History: Reclaiming the Lesbian and Gay Past,* ed. Martin Bauml Duberman, Martha Vicinus, and George Chauncey, Jr., 426–40. New York: New American Library, 1989.

Davis, Natalie Zemon. *Society and Culture in Early Modern France.* Stanford: Stanford Univ. Press, 1975.

de Lauretis, Teresa. *Technologies of Gender.* Bloomington: Indiana Univ. Press, 1987.

D'Emilio, John, and Estelle B. Freedman. *Intimate Matters: A History of Sexuality in America.* New York: Harper, 1988.

Deming, Robert H. *"Kate and Allie:* 'New Women' and the Audience's Television Archive." *Camera Obscura* 16 (Jan. 1988).

"Diahann Carroll's Juggling Act." *Good Housekeeping,* May 1969, 38–51.

Dichter, Ernest. *The Strategy of Desire.* Garden City, N.Y.. Doubleday, 1960.

Dill, Bonnie Thornton. "The Dialectics of Black Womanhood." In *Feminism and Methodology*, edited by Sandra Harding, 97–108. Bloomington and Indianapolis: Indiana Univ. Press, 1984.

Doane, Mary Ann. *The Desire to Desire: The Woman's Film of the 1940s.* Bloomington: Indiana Univ. Press, 1987.

Docherty, Thomas, ed. *Postmodernism: A Reader.* New York: Columbia Univ. Press, 1993.

Douglas, Mary. *Purity and Danger: An Analysis of the Concept of Pollution and Taboo.* London: Routledge, 1984.

Dunne, Michael. *Metapop: Self-referentiality in Contemporary American Popular Culture.* Univ. Press of Mississippi, 1992.

Dyer, Richard. *Stars.* London: British Film Institute, 1979.

———. "White." *Screen* 29, no. 4 (autumn 1988): 44–64.

Eaton, Mick. "Television Situation Comedy" In *Popular Film and Television,* edited by Tony Bennett, Susan Boyd-Bowman, Colin Mercer, and Janet Woollacott, 26–52. London: William Collins and Sons, 1981.

Echols, Alice. *Daring to Be Bad: Radical Feminism in America, 1967–1975.* Minneapolis: Univ. of Minneapolis Press, 1989.

Eddy, Bob. "Private Life of a Perfect Papa." *Saturday Evening Post,* Apr. 27, 1957.

Edmerson, Estelle. "A Descriptive Study of the American Negro in United States Professional Radio, 1922–1953." Masters thesis, Univ. of California, Los Angeles, 1954.

Ehrenreich, Barbara. *The Hearts of Men: American Dreams and the Flight from Commitment.* Garden City, N.Y.: Anchor, 1983.

Eisenman, Stephen. *Gauguin's Skirt.* London: Thames and Hudson, 1996.

Eisler, Benita. *Private Lives: Men and Women of the Fifties.* New York: Franklin Watts, 1986.

Elder, Sean. "Is TV the Coolest Invention Ever Invented?" *Mother Jones,* Dec. 1989, 28–31.

Ellis, John. *Visible Fictions Cinema: Television: Video.* London: Routledge and Kegan Paul, 1982.

Esslin, Martin. *The Age of Television.* San Francisco: W. H. Freeman, 1982.

Evers, Mrs. Medgar. "A Tale of Two Julias." *Ladies Home Journal,* May 1970, 60–65.

Ewen, Stuart, and Elizabeth Ewen. *Channels of Desire: Mass Images and the Shaping of American Consciousness.* New York: McGraw-Hill, 1982.

Farwell, Marilyn R. "Heterosexual Plots and Lesbian Subtexts: Toward a Theory of Lesbian Narrative Space." In *Lesbian Texts and Contexts: Radical Revisions,* edited by Karla Jay and Joanne Glasgow. New York and London: New York Univ. Press, 1990.

Ferguson, Marjorie. *Forever Feminine: Women's Magazines and the Cult of Femininity.* London: Heinemann, 1983.

Feuer, Jane. "Genre Study and Television." In *Channels of Discourse, Reassembled,* 2d edition, edited by Robert C. Allen, 138–60. Chapel Hill: Univ. of North Carolina Press, 1992.

———. "Melodrama, Serial Form, and Television Today." *Screen* 25, no. 1 (1984): 4–16.

———. "The MTM Style." In *Television: The Critical View,* edited by Horace Newcomb, 52–84. New York: Oxford Univ. Press, 1987.

———. "Narrative Form in American Network Television." In *High Theory/Low Culture: Analyzing Popular Culture and Film,* edited by Colin MacCabe, 104–14. Manchester: Manchester Univ. Press, 1998.

Fife, Marilyn Diane. "Black Images in American TV: The First Two Decades." *The Black Scholar,* Nov. 1974: 13–14.

Finnigan, Joseph. "Cameraperson in Hotpants." *TV Guide,* Sep. 9, 1972.

Fishbein, L. "Roots: Docudrama and the Interpretation of History." In *American History/American Television: Interpreting the Video Past,* edited by John E. O'Connor, 279–305. New York: Ungar, 1983.

Fishwick, Marshall. "Icons of America." In *Icons of America,* edited by R. Browne and M. Fishwick. Bowling Green, Ohio: Bowling Green State Univ. Popular Press, 1978.

———. "Entrance." In *Icons of Popular Culture,* edited by M. Fishwick and R. Browne. Bowling Green, Ohio: Bowling Green State Univ. Popular Press, 1970.

Fiske, John. *Television Culture.* New York: Methuen, 1987.

———. "Television: Polysemy and Popularity." *Critical Studies in Mass Communication* 3, no. 4 (1986): 391–405.

———. *Understanding Popular Culture.* Boston: Unwin Hyman, 1989.

Fiske, John, and John Hartley. *Reading Television.* London: Methuen, 1978.

Forbes, Kathryn. *Mama's Bank Account.* New York: Harcourt, 1943.

Foster, Hal, ed. *The Anti-Aesthetic: Essays on Postmodern Culture.* Port Townsend, Washington: Bay Press, 1983.

Foucault, Michel. *The History of Sexuality: Volume I: An Introduction.* Translated by Robert Hurley. New York: Vintage, 1980.

———. *Power/Knowledge: Selected Interviews and Other Writings, 1972–77.* Edited by Colin Gordon. Brighton, England: Harvester, 1980.

———. *Les mots et les choses.* Paris: Gallimard, 1969.

Frazier, E. Franklin. *The Family: Its Function and Destiny.* New York: Harper and Row, 1959.

———. *The Negro Family in the United States.* Chicago: Univ. of Chicago Press, 1939.

Freud, Sigmund. "Humour." *The Standard Edition of the Complete Psychological Works of Sigmund Freud,* vol. 21. London: Hogarth, 1964.

———. *Jokes and Their Relation to the Unconscious.* Translated and edited by James Strachey. New York: Norton, 1960.

Friedan, Betty. *The Feminine Mystique.* New York: Dell, 1963.

Friend, Tad. "Sitcoms, Seriously." *Esquire,* Mar. 1993, 112–24.

Garnham, Nicholas. *Structures of Television*. London: British Film Institute, 1978.

Genette, Gerard. *Figures III*. Paris: Seuil, 1970.

Gerani, Gary, with Paul H. Schulman. *Fantastic Television*. New York: Harmony Books, 1977.

Gerbner, George. "Mass Media and Human Communication Theory." In *Human Communication Theory*, edited by Frank Dance. New York: Holt, Rinehart, and Winston, 1967. Also in Dennis McQuail, ed. *Sociology of Mass Communications*. Harmondsworth, England: Penguin, 1972.

Gibson, William. "Network News: Elements of a Theory." *Social Text* 3 (fall 1980).

Gilbert, Matthew. "Trivial Pursuit." *New York Times,* May 10, 1998, N1, N8.

Ginzburg, Carlo. "Morelli, Freud, and Sherlock Holmes: Clues and Scientific Method." *History Workshop* 9 (spring 1980): 5–36.

Gitlin, Todd. *Inside Prime Time*. New York: Pantheon, 1983.

Gitlin, Todd, ed. *Watching Television*. New York: Pantheon, 1982.

Glasgow University Media Group. *Bad News*. London: Routledge and Kegan Paul, 1976.

———. *More Bad News*. London: Routledge and Kegan Paul, 1980.

Glut, Donald F., and Jim Hutton. *The Great Television Heroes*. New York: Doubleday, 1975.

Goethals, Gregor. *The TV Ritual: Worship at the Video Altar*. Boston: Beacon, 1981.

Golding, P. "Media Professionalism in the Third World: The Transfer of an Ideology." In *Mass Communication and Society,* edited by J. Curran et al., 291–308. London: Edward Arnold, 1977. Reprint, Newbury Park, Calif.: Sage, 1979.

Goldman, Eric. *The Crucial Decade and After: America 1945–1960*. New York: Vintage, 1960.

Goodall, Brian, and Gregory Ashworth. *Marketing the Tourism Industry: The Promotion of Destination Regions*. New York: Croom Helm, 1998.

Gordon, Linda. "On Difference." In *Women, the State, and Welfare,* edited by Linda Gordon. Madison: Univ. of Wisconsin Press, 1990.

Grossberg, Lawrence. "The In-Difference of Television." *Screen* 28, no. 2 (1987): 28–45.

Grote, David. *The End of Comedy: The Sit-Com and the Comedic Tradition*. Hamden, Conn.: Archon, 1983.

Hall, Stuart. "Culture, Media and the 'Ideological Effect.' " In *Mass Communication and Society,* edited by James Curran, Michael Gurevitch, and Janet Woollacott. Beverly Hills, Calif.: Sage, 1979.

———. "Encoding and Decoding the Television Discourse." In *Stenciled Occasional Papers,* no. 7. Birmingham, England: Birmingham Univ., Centre for Contemporary Cultural Studies, 1973.

———. "Encoding/Decoding." In *Culture, Media, Language,* edited by Stuart Hall et al., 128–38. London: Hutchinson, 1980.

———. "The Re-discovery of 'Ideology': Return of the Repressed in Media Studies." In *Culture, Society, and the Media,* edited by Michael Gurevitch et al., 56–90. London: Methuen, 1982.

———. "Television as a Medium and Its Relation to Culture." In *Stenciled Occasional Papers,* no. 4. Birmingham, England: Birmingham Univ., Centre for Contemporary Cultural Studies, 1971.

Hallin, D. "We Keep America on Top of the World." In *Watching Television,* edited by Todd Gitlin, 9–41. New York: Pantheon, 1986.

Hamamoto, Darrell Y. *Nervous Laughter: Television Situation Comedy and Liberal Democratic Ideology.* New York: Praeger, 1989.

Harding, Sandra, ed. *Feminism and Methodology.* Bloomington and Indianapolis: Indiana Univ. Press, 1974.

Harmetz, Aljean. "He Stars as a Salesman of Shows to the Networks." *New York Times,* Jun. 27, 1982, 27, 28.

Harris, Jay S., ed. *TV Guide: The First Twenty-Five Years.* New York: Simon and Schuster, 1978.

Hartley, John. "Encouraging Signs: Television and the Power of Dirt, Speech, and Scandalous Categories. In *Interpreting Television: Current Research Perspectives,* edited by W. Rowland and B. Watkins, 119–41. Newbury Park, Calif.: Sage, 1984.

Hayden, Dolores. *Redesigning the American Dream: The Future of Housing, Work, and Family Life.* New York: Norton, 1984.

Heath, Stephen. "Body, Voice." *Questions of Cinema,* 176–93. Bloomington: Indiana Univ. Press, 1981.

Henley, Nancy M. *Body Politics: Power, Sex, and Non-verbal Communication.* Englewood Cliffs, N.J.: Prentice-Hall, 1977.

Herron, Jerry. "Homer Simpson's Eyes and the Culture of Late Nostalgia." *Representations* 43 (1993): 1–26.

Higham, Charles, and Joel Greenberg. *The Celluloid Muse: Hollywood Directors Speak.* New York: Signet/New American Library, 1972.

Himmelstein, Hal. *Television Myth and American Mind.* New York: Praegar, 1984.

Hirschberg, Lynn. "So What's to Become of Our Jerry?" *Vanity Fair,* May 1998, 185–92, 242–46.

Hoberman, J. "Ralph and Alice and Ed and Trixie." *Film Comment* 21, no. 5 (Oct. 1985): 62–68.

Holmlund, Christine. "When Is a Lesbian Not a Lesbian? The Lesbian Continuum and the Mainstream Femme Film." *Camera Obscura* 25/26 (Jan.-May 1991): 145–46.

Horowitz, Susan. "Life with Kate and Allie—The Not-So-Odd Couple on TV." *Ms.,* Sep. 1984, 32–33.

Hutcheon, Linda. *The Politics of Postmodernism.* New York: Routledge, 1989.

Jacobs, A. J. "You've Been a Great Audience! Good Night!" *Entertainment Weekly,* May 4, 1998, 5–8.

James, Caryn. "For Fall, TV Looks Back, and Back." *New York Times,* May 18, 2002, B7.

———. "Good-bye Already! For *Seinfeld* and Others, Parting Is Such Sweet Sitcom." *New York Times Online,* May 12, 1998, 1–2.

Jameson, Fredric. "Postmodernism and Consumer Society." In *The Anti-Aesthetic: Essays on Postmodern Culture,* edited by Hal Foster, 111–25. Port Townsend, Wash.: Bay Press, 1983.

———. "Postmodernism, or, The Cultural Logic of Late Capitalism." *New Left Review* 146 (1984): 53–92.

Johnson, Carla. "The Schlemiel and the Schlimazl in *Seinfeld.*" *Journal of Popular Film and Television* (fall 1994): 117–24.

Johnson, Nicholas. "Towers of Babel: The Chaos in Radio Spectrum Utilization and Allocation." *Law and Contemporary Problems,* summer 1969.

Jones, Gerard. *Honey, I'm Home! Sitcoms: Selling the American Dream.* New York: Grove, 1992.

Jones, Jacqueline. *Labor of Love, Labor of Sorrow: Black Women, Work, and the Family, from Slavery to the Present.* New York: Vintage, 1985.

Kagan, Norman. "Amos 'n' Andy: Twenty Years Late or Two Decades Early? *Journal of Popular Culture* 6 (summer 1972): 71–75.

Kaminski, Stuart M. *American Television Genres.* Chicago: Nelson Hall, 1985.

Kanfer, Stefan. *A Journal of the Plague Years.* New York; Atheneum, 1973.

Kehr, Dave. "Travolta vs. Winkler: Transfers from Other Media." In *The Movie Star,* edited by Elisabeth Weis, 34–44. New York: Penguin, 1981.

Kellner, Douglas. *Herbert Marcuse and the Crisis of Marxism.* London: Macmillan, 1984.

———. "Network Television and American Society: Introduction to a Critical Theory of Television." *Theory and Society* 10 (1981): 31–62. Also in E. Wartella and C. Whitney, eds., *Mass Communication Yearbooks,* 411–442. Beverly Hills, Calif.: Sage, 1982.

———. "Postmodernism as Social Theory: Some Challenges and Problems. *Theory, Culture and Society* 5 (1988): 2–3.

———. "Television Images, Codes, and Messages." *Television* 7 (1980): 1–19.

———. "Television, Mythology, and Ritual." *Praxis* 6 (1982): 133–155.

———. "TV, Ideology, and Emancipatory Popular Culture." *Socialist Review* (May-Jun. 1979): 13–53.

Kirby, John B. *Black Americans in the Roosevelt Era: Liberalism and Race.* Knoxville: Univ. of Tennessee Press, 1980.

Koch, Neal. "Bartenders with Class." *Channels* (Nov. 1988): 59+.

Kozloff, Sarah Ruth. "Narrative Theory and Television." In *Channels of Discourse,* edited by Robert C. Allen, 42–73. Chapel Hill: Univ. of North Carolina Press, 1987.

Langer, John. "Television's Personality System." In *Media, Culture, and Society,* edited by Richard Collins et al., 351–66. London: Sage, 1981.

Lasfargues, Alain. "Dix ans de télévision aux USA." *Cahiers du cinema* (Jan. 1982): 331.

Laurent, Lawrence. "Wanted: The Complete Television Critic." In *The Eighth Art,* edited by Robert Shayon, 155–71. New York: Holt, Rinehart and Winston, 1962.

Lazarsfeld, Paul. *Radio and the Printed Page.* New York: Arno, 1940.

Lee, Janet. "Subversive Sitcoms." *Women's Studies* 21, no.1: (1992): 87–101.

Lewis, P. "Joke and Anti-Joke: Three Jews and a Blindfold." *Journal of Popular Culture* 21, no. 1 (1987): 63–74.

Lewis, Richard Warren. "The Importance of Being Julia." *TV Guide,* Dec. 14, 1968, 26.

Linden, Fabian. *Women: A Demographic Social and Economic Presentation.* New York: The Conference Board, 1973.

Littwin, Susan. "Not Just Whistlin' Dixie." *TV Guide,* Dec. 15, 1990, 4–5, 7, 9–10.

Long, Rob. "Jerry Built: The Success of 'Seinfeld' was an Implicit Rebuke to PC Pieties." *National Review Online,* Feb. 9 1998, 1–4.

Lovell, Terry. *Pictures of Reality.* London: British Film Institute, 1983.

MacDonald, J. Fred. *Blacks and White TV: Afro-Americans in Television since 1948.* Chicago: Nelson-Hall, 1983.

———. "Stride Toward Freedom—Blacks in Radio Programming." In *Don't Touch That Dial.* Chicago: Nelson Hall, 1979.

———. "Radio's Black Heritage: *Destination Freedom,* 1948–50." *Phylon* 39 (Mar. 1978): 66–73.

Macherey, Pierre. "Jules Verne: The Faulty Narrative." In *A Theory of Literary Production,* translated by Geoffrey Wall. New York: Routledge, 1985.

Marc, David. *Comic Visions: Television Comedy and American Culture.* Boston: Unwin Hyman, 1989.

———. *Demographic Vistas: Television in American Culture.* Philadelphia: Univ. of Pennsylvania Press, 1984.

Marouby, Christian. *Utopie et primitivisme.* Paris: Editions du Seuil, 1990.

Masterman, Len, ed. *Television Mythologies: Stars, Shows, and Signs.* New York: Marion Boyers, 1984.

Mayer, Jane. "The High Road: NBC's Grant Tinker Wins Critical Acclaim but Not Big Audiences." *New York Times,* Dec. 16, 1982: 1:1.

Mayne, Judith. "Marlene Dietrich, The Blue Angel, and Female Performance." In *Seduction and Theory,* edited by Dianne Hunter. Urbana: Univ. of Illinois Press, 1989.

McConnell, Frank. " 'Real' Cartoon Characters." *Commonweal,* Jun. 15, 1990, 389–90.

McCrohan, Donna. *The Honeymooners' Companion: The Kramdens and the Nortons Revisited.* New York: Workman, 1978.

McHale, Brian. *Constructing Postmodernism.* London: Routledge, 1992.

Meier, August. *Negro Thought in the Age of Booker T. Washington, 1885–1915.* Ann Arbor: Univ. of Michigan Press, 1965.

Mellencamp, Patricia. "Jokes and Their Relationship to the Marx Brothers." In *Cinema and Language,* edited by Stephen Heath and Patricia Mellencamp. Frederick, Md.: University Publications of America, 1983.

———. "Situation Comedy, Feminism, and Freud: Discourses of Gracie and Lucy." In

Star Texts: Image and Performance in Film and Television, edited by Jeremy G. Butler, 316–32. Detroit: Wayne State Univ. Press, 1991. Also in *Studies in Entertainment: Critical Approaches to Mass Culture,* edited by Tania Modleski, 80–95. Bloomington: Indiana Univ. Press, 1986.

Mellencamp, Patricia, ed. *Logics of Television: Essays in Cultural Criticism.* Bloomington: Indiana Univ. Press, 1990.

Metz, Christian. *Le signifiant imaginaire.* Paris: UGE, 1977. Reprinted as "Le signifiant imaginaire." *Communications* 23. Paris: Seuil, 1977.

Mintz, Lawrence E. "Situation Comedy." In *TV Genres: A Handbook and Reference Guide,* edited by Brian G. Rose and Robert S. Alley, 107–30. Westport, Conn.: Greenwood, 1985.

Mitchell, Juliet. *Women: The Longest Revolution.* London: Virago, 1984.

Mitz, Rick. *The Great TV Sitcom Book.* New York: Richard Marek, 1980.

Modleski, Tania. "Femininity as Mas(s)querade: A Feminist Approach to Mass Culture." In *High Theory/Low Culture,* edited by Colin McCabe. New York: St. Martin's, 1986.

Montgomery, K. "Gay Activists and the Networks." *Journal of Communication* 31 (1981): 49–57.

Morley, David. *The Nationwide Audience.* Chapel Hill and London: Univ. of North Carolina Press, 1985.

Moynihan, Daniel. *The Negro Family: The Case for National Action.* Washington, D.C.: U.S. Department of Labor, Office of Planning and Research, Mar. 1965.

Murdock, Graham. "Misrepresenting Media Sociology: A Reply to Anderson and Sharrock. In *Mass Communication Review Yearbook,* vol. 3, edited by D. Whitney et al., 755–66. Beverly Hills, Calif.: Sage, 1982.

Murdock, Graham, and Peter Golding. "Capitalism, Communication, and Class Relations." In *Mass Communication and Society,* edited by James Curran, Michael Gurevitch, and Janet Woollacott. Beverly Hills: Sage, 1979.

Murphy, Mary, and Frank Swertlow. "Delta Redesigned" *TV Guide,* Jul. 4–10, 1992, 10–16.

Murray, Lawrence. "Universality and Uniformity in the Popular Arts: The Impact of Television in Popular Culture." In *Screen and Society,* edited by Frank Coppa. Chicago: Nelson Hall, 1979.

Naremore, James. *Acting in the Cinema.* Berkeley: Univ. of California Press, 1988.

Nath, Ram. *Smoking: Third World Alert.* New York: Oxford Univ. Press, 1986.

Neale, Steve, and Krutnik, Frank. "Broadcast Comedy and Sit-com." In *Popular Film and Television Comedy,* edited by Steve Neale and Frank Krutnik, 209–61. New York: Routledge, 1990.

Neale, Stephen. *Genre.* London: British Film Institute, 1980.

Nielson, David G. *Black Ethos.* Westport, Conn.: Greenwood, 1980.

Nesde, Joan. "The Fem Question." In *Pleasures and Dangers: Exploring Female Sexuality,* edited by Carole Vance, 232–41. London: Pandora, 1989.

Nestle, Joan. *A Restricted Country.* Ithaca, N.Y.: Firebrand, 1987.

Nestle, Joan, ed. *The Persistent Desire: A Butch-Femme Reader.* Boston: Alyson, 1992.

Newcomb, Horace. "One Night of Prime-time: An Analysis of Television's Multiple Voices." In *Media, Myths, and Narratives: Television and the Press,* edited by James Carey, 88–112. Newbury Park, Calif.: Sage, 1988.

———. *TV: The Most Popular Art.* New York: Anchor, 1974.

Newcomb, Horace, ed. *Television: The Critical View.* New York: Oxford Univ. Press, 1987.

Newcomb, Horace, and Robert S. Alley, eds. *The Producer's Medium: Conversations with Creators of American TV.* New York: Oxford Univ. Press, 1983.

O'Connor, John E., ed. *American History, American Television: Interpreting the Video Past.* New York: Ungar, 1983.

O'Donnell, Patrick, and Robert Con Davis, eds. *Intertextuality and Contemporary American Fiction.* Baltimore: Johns Hopkins Univ. Press, 1989.

Oliver, Charles. "Box of Babel? Television and American Culture." *Current* 356 (1993): 10–14.

Parker, Patricia. *Literary Fat Ladies: Rhetoric, Gender, Property.* New York: Methuen, 1987.

Paulsen, P. "Sit-com Sermons Preach Loving Lessons. *Media and Values* (summer/fall 1987): 26–27.

Peary, Danny. "Remembering '*Father Knows Best.*' " In *TV Book,* edited by Judy Fireman, 173–75. New York: Workman, 1977.

Perry, Gill. "The 'Going Away': A Preparation for the Modern." In *Primitivism, Cubism, Abstraction: The Early Twentieth Century,* edited by Charles Harrison, Francis Frascina, and Gill Perry. New Haven, Conn.: Yale Univ. Press/Open Univ. Press, 1993.

Pleck, Joseph L. *The Myth of Masculinity.* Cambridge, Mass.: MIT Press, 1981.

Pogrebin, Letty Cottin. "Woman's Place: A Personal View of What It's Like to Grow Up Female." *TV Guide,* Sep. 1, 1973.

Polenberg, Richard. *One Nation Divisible: Class, Race, and Ethnicity in the United States Since 1938.* New York: Penguin, 1980.

Pollock, Griselda. *Avant-garde Gambits: Race and the Gender of Art History.* London: Thames and Hudson, 1992.

Pollock, Griselda, and Fred Orton. "Les Données Bretonnantes: La Prairie de Répresentation." *Art History* (Sep. 1980): 314–45.

Rebeck, Victoria A. "Recognizing Ourselves in The Simpsons." *The Christian Century,* Jun. 27, 1990, 622.

Real, Michael. *Mass-Mediated Culture.* Englewood Cliffs, N.J.: Prentice-Hall, 1977.

———. *Super Media: A Cultural Studies Approach.* Newbury Park, Calif.: Sage, 1989.

Rebeck, Victoria A. "Recognizing Ourselves in the Simpsons." *Christian Century,* Jun. 27, 1990, 622

Reeves, Jimmie. "Television Stars. The Case of Mr. T." In *Television: The Critical View*, 4th ed., edited by Horace Newcomb, 445–54. New York: Oxford Univ. Press, 1987.

Reid, Stanley D., and Laurel J. Reid. "Tourism Marketing Management in Small Island Nations: A Tale of MicroDestinations:" In *Global Tourist Behavior*, edited by Muzalfer Uysal. London/New York: Haworth, 1994.

"Requiem for the Kingfish." *Ebony*, July 1959: 57–64.

Rhodes, Kenneth. "Father of Two Families." *Cosmopolitan*, Apr. 1956, 125.

Rich, Adrienne. "Compulsory Heterosexuality and Lesbian Existence." In *Powers of Desire: The Politics of Sexuality*, edited by Ann Sitnow, Christine Stansell, and Sharon Thompson, 177–205. New York: Monthly Review Press, 1983.

Rollin, Roger. "In the Family: Television's Re-Formulation of Comedy." *The Psychocultural Review* 2, no. 4. (fall 1978).

Rose, Arnold M. "TV Bumps into the Negro Problem." *Printers' Ink*, Jul. 2, 1951, 36.

Rosen, Diane. "TV and the Single Girl." *TV Guide*, Nov. 6, 1971, 12.

Rovin, Jeff. *The Great Television Series*. New Jersey: A. S. Barnes, 1979.

Rowe, John Carlos. "Metavideo: Fictionality and Mass Culture in a Postmodern Economy." In *Intertextuality and Contemporary American Fiction*, edited by Patrick O'-Donnell and Robert Con Davis, 214–35. Baltimore: Johns Hopkins Univ. Press, 1989.

Rowe, Kathleen K. "Roseanne: Unruly Woman as Domestic Goddess." *Screen* 31, no. 4 (winter 1990): 408–19.

Russell, Cheryl. "Why Baby Boomers Are Cartooners." *TV Guide*, Dec. 19–25, 1992: 10–12.

Russo, Mary. "Female Grotesque: Carnival and Theory." In *Feminist Studies/Critical Studies*, edited by Teresa de Lauretis, 213–29. Bloomington: Indiana Univ. Press, 1986.

Ryan, Suzanne C. "Prime-time Develops a Conscience: New TV Shows Echo Post-Sept. 11 Themes." *Boston Globe*, May 22, 2002, E1.

Sartre, Jean-Paul. "The Comic Actor." In *Sartre on Theater*, translated by Frank Jellinek. New York: Pantheon Books, 1976.

Sausser, Gail. *Lesbian Etiquette*. Trumansburg, N.Y.: Crossing, 1986.

Scarry, Elaine. *The Body in Pain: The Making and Unmaking of the World*. New York: Oxford Univ. Press, 1985.

Schatz, Thomas. *"St. Elsewhere*: Evolution of the Ensemble Series." In *Television: The Critical View*, edited by Horace Newcomb, 85–100. New York: Oxford Univ. Press, 1987.

Schiller, Herbert. *Information and the Crisis Economy*. Norwood, N.J.: Ablex, 1984.

Schramm, Wilbur, Jack Lyle, and Edwin B. Parker. *Television in the Lives of Our Children*. Toronto: Univ. of Toronto Press, 1961.

Schwartz, Sherwood. *Inside Gilligan's Island: From Creation to Syndication*. Jefferson, N.C.: McFarland, 1988.

Schwartz, Tony. *Media: The Second God*. New York: Doubleday, 1984.

———. "Why the TV Season Went Wrong." *New York Times,* May 9, 1982, II: 1.

Seiter, Ellen. "Promise and Contradiction: The Daytime Television Serials." *Screen* 23 (1982): 150–63.

"Selling the Negro Market." *Tide,* Jul. 20, 1951.

Shayon, Robert Louis. " 'Julia': Breakthrough or Letdown?" *Saturday Review,* Apr. 20, 1968, 49.

———. " 'Julia': A Political Relevance?" *Saturday Review,* Jul. 20, 1968, 37.

———. " 'Julia' Symposium: An Opportunity Lost." *Saturday Review,* May 25, 1968: 36.

Sherman, Ellen. "Femme Scribes Cop Top Jobs." *Ms.,* Dec. 1974.

Silverman, Kaja. *The Acoustic Mirror.* Bloomington: Indiana Univ. Press, 1988.

Silverstone, Roger. *The Message of Television: Myth and Narrative in Contemporary Culture.* London: Heinemann Educational Books, 1981.

Smith, Bernard. *European Vision and the South Pacific: 1768–1850.* New York/London: Oxford Univ. Press, 1960.

Snead, J. *"Recoding Blackness: The Visual Rhetoric of Black Independent Film."* Speech given at "The New American Filmmakers Series: Exhibitions of Independent Film and Video." No. 23, Whitney Museum of American Art, New York, Jun. 20, 1985.

Solomon-Godeau, Abigail. "Going Native." *Art in America* 77 (Jul. 1989): 8–29.

Spigel, Lynn. *Make Room for TV—Television and the Family Ideal in Postwar America.* Chicago: Univ. of Chicago Press, 1992.

Sporkin, Elizabeth, Lois Armstrong, Tom Cunnett, and Jack Kelly. *People,* Jul. 29, 1991, 46–51.

Stabiner, Karen. "For Bob Newhart, Affection Is Still the Essence of Successful Comedy." *New York Times,,* Dec. 26, 1982, II, 25:1.

Stallybrass, Peter, and Allon White. *The Politics and Poetics of Transgression.* Ithaca, N.Y.: Cornell Univ. Press, 1986.

Stam, Robert. "Bakhtin. Eroticism and the Cinema: Strategies for the Critique and Trans-Valuation of Pornography." In *CineAction!* 10 (fall 1987): 13–20. Reprinted as "The Grotesque Body and Cinematic Eroticism." In *Subversive Pleasures: Bakhtin, Cultural Criticism, and Film,* edited by Robert Stam, 157–86. Baltimore: Johns Hopkins Univ. Press, 1989.

Stanley, Alessandra. "Wearied by Reality, Television Returns to a 1980's Mindset," *New York Times,* Jul. 24, 2002, B1, B7.

Stark, Steven. *Glued to the Set.* New York: Delta, 1997.

Stauth, Cameron. *"Cheers:* The Hit That Almost Missed. *Esquire,* Feb. 1984, 85+

Steiner, Gary A. *The People Look at Television.* New York: Alfred A. Knopf, 1963.

Stoddard, Sylvia. *TV Treasures: A Companion Guide to Gilligan's Island.* New York: St. Martin's Paperback, 1990.

Straayer, Chris. "Voyage en douce, entre nous: The Hypothetical Lesbian Heroine." *Jump Cut* 35 (1990).

Surgeon General's Scientific Advisory Committee on Television and Social Behavior.

Television and Growing Up: The Impact of Violence. Washington, DC: Government Printing Office, 1972.

"Television." *Ebony,* Jun. 1950, 20–25.

Terrace, Vincent. *The Complete Encyclopedia of Television Programs 1947–1976.* 2 vols. South Brunswick, N.J.: A. S. Barnes, 1976.

"The Case of the Missing Roast Beef." *Ebony,* Apr. 1958, 143.

"The Forgotten 15,000." *Sponsor,* Oct. 1949, 24–25, 54–55.

Theweleit, Klaus. *Male Fantasies: Volume I: Women, Floods, Bodies, History.* Translated by Stephen Conway et al. Minneapolis: Univ. of Minnesota Press, 1987.

———. *Male Fantasies: Volume II: Male Bodies: Pschoanalyzing the White Terror.* Translated by Erica Carter et al. Minneapolis: Univ. of Minnesota Press, 1989.

Thorburn, David. "Is TV Acting a Distinctive Art Form?" *New York Times* Sec. 2, Aug. 14, 1977: 19.

———. "Television as an Aesthetic Medium." In *Media, Myths, and Narratives: Television and the Press,* edited by James Carey. Newbury Park, Calif.: Sage, 1988.

Todorov, Tzvetan. *Introduction à la littérature fantastique.* Paris: Seuil, 1970.

Tuchman, Gaye. *Making News: A Study in the Construction of Reality.* New York: Free Press, 1978.

Tuchman, Gaye, et al., eds. *Hearth and Home: Images of Women in the Mass Media.* New York: Oxford Univ. Press, 1978.

Tucker, Ken. "Toon Terrific." *Entertainment Weekly,* Mar. 12, 1993, 49–50.

Twitchell, James B. *Carnival Culture: The Trashing of Taste in America.* New York: Columbia Univ. Press, 1992.

Urry, John. *The Tourist Gaze: Leisure and Travel in Contemporary Societies.* Thousand Oaks, Calif.: Sage, 1990.

U.S. Commission on Civil Rights. *Window Dressing on the Set: Women and Minorities in Television.* Washington, D.C.: U.S. Commission on Civil Rights, Aug. 1977.

Vance, Vivian. "Lucy and I Adored Each Other—Then People Began to Whisper That We Were Lovers." *National Enquirer,* Aug. 29, 1989, 20–21.

Van Druten, John. *I Remember Mama.* New York: Dramatists Play Service, 1944.

Verne, Jules. *The Mysterious Island.* 1875. Reprint, New York: Dodd, Mean, 1958.

Waldron, Vince. *Classic Sitcoms.* New York: Macmillan, 1987.

Walls, Bishop J. "What about Amos 'n' Andy?" *Abbotts Monthly,* Dec. 1930, 38–40. James Weldon Johnson Memorial Collection, Beineke Library, Yale.

Walsh, Andrea. *Women's Film and Female Experience.* New York: Praegar, 1984.

Warren, Elaine. "Shake-Up at the Sugarbakers: It's Now Re-Designing Women." *TV Guide,* Sep. 21, 1991, 10–17.

Waters, Harry F. "Family Feuds." *Newsweek,* Apr. 23, 1990, 58–62.

Waugh, Patricia, ed. *Postmodernism: A Reader.* London: Edward Arnold, 1992.

Weber, Samuel. *The Legend of Freud.* Minneapolis: Univ. of Minnesota Press, 1982.

Wells, Paul. "Where Everybody Knows Your Name: Open Convictions in Closed Contexts in the American Situation Comedy." In *Because I Tell a Joke or Two: Comedy,*

Politics, and Social Difference, edited by Stephen Wagg, 180–201. New York: Routledge, 1998.

Welter, Barbara. "The Cult of True Womanhood: 1820–60" *American Quarterly* 18, no. 162 (1966): 152.

Wexman, Virginia Wright. "Returning from the Moon: Jackie Gleason, the Carnivalesque, and Television Comedy." *Journal of Film and Video* 42, no. 4 (winter 1990): 20–31.

White, A. "Telling It on the Mountain. *Film Comment* (Oct. 1985): 39–41.

White, Hayden. "The Value of Narrativity in the Representation of Reality." *Critical Inquiry* 7, no. 1 (1980).

White, Mimi. "Ideological Analysis and Television." In *Channels of Discourse,* edited by Robert C. Allen, 161–202. Chapel Hill: Univ. of North Carolina Press, 1987.

White, R. "Mass Communication and Culture: Transistion to a New Paradigm." *Journal of Communication* 33, no. 3 (1983): 279–301.

White, Walter. "Negro Leader Looks at TV Race Problem." *Printers' Ink,* Aug. 24, 1951, 31.

Whitney, Dwight. "You've Come a Long Way, Baby: Happy Hotpoint Is Now Mary Tyler Moore Moviestar. *TV Guide,* Sep. 19, 1970, 34.

Wilde, Alan. *Horizons of Assent.* Philadelphia: Univ. of Pennsylvania Press, 1987.

Williams, Raymond. *The Long Revolution.* New York: Columbia Univ. Press, 1962.

———. *Television: Technology and Cultural Form.* London: William Collins and Sons, 1974.

Wolcott, James. "Holy Mack'ell: Amos 'n' Andy Videotapes Are Hot Items on the Nostalgia Market." *Esquire,* Jan. 1981, 11–12.

Woollacott, Janet. "Fictions and Ideologies: The Case of the Situation Comedy." In *Popular Culture and Social Relations,* edited by Tony Bennett, Colin Mercer, and Janet Woollacott, 196–218. Philadelphia: Open Univ. Press, 1986.

Wright, Gwendolyn. *Building the Dream: A Social History of Housing in America.* Cambridge: MIT Press, 1981.

Wright, Will. *Six Guns and Society: A Structural Analysis of the Western.* Berkeley: Univ. of California Press, 1977.

Index

ABC (American Broadcasting Company): color broadcasting, 89; in early 1990s, 247; *Ellen*, 248–49; "family" hour programs, 153; *Jackie Robinson Show*, 28; *Love on a Rooftop*, 89; *Mod Squad*, 89; *Roots*, 239; *Roseanne*, 247, 259; "second season," 89; after September 11, 2001, 250; Silverman at, 217; *Small Sacrifices*, 259; *Soap*, 153; *Taxi*, 210; in television development, 1; *That Girl*, 89, 159; *Three's Company*, 153

action-adventure shows, 89

Action for Children's Television, 244

Adams, Julius, 29

Addams Family, The, 88, 120

Adelman, Sybil, 160

Adorno, T. W., 22

Adventures of Ozzie and Harriet, The: down-to-earth characters on, 60; idealized nuclear family in, 4, 5, 157, 265, 297n. 4, 298n. 25; identification of stars and characters in, 57; Ozzie as not having a profession, 233

African Americans: *Beulah*, 3, 129, 136, 297n. 4; as "black," 239; the black family, 145, 146–47; black male stereotypes, xviii, 224, 230, 232, 239, 245; call for recoding blackness, 230–31; *Ebony* magazine, 29, 144, 291n. 15; Fox network appealing to, 249; interracial sexuality, 141; *The Jeffersons*, xviii, 96, 152; mythologies about, 225, 226; Otherness of, 135–36; performers breaking into television, 29; presence on television in 1960s, 142; on radio, 27–29; restrictive covenants, 76; *Roots*, 238–39; *Sanford and Son*, xviii, 153, 243; television production companies of, 30. *See also Amos 'n' Andy;* black middle class; *Cosby Show, The; Julia*

Alexander, Marguerite, 272

Alexander, William D., 30

Alice, 189, 306n. 8

All America company, 30

Allen, Gracie: language as used by, xiv; as vaudeville and radio performer, xiv, 2. *See also Burns and Allen Show, The*

Allen, Robert C., 66

Allen, Steve, 296n. 13

All in the Family: Archie as rarely shown working, 233; class in, 110, 151, 264, 265; as much discussed, 95; popularity of, 151; racial and ethnic epithets in, 151; realism of, 108; sexuality in, 111, 112; social issues as topics of, 152; as socially relevant sitcom, xvi, 92–93, 96, 109, 149, 216; spinoffs of, 152; as taped before live audience, 229

Althusser, Louis, 213, 214

Altman, Rick, 67, 260

American Jewish Committee, 32, 293n. 34

Amos 'n' Andy, 25–40; Julius Adams on, 29; black actors on, 31, 38; black dialect on, 36–37; black middle class and protest against, xiii–xiv, 25–26, 27, 39; black middle class as portrayed on, xiii, 33, 34–35; budget of, 31; characters of, 31–32; Christmas story on, 36–38; *The*